Migration and Development in the Caribbean

Westview Special Studies

The concept of Westview Special Studies is a
response to the continuing crisis in academic and
informational publishing. Library budgets are being
diverted from the purchase of books and used for data
banks, computers, micromedia, and other methods of
information retrieval. Interlibrary loan structures
further reduce the edition sizes required to satisfy
the needs of the scholarly community. Economic
pressures on university presses and the few private
scholarly publishing companies have greatly limited the
capacity of the industry to properly serve the academic
and research communities. As a result, many
manuscripts dealing with important subjects, often
representing the highest level of scholarship, are no
longer economically viable publishing projects--or, if
accepted for publication, are typically subject to lead
times ranging from one to three years.
Westview Special Studies are our practical
solution to the problem. As always, the selection
criteria include the importance of the subject, the
work's contribution to scholarship, and its insight,
originality of thought, and excellence of exposition.
We accept manuscripts in camera-ready form, typed, set,
or word processed according to specifications laid out
in our comprehensive manual, which contains
straightforward instructions and sample pages. The
responsibility for editing and proofreading   lies with
the author or sponsoring institution, but our editorial
staff is always available to answer questions and
provide guidance.
The result is a book printed on acid-free paper
and bound in sturdy library-quality soft covers. We
manufacture these books ourselves using equipment that
does not require a lengthy make-ready process and that
allows us to publish first editions of 300 to 1000
copies and to reprint even smaller quantities as
needed. Thus, we can produce Special Studies quickly
and can keep even very specialized books in print as
long as there is a demand for them.

About the Book and Editor

Is emigration from the Caribbean area to the
United States an essential escape valve, releasing
destabilizing population pressures and permitting space
for economic development? Or do the talented, skilled,
and professional people exit, reducing the
possibilities for development? In answering these
questions, the contributors to this book offer the
first in-depth analysis of the unexplored relationship
between two crucial phenomena shaping the region:
migration and development. The contributors break new
ground in challenging old assumptions that underlie
current policies. They offer new proposals that aim to
multiply the benefits of migration to Caribbean
development while reducing the costs. They examine the
impact of various development strategies on migration
and suggest projects and strategies that could reduce
the pressures of migration. Finally, they assess the
impact of U.S. immigration policies on Caribbean
economic development and U.S.-Caribbean relations and
offer proposals to modify such policies.

Robert A. Pastor is currently Professor of
Political Science at Emory University and Director of
the Latin American and Caribbean Program at the Carter
Center. He is on leave of absence in 1985-86 as a
Fulbright Professor at El Colegio de Mexico. He
directed a two-year research project on "Migration and
Development in the Caribbean" at the School of Public
Affairs of the University of Maryland at College Park.

Migration and Development in the Caribbean
The Unexplored Connection

edited by
Robert A. Pastor

Westview Press / Boulder and London

Westview Special Studies on Latin America and the Caribbean

This Westview softcover edition was manufactured on our own premises using equipment and methods that allow us to keep even specialized books in stock. It is printed on acid-free paper and bound in softcovers that carry the highest rating of the National Association of State Textbook Administrators, in consultation with the Association of American Publishers and the Book Manufacturers' Institute.

Published in 1985 in the United States of America by Westview Press, Inc.; Frederick A. Praeger, Publisher; 5500 Central Avenue, Boulder, Colorado 80301

Library of Congress Cataloging in Publication Data
Main entry under title:
Migration and development in the Caribbean.
    (Westview special studies on Latin America and the Caribbean)
    Bibliography: p.
    Includes index.
    1. Caribbean Area--Emigration and immigration--Economic aspects--Addresses, essays, lectures. 2. Caribbean Area--Economic conditions--Addresses, essays, lectures. 3. United States--Emigration and immigration--Addresses, essays, lectures. I. Pastor, Robert A.
JV7321.Z7E285   1985   325.729   85-3246
ISBN: 0-8133-7056-6

Composition for this book was provided by the editor
This book was produced without formal editing by the publisher

Printed and bound in the United States of America

The paper used in this publication meets the minimum requirements of the American National Standard for Permanence of Paper for Printed Library materials Z39.48-1984.

6   5   4   3   2

For Margy

Contents

Tables

Preface

This book represents the product of a two-year research project and a four-year personal journey to explore the relationship between migration and economic development in the Caribbean area. Does Caribbean immigration to the United States assist or impede the economic development of the Caribbean? Would the curtailment of immigration affect the stability of the Caribbean? Can a certain mix of development strategies significantly reduce the pressures for migration? What can the United States and the Caribbean countries do separately and together to improve the prospects for economic development while permitting migration at manageable levels? This book begins with these questions and ends with some answers.

In 1981, Dr. Mary Kritz, Assistant Director of the Population Sciences Division of the Rockefeller Foundation, first approached me to ask if I would undertake some research on the policy implications of emigration from the Caribbean Basin to the United States. Although the Caribbean Basin had been a principal area of interest to me both from a policymaking and scholarly perspective for about fifteen years, most of my time had been devoted to questions of national security and economic development. As the Director of Latin American and Caribbean Affairs on the National Security Council from 1977 to 1981, I had been indirectly involved in developing the immigration legislation sent to Congress in August 1977, and I had been deeply enmeshed in the Mariel exodus of 1980. However, I had never really focused my attention on the connection between migration, economic development, and national security. As I began my research for the Rockefeller Foundation, I soon realized that no one else had explored the connections either. As my research only scratched the outline of the issues, I decided to seek support to delve more deeply into them.

With the encouragement and financial support of the Ford and Rockefeller Foundations, I began a research project on this subject at the School of Public Affairs, University of Maryland, College Park. As the project developed, additional support from the World Bank, the Agency for International Development, and the Inter-American Foundation was obtained. Dr. Sergio Diaz-Briquets served as my Associate Director. Our substantive objectives will be discussed in my introductory chapter; let me say a word about our procedural objectives here.

In the United States, research on the relationship between migration and development is likely to be viewed as worthwhile by some or as a harmless academic pursuit by others. In the Caribbean, the subject generates controversy or, at a minimum, intense unease. Very few people in governments or at the universities in the region want to address this issue. Most fear that even discussion could be used as justification for the United States to curtail immigration, which is assumed to be a social benefit and an inalienable personal right. When pressed, some would recognize that there are social costs and that the United States has the right--which is exercised by all Caribbean governments--to restrict immigration, but few want to pursue these implications further. It would therefore have been tempting to pursue this project without substantial Caribbean participation, but it would also have defeated two of the project's purposes--to open a dialogue between the United States and the Caribbean countries and to seek a common approach and, if possible, cooperative solutions. Paul Balaran and Jeffrey Puryear of the Ford Foundation helped us to understand that the substantive goals could only be achieved if the issue was addressed from a cross-cultural perspective.

The overall objective of the project was to analyze and recommend policies for the United States, the Caribbean countries, and international development organizations in the twin areas of migration and development. To accomplish this, we decided to involve policymakers as well as scholars in every stage of the project and to ensure the participation of as many national perspectives as possible. Nearly half the contributors to this book are from the Caribbean, and the conference at the Wye Center in Maryland in September 1984 to review the research papers had a similarly diverse group of participants. The dialogue was sometimes awkward but always fruitful among the Caribbean representatives, between them and those from the United States, Mexico, and Canada, and most of all, between those representing different disciplines-- economists, political scientists, policymakers and analysts, demographers, and sociologists. Ransford Palmer, a Jamaican-born Professor of Economics at Howard University, commented that "scholars from different disciplines emerged with a better understanding of the limitations of their own approaches and of the potential benefits of a holistic approach." This statement was also true for the crossnational exchange.

Because of the important role played by the participants at the research conference at the Wye Center and at a policymakers conference at the Woodrow Wilson Center on January 23, 1985, a list of those participants is included at the back of this book. Let me, however, acknowledge several persons whose written and oral comments were of special use to us as we revised our chapters: Patricia Pessar of Georgetown University's Center for Immigration Policy; Alejandro Portes of the Johns Hopkins University; Ransford Palmer; Nicholas Carter of the World Bank; Edwin P. Reubens, formerly of the City College of New York; Jagdish Bhagwati of Columbia University; Michael Teitelbaum of the Sloan Foundation; and Hollis Chenery of Harvard University. Their generosity in offering their advice should not be interpreted as responsibility for the product; the authors alone assume that responsibility.

The personal debts accumulated in organizing the research project, revising and editing the papers, and assembling the book provided me with a new appreciation for the term "debt crisis." A separate book would be needed to thank all the people who contributed to this project, but in lieu of that, let me express my gratitude to the Ford and Rockefeller Foundations, the World Bank, the Agency for International Development, and the Inter-American Foundation for their generous financial support, and to Peter Brown and George Eads, Deans of the School of Public Affairs, for their encouragement and assistance. Louis Goodman and Richard Morse of the Latin American Program of the Woodrow Wilson Center for International Scholars were helpful collaborators in organizing a follow-up conference for Congressional staff and policy-makers on January 23, 1985.

It is hard to see how the project could have been accomplished without Sergio Diaz-Briquets, whose expertise and organizational skills were invaluable. Charles Becker did a superb job as Coordinator of the

Conference and in preparing this volume. Mary Barberis rendered exceptional and timely work editing several of the manuscripts, and David Birdsell, Sara Grusky, and Kim Cameron helped proof the manuscript. Without question, however, the most indispensable contributor to the project was Rosemary Blunck, whose patience, perspective, and humor permitted her to rise above both the project and the manuscript, which she typed and proofed, but not so high above that she wasn't able to see the project to its conclusion.

Robert Pastor

1. Introduction:
The Policy Challenge

Robert A. Pastor

I. The Unexplored Connection

Recent events in the Caribbean area have attracted
the attention of the United States again. The rise and
fall of the New Jewel Movement in Grenada, the covert
war in Nicaragua, the civil war in El Salvador, the
Mariel exodus of 125,000 Cubans--these events and
others have reminded the United States that it could
not shield itself from the effects of instability on
its "third border" even if it were so inclined, and
twentieth-century history reveals no such inclination.

Generally, the United States begins a search for a
new Caribbean policy in the middle of a security crisis
in the region. The U.S. style is to react to crises
and then react to criticism that the United States only
reacts to crises. To prove the criticism inaccurate,
U.S. foreign-policy makers propose long-term social and
economic strategies to address the underlying causes of
instability. Such are the origins of the Alliance for
Progress and the Reagan administration's Caribbean
Basin Initiative.

Added to the strategic imperative to prevent
Communist expansion and a general humanitarian impulse,
the United States has acquired a more subtle and
compelling motive for promoting social reform and
economic development in the Caribbean as a means for
achieving political stability: immigration. In the
last two decades, the Caribbean Basin has become the
largest source of immigrants and refugees to the United
States. In a sense, migration has become a link
whereby the United States shares the consequences of
instability and underdevelopment in the region, and as
such, it has become a rationale for U.S. security
policy. In an interview in April 1984, William J.
Casey, the director of the Central Intelligence Agency,
stated: "If we have another Cuba in Central America,
Mexico will have a big problem, and we're going to have

1

a massive wave of immigration." He went on to stress
that a principal motive of U.S. policy is "to prevent
this from happening."[1]
During the last three decades, about 10 percent of
the Caribbean region's population emigrated to the
United States. Of the two million Caribbean emigrants
who have come to the United States to live since 1820,
nearly one-half have arrived in the last decade.[2]
Leaving aside Casey's concerns, this new Caribbean
presence has generated new interest in Caribbean
economic development, albeit for somewhat contrary
reasons: Some argue that the United States has an
obligation to assist a neighbor who is also becoming a
relative; others argue that the United States should
promote development in order to reduce the pressures
for further emigration.
Regardless of the perspective on this issue,
Caribbean emigration clearly is related to the region's
economic development and political stability in a
number of ways, none of which is clearly understood.
When emigration is the search abroad for economic
opportunity not available at home, it can be said to be
caused by underdevelopment. Emigration can impede
development when managers and professionals leave.
U.S. immigration policy undoubtedly affects both the
magnitude of emigration and the kinds of emigrants from
the region, a relationship that in turn affects
economic development and political stability.
Yet despite the increasing importance of migration
and development and their obvious relationship, few
nations have considered relating their policies on
migration with their development strategies, let alone
systematically doing so. The United States has
undertaken a new economic approach to the region--the
1983 Caribbean Basin Initiative (CBI)--with little
understanding of its impact on migration and has
debated a major immigration reform with little
understanding of its impact on the region's
development. It is entirely plausible that the two
policies could undermine each other. The effect of the
CBI could be to stimulate emigration pressures even
while the new immigration law could deny those
pressures an outlet. So instead of promoting
development and manageable migration, the United
States--having failed to relate its policies to one
another--could unintentionally provoke instability and
frustrate development. In other words, the failure by
the United States to relate migration and development
could unwittingly undermine its two central interests
in the region.
This ironic contradiction has its counterpart in
the Caribbean, where regional leaders view development
as a core objective yet sometimes pursue policies that

encourage emigration by those most needed to manage
their nation's development. By failing to relate
migration to development, Caribbean leaders have
reduced their ability to manage either.

How are we to explain these parallel
contradictions? Briefly, neither the United States nor
the Caribbean has tried to comprehend the relationship
between migration and development, despite the fact
that these two crucial phenomena are reshaping the
nations of the Caribbean region and their relationship
with the United States. Neither seems aware that this
new bond of migration is both a unique opportunity and
a new source of vulnerability.

The purpose of this book is to explore the
connection between these two phenomena: to examine the
impact of development on migration and of migration on
development. With a better understanding of the
relationship, we recommend ways to modify both U.S. and
Caribbean migration policies, Caribbean development
strategies, and U.S. and international development
assistance policies so they serve common objectives in
economic development and manageable migration. In
addition, the book evaluates mechanisms and proposals
that could use migration to enhance development. We
recognize that the data are limited and often uneven
and that the issues are controversial. Nonetheless, we
believe that we are more likely to advance the
development--in the fullest sense of the word--of
individuals and nations in the entire region if we
focus on these issues than if we ignore them.

Our objectives are modest. Migration is not
viewed as a problem to be solved but as a phenomenon to
be understood and a policy issue of urgent concern to
the entire Caribbean area. We do not seek to locate
the answer to development and migration but rather to
offer some ideas to improve development prospects in
the area and to reduce needless dislocations associated
with some migration flows.

The contributors to this book approach the subject
from diverse perspectives--from that of the United
States as well as that of the Caribbean countries, as
scholars as well as policymakers, from the private
sector as well as from governments and international
organizations, and from a variety of academic
disciplines, including economics, demography, political
science, and sociology. By this diversity, we attempt
to make the analysis relevant to the entire region and
the proposals feasible and sensitive to all national
perspectives.

Chapter 1 will introduce the many dimensions of
the policy challenge. First, I will define the subject
and the geographical focus; then I will examine the
conventional assumptions of the relationship between

migration and development, and review the literature on
other regions as well as on the Caribbean. Finally, I
will describe the specific policy questions and
challenges to be addressed by the other authors.

II. The Caribbean and Its People: Defining a Moveable Object

The Caribbean area is defined as the islands in
the Caribbean Sea plus the three nations and one
dependency on the rim that share a northern European
colonial heritage--Belize, Guyana, Suriname, and French
Guiana. Altogether, there are sixteen independent
nations and ten dependencies--twelve including Puerto
Rico and the U.S. Virgin Islands (see Table 1.1). The
nations range in size and population from St. Kitts-
Nevis, which became independent in 1983 and has a
population of 44,404 and an area of 104 square miles,
to Cuba with a population of nearly 10 million and an
area of 44,000 square miles. The per capita gross
domestic product (GDP) of the countries ranges from
Haiti with $288 to Trinidad and Tobago with $4,847.

Although the primary geographical focuses in the
book are the Caribbean as a sending region and the
United States as the receiving country, we will
frequently try to widen that focus to include Mexico
and Central America (which together with the Caribbean
are referred to as the Caribbean Basin) and sometimes
other sending regions and occasionally Canada and other
receiving nations. The reason for expanding the focus
is to test hypotheses generated by our research on the
Caribbean through comparative analysis with other
regions and to propose policies relevant to the entire
basin and solid enough to apply to other regions. The
Caribbean nations seem a natural focus as they share
with Mexico a relatively long history of emigration to
the United States, and, like the Central American
countries, they have small and vulnerable economies.

Despite the seemingly vast political, economic,
and cultural diversity, the nations of the Caribbean
share many similar problems and opportunities. As
relatively small, open, vulnerable countries on the
border of the world's richest and most powerful country,
they all confront a similar strategic dilemma--how to
retain autonomy while seeking regional integration, how
to elude the dominance of the United States while
securing improved access to the U.S. market. Although
it possesses limited markets and resources, the
region's proximity to the U.S. market and its access to
external capital contribute to its position in the
middle class of the developing world. However, because
of advertising, trade, migration, and proximity to the
United States, the Caribbean's principal competitor for

Table .1.1

Population, Area, and Gross Domestic Product Data
for Caribbean Countries
(per sq. mi.)

Country (date of Independence	Population	Area (sq.mi.)	Pop. Density (per sq.mi.)	GDP (US$ million)	Per capita GDP
Anguilla (U.K.)	6,500	35	185	3.0	461
Antigua (1981)	77,226	108	715	79.1	1,039
Bahamas (1973)	209,505	5,382	38.9	1.0[a]	4,760[a]
Barbados (1966)	252,000	166	1,518	950.4[a]	3,817[a]
Belize (1981)	146,000	8,864	16	184.5[a]	1,200[a]
Bermuda (U.K.)	72,000	20.6	3,496	598	10,894
Cayman Islands (U.K.)	17,035	100	170	72	4,800
Cuba (1902)	9,771,000	44,000	222	13,000	1,360
Dominica (1978)	74,100	289	256	49.7[a]	598[a]
Domin. Republic (1844)	5,762,000	18,700	308	5,500[a]	990[a]
Grenada (1974)	107,000	133	809	50.2	459
Guadeloupe (France)	317,000	687	461	987	3,040
Guiana (France)	66,000	35,135	1.9	120	1,935
Guyana (1966)	795,000	83,000	9.6	560.7[a]	690[a]
Haiti (1804)	6,000,000	10,714	540	1,500[a]	288.6[a]
Jamaica (1962)	2,225,000	4,411	504	2,979	1,339
Martinique (France)	312,000	425	734	1,135	3,559
Montserrat (U.K.)	12,034	39.5	304	20[a]	1,736[a]
Neth. Antilles (Ncth.)	243,000	383	634	864	3,472
St. Kitts-Nevis (1983)	44,404	104	427	48.1[a]	920[a]
St. Lucia (1979)	122,000	238	513	210	1,696
St. Vincent (1979)	115,000	150	767	59[a]	513[a]
Suriname (1975)	388,000	63,227	6.1	822.4[a]	2,370[a]
Trinidad & Tob. (1962)	1,176,000	1,980	594	5,700	4,847
Turks & Caicos (U.K.)	7,436	192	38.7	15[a]	2,000[a]
Virgin Isl. (U.K.)	12,244	59	210	28.5[a]	2,456[a]
Total	28,329,484	278,542.1		35,806.6	
United States	226,504,825	3,618,770	64	2,626,100[a]	11,536[a]
Puerto Rico	3,240,000	3,435	943	11,771	3,001
U.S. Virgin Is.	98,307	132	745	542[a]	4,743[a]

[a] GNP

Sources: Caribbean/Central American Action, Caribbean Databook, 1983 (Washington, D.C.: Caribbean/Central American Action, 1983); for the U.S.: U.S. Dept. of Commerce, Bureau of the Census, Statistical Abstract of the United States, 1981 (Washington, D.C.: Government Printing Office, 1981). The years in which these were measured vary. Some are at constant dollars. The figures are based on UN and national data.

its skilled population and product is the United
States, not the countries of the Third World. The
United States is therefore both solution and problem,
source of aid and competitor, destination for emigrants
and magnet for the region's talent.

Though differences in political and economic
systems in the region sometimes appear immense, they
should not obscure common structural problems and the
need for cooperative or at least similar solutions.
For example, consider the two "model systems," the
Puerto Rican and the Cuban, which are often taken as
the polar options available to the region, and examine
one critical development problem--employment. Both
islands sustained rather steep increases in population,
which contributed to serious employment problems
fifteen years later. Despite the different
orientations of the two governments, both essentially
relied on the same two solutions to address their
employment problem: a vast expansion in government
employment and out-migration. The expansion of the
Cuban government and the out-migration of nearly one
million Cubans in the last two decades are well-known,
as is Puerto Rican out-migration. Less well known is
the continuous enlargement of the public sector in
Puerto Rico--the supposed bastion of the free
enterprise system in the Caribbean. From 1940 to 1970,
public-sector employment in Puerto Rico increased at an
annual average of 7.2 percent, as compared to 1 percent
for the entire economy and 2.6 percent for the
manufacturing sector. By 1979, the Puerto Rican
government employed nearly one-fourth of the island's
labor force.[3]

The pressures to emigrate from the Caribbean
increased markedly in the postwar period, and the
United States became the major destination,
particularly after the passage of the 1965 immigration
law. In the 1940s, Caribbean legal immigration to the
United States averaged less than 5,000 persons per year
(see Table 1.2). This number nearly tripled in the
1950s; the new number then almost quadrupled in the
1960s and that figure nearly doubled in the 1970s.
Between 1965 and 1979, immigration to the United States
from Jamaica and Trinidad increased almost tenfold.[4]
Of all the world's countries, Mexico has been the
largest source of immigrants during the last two
decades. Yet with a population more than twice that of
the entire Caribbean during the last two decades,
Mexico has been the source of fewer legal immigrants.
For a more detailed breakdown of immigration data from
the Caribbean, broken down by country during the last
two decades, see Table 1.3. (When one takes into
account the fact that the statistics in Tables 1.2 and
1.3 reflect a considerable undercounting of Cuban

Table 1.2

Caribbean Immigration into the United States, 1820-1983

Region of Last Residence	1820-1860	1861-1900	1901-1920	1921-1930	1931-1940	1941-1950	1951-1960	1961-1970	1971-1980	1981-1983	1820-1983 Total
All countries	5,062,414 (123,474)	14,061,192 (351,530)	14,532,297 (726,615)	4,107,209 (410,721)	528,431 (52,843)	1,035,039 (103,504)	2,515,479 (251,548)	3,321,677 (332,168)	4,493,314 (449,331)	1,750,494 (583,498)	51,407546 (313,461)
Caribbean	40,487 (987)	85,111 (2,128)	230,972 (11,549)	74,899 (7,490)	15,502 (1,550)	49,725 (4,973)	123,091 (12,309)	470,213 (47,021)	741,126[c] (74,113)	213,986 (71,329)	2,045,112 (12,470)
Caribbean as % of total	.8	.6	1.6	1.8	2.9	4.8	4.9	14.2	16.5	12.2	4.0
Mexico[d]	17,766 (433)	10,237 (256)	268,646 (13,432)	459,287 (45,929)	22,319 (2,232)	60,589 (6,059)	299,811 (29,981)	453,937 (45,394)	640,294 (64,029)	216,453 (72,151)	2,449,339 (14,935)
Central America	968 (24)	1,205 (30)	25,351 (1,268)	15,769 (1,577)	5,861 (586)	25,665 (2,567)	44,751 (4,475)	101,330 (10,133)	134,640 (13,464)	72,736 (24,245)	428,276 (2,611)
Colombia[b]	NA	NA	NA	14,071 (1,407)	2,601 (260)	7,277 (728)	18,048 (1,805)	72,028 (7,203)	77,348 (7,735)	28,601 (9,534)	243,735 (1,486)
Caribbean Basin	59,221 (1,444)	96,553 (2,414)	524,969 (26,249)	564,026 (56,403)	46,283 (4,628)	143,256 (14,326)	485,701 (48,570)	1,097,508 (109,751)	1,593,408 (159,341)	531,776 (177,259)	5,166,462 (31,478)
Caribbean Basin as % of total	1.2	.7	3.6	13.7	8.8	13.8	19.3	33.0	35.5	30.4	10.1

[a] No record of immigration from Mexico from 1886 to 1893

[b] No figures available for individual periods. Total 1820-1920 = 23,761 and figures from 1921 to 1950 are also from 1981 Statistical Yearbook. Those numbers are added to those figures from 1951 to 1983 in the 1983 Statistical Yearbook to arrive at the total number.

[c] Includes Mariel Cuban entrants (124,789) and Haitian legalized entrants (10,211)

Source: U.S. Department of Justice/INS, 1983 Statistical Yearbook of the Immigration and Naturalization Service (Washington, D.C.: Government Printing Office), Table 1, pp. 4-5. An immigrant is an alien admitted for permanent residence. The figures in parenthesis are the average annual members of immigrants per period. The Caribbean includes Anguilla, Antigua, Bahamas, Barbados, Bermuda, Br. Virgin Islands, Cayman Islands, Cuba, Dominica, Dominican Republic, Grenada, Guadeloupe, Haiti, Jamaica, Martinique, Montserrat, Neth. Antilles, Puerto Rico, St. Nevis, St. Lucia, St. Vincent & Grenadines, Trinidad and Tobago, Turks and Caicos Islands, and the U.S. Virgin Islands.

8

Table 1.3

Immigration by Country or Region of Birth from the Caribbean, 1960-1983

Country/Region of Birth	1960-1965	1966-1970	1971-1975	1976-1980	1981-1983	1960-1983 Total
All countries	1,715,710	1,871,365	1,936,281	2,557,033	1,750,494	9,830,883
Caribbean[a]	159,354	381,386	341,631	608,689	244,673	1,735,733
Cuba	84,979	180,073	110,691	291,332[b]	28,045	695,120
Dominican Republic	36,128	58,744	67,051	80,965	57,729	300,617
Haiti	10,820	27,648	27,130	41,786[c]	23,886	131,270
MDC's[f]	16,084	98,115	116,921	155,329	105,088	491,537
Barbados	2,377	7,312	7,878	13,070	6,204	36,841
Guyana	1,434	5,760	14,320	33,211	25,782	80,507
Jamaica	9,675	62,676	61,445	80,550	61,815	276,161
Trinidad & Tobago	2,598	22,367	33,278	28,498	11,287	98,028
OECS[f]	NA	NA	11,349	25,152	20,795	57,296
Antigua	NA	NA	1,969	4,131	6,171	12,271
Dominica	NA	NA	1,182	3,399	1,836	6,417
Grenada	NA	NA	2,388	5,377	2,230	11,105
Montserrat	NA	NA	932	1,007	503	2,442
St. Kitts-Nevis	NA	NA	1,960[d]	4,474	4,679	11,113
St. Lucia	NA	NA	1,305	3,642	1,981	6,928
St. Vincent and Gren.	NA	NA	1,613	3.122	2,285	7,020
Other [e]	11,343	16,806	8,489	14,125	8,755	59,518

[a]Discrepancy between these Caribbean data and those in aggregate table (Caribbean Immigration to the United States, 1820-1983) is caused by the inclusion of data for Guyana and Belize in above figure for the Caribbean.

[b]Includes 124, 789 refugees and "entrants" from Cuba, Mariel exodus 1980. Source: U.S. Department of the Census, Statistical Abstract of the United States 1982/83 (Washington, D.C.: Government Printing Office), p. 92.

[c]Includes 10,211 Haitian "entrants" legalized simultaneously with the Mariel Cubans, 1980.

[d]Prior to FY 1977, historical data for Anguilla were included in St. Kitts-Nevis.

[e]From 1960 to 1970, we assume that "other" includes the OECS nations, which were not yet independent. There is no specific reference to that effect. From 1971 to 1981, "other" includes Anguilla, Bahamas, Belize, Br. Virgin Islands, Cayman Islands, Guadeloupe, Martinique, Neth. Antilles, Puerto Rico, Turks & Caicos Islands, and the U.S. Virgin Islands.

[f]"MDC's" are the four largest English-speaking, "middle developing countries;" and OECS is the Organization of Eastern Caribbean States.

Source: U.S. Department of Justice, 1969, 1980, 1980, 1981, and 1983 Statistical Yearbooks of the Immigration and Naturalization Service (Washington, D.C.: Government Printing Office), Tables 1, 13, and 14. Years ended June 30, 1960-1976, July-September 1976, and years ended September 30, 1977-1981.

immigrants, the gap between the Caribbean and Mexico as sources of immigration widens.)

The figures in Tables 1.2 and 1.3 do not include the 10,000 to 20,000 temporary workers who come to the United States each year (see Chapter 8 by Terry McCoy) or the large numbers of people from the region who have entered or remain illegally in the United States. The Select Commission on Immigration and Refugee Policy estimated that the majority of undocumented workers in the United States--three to six million in 1981--were from Mexico but "an increasing proportion . . . appear to come from countries other than Mexico--from the Dominican Republic, Jamaica, El Salvador, Trinidad and Tobago, Guatemala, Haiti, and Colombia. . . ."[5] Morris and Mayio estimated that five of the top nine source countries of undocumented workers in 1975 to 1977 were Caribbean islands. Rough estimates in the late 1970s suggested a total illegal Caribbean population in the United States of slightly less than one million people.[6]

Unlike illegal workers from Mexico and Central America who travel overland by stealth, many undocumented workers from the Caribbean are said to arrive in the United States legally and just overstay their visas. Although estimates of the percentage of visa-abusers are not yet reliable, during the decade of the 1970s, Caribbean people received nearly 6 million nonimmigrant visas--representing 10 to 20 percent of the population, depending on the estimates of the numbers of multiple entries.[7] (See Table 1.4)

An analysis of the likely demographic, social, and economic changes in the region suggests that the pressures to emigrate are likely to remain strong in the next two decades. Although the rate of population growth has begun to decline, the population will continue to increase and so too will the labor force and the level of unemployment. As the level of education continues to rise, and innovations and efficiencies in communications and transportation continue to narrow the distances between countries, a larger proportion of the population will find the United States more accessible. As Caribbean communities become more settled in the United States, new emigrants will find the trip and the transition easier. Surveys taken in the region show an increasing number of people who have lived in the United States for an extended period and an even higher percentage of respondents interested in moving there permanently.[8]

Two other factors--political instability and immigration policy--are important as one considers the possible magnitude of emigration from the region to the United States in the next two decades. The case of Central America during the last five years poignantly

Table 1.4

Caribbean Nonimmigrant Visas, by Country or Region of Birth, 1970s

Country/Region of Birth	1970	1971	1972	1973	1974	1975	1976	1977	1978	1979	Ten-Year Total
All countries (millions)	4.432	4.404	5.171	5.977	6.909	7.084	10.328	8.036	9.344	7.060	68.745
Caribbean	529,627	420,542	501,811	562,234	598,058	591,848	861,292	639,133	732,767	547,051	5,984,363
Anguilla	-	-	-	-	-	-	-	1,002	1,083	1,529	3,614
Antigua	20,697	12,507	12,586	14,279	14,763	11,445	12,838	8,657	8,213	6,601	122,586
Bahamas	101,739	89,090	84,372	87,378	83,594	71,165	101,050	87,062	107,632	74,266	887,348
Barbados	11,552	9,972	11,633	13,641	15,444	13,116	21,234	19,111	17,959	10,706	144,368
Belize	4,393	3,697	3,695	4,404	6,153	6,866	9,962	6,986	9,828	6,298	62,282
Bermuda	14,321	14,059	17,710	20,147	20,352	18,063	29,462	24,157	23,761	17,622	199,644
Br. Virgin Is.	9,571	5,933	5,896	7,200	7,550	9,368	10,781	9,091	8,902	11,063	85,454
Dominica	7,578	9,294	11,276	6,458	7,130	5,692	4,318	2,726	2,526	1,736	58,234
Dominican Rep.	105,191	74,252	111,845	124,528	143,512	149,386	207,435	154,964	166,519	134,461	1,372,093
Guyana	12,697	9,266	9,793	12,443	14,151	11,119	19,752	14,933	18,228	12,053	134,435
Haiti	24,535	25,299	28,351	32,523	37,287	42,589	70,934	52,091	62,405	37,358	413,372
Jamaica	81,727	70,743	97,337	113,300	123,073	124,312	188,896	127,990	142,538	98,466	1,168,382
Neth. Antilles	11,201	9,197	9,710	12,405	21,871	13,672	19,940	15,868	18,851	12,862	145,577
St. Kitts-Nevis	27,244	13,656	14,695	14,620	14,771	12,626	14,166	8,605	6,906	6,372	134,661
St. Lucia	8,722	4,075	4,447	5,072	5,486	4,055	5,325	3,480	3,745	3,038	47,445
Trinidad & Tob.	41,788	34,570	37,466	44,605	48,295	42,631	68,102	51,976	61,690	41,948	473,071
Other	46,671	33,932	41,000	49,131	34,626	55,573	77,097	50,434	71,981	70,672	531,297

Source: U.S. Department of Justice, 1979 Statistical Yearbook of the Immigration and Naturalization Service (Washington, D.C.: Government Printing Office), p. 40. Years ended June 30, 1970-75, and years ended September 30, 1977-79; 1976 includes July-September transition quarter. A nonimmigrant is an alien admitted in temporary status. Data exclude border crossers, crewmen, and insular travelers. Students and others entering with multiple entry documents are only counted on the first admission.

demonstrates the impact of political instability on migration flows. Though the population of Central America tripled since 1950, the impact on migration to the United States until 1979 was modest. Since then, violence and political instability provided the impetus for a massive, mostly illegal migration. Only 5,000 Nicaraguans and 14,311 Salvadorans legally immigrated to the United States in 1980 and 1981, but estimates in a U.S. Bureau of the Census study range from 25,000 to 100,000 Nicaraguans and up to 500,000 Salvadorans who have emigrated illegally to the United States from 1978 to 1983.[9] Most of these migrants fall into a bureaucratic gray area between an economic migrant and a political refugee: people who may have considered emigration for economic reasons but were finally impelled to move because of the violence.[10]

The propensity to emigrate is often transformed into movement by political instability, but the prime factor determining where people go is immigration policy and its implementation. "Whatever factors incline individuals to stay in their country or to leave it, the countries of potential destination determine the actual level and character of transnational flows."[11] Many from the Caribbean and Central America will emigrate if it is legally permissible; fewer will consider emigrating if it is illegal; and many fewer will attempt to emigrate if laws are effectively administered to deny illegals entry at the border or access to a job. Political instability and violence would increase the numbers in each category.

The human ties binding the United States and the nations of the Caribbean have grown thicker and stronger, and mean more migration can be expected in the future. In a nation of 233 million people like the United States, however, the Caribbean presence is generally not as obvious or as important as the emigrants' absence from their home nations. The minimum proportion of Caribbean people who have migrated to the United States in the last thirty years as a percent of the current populations in their homelands ranges from nearly 9 percent in Haiti to over 25 percent in Barbados, with a regional average of 10 percent. Table 1.5 does not include data for the migration of Puerto Ricans, since they have been U.S. citizens since 1917. Emigration by Puerto Ricans from the island to the mainland has left two million people on the mainland (about 60 percent of these in New York City) and 3.2 million on the island.

The asymmetry in the relationship between the small nations of the Caribbean and the United States influences virtually all international transactions, and migration is no exception. For example, Jamaica

Table 1.5

Caribbean Migration to the United States: The Reciprocal Impact

Country	Population[a]	Total Immigration 1950-1983[b]	Est. Illegal Population in the U.S.[c]	Migrants to the U.S. as % of Home Population[d]
Cuba	9,771,000	910,867	-	9.3
Dominican Republic	5,762,000	318,644	225,000	9.4
Haiti	6,000,000	132,610	400,000	8.9
Commonwealth Caribbean				
Barbados	252,000	38,183	25,000	25.1
Guyana	795,000	80,462	-	10.1
Jamaica	2,225,000	288,464	250,000	21.4
Trinidad & Tobago	1,176,000	100,305	60,000	13.6
Total Caribbean	28,329,484	1,869,535	960,000	10.0

[a]Table 1.1

[b]Figures for 1950 to 1969 are for immigration by country/region of last permanent residence. Those for 1970 to 1983 are for country/region of birth. Note that these figures for immigration flows, not stocks. Return migration is not considered. Source: U.S. Department of Justice, INS Statistical Yearbooks (Washington, D.C.: Government Printing Office) for those years.

[c]Estimated stock of illegal population--from testimony by Virginia Dominiquez, Hearings before the Subcommittee on Inter-American Affairs of the Committee on International Relations, U.S. House of Representatives, 95th Congress, Second Session, May-August 1978, pp. 217-218. Estimates on the illegal Haitian population are from James Allman, "Haitian Migration: Thirty Years Assessed," Migration Today, vol. 10, no. 1, p. 8.

[d]These figures are imprecise. They are underestimates of the total numbers who migrated in the past thirty years as a percent of the home populations, since they do not take flows of illegals, nor of legal temporary migrants, into account. But they are overestimates of the populations outside their countries at the present time, since they have not been adjusted for the return of legal immigrants. See the discussion on statistics for Cuban refugees in Robert A. Pastor, "Migration in the Caribbean Basin: The Need for an Approach as Dynamic as the Phenomenon," in Mary M. Kritz, ed., U.S. Immigration and Refugee Policy: Global and Domestic Issues (Lexington, Mass.: Lexington Books, 1983), p. 98.

had a population of 1.4 million in 1950. One in five
left during the next twenty years and were joined by
another 190,000 born after 1950 and leaving before
1980. Without emigration, one scholar estimated that
the Jamaican population would have had more than
600,000 more people than it has today, and an
additional 330,000 jobs would have been needed during
the 1970s. Even though emigration reduced population
growth and the size of the labor force, there were also
significant costs. During the 1970s, the equivalent of
more than half of the graduates of all Jamaica's
university and vocational schools left Jamaica for the
North American labor force.[12] But from the U.S.
perspective, the 18,600 Jamaican professionals and
managers who emigrated represented a miniscule
percentage of the number who graduated from U.S.
universities during this same period. In short, the
emigration may have cost Jamaica relatively more
economically than it benefited the United States.

Because of the asymmetry in the relationship, a
minor decision by the U.S. government or even by a U.S.
company can have a major impact on a nation in the
region. A decision to reduce the sugar quota can erase
overnight one-fifth of a country's foreign exchange. A
decision by ten medium-sized U.S. companies to invest
in Dominica and generate 5,000 jobs would reduce
unemployment from over 20 percent to nothing. The
tourist industry that supported about 25,000 jobs in
Haiti almost suffered a complete collapse because
rumors surrounding the disease AIDS reduced the number
of tourists from 70,000 in 1981 to 10,000 in 1982.[13]
Or a new U.S. immigration law that reduced current
levels of legal and/or illegal immigration--like the
Simpson-Mazzoli Immigration Reform and Control Act--
could have serious effects on the Caribbean. However,
the nature of such effects cannot be predicted with any
precision because still too little is known about the
relationship between migration and development in the
region.

III. Errant Assumptions, Faulty Policies

The conventional wisdom concerning the
relationship between migration and development in the
Caribbean--and elsewhere--can be summarized with two
propositions. First, that emigration from the
overpopulated, underemployed nations of the Caribbean
functions as an essential escape valve, contributing to
the economic development (and the political stability)
of the sending nations by releasing large numbers of
unemployed persons and by generating remittances. The
corollary to this proposition is that closure of the
U.S. labor market to emigrants from the Caribbean would

lead to higher rates of unemployment, and lower growth, and perhaps to political and social instability. Second, that the only way to solve the problem of migration is to "go to the source" and promote the economic development of the sending countries.

These two propositions continue to hold court and influence U.S. government policy. The first proposition, for example, was a premise of the December 1982 hearings of the Subcommittee on Census and Population of the House of Representatives on the Simpson-Mazzoli bill. The hearings' explicit purpose was to examine the implications of the bill for the Caribbean Basin, but their implicit intent was to impede passage of the bill by suggesting that it would hurt relations with the Caribbean and exacerbate instability there.[14]

The second proposition was one of the Reagan administration's arguments in favor of the Caribbean Basin Initiative--a comprehensive trade and investment policy for the region. Testifying for the bill, a senior administration official said it was needed for "alleviating the root causes of human misery which have stimulated a major and sustained flow of people from the Caribbean Basin into the United States. . . ."[15] President Reagan posed the issue more starkly in an address to the nation on May 9, 1984, when he warned of "the prospect of hundreds of thousands of refugees" from Central America coming to the United States if Congress did not approve his request for aid and if Marxists took power.[16]

These propositions not only continue to shape U.S. policy, but they also reflect the predominant view of Caribbean (and Mexican) leaders and influence Caribbean emigration policy--or, rather, lack of policy--as well. Emigration from the Caribbean is viewed as a "fact of life," "a survival strategy," a "structural reality"--all variations on the safety-valve thesis.[17]

Much research, however, raises questions about these two propositions. The average Caribbean migrant is above the average national in education, health, and income, and most legal migrants are considerably above the average.[18] Moreover, most migrants were employed until the time of their departure. Unless these migrants are immediately replaced by equally well-qualified and well-trained fellow citizens, the proposition that emigration from the Caribbean is a safety valve, releasing population and unemployment pressures, may very well be inaccurate. On the contrary, many islands are exporting highly motivated labor with scarce skills; this emigration can hardly be considered beneficial to the economic development of the region. Remittances can support families and

provide foreign exchange, but they can also contribute
to inflation and to dependence on luxury goods.

Even the precise effect of closure on the sending
country is not clear cut. Regarding the classic case
of the deportation of West Indians during the
depression, interpretations differ as to whether that
caused the riots of 1935-1938. Some authors argue that
the link is indisputable: "The cutoff of emigration
outlets for laborers of the smallest islands was a
fundamental cause of West Indian unrest."[19] But others
attribute the unrest to the depression and to the
organization of labor unions.[20]

In approaching the relationship from the other
direction, some continue to recommend development as a
strategy for reducing the pressures of migration;
however, development has almost always resulted in
considerable internal dislocations from rural to urban
areas and subsequently toward international
migration. The case of Puerto Rico, where nearly 40
percent of the population migrated to the United States
during the period of accelerated growth, is
illustrative, as is the more recent case of the
Dominican Republic's rapid economic growth in the mid-
1960s, which coincided with the departure of large
numbers of emigrants.

Both the rate and the kind of economic development
affect urbanization and emigration, but it is not clear
which policies are most effective in reducing migration
pressures. Rapid urbanization in the Caribbean area is
a serious problem in and of itself and often the first
step in a two-step process leading to emigration to the
United States. Therefore, it is also important to
examine policies that hinder or accelerate rural-to-
urban migration.[21]

Between 1950 and 1970 the urban population in the
Caribbean grew twice as fast as the rural population,
but between 1970 and 1980 it grew four times as fast.
By the year 2000, nearly two-thirds of the Caribbean
population is expected to live in urban areas as
compared to 38 percent in 1960.[22] One study found that
internal migration is reduced by programs that increase
cultivable land, reduce population fertility, or permit
greater equity in the distribution of income or land.
Conversely, migration is stimulated by programs that
increase access to cities, commercialize agriculture,
increase rural inequalities, or raise education or
skill to a level inappropriate to the particular rural
area.[23]

Still another, rather innovative theory regards
migrants not as risk-takers, as conventional wisdom
would call them, but risk-avoiders who emigrate as part
of a family insurance strategy. The policy implication
of this theory would be to provide more security to

families rather than, say, more income to farmers as the best way to reduce migration.[24]

Former Mexican President Jose Lopez Portillo repeatedly expressed his country's preference for exporting goods, not people, as a way of encouraging the United States to open its markets further. The assumption that receiving nations have a choice between accepting goods or illegal aliens, however, is also weak. Indeed, certain export-oriented development strategies, like Operation Bootstrap and the U.S.-Mexican Border Industrialization Program, appear to have stimulated both exports and migrants. Both programs were quite effective in attracting assembly-type industries, which created jobs. In Puerto Rico, the program accelerated the movement from the rural areas, and in Mexico, the program encouraged movement to the border areas. The journey to the continental United States was shortened. If the Caribbean Basin Initiative succeeds in attracting assembly operations to the region, it might produce a similar result—increased not reduced migration.[25]

In the few efforts to assess whether U.S. aid could reduce the pressures of migration, analysts have been cautious, suggesting that job-creation efforts could relieve some pressures in the short run, and population programs and better income distribution could help in the long run, but U.S. aid programs could only have a modest, marginal impact on both.[26]

The relationship between migration and development is more complex than conventional wisdom considers it to be. Some aspects of migration assist development whereas others impede it; similarly, some aspects of the development process can encourage migration whereas others do not. Before describing the specific policy issues, I will review the literature.

IV. Review of the Literature: Other Regions

Much of the literature on international migration has focused on the causes of migration (the "push" factors) and on the costs and benefits to receiving nations rather than sending nations.

At least four theories are put forth to explain migration.[27] The most well known is the push-pull theory, which explains why individuals move—in response to population pressure, to lack of economic opportunity, to political change, or to the promise of a better life. A second theory—referred to alternately as "household networks" or "transnational communities"—explains why entire villages appear to move and to facilitate movement by others. A third theory—the historical/structural one—explains why people from the developing world move to industrialized countries; the international economic system siphons off cheap, surplus labor from the periphery to man the factories of the metropole. Finally, a public policy theory suggests that laws or the absence of a clear, enforceable policy can encourage, discourage, or divert the flows of people.

These theories are compatible in part because they address slightly different questions. The push-pull framework has been most often used empirically to understand the main causes of migration. A consensus among scholars is that the poorest people in the most isolated communities are not the ones migrating to the United States. Beyond that, scholars also agree that no single factor explains emigration, but rather a combination of factors related to economic and social development and political change. These push factors are wide ranging and numerous, including agricultural stagnation or modernization, urbanization, unemployment, inadequate educational or health facilities, limited markets, political instability or violence, and income differentials. Even if one could reduce virtually every source of pressure for emigration, at least one cause, say income differentials, will always exist to push or pull prospective emigrants. As long as better opportunities exist abroad, there will always be pressure to emigrate. However, the magnitude of the flow is likely to be affected by the number and kind of pressures so that if all pressures but one could be reduced, the overall flow might be reduced as well.

Before reviewing the limited research on migration and development in the Caribbean region, I will review the more extensively studied case of migration to northern Europe in the postwar period. Initially, this migration was viewed as benefiting the receiving countries in northwestern Europe--by furnishing needed and inexpensive labor on a temporary basis. It was also viewed as helping the Mediterranean sending countries by providing jobs and new skills to people unemployed at home. Remittances also helped Mediterranean families with income support and the governments with hard currency.

In the late 1960s and early 1970s, when the labor influx grew most rapidly, there was a reassessment. Most European host governments had not anticipated some of the social and cultural consequences of these migrations; after considering them, some concluded that the social costs may have outweighed the economic benefits. The reassessment of the impact of migration on the sending countries also produced mixed results. The original expectation that migration would significantly upgrade the skills of emigrants, which together with remittances would provide a substantial

stimulus to economic development in the sending
countries, was simply not fulfilled.[28]
    Research on migration in the Middle East and North
Africa also notes that developmental results for the
sending countries fell considerably below
expectations. In a major study for the World Bank,
researchers concluded that labor migration from nine
Middle Eastern countries to the oil-exporting states in
the region "cannot be seen as having contributed
greatly to accelerated long-term economic growth
amongst the labor-supplying countries. It appears to
have brought rather limited benefits, which in the
social account and the longer term, may be outweighed
by costs incurred."[29]
    The World Bank study found that unemployment was
hardly affected since most of the migrants were
previously employed. Because of the rigidities in the
labor markets of these countries, those jobs requiring
some level of education and skill were not always
filled. Remittances may have been considerable but
"appear to cause demand-led inflation, which if often
aggravated by cost-push inflation, caused further labor
out-migration." Instead of stimulating demand for
local products, remittances and the movement of
migrants altered consumption patterns toward more
expensive imports. Even though labor migration did not
appear to greatly benefit sending countries, the
authors concluded that this result may have had more to
do with the absence of government policy than with the
migration itself:

> A laissez-faire attitude towards migration
> for employment on the part of the labor
> exporters should be ruled out. Greater
> benefits can be extracted for the labor-
> exporting countries with plans that invest
> remittances, that utilize more effectively the
> new skills learned by the migrants, and that
> carefully take into account the skilled
> manpower needs of the sending country.[30]

    In a study on labor migration from Bangladesh to
the Middle East, also sponsored by the World Bank, the
authors made similar assumptions and reached similar
conclusions. Eight million of a labor force of nearly
30 million in 1978, were unemployed; yet the number of
Bangladeshis migrating for labor to the Middle East was
insignificant--less than 60,000. The authors assumed
that migration constituted a benefit to the sending
country; they only questioned the extent of that
benefit. Given the magnitude of Bangladesh's
development problem and the size of the migration, not
surprisingly they found that the program had a limited

impact. Still, the study concluded that there were
ways to multiply the positive impact of the migration
program, and the government would be better served
identifying those ways: "The question is not whether
Bangladesh should allow migration, but whether it has
the determination and capability to formulate and
administer an appropriate migration policy."[31]
      A different study of the same region reached
similar conclusions--that the impact of emigration on
the sending country was "not so unambiguously benign"
and that well-formulated policies should replace the
"highly questionable" laissez-faire approach.[32]

V. Review of the Literature: Migration and Development in the Caribbean

      Research on migration from the Caribbean also
identifies both positive and negative effects on
economic development. The most compelling positive
effect is remittances, which one scholar described as
"impressive." In a study of three communities in the
Dominican Republic, Grasmuck found that more than one-
third of all households reported receiving remittances.
Typically, the foreign exchange was spent on food,
clothing, radios, televisions, and other consumer goods.[33]
      The U.S. temporary worker program (II-2 labor) may
be extremely small in numbers, but it can have a
disproportionately large and positive impact on the
small countries in the Caribbean. In a preliminary
study of temporary worker remittances to St. Vincent
from the United States, Dawn Marshall found that
remittances accounted for 3 to 6 percent of St.
Vincent's gross domestic product and 9 to 28 percent of
total exports for the years 1965 to 1979. This amount
accrued from only 250 to 500 workers. Another study by
two scholars from the University of Florida found that
in 1980-81, H-2 workers remitted about $19 million to
the Caribbean.[34]
      In 1976, the U.S. State Department estimated that
Belize had 30,000 of its citizens working in the United
States--most of them illegally--and that they remitted
$10 million to $15 million annually. The number of
migrants was roughly equal to the labor force remaining
in Belize, and the remittances approximated Belize's
earnings from sugar exports. Despite an annual birth
rate approaching 4 percent, emigration was so
substantial that the country's population had been
decreasing since 1972.[35]
      One scholar estimated that from 1960 to 1970,
emigration reduced the natural population increase of
the Caribbean by half--enough to cause a 12 percent
decline in the size of the labor force in fourteen

Commonwealth Caribbean countries.[36] Another study of
the period 1969 to 1970 found that the average annual
rate of emigration as a percent of the natural increase
in the population ranged from 53 percent in Trinidad to
142 percent in St. Kitts.[37] Unemployment, which ranges
from 20 to 30 percent in the Caribbean, would
doubtlessly be severely exacerbated without such
sizable emigration.[38]

Emigration has also helped Haiti keep its annual
population growth to about 1.6 percent, "which is very
low for a developing country with little use of modern
contraception." And the level of remittances was
estimated at 5 percent of Haiti's gross national
product (GNP), or approximately $50 million in 1977.
This is more money than the Haitian government spent
that year on wages.[39]

The most extreme cases of dependence on
remittances occur perhaps in the rural areas of
Mexico. In their study of a small Indian community in
Mixteca, Stuart and Kearney referred to the impact of
migration on development as nothing less than
"overwhelming. Without the possibility of migration
earnings, the village could not exist as a viable
community at its present population." The authors
concluded that for most households "migration is the
only alternative to starvation." Remittances mainly go
for subsistence needs and for improved housing. Their
study provides the classic illustration of the safety
valve theory, in which migration is "a palliative for
unemployment, land shortage, lack of credit, and all
the other typical conditions of rural stagnation." But
the authors noted that, even though migration keeps the
village from collapsing and its people from starving,
it also inhibits growth. Indeed, they found that the
village remains in its primitive form precisely because
the "safety net" of foreign remittances has made
adaptation less necessary. The community, in short,
has become "dangerously dependent on migration." It
survives, but barely.[40]

As with Mexico, virtually every study on the
Caribbean found that remittances are used for
consumption rather than investment, and that migration
leads to an increase in the number of dependent,
female-headed households.[41]

Since 1978, the World Bank has published more than
100 economic reports on the Caribbean, and one
consistent theme running through many of these reports
is that "the paucity of management resources in the
public sector" as well as in the private sector is a
major constraint on economic development, and in many
cases, on absorbing foreign aid.[42] The scarcity of
skilled manpower is caused by two factors: the lack of
quality education relevant to the region's needs and

the emigration of skilled workers--the so-called
"brain-skill drain." This drain affects both the
public and private sectors. Hope reported that in
1975, 40 percent of the private firms surveyed in
Trinidad and Tobago felt that a shortage of skilled and
professional labor was "hindering their plans for
expansion."[43]

According to Palmer, the percentage of
professional and technical workers emigrating to the
United States from the Caribbean as a percent of all
Caribbean emigrants has ranged consistently from about
10 to 20 percent since records have been kept.[44] From
the U.S. perspective, the numbers are not particularly
large, but when they are broken down by country of
origin, it becomes evident that the impact on some
countries is substantial. Jamaica has been a major
source of professional personnel migrating to the
United States, contributing anywhere from 37 percent in
1962 to 70 percent in 1969 of all Commonwealth
Caribbean professionals.[45] Girling found that from
1967 to 1968, 4,140 technical and professional workers
emigrated from Jamaica to the United States. Although
only 4 percent of the Jamaican labor force was composed
of professional and technical workers, 17 percent of
all emigrants were in this category.[46] Foner observed
that Jamaican migrants to the United States "have been
more skilled than the average Jamaican and that the
typical emigrant worker was not unemployed back
home." She estimated that 51 percent of the Jamaicans
trained in professional and management skills between
1977 and 1981 immigrated to the United States.[47]

In a study of a small community in Haiti, Maguire
concluded that "migration does not lead to human or
social change in the parish. To the contrary,
migration tends to drain off the more energetic people,
which must retard the community's development."[48]
Grasmuck arrived at a similar conclusion in her study
of the Dominican Republic: Emigration "does not draw
from the displaced, jobless--the 'labor surplus.' On
the contrary, in the case of Juan Pablo [a fictional
name for an agricultural community in the Dominican
Republic], out-migration has increased unemployment by
undermining the economic base of the community." She
further suggested that in the Dominican Republic,
emigration may have decreased the pressure for agrarian
reform, thus further debilitating an already weak
agricultural base and leading to an increased
dependency on cash payments.[49]

Allman implied that emigration has reduced the
pressure on the Haitian government to develop a
coherent population policy.[50] It should also be
recalled that Mexico only developed a population policy
in 1974 and did not really focus on encouraging labor-

intensive investments until 1980--nearly two decades
too late. One might legitimately ask whether the
reduced pressures caused by decades of legal and
illegal migration led the Mexican government to
calculate the country's domestic needs in a way that
permitted it to avoid the population issue and the
unemployment problem for so long.

The effects of migration on agricultural
production in the Caribbean are not clear. In a small,
poor agricultural community in the Dominican Republic,
Grasmuck found that the effects of outmigration were
"decidedly negative": poor utilization of land by
intensive grazing reduced production. But the pattern
was different in a more prosperous and dynamic
agricultural community where agricultural production
did not decline. Grasmuck attributed this to the
already developed infrastructure.[51] The pattern is
similarly ambiguous at a macroeconomic level, as
agriculture has been declining everywhere in the
Caribbean--in countries of high as well as low
emigration.

In summary, the literature suggests that migration
clearly has both positive and negative effects on
individuals, households, and national economic
development. The effects on individuals and households
are generally positive, though there are some
drawbacks. Although raising the levels of income
through remittances, emigrants also tend to leave
behind dependent (nonproductive) families.

At the macro level, emigration often lowers
population growth and unemployment, but it can also
produce a brain or skill drain. Immigrants are often
among the most highly motivated in the population, and
their departure may lead to economic stagnation in
their home communities. Finally, large-scale
emigration can provide confused signals to home
governments, leading them to think that they have less
cause to promote population planning or manpower
programs, or to encourage labor-intensive rather than
capital-intensive investments.

VI. The Policy Issues

Powerful structural--geographical, economic, and
familial--and psychological reasons explain why
emigration is a part of the Caribbean reality. Since
these determinants can be neither ignored nor changed
to any great degree, policy should focus on the
margins: (a) to reduce the costs and multiply the
benefits of emigration to the development of the
sending countries; (b) to identify and promote those
development policies that minimize the pressures to
migrate (internally and internationally) without

hampering unduly either personal or national development; (c) to redirect development projects and plans to take account of migration; and (d) to increase productive employment opportunities in home countries. Precluding emigration is no more an option than precluding development. This does not mean that small changes in policy are of little consequence to the region. Because of the asymmetry in size and wealth, even a marginal change in U.S. policy can have a very large impact on the Caribbean. Moreover, given the importance of migration and development to the region, and the small size and openness of the nations, relatively minor changes in the policies of these nations could have significant repercussions for their people.

To address these issues, the nineteen chapters of this book are divided into the following six parts: (I) the impact of development on migration; (II) the impact of emigration on development: case studies; (III) the impact of different types of migration on development; (IV) Caribbean policies; (V) international and U.S. options; and (VI) a synthesis of theory and policy. In the next section, I will describe each part and introduce each chapter.

(I)   The Impact of Development on Migration

In deciding on policies and forging these policies into a development strategy, a government must balance or select from several different development objectives: growth, equity, employment, agricultural productivity, education, health care, and so on. In pursuing one objective, a government might preclude the achievement of another objective. For example, many governments keep food prices low to permit more consumption by the urban poor, but such a policy often discourages food production, encourages food imports, and accelerates urbanization. Still this policy might be maintained for one of three reasons: (a) The value of social peace in the urban areas may be calculated to exceed the economic costs of the policy; (b) the implications and costs are not known or calculated; or (c) the costs may be "concealed" by a variety of means, e.g., food aid or illegal migration abroad. We would not presume to try to influence the first reason but to provide data on (b) or (c) to permit an informed decision.

Diaz-Briquets explores the impact of alternative development policies and strategies on international migration by comparing cases involving large and small flows of emigration. Diaz-Briquets identifies nine distinct causes of migration, and addresses the questions of which development policies and strategies

appear to increase the level of emigration, and which
do not?

In considering the relationship between migration
and development, Anthony Maingot focuses on the
political and social ramifications. What are the
social and political causes and consequences of
emigration? Maingot suggests that the conventional
dichotomy between internal and international migration
is less relevant in the Caribbean area because it is a
single socio-cultural area. The social network that
connects Caribbean communities in the United States and
the Caribbean has historically been used to assist
individuals to advance socially and economically in the
United States and politically in the Caribbean. These
social and political ties have become the parameters
within which leaders in the Caribbean must work. To
ignore them, Maingot argues, is politically perilous.

(II) The Impact of Emigration on Development: Case Studies

Although the emphasis of recent literature on
immigration has been on the consequences for the
receiving society, attention has begun to shift toward
understanding the consequences for the sending
countries. Three separate case studies on different
countries and subregions of the Caribbean identify and
assess the developmental costs and benefits of
emigration on the sending areas. Both Marshall and
Anderson build on their own survey research conducted
over a number of years, and Preeg draws on his
experience as a former U.S. Ambassador to Haiti as well
as on recent research on Haitian and Dominican
development. The three cases provide a good
opportunity to test the broader validity of certain
hypotheses on the net developmental impact of
emigration.

Although addressing most of the same questions,
the three authors use different styles and approaches,
which together deepen the understanding of the impact
of migration on Caribbean development. Dawn Marshall
describes the evolution of development planning in the
Eastern Caribbean, and after discussing the case of St.
Vincent in greater detail, she concludes that
emigration has had a detrimental impact on the region's
desperate need for good management. Overall, Marshall
finds that emigration has had a positive impact on
reducing population growth; it has had an uncertain
impact on unemployment; and the impact of remittances
is in inverse proportion to the size of the nation's
economy, with the smallest islands being aided most.

Using the case of Jamaica, Patricia Anderson
suggests that the political as well as the economic

costs and benefits of emigration need to be weighed,
while recognizing that emigration is only one dimension
of a dependent model of economic development. Using
this model, she describes how any attempt to interrupt
the flow of capital or to fundamentally transform the
social and economic structure is likely to have a
similarly disruptive impact on the flow of labor. This
situation is precisely what occurred in the 1970s when
white-collar emigration severely retarded Jamaica's
economic development. At the same time, this
emigration benefited the government politically in two
ways: Opponents of the region departed and their
departure sometimes opened up positions for young
graduates. In addressing the question of what would
have happened if these emigrants had not left, Anderson
distinguishes between "social need" and "effective
demand": Even though managers are needed, the system
does not always create opportunities for their
productive employment.

Finally, Ernest Preeg finds that the massive
migration flows from both Haiti and the Dominican
Republic in the last two decades have probably hurt
more than helped their two economies. Preeg offers an
interesting rebuttal to the safety-valve thesis: He
suggests that the flow of Haitian boat people
distracted small farmers and significantly lowered
productivity. He believes that the effective
interdiction efforts--which reduced the number of boat
people from more than 15,000 in 1980 to 134 in 1982--
will improve the development prospects of Haiti.

(III) The Impact of Different Types of Migration on Development

As one dives into the immigration issue, one swims
past two simple and contradictory assumptions. The
first is that all immigration is the same. The second
is that each type of migration is totally different
from the others: legal or illegal; temporary or
permanent; economic or political; out of the country
(emigration), into the country (immigration), or return
to the country. In Part II, three authors explore the
developmental impact of permanent legal migration from
three sets of countries, and in Part III, four authors
assess these assumptions by exploring the developmental
impact of four types of migration.

Deeply rooted in the culture of Caribbean
emigration is the "ideology of return"--the belief that
the trip abroad is temporary. In Chapter 7, Elizabeth
Thomas-Hope finds that this phenomenon retains a strong
hold on Caribbean psychology even if not on Caribbean
behavior. Are these returning migrants catalysts for
economic development or burrs of social frustration?

Although existing data are insufficient to reach a definitive conclusion, Thomas-Hope finds that the returning migrant has not significantly upgraded his skills, and, though he often returns with some funding that could be used for investment, it generally is not.

Like the returning migrant, the temporary worker goes abroad for a fixed period. Even though the profiles of the average temporary agricultural workers differ markedly from those of other types of migrants, their impact on development is often quite similar. For example, all transmit remittances to raise the income level in their households in their homeland. Terry McCoy surveys the history of the temporary worker program and then focuses on the specific case of the developmental impact on the Caribbean of West Indians brought to cut sugarcane in Florida.

Demetrios Papademetriou addresses a similar set of questions in his chapter on illegal aliens. Extrapolating from a large sample he has developed of illegal Caribbean immigrants in the New York-New Jersey metropolitan area, Papademetriou suggests that the developmental impact of Caribbean illegals does not differ greatly from that of legal immigrants; however, all Caribbean emigrants have a different impact than, say, Mexicans, as they reflect a higher level of education and better wage-earning capacity. In one of his samples, the illegals remitted on average more than $1,000 per year, "very substantial figures when considering the average household's annual income."

Perhaps the most unexplored type of Caribbean migration in the twentieth century is the immigrant who settles in the Caribbean. Trevor Hope's chapter is therefore a most valuable and interesting contribution to this book. He finds that a much larger proportion of immigrants to the Caribbean as compared to the native population make a substantial contribution to their adopted nation's economy. (Of course, this is true of the impact of many immigrants to the United States and elsewhere.) However, legal restrictions on immigration to the Caribbean make it difficult for more than a few to use this opportunity. Although the developmental impacts of legal, illegal, temporary, and return migration contain many similarities, the policy implications of each are quite different. McCoy and Trevor Hope explore some of these considerations and offer some useful policy recommendations, which are summarized in the final chapter.

(IV) Migration and Development: Caribbean Policies

Since migration is so much a part of Caribbean consciousness, it is not surprising that migration should reflect and affect the broad panorama of Caribbean development. In Part IV, four Caribbean men of diverse backgrounds and perspectives open new paths in attempting to integrate migration with development strategy. Courtney Blackman, the governor of the Central Bank of Barbados, readily acknowledges the reluctance of Caribbean governments to formulate either migration policies or development strategies that incorporate migration; he concludes that this approach represents a serious oversight. After taking issue with the dependency theory as articulated by Patricia Anderson and Ralph Henry (with Kim Johnson), Blackman offers an alternative "open-systems" theory to describe Caribbean economies and to help guide the development of new policies that relate migration to development. Blackman's chapter represents one of the few efforts by a senior Caribbean government official to propose a wide ranging set of development policies that aim to use migration to benefit the Caribbean nations. (Jamaica's Prime Minister, Edward Seaga, also has recently suggested a number of specific ideas in this area.)[52] The most encouraging aspect of Blackman's ideas is their provocativeness; they will no doubt generate further discussion on these issues.

In addition to Blackman's more comprehensive approach, the other chapters in this part focus on two separate micro-development issues: manpower policy and employment generation. During the last two decades, the most reliable export of the Caribbean has been its skilled manpower. At the same time, most economic studies of the region point to the lack of skilled manpower as the most significant obstacle to economic development. Obviously, manpower policy significantly fails to connect skills to jobs, training to placement. If such policies exist, they are clearly not working properly.

One would expect a certain level of emigration of trained personnel from the Caribbean, but the scale reflects a larger problem. Governments are expending large amounts of scarce resources to train people, but they cannot find them jobs, and many emigrate.

Ralph Henry and Kim Johnson view emigration as symptomatic of a larger development failure, which they attribute mostly to dependency, but also to inadequate and ineffective manpower policies. Henry surveys the history of labor strategies and manpower policies in the region and then undertakes a comparative analysis of manpower policies of the four countries that have attempted the most radical economic re-structuring-- Guyana, Jamaica, Trinidad, and Grenada. With the exception of Trinidad, the other three governments provoked an exodus of talent, which retarded their development. He concludes that the increased emigration was "a good index of the failure of their attempts at economic re-structuring." Henry offers an alternative "human-resources strategy" modeled on the successful policies of Singapore and three other Asian countries.

The second micro-development study by Luther Miller focuses on ways to exploit the region's comparative advantage in tourism to stimulate answers to three other development problems: food production, job creation, and the need for foreign exchange. Two approaches are generally advocated to address the problem of a limited market: regional integration and/or improved and guaranteed access to a metropolitan market (the Lome agreement of the European Economic Community and the Caribbean Basin Initiative of the United States). However, the greatest untapped market opportunity is the one that accompanies North American tourists to the region. The Caribbean is saved the problem of exporting its goods; all it has to do is produce for an artificially expanded local market. Instead, however, the region has imported the tastes of the tourists and then the food to satisfy these tastes.[53]

Agriculture has declined, scarce foreign exchange is being wasted; urbanization increases, and unemployment has worsened throughout the region, as young people leave the farms but cannot find jobs in the towns.[54] In its 1981 report, the Group of Caribbean Experts, representing the most distinguished economists of the region, concluded its analysis of the agricultural problem with the following warning: "The gravity of the unemployment situation, especially as it affects young people, is the most explosive problem facing the region today."[55] Luther Miller explores this subject and suggests specific steps for generating employment opportunities by linking local agriculture with tourism.

(V) Migration and Development: International and U.S. Options

In an interview in which he referred to the "lack of managerial and entrepeneurial skills" as the single most significant impediment to development in the Caribbean, William Demas, president of the Caribbean Development Bank, acknowledged that the bank does not take migration into account in preparing its development projects. This is also true of the U.S. and Canadian aid agencies and the international development banks (the World Bank, the Inter-American Development Bank), and United Nations (UN) agencies.[56] Altogether, these external donors represent the principal sources of capital and

technical assistance for the region. G. Arthur Brown
reviews the effects and impediments to regional
economic integration, and the role played by
international agencies in the region's development.
Brown focuses on the failure of development agencies to
take more fully into account surplus labor and offers
recommendations for establishing a more direct link
between development projects and labor utilization.

Pastor and Rogers address the question of whether
international mechanisms could be devised to use
migration to enhance economic development in the
sending countries. They examine migration-for-
development programs from other regions and adapt them
to the Caribbean. The two authors propose Caribbean
remittance banks, four separate return incentive
programs to close the management gap, and several
strategies to encourage young Caribbean graduates to
remain home or return after studying abroad.

U.S. immigration policies historically have been
sensitive to Latin America and to a slightly lesser
extent to the Caribbean as compared with the rest of
the world.[57] Since 1976, however, U.S. immigration
policy has treated the region as it does the rest of
the world. The Simpson-Mazzoli bill would permit a
doubling in the legal country quota for immigrants from
Mexico and Canada, but not for the Caribbean. Should
the United States consider special preferences for the
rest of the Caribbean Basin? What will be the impact
of the Simpson-Mazzoli bill on the region? Should U.S.
immigration policies be revised to improve the
prospects for economic development in the Caribbean?

Should any special steps be taken to reduce the
brain drain? In the Report of the Select Commission on
Western Hemisphere Immigration in January 1968, the
commission concluded after some deliberation on the
brain-drain issue that "this matter is rather more one
for the consideration of the countries of emigration
than it is for the U.S. To deliberately forbid the
immigration of skilled persons would seem to do a
disservice to the interests of all parties concerned,
mindful as we may be of the problem which many Western
Hemisphere countries face in this regard."[58] Is there
any reason to change that evaluation?

The brain-drain remains a very thorny issue--for
the receiving nation as well as for the sending
nation. In May 1984, a task force of Republican
Congressmen issued a report on improving U.S.
competitiveness. One of its recommendations was to
permit more foreign students in engineering and science
to remain permanently in the United States.[59] Should
the United States follow this recommendation or adopt
an opposite policy--such as requiring professionals who
emigrate to pay an education tax to compensate the

sending countries for their investment? These
questions are addressed by Harris Miller in his
chapter.

What is the impact of U.S. aid programs and the
Caribbean Basin Initiative on migration? Should these
be altered to take migration into account? If so,
how? Hakim and Weintraub discuss these and other
issues for U.S. development policy in their chapter.

(VI) Toward a Synthesis in Theory and Policy

The last two chapters represent an effort to weld
the previous analyses into a coherent theoretical
(Chapter 18) and policymaking (Chapter 19) synthesis.
In Chapter 18, Reynolds approaches the issues from the
perspective of the entire Caribbean Basin and sets two
tasks for himself as he frames the conceptual issues
underlying the research project: to devise a relevant
new economic theory of migration and to use that theory
to propose a new development strategy for the Caribbean
Basin.

First, Reynolds assesses existing economic theory
on migration in the light of the data and insights
developed by the other authors, and he offers an
alternative theory. He finds both neoclassical theory,
which assumes away the issue of cross-national labor
mobility, and "segmentation" or "dualistic" theories of
labor markets incapable of explaining migration and its
relationship to development in the contemporary
world. Instead, he suggests that a dynamic new pattern
of movement of goods, technology, capital, and people
is emerging that breaks down traditionally segmented
markets.

Second, given this new internationalization of
production and migration, Reynolds argues that a
totally new approach is needed by the region to exploit
the new economic opportunities. He recommends a
"mutual development strategy" for the entire Caribbean
Basin to deal with regional migration and labor welfare
through innovative new production and market-sharing
arrangements.

In the final chapter, I try to do for policy what
Reynolds does for theory--summarize and synthesize the
principal findings and conclusions of the previous
chapters as well as those suggested by the participants
in the two conferences we held. In assembling the
various policy recommendations suggested by all the
authors and building on the Caribbean Basin conceptual
approach proposed by Reynolds, I also suggest ways to
shape the recommendations into a Caribbean Basin
Compact.

Notes

This paper has benefited from the comments of Sergio Diaz-Briquets, Peter Hakim, and Anthony Maingot. Carola Weil, Kim Cameron, and Charles Becker deserve a special note of gratitude for compiling the tables and checking some of the data in this chapter.

1. "C.I.A. Chief Sees Migration, Not Mining, as Public Worry," New York Times, April 16, 1984, p. A8.

2. The statistics are from the U.S. Department of Justice, 1983 Statistical Yearbook of the Immigration and Naturalization Service, Table 1, pp. 4-5.

3. Comptroller General of the United States, Report to the Congress: Puerto Rico's Political Future: A Divisive Issue With Many Dimensions (Washington, D.C.: General Accounting Office, March 2, 1981), pp. 26-32.

4. U.S. Department of Justice Annual INS Reports, developed in Tables 3 and 4 of "Caribbean Emigration and U.S. Immigration Policy: Cross Currents," by Robert Pastor, paper prepared for a Conference on the "International Relations of the Contemporary Caribbean," sponsored by the Caribbean Institute and Study Center for Latin America (CISCLA) of Inter-American University of Puerto Rico, San German, Puerto Rico, April 22-23, 1983.

5. U.S. Select Commission on Immigration and Refugee Policy, U.S. Immigration Policy and the National Interest: Staff Report (Washington, D.C., 1981), p. 66.

6. Milton Morris and Albert Mayio, Illegal Immigration and United States Foreign Policy (Washington, D.C.: Brookings Institution, October 1980), Chapter 4. Also see Table 1.4 in this paper for estimates of illegal migrants from the Caribbean area. When countries are ranked by the average annual expulsions of their nationals as reported by INS, nine of the top ten during the past ten years have been neighboring countries in the western hemisphere. (Milton D. Morris, Immigration: The Beleaguered Bureaucracy, Washington, D.C.: Brookings Institution, 1985, p. 59).

7. In 1983, for the first time, the Immigration and Naturalization Service kept computerized files on

the arrivals and departures of people with temporary
visas. While there is not yet a breakdown by region,
the agency had no record of departure for 2.1 million
people of the 10 million who entered in that year on a
non-immigrant visa. ("Closing the Door?" Newsweek,
June 25, 1984, p. 22). However, these figures may be
subject to as much as a 50% error in over-estimation.
(Telephone conversation, Dr. Dorothy Krahn, I.N.S.,
June 27, 1984)

8. For a review of the surveys, see Anthony P.
Maingot, "The Difficult Path to Socialism in the
English-Speaking Caribbean," in Richard R. Fagen (ed.),
Capitalism and the State in U.S.-Latin American
Relations (Stanford: Stanford University Press, 1979),
pp. 273, 281; and Anthony P. Maingot, "Options for
Grenada," Caribbean Review, Vol. XII, No. 4, p. 27.

9. Linda S. Peterson, U.S. Bureau of the Census,
"Central American Refugee Flows: 1978-1983," mimeo.,
January 11, 1984, pp. 6-9.

10. Astri Suhrke used the term "quasi-refugee" to
refer to another gray-area category of economic
migrants who left Communist states to take advantage of
generous refugee programs. She placed recent migrants
from Cuba, Indo-China, and East Germany in this
category. This is different from the category I
describe. (Astri Suhrke, "Global Refugee Movements and
Strategies of Response," in Mary M. Kritz (ed.), U.S.
Immigration and Refugee Policy: Global and Domestic
Issues (Lexington, Mass.: D.C. Heath and Company,
1983), p. 165.)

11. Aristide R. Zolberg, "The Political Economy
of Immigration," in Wayne A. Cornelius and Ricardo
Anzaldua Montoya (eds.), America's New Immigration
Law: Origins, Rationales, and Potential Consequences
Monograph Series 11 (San Diego: Center for U.S.-
Mexican Studies, 1983), p. 1.

12. Lorna Murray, National Planning Agency,
Ministry of Finance, Government of Jamaica, "Emigration
to North America from Jamaica, 1970-1980," mimeo.,
January 1982; Loy Bilderback, International Labor
Migration Project, Organization of American States,
"The Jamaican Experience: Population and Labor
Migration, 1950-2000," July 15, 1983, Washington, D.C.,
mimeo.

13. Latin America, Weekly Report, 9 December
1983, p. 12.

14. Hearings on the implications of H.R. 6514, the Immigration and Reform and Control Act of 1982, Subcommittee on Census and Population, Committee on Post Office and Civil Service, U.S. House of Representatives, 97th Congress, 2nd session, December 9, 1982.

15. Statement by Deputy Secretary of State Walter J. Stoessel, Jr. before the Senate Foreign Relations Committee, Hearings: Caribbean Basin Initiative, March 25, 1982, p. 47.

16. President Ronald Reagan, "U.S. Interests in Central America," Department of State, Bureau of Public Affairs, Washington, D.C., May 9, 1984.

17. Dawn Marshall, "Toward an Understanding of Caribbean Migration," in Mary M. Kritz (ed.), U.S. Immigration and Refugee Policy: Global and Domestic Issues (Lexington, Mass.: D.C. Heath and Company, 1983), p. 115; Anthony P. Maingot, "Caribbean Migration as a Structural Reality," revised version of paper presented to the Conference on Caribbean Migration sponsored by Georgetown University and Greater Miami United, Miami, Florida, December 8, 1982, p. 3; for an insightful description of Caribbean migration as a "strategy of survival," see Bonham Richardson, Caribbean Migrants: Environment and Human Survival on St. Kitts and Nevis (Knoxville: The University of Tennessee Press, 1983).

18. For the profile of the average migrants, see Wayne Cornelius, Mexican Migration to the United States (with Comparative Reference to Caribbean-Basin Migration: The State of Current Knowledge and Recommendations for Future Research), Center for U.S.-Mexican Studies, University of California, San Diego, Working Paper #2, May, 1979, pp. 91-98. Although the literature on migration and development in the Caribbean Basin is sparse, there have been some notable contributions. See the Winter issue, 1982-83 of International Migration Review, Vol. 16, and in particular the article by Thomas K. Morrison and Richard Sinkin, "International Migration in the Dominican Republic: Implications for Development Planning," pp. 819-836; Thomas K. Morrison, "The Relationship of U.S. Aid, Trade and Investment to Migration Pressures in Major Sending Countries," International Migration Review, Spring, 1982; Allen R. Newman, "The Impacts of Emigration on the Mexican Economy," Migration Today, Vol. X, No. 2, 17-21; Sidney Weintraub, "U.S. Foreign Economic Policy and Illegal Migration," Population Research and Policy Review, 2

(1983): 211-231; and Robert Pastor, "Migration in the Caribbean Basin: The Need for an Approach as Dynamic as the Phenomenon," in Mary M. Kritz (ed.), U.S. Immigration and Refugee Policy: Global and Domestic Issues. For an excellent case study, see Stanley Friedlander, Labor Migration and Economic Growth: A Case Study of Puerto Rico (Cambridge: The M.I.T. Press, 1965).

19. Bonham Richardson, Caribbean Migrants: Environment and Human Survival on St. Kitts and Nevis, Supra fn. #17, p. 142.

20. E.H. Carter, G.W. Digby, and R.N. Murray, History of the West Indian Peoples: 18th Century to Modern Times (London: Thomas Nelson, 1981), pp. 166-168.

21. On the two-step migration pattern from rural to urban to international, see D. Conway, "Step-Wise Migration: Toward a Clarification of the Mechanism," International Migration Review, Vol. XIV, No. 1: 3-14. Dr. Manuel Gollas, a Professor at El Colegio de Mexico, citing studies on the impact of development on migration, noted that an increase in the wage differential between Mexico City and outlying rural areas by 10% led to an increase in the flow of migration to the capital by 20%. (Cited in Structural Factors in Mexican and Caribbean Basin Migration: Proceedings of a Brookings Institution-El Colegio de Mexico Symposium, June 28-30, 1978 (Washington, D.C.: Brookings Institution), p. 128.

22. Kempe Ronald Hope, "Urban Population Growth in the Caribbean," Cities, November 1983, p. 167.

23. Richard Rhoda, "Rural Development and Urban Migration: Can We Keep Them Down on the Farm?" International Migration Review, Vol. XVII, 34-64. August Schumacher also discusses Mexican agricultural policies, which accelerated migration, and a new program (PIDER), one of whose purposes is to reduce the flow. (See his chapter, "Agricultural Development and Rural Employment: A Mexican Dilemma," in Peter G. Brown and Henry Shue (eds.), The Border That Joins: Mexican Migrants and U.S. Resonsibility (Totowa, N.J.: Rowman and Littlefield, 1983): 141-161). Simmons also points to the urban-bias in development as one reason for increased migration. (Alan B. Simmons, "Migration and Rural Devlopment: Conceptual Approaches, Research Findings, and Policy Issues," paper prepared for United Nations Population Division, Expert Group Meeting on Population Distribution, Migration and Development,

March 1983, p. 20.) Also see Michael P. Todaro, Economic Development in the Third World, (New York: Longman, 1977), Chapter 9, "Rural-Urban Migration: Theory and Policy," pp. 186-203.

24. Oded Stark and David Levhari, "On Migration and Risk in LDC's," Economic Development and Cultural Change, Vol. 31, No. 1, October 1982: 191-6.

25. For Lopez Portillo's comment and a brief description of the impact of the Border Industrialization Program, see Stephen P. Mumme, "Mexican Politics and the Prospects for Emigration Policy: A Policy Perspective," Inter-American Economic Affairs, Vol. 32, Summer 1978, p. 85. For an analysis of the impact of Operation Bootstrap and its relevance to the CBI, see Robert Pastor, "Sinking in the Caribbean Basin," Foreign Affairs, Summer 1982, Vol. 60, No. 5: 1038-1058.

26. See the articles by Thomas K. Morrison and Richard Sinkin, Thomas K. Morrison, and Sidney Weintraub, Supra. fn. #18.

27. My summary of existing theories is necessarily brief. For a more extended discussion, see the six introductory essays in Part I of Global Trends in Migration: Theory and Research on International Population Movements, edited by Mary M. Kritz, Charles B. Keely, and Silvano M. Tomasi, (N.Y.: Center for Migration Studies, 1981).

28. A summary of the recent literature is contained in Demetrios G. Papademetriou, "Emigration and Return in the Mediterranean Littoral," Comparative Politics, Summer 1985. See also Rosemarie Rogers, "Return Migration in Comparative Perspective," in Daniel Kubat (ed.), The Politics of Return Migration (Rome: Center for Migration Studies, 1984).

29. Ismail Serageldin, James Socknat, and Stace Birks, International Labor Migration in the Middle East and North Africa, Summary Report of Research Project on International Labor Migration and Manpower in the Middle East and North Africa, World Bank, March 1981, pp. 46-49.

30. Ibid.

31. Syed Ashraf Ali et. al., Labor Migration from Bangladesh to the Middle East, World Bank Staff Working Paper No. 454, April, 1981, p. xiii.

32. Alan Richards and Phillip L. Martin, "The Laissez-Faire Approach to International Labor Migration: The Case of the Arab Middle East," Economic Development and Cultural Change, Vol. 31, No. 3, April 1983, pp. 469-470.

33. Sherri Grasmuck, "The Impact of Emigration on National Development: Three Sending Communities in the Dominican Republic," Occasional Paper #33, New York University Center for Latin American and Caribbean Studies, June 1982, pp. 9-10.

34. Terry L. McCoy and Charles H. Wood, "Caribbean Workers in the Florida Sugar Cane Industry," Paper #2, Gainesville: Center for Latin American Studies, University of Florida, December 1982, p. 54. Data from St. Vincent Digest of Statistics, 1976 and 1979; World Bank Economic Memorandum on St. Vincent, 1981. From presentation by Dawn Marshall at Conference on the Caribbean, Bridgetown, Barbados, October 1982. Also see Chapter 4, Table 7 in this book.

35. U.S. Department of State, "Belize Experiences Serious Labor Drain to the U.S.," unclassified memorandum, May 14, 1976.

36. George W. Roberts, "Work Force of the Commonwealth Caribbean at 1970," cited by Wayne Cornelius, Mexican Migration to the United States (with Comparative Reference to Caribbean-Basin Migration): The State of Current Knowledge, San Diego: Center for United States-Mexican Studies, May 1979, p. 157.

37. Hilbourne A. Watson, "International Migration and the Political Economy of Underdevelopment: Aspects of the Commonwealth Caribbean Situation," in Roy Bryce-Laporte and Delores Mortimer (eds.), Caribbean Immigration to the United States, (Washington, D.C.: Research Institute on Immigration and Ethnic Studies, 1983), p. 31. The Population Reference Bureau in Washington, D.C. published in 1984 an excellent series of papers on eight countries in the eastern Caribbean, describing demographic trends and their implications for employment, migration, and development.

38. Bureau of Latin America and the Caribbean, Agency for International Development, "The Eastern Caribbean Economies: Current Status and Prospects," November 3, 1980, p. 7.

39. James Allman, "Haitian Migration: Thirty Years Assessed," Migration Today, Vol. X, No. 1, p. 7; James Allman and John May, "Haitian International

Migration, 1950-80, Recent Trends and Their Implications," June 1980, pp. 15-16.

40. James Stuart and Michael Kearney, "Causes and Effects of Agricultural Labor Migration from the Mixteca of Oaxaca to California," University of California, San Diego Program In U.S.-Mexican Studies, Working Paper #28, 1981, pp. 7, 26, 30-37.

41. Sherri Grasmuck, Supra. fn. #32, p. 8.

42. World Bank, Caribbean Group: Current Situation and Prospects, Report No. 3937-CRG, May 24, 1982, pp. 8-9. This report cited the conclusion of a World Bank study group on the economic problems of the micro-states at a meeting in Antigua in April 1981. For a discussion of the "management gap" in the Caribbean and some proposals for addressing it, see Chapter 15 in this book.

43. Kempe R. Hope, "The Emigration of High-Level Manpower from Developing to Developed Countries (with reference to Trinidad and Tobago)," Second Seminar on Adaptation and Integration of Permanent Immigrants, Geneva, 19-21 November 1975, p. 212. In a study for the World Bank, Joseph Pelzman concluded: "For all of the countries of the Caribbean, the outflow of skilled labor represents the greatest disincentive to attracting new capital." ("The Impact of the Caribbean Basin Initiative on Caribbean Exports," World Bank, June 1982, p. 38).

44. Ransford W. Palmer, "Migration from the Caribbean to the States: The Economic Status of the Immigrants," in Bryce-Laporte and Mortimer (eds.), Supra. fn. #37, p. 46.

45. Ibid, p. 48.

46. Cited in Rawle Farley, "Professional Migration: The Brain Drain From the West Indies and Africa," in Bryce-Laporte and Mortimer, Ibid, p. 178.

47. Nancy Foner, "Jamaican Migrants: A Comparative Analysis of the New York and London Experience," unpublished paper for New York University Research Program in Inter-American Affairs, 1982.

48. Robert Maguire, "Bottom-Up Development in Haiti," (Rosslyn, Va.: Inter-American Foundation, April 1981), p. 32.

49. Sherri Grasmuck, Supra. fn. #33, p. 14.

50. James Allman, Migration Today, Supra. fn. #39, p. 11.

51. Sherri Grasmuck, Supra. fn. #33, pp. 10-13.

52. See Lorna Murray, National Planning Agency of Jamaica, Supra. fn. #12, p. 4 and Chapter 15 in this book.

53. "Agricultural Development and the Caribbean Basin," statement by Robert Pastor, before the Subcommittee on Department Operations, Research and Foreign Agriculture, House Committee on Agriculture and the Subcommittee on Inter-American Affairs, House Foreign Affairs Committee, Joint Hearings: Agricultural Development in the Caribbean and Central America, July 20 and 22, 1982, pp. 75-106; U.S. Department of Agriculture, "U.S. Caribbean Trade Ties Remain Strong," Foreign Agriculture, November 1981; The Report of the Group of Caribbean Experts, "The Caribbean Community in the 1980s," CARICOM Secretariat, January 1981, p. 44.

54. Jack Harewood, "Unemployment and Related Problems in the Commonwealth Caribbean," in Occasional Papers, Human Resources #2, October 1978, Institute of Social and Economic Research, University of the West Indies, St. Augustine, Trinidad, pp. 1-68. For a graph on the decline of agriculture in the Caribbean, see testimony of Dr. Richard Weisskoff, "The Caribbean Basin Policy: Hearings," House Foreign Affairs Subcommittee on Inter-American Affairs, July 14, 21, and 28, 1981, p. 51.

55. The Report of the Group of Caribbean Experts, "The Caribbean Community in the 1980s," Supra. fn. #53, p. 39.

56. Interview by the author with William Demas, President of the Caribbean Development Bank, Barbados, February 2, 1984, and with William Wheeler, Director, Caribbean Office, Agency for International Development, Barbados, February 3, 1984.

57. Though immigration policy has been "sensitive," this does not mean that it has taken into account the impact of migration on development, because it hasn't. Robert Pastor, "U.S. Immigration Policy and Latin America: In Search of the 'Special Relationship'," Latin American Research Review, Fall, 1984, Vol. 19, No. 3, Fall 1984.

58. _Report of the Select Commission on Western Hemisphere Immigration_ (Washington, D.C.: Government Printing Office, January 1968), p. 14.

59. Peter Behr, "GOP Task Force Urges New U.S. Role To Help Industries Compete," _Washington Post_, May 2, 1984, pp. C 1, 4.

Part 1

The Impact of Development on Migration

2. Impact of Alternative Development Strategies on Migration: A ComparativeAnalysis

Sergio Diaz-Briquets

As emigration from the Caribbean Basin countries to the United States intensified during the past two decades, researchers began to focus their attention on the reasons behind this development. This concern is justified, since large-scale emigration from this region to the United States has important domestic and international ramifications. Despite the interest and research it has generated, we still lack a fully articulated understanding of the reasons for these large population displacements. Earlier, broad explanations are giving way to more intricate and detailed formulations positing that emigration from the region results from a multiplicity of causes, many of which are related to the process of social and economic change experienced by these countries,[1] and to how these changes are influenced by the operation of a global economic system.[2] Some of these determinants are regarded as having universal applicability whereas others are understood to have explanatory power only in relation to specific socioeconomic and political circumstances.

Few analysts have tried to contrast the experience of countries differing in the relative number of departing emigrants. Although every country in the Basin is a supplier of U.S.-bound emigrants, substantial differences in emigration rates are evident within the region. In this chapter, I attempt a comparative analysis of emigration experiences for selected countries by assessing how developments commonly associated with emigration evolved during the last two decades. This approach may prove useful and of more than academic interest, since it can assist in identifying how national development strategies and foreign assistance programs can help lessen emigration pressures.

The conclusions that follow are only inferential because of the difficulty of isolating cause-and-effect

41

relationships in a social and economic phenomenon as complex as international migration. As Simmons indicated, researchers have found it nearly impossible to derive broad generalizations about migration that are valid across different national contexts.[3] Nevertheless, certain development patterns across nations do appear to lead to higher levels of emigration than others. This chapter aims to identify these patterns.

I. Determinants of Emigration

In essence, nine major determinants of Caribbean Basin emigration can be identified in the literature. Disagreements that persist as to their significance reflect, to an extent, conceptual and disciplinary approach differences. Without attempting to rank them in order of importance, the causes of emigration may be summarized as follows:

1. high population and labor force growth rates;

2. development strategies that have failed to generate sufficient employment opportunities, although in some cases they have been quite successful in promoting high economic growth rates;

3. social and economic change unaccompanied by necessary structural and political transformations: The resilience of traditional structures has come into conflict with popular expectations and aspirations largely acquired from the model provided by more economically developed countries;

4. social and political strife;

5. advances in transportation and communications that have lowered the economic and psychic costs of emigration;

6. the establishment of ethnic colonies in the United States that tend to perpetuate migratory flows by encouraging the flows and easing the assimilation of newly arrived immigrants;

7. vast differences in wage levels and standards of living between the United States and the Caribbean Basin countries;

8.   the need for cheap and abundant unskilled
      labor in U.S. agriculture, industry, and
      services; and

9.   U.S. immigration policy that encourages family
      reunification, and does not actively
      discourage illegal migration.

In this chapter I focus on the first three
determinants, while briefly noting that U.S policy can
affect some of the others. Enforcement of border
controls, for example, can substantially reduce the
volume of illegal immigration flows, although the
domestic and international costs of tight enforcement
can be high. Modifying the preference system for
legally admitted immigrants can weaken the strength of
ethnic and familial bonds. Not much can be done about
modern means of transportation and communication or
about short-term reduction of differences in living
standards between the United States and the Caribbean
Basin countries. U.S. policies, finally, can help
reduce social, economic, and political tensions in the
region, but this is an enduring objective of U.S.
foreign policy. The current debate in the United
States is over how best to achieve this objective.
     Understanding how these determinants can be
modified to enhance the region's ability to
productively employ a growing labor force is critical
to the future. This is even more important for those
countries that face an excess labor situation and the
potential implementation of policies to limit
immigration by countries that, in the past, were large
recipients of emigrants from the region.
     My specific aim in this chapter is to explore what
development strategies have succeeded in creating
productive employment and in raising living standards
and thus in diminishing the need for emigration, even
though this has not been one of the goals of national
economic development strategies. A secondary objective
is to evaluate how these development strategies and the
results thereof have interacted with demographic
factors, in particular, labor force growth. My
contention is that differences in emigration rates--
except in cases of the complete breakdown of civil
order--can be substantially explained by the effect of
development strategies on job creation and labor-force
growth. The strength of other emigration determinants
depends on specific national and transnational (e.g.,
preexisting social networks) circumstances.
     To investigate this complex nexus, I will review
the recent socio-economic and pertinent political
histories of four of the Spanish-speaking Caribbean
Basin countries--Costa Rica, Cuba, the Dominican

Republic, and Panama. These countries provide an interesting mix of emigration and development experiences. Cuba and the Dominican Republic, despite enormous differences in their histories in the last two decades, were among the principal contributors of emigrants to the United States. The other two are among those countries from which relatively few migrants have left; in fact, they have been recipients of limited numbers of immigrants from neighboring countries.[4] The Dominican Republic is the only country among the four from which hundreds of thousands of emigrants have departed and at the same time it has received large contingents of immigrants, both temporary and permanent, from its poverty stricken neighbor, Haiti.

"Why Cuba?" the reader may ask. Although many of the determinants of Cuban emigration are very specific to the revolution, the Cuban experience sheds light on the determinants of emigration in other countries. For example, analysts not uncommonly propose policy measures (e.g., full employment, more equitable income distributions) to alleviate emigration pressures in the region very similar to policies followed in Cuba over the past quarter of a century. Yet the Cuban emigration history suggests that these measures, unless accompanied by other developments, may be ineffective in reducing emigration pressures: In fact, they may have the opposite effect.

II. Emigration Trends

Table 2.1 presents a summary of the Immigration and Naturalization Service (INS) statistics on legal immigration to the United States from each of the countries between 1960 and 1980. These statistics show that, in relation to their populations, legal immigration rates from Costa Rica and Panama have been substantially lower than that from the Dominican Republic. A crude estimate of country differentials in immigration levels can be obtained by relating the total number of legal immigrants admitted during the 1960-1980 period to the average population size in 1960 and 1980 for each country. The resulting ratios are shown at the bottom of Table 2.1. The Dominican Republic ratio is three times higher than Costa Rica's and nearly twice as high as Panama's. By far the highest ratio is the one for Cuba, which is even higher when the 1980 Mariel entrants are added to the numerator. The problems associated with the figures for Cuban immigration are well known. Many Cuban immigrants, but not all, have adjusted their

Table 2.1

Immigrants from Selected Caribbean Basin Countries,
1960 to 1980

Year[a]	Costa Rica	Cuba	Dominican Republic	Panama
1960	803	8,283	756	1,722
1961	749	14,287	3,045	1,875
1962	1,407	16,254	4,603	2,098
1963	1,754	10,587	10,683	2,184
1964	2,729	15,808	7,537	1,750
1965	2,911	19,760	9,504	1,933
1966	1,582	17,355	16,503	1,594
1967	1,175	33,321	11,514	1,676
1968	1,668	99,312	9,250	1,976
1969	1,925	13,751	10,670	1,585
1970	1,456	16,334	10,807	1,630
1971	968	21,611	12,624	1,457
1972	907	20,045	10,760	1,507
1973	901	24,147	13,921	1,612
1974	752	18,929	15,680	1,664
1975	889	25,955	14,066	1,694
1976	1,452	35,996	15,088	2,162
1977	1,664	69,708	11,655	2,389
1978	1,575	29,754	19,458	3,108
1979	1,467	15,585	17,519	3,472
1980	1,535	15,054	17,245	3,572
Total 1960-1980	30,269	541,836	242,888	42,660

Ratio of total arrivals (1960-1980) to average population
(1960 and 1980)   1.76   6.46   5.28   2.85

With Mariel arrivals
included   7.96

[a]Years ended June 30 for 1960-1975; 1976; July 1, 1975, to
September 1976; and years ended September 30, for 1977-1980.

Source: Immigration and Naturalization Service, U.S. Department
of Justice, 1979 Statistical Yearbook of the Immigration and
Naturalization Service, Washington, D.C., Table 14, p. 39, and
for 1960 to 1969 and 1980, unpublished data furnished by the INS.

immigration status since arriving in the United
States.[5] Yearly totals, therefore, do not reflect the
ebbs and flows of Cuban immigration. The magnitude of
Cuban immigration has varied significantly over the
period in question because of the easing
or tightening of restrictions by the Cuban and U.S.
governments. In total, well over 700,000 Cubans
arrived in the United States between 1959 and 1980; the
latest wave of over 125,000 immigrants came via the
Mariel sealift.

The INS figures in Table 2.1 do not take into
account the considerable illegal immigration flows.
The Dominican Republic is known to be one of the
principal sources of illegal immigration, the number of
illegal Dominican immigrants perhaps exceeding the
number of legal entries. In contrast, illegal
immigration flows from Costa Rica and Panama seem to be
relatively less important. Data on undocumented
immigrants by country of origin expelled from the
United States support this conclusion. Annual
expulsion ratios per 100,000 population are higher for
the Dominican Republic than for Costa Rica or
Panama.[6] If legal and illegal immigration are
considered together, emigration rates from the
Dominican Republic are even higher than those from
Costa Rica and Panama.

III. Population and Labor Force Growth

Before examining development strategies, it is
useful to briefly review the four countries' recent
population histories. Two of them, Costa Rica and the
Dominican Republic, are archetypical examples of the
so-called population explosion. The population of
these countries began to increase rapidly after the
Second World War. By the 1960s they were among the
countries in the world with the highest natural
increase rates, over 3 percent per year. Panama's
natural increase rate, though also high, was slightly
lower. Natural increase rates in these countries,
despite significant fertility declines in recent years,
are still high. In 1984 they were estimated at 2.7
percent for Costa Rica and the Dominican Republic and
just below 2 percent in Panama.

More crucial here is that the persons born during
the postwar period began reaching working age during
the 1960s and 1970s--the years associated with the
onset of large-scale emigration to the United States.
Yet only the Dominican Republic was a disproportionate
contributor of emigrants to the United States. Panama
was a relatively minor contributor and Costa Rica even
less so. These differences suggest that rapid

population growth may be a necessary but not sufficient
condition for large-scale emigration.

The case of Cuba is particularly interesting since
strong evidence indicates that the latest wave of
emigration from this country--the Mariel sealift--was
to an extent the result of demographic pressures on the
employment and housing markets provoked by the arrival
at early adulthood of the children born during the
1960s, when Cuba experienced a spectacular baby
boom.[7] As the children grew up, the number of new
entrants to the labor force increased at a much faster
rate than in the past. Added to this was a severe
housing shortage that would be further aggravated by
the upcoming establishment of separate households as
the baby-boom generation reached marriage age. Many
Cubans, of course, were seeking to emigrate for
political and economic reasons. Economic conditions at
the time had taken a turn for the worse. A great deal
of internal unrest also was caused by visits made by
large numbers of Cubans residing in the United
States. The stories that visitors told and the
presents they brought magnified the contrast between
Cuba's spartan life-style and U.S. prosperity.

Many explanations of international migration
assume that U.S.-bound emigration is in part determined
by prevailing imbalances associated with the operation
of market forces within peripheral and central
countries in the international capitalist economy.
Cuba is largely, although not completely, isolated from
those forces. The Cuban experience suggests that
sizable increases in the labor force can be and are,
under certain circumstances, one of the main
determinants of emigration. How labor force increases
interact with the ability of a country's development
strategy and resource endowment to generate productive
employment is the crucial intersection where attention
should be focused.

IV. Economic and Political Systems

The policies of the four countries being studied
encompass a wide range of economic and social
development strategies. At one extreme is Cuba, in
which most means of production are owned by the state
and where investment allocations and other economic
decisions are made, in principle if not always in
practice, by a central planning apparatus. The nature
of the political-economic system is such that certain
social goals--satisfaction of basic necessities for
all--are pre-eminent. Because of economic
inefficiencies and other factors, the Cuban government
requires heavy Soviet subsidies to meet the social
goals set by the revolution. The subsidies and the

country's membership in the Council for Mutual Economic
Assistance (COMECON) help insulate the national economy
from the disruptions often experienced by more open
free-market economies.

Costa Rica, Panama, and to a lesser extent the
Dominican Republic are examples of countries with mixed
economies in which the state plays a guiding role and
is also a direct participant in the economy. They are
extremely open economies, highly sensitive to the
swings of the international market place. Because of
their heavy reliance on the export of a few
commodities, or, in the case of Panama, services, they
are very vulnerable to external shocks beyond their
control.[8] Costa Rica and Panama, although not as
heavily advertised and acclaimed as Cuba, also have
emphasized social development. These two countries,
like Cuba, have been very successful in the health and
education fields and have achieved equitable patterns
of income distribution, although to a lesser extent
than Cuba. The achievements of the Dominican Republic
in these areas have also been significant, though not
as great as in the other countries.

All four countries have had relatively stable
governments for at least the last fifteen years. Costa
Rica has been the most stable and democratic country in
Latin America during the last thirty years. After
periods of upheaval in the 1960s, the political
situation in the Dominican Republic and Panama has been
characterized by relative continuity. Although the
political systems of these two countries are different,
they are both pluralistic and participatory. Cuba has
a totalitarian political structure governed by a
Communist Party.

Political stability is a necessary condition for
the attainment of sustained economic development. This
statement does not imply, however, that political
stability should be equated with continuity of
development strategies, as Cuba's economic development
strategies have shifted direction several times over
the last quarter-century.[9] The other three countries
also reformulated earlier development strategies that
had attained relative success during the 1970s.[10]

All four countries have had serious economic
difficulties since the mid-to-late 1970s, primarily
because of the international recession. Cuba has
suffered less than the other countries since its
economy is heavily subsidized and because of its
economic integration with the socialist bloc, but all
four countries are heavily in debt to international
lenders. Over the years, Cuba has accumulated a huge
debt to the Soviet Union and owes some $3 billion to
Western banks. In the other countries, borrowing
escalated dramatically in the second half of the last

decade, in part as these countries tried to ameliorate
the effects of the recession and the oil price rise
through heavy infusions of foreign capital. Between
1970 and 1982, the external public debt of the
Dominican Republic rose from $212 million to $1,620
million, Costa Rica's from $134 million to $2,475
million, and Panama's from $194 million to $2,820
million.[11]

V. Employment Generation and Development Strategies

In the key area of employment generation, the
picture is mixed and mired in statistical
shortcomings. Throughout most of the 1960s and up to
the mid-1970s, Costa Rica and Panama appear to have
done well in generating new productive jobs--having
developed nearly enough to keep pace with labor force
growth. Between 1960 and 1970 and up to 1975, open
unemployment in Costa Rica declined from 7 to 4
percent. This remarkable performance was induced by a
balanced development strategy that resulted from the
confluence of several factors. First, the market for
Costa Rican manufacturers expanded by the creation of
the Central American common market. Second, the
diversification and expansion of agricultural
production was achieved through intensive rural
development efforts that included agrarian reform,
colonization of virgin lands, and the increased use of
modern agricultural inputs. The strong guiding role of
the state and considerable foreign investments played
an important role in the country's development at this
time. The traditional dependency of Costa Rica on
coffee and banana exports--accounting for 75 percent of
all exports in 1960--was reduced. By 1975, these two
commodities represented slightly less than 50 percent
of all exports, with the rising share of industrial
exports accounting for a major portion of the
balance.[12]

The economic growth of Panama was tied more
tightly to the expansion of urban activities, many of
them associated with the operation of the canal and the
country's geo-economic position, including banking,
finance, and other services. As a result, employment
opportunities and income levels grew rapidly.
Employment growth in services appears to have favored
disproportionately the better educated and skilled,
however. Problems of unemployment and underemployment
for the unskilled persist. This is true in the cities,
partly because of high rates of rural to urban
migration, and in the countryside.[13] In the late
1960s, major rural development projects were initiated,
and the availability of virgin lands contributed to the
absorption of otherwise surplus rural labor.

In both countries the effects of the recession since the mid-1970s began to magnify certain weaknesses associated with the development strategies they had pursued. The limits of the early and easy phases of import substitution were reached, and costly social programs weighed heavily in national budgets.[14] In addition, uncertainties over the future status of the canal retarded private investments in Panama, and the erosion of the Central American common market had negative consequences for Costa Rica. Last, rising energy bills began to consume an increasing share of the countries' foreign exchange and the servicing of an ever-growing foreign debt contributed to economic deterioration. Unemployment levels began to rise in both countries, reaching nine percent by about 1980.[15] The civil wars in other Central American countries worsened the situation.

In summary, up to the mid-1970s the economies of Costa Rica and Panama grew at satisfactory rates, large numbers of new productive jobs were created, living standards were raised, and significant gains in social areas were recorded. In Panama, the rapid expansion in employment opportunities for the more skilled probably acted as a particularly effective deterrent to emigration. The most aspiring and better educated workers are more likely to emigrate if opportunities for social advancement in the home country are limited.

By any measurable criterion, the development strategies pursued in the Dominican Republic were far less successful in promoting productive employment growth. Although economic growth rates were exceptionally high--between 1968 and 1974 the economy grew at an annual rate of 11 percent, one of the highest growth rates in the world--unemployment and underemployment remained persistent problems. In 1973, just before the worldwide economic recession, urban unemployment was estimated at 20 percent. In rural areas, as much as 60 percent of the labor force was underemployed.[16]

The reasons for such high levels of labor underutilization are complex, but several factors appear to have been specifically implicated. A major one was that development strategies disproportionately favored the use of capital-intensive inputs over labor-intensive methods. Studies by World Bank researchers have indicated that much of the industrial growth in the Dominican Republic, as well as many of the significant infrastructural development projects undertaken, was achieved through heavy reliance on highly efficient, capital-intensive approaches that use little labor.[17] Industrial-incentive policies that gave preference to high capital inputs were identified in the World Bank studies as the main contributor to this problem.

The performance of the agricultural sector can also help explain the low rates of labor utilization. The poor allocation of agricultural investments is part of the story. Rural areas of the country have been neglected to the benefit of cities. Only limited efforts have been made to increase and diversify agricultural production, and these have been geared primarily to infrastructural development. The rural infrastructure also has been expanded with highly capital-intensive methods that use little labor. In addition, rural social services are highly inadequate in relation to what is offered in urban areas.[18]

The Dominican Republic remains highly dependent on sugarcane production, a traditionally seasonal activity very vulnerable to the vagaries of the international market. Furthermore, working conditions in this sector for a long time have been unappealing to Dominican workers: Wages and working conditions are poor, and employment in the sugar fields is equated with low social status. This situation is common throughout the sugarcane producing countries of the Caribbean. These conditions are aggravated by the officially channeled or tolerated importation of low wage labor from Haiti.[19] It has been estimated that as much as 90 percent of the work force in the sugar fields is Haitian.[20] Thus, as rural Dominicans sought jobs in the cities and in the United States, a large influx of Haitian labor replaced them in the cane fields.

High rates of rural to urban migration tend to depress wages in the cities and to increase competition for available jobs. Therefore, at least indirectly, rural stagnation contributes to high rates of emigration. Survey work has established that the vast majority of Dominican emigrants have an urban background and educational levels above the national average. Also involved in the failure of rural areas to absorb more labor was a dearth of virgin, unoccupied lands. As noted, the settlement of virgin territories in Costa Rica and Panama helped absorb part of the excess rural labor force.

Cuba's successes in absorbing labor responded to causes very different from those in Costa Rica and Panama: These causes are primarily demographic and sociopolitical. As discussed, labor force growth rates in Cuba until the late 1970s were far lower than in the other countries. The capacity to absorb labor was enhanced, furthermore, by the flight of hundreds of thousands of people dissatisfied with political and economic conditions in Cuba. The nature of the earlier waves of emigration was very different from that characterizing other countries, and large-scale emigration began much earlier. The earlier Cuban migrants were drawn from the higher socioeconomic and better educated strata. Nevertheless, the initial period of emigration from Cuba may have only anticipated by a few years the period of intensified labor emigration from other Caribbean Basin countries. This view is supported by an earlier history of limited Cuban emigration dating to years before the revolution, but not by other factors such as relatively low labor force growth rates.

The most important factors leading to high rates of labor absorption in Cuba--witness the high levels of female labor force participation in the Cuban economy-- were social and political. The revolutionary leadership promised full employment. Several measures were implemented to achieve that objective. The bureaucracy was expanded, and year-round employment was provided to the peasantry. Moreover, increased school enrollment rates, an expansion of the social security system, and the creation of a large military machine removed many potential workers from the labor force.[21] Open unemployment was reduced to almost negligible levels, but underemployment--one of the most serious drawbacks of the national economy--grew worse. As the economy continued to have difficulties into the late 1970s, and as the demographic picture changed, unemployment and labor force pressures reappeared. The Mariel exodus followed.

Cuba has had little success in diversifying its exports. In fact, between 1960 and 1980, Cuba's dependency on sugar exports grew worse: They ranged from 80 to 86 percent of total exports. Like the other countries, Cuba followed a strategy of import substitution. This strategy has permitted Cuba to reduce its dependence on foreign imports. Significantly, however, the share of industry in the national production aggregate has declined over the period by about 25 percent. This contradiction reflects the low levels of material consumption in Cuba's austere social system. The share of nonproductive services, not surprisingly, has exhibited the greatest dynamism over this period.

Cuba's development strategies have had mixed results: high scores in social development, poor ratings in economic growth, and satisfactory results in labor absorption but not in the generation of productive employment. Low labor productivity is widespread in the economy. Thus, despite very generous Soviet subsidies, Cuba's economy can only support austere living standards. This austerity, and the political oppressiveness related to it, explains the high emigration propensities of the Cuban population in recent years.

VI. Development Strategies and Emigration

The preceding discussion has illustrated the multiplicity of factors that determine emigration and the complex interactions among them. Several features seem to distinguish countries with relatively low emigration propensities from those with high propensities. Emigration rates were substantially lower from those countries (Costa Rica and Panama) that pursued balanced development strategies in which both social and economic objectives received the required attention and, most importantly, where both objectives were more or less met. At opposite extremes are Cuba and the Dominican Republic. The former country, although making substantial social gains, fared poorly in promoting sustained economic growth. In the latter country, very high rates of economic growth were recorded, but achievements in social areas fell far short of those in the other countries. Equitable income distribution is insufficient if economic stagnation interferes with the satisfaction of increasing material wants; likewise, high rates of economic growth must lead to measurable improvements in living standards for all socioeconomic strata. The pie not only must grow; it also should be more equitably divided.

Associated with the need for balanced strategies is a need for national economies to diversify, both in their internal markets and in their relations with the outside world. The vulnerability of the small Caribbean Basin economies to outside forces can be reduced by economic diversification. Diversification will also result in more domestic productive employment opportunities. In this manner, these economies are less likely to be subject to the pains inflicted by cyclical international demand changes for a limited number of key goods. This translates into greater stability and thus into more effective means to ensure a continuity of minimum levels of job security and living standards. Costa Rica was able to reach these objectives through increased diversification and trade in agriculture and industry. Panama did so by diversifying its internal production, by taking advantage of its strategic international situation, by placing a premium on the strengthening of service sectors catering to international needs. Cuba and the Dominican Republic, although diversifying their internal production structures, failed to loosen the grip of overdependence on monoculture in their international trade.

The ability to adapt to differential and often competing aspirations of various social segments—whether politically, socially, or economically—seems

to be another dimension closely associated with
emigration. All countries being studied experienced
vast social changes in the last two decades.
Educational standards improved considerably. Better
educational standards led to increased aspirations, the
emergence of new wants, more sophisticated worldviews,
and alternative perceptions of the future. The
governments of those countries that were more
responsive to those needs--in their widest dimensions--
fared much better in enhancing domestic prospects for
their populations. In these countries, sufficient
outlets were available to help ease conflicts among
different social sectors and thus avoid deep
polarizations. In the Dominican Republic, in contrast,
the short-term needs (in the form of the importation of
cheap foreign labor) of some economic sectors took
precedence over the welfare of vast sectors of the
rural population and indirectly over living conditions
in cities. In Cuba, a dogmatic and personalistic
approach to economic and political issues has prevented
the required evolution of the social system long after
the revolution was consolidated. In these two
countries, although for different reasons, the only
available option for the satisfaction of many
aspirations has been emigration.

Crucially important, too, is the creation of the
necessary conditions for the gradual and uninterrupted
achievement of social and economic development goals.
No better example of this imperative can be given than
by recalling the severe economic blows produced by the
recent international recession in these countries. The
accomplishments of Costa Rica and Panama were severely
eroded by this discontinuity. Its effect on emigration
may have been felt immediately.[22] The consequences of
the international crisis on the more vulnerable economy
of the Dominican Republic were perhaps worse, but they
were also felt in Cuba.

Several hypotheses can be advanced regarding the
links between development strategies and emigration.
These hypotheses are broad in scope and based on the
experiences of a few countries and are suggestive of
how development strategies can take into account the
migration factor. They are also relevant to the design
of bilateral and multilateral foreign-assistance
programs, if these programs are to take into account
the social and economic circumstances responsible for
high emigration. Some of them may apply to other
Caribbean countries; others may not. The regional
diversity is such, and the emigration processes so
intricate, that their relevance in other national
situations may be more restricted. They are as
follows:

1. Emigration rates are likely to be lower in
    those countries in which development
    strategies have achieved a relative balance
    between economic growth and social objectives.

2. High rates of economic growth for their own
    sake are insufficient to reduce emigration
    pressures if unaccompanied by policies that
    contribute to the expansion of productive
    employment.

3. Balanced sectoral growth is necessary,
    including economic diversification, if
    excessive dependency on a few export
    commodities is to be reduced and a country's
    economic base is to be broadened.

4. Expansion and diversification of international
    economic relations, in agriculture, industry,
    and services, can contribute to the reduction
    of emigration pressures, particularly when
    diversification occurs through the maximum
    utilization of national natural resource
    endowments and opportunities and when it leads
    to a more complex economic base.

5. Emigration pressures are lower in those
    countries in which the political system has
    the ability to adapt to changing circumstances
    and in which socio-economic structures can be
    transformed to accommodate increased
    expectations.

6. The achievement of equity and other social
    objectives at all costs is insufficient to
    stem emigration pressures if increased
    economic expectations are not satisfied.

7. The fragility and openness to outside forces
    of most Caribbean Basin countries' economies
    can erode overnight substantial gains achieved
    over many years.

8. High rates of labor force growth--at least in
    the short to medium term--are not necessarily
    associated with high rates of emigration, as
    long as some of the above-named conditions are
    fulfilled. In the absence of those
    conditions, they are crucial determinants of
    emigration.

In short, economies that are more broadly
diversified, that can generate adequate rates of

economic growth, and that give sufficient attention to
social objectives appear to be more likely to produce
adequate numbers of productive jobs and more capable of
satisfying latent needs of the population. Under these
conditions, and as long as a situation conducive to
substantial economic growth persists, these economies
can successfully reduce push factors usually associated
with emigration.

Of course, identifying what is necessary is far
easier than accomplishing such objectives.
Significant, and, at times, poorly understood trade-
offs between sustained economic growth and social
equity objectives have a tendency to frustrate well-
intentioned development plans. Cuba and Costa Rica's
experience serves as testimony to this assertion.[23]

This chapter sought to establish if emigration
responds to different development patterns. An
underlying premise of the analysis was that emigration,
at least in the Caribbean Basin context, is an
inevitable product of the development process, but that
the rate at which emigration occurs is influenced by
the type of development. The precise degree of effect
is difficult to determine because so many factors
influence the magnitude and character of migratory
flows, but this analysis suggests that unbalanced
development patterns lead to more emigration, all other
things held constant. In this closing section, I will
explore whether or not this hypothesis applies to other
countries in the Basin.

Most countries in the Caribbean Basin have had
development experiences in some ways comparable, at
least in their broad outlines, to those of the high-
emigration countries examined in this chapter.
Political conflicts among different social strata in
Guyana and Jamaica, for example, retarded
development. Haiti's political system is as notorious
as its social and economic backwardness.

Few if any of these countries have been able to
reduce their extreme dependence on outside economic
forces, and their economies remain highly dependent on
the production of a limited number of export
commodities. In Central America, the situation is
aggravated by an explosive political situation. Income
distribution is highly inequitable, and in many cases,
despite impressive achievements in economic growth,
vast sectors of the population have yet to receive the
social benefits of development. In most countries of
the region, the neglect of the rural sector has
resulted in extremely uneven patterns of development
with attendant high emigration rates to cities. Mexico
shares many of these characteristics.

The smaller Eastern Caribbean countries, despite
their more open and democratic political systems,

continue to struggle in their nearly nonviable economic states. Their small size, limited human and natural resources, and minute internal markets act as powerful constraints to economic activity. Their economies only provide limited employment opportunities and even fewer channels for social mobility, and are always vulnerable to the vagaries of international markets and the whims of the tourist industry. These countries have been unable to develop reasonable linkages between tourism and other sectors of the economy and have had little success in diversifying their economic base. All these countries are major sources of emigrants to the United States and other developed countries, and are also senders of migrants to other relatively more prosperous countries in the region.

This chapter's hypotheses would not seem to apply to Barbados and Trinidad and Tobago. By regional standards, they are among the more prosperous and politically stable countries and have achieved a high level of social development. Yet, emigration rates from these two countries are high. Several factors can explain their high emigration propensities.

Possibly the most important one is their limited size and the limited opportunities that such small size affords. In this sense, these two countries inevitably share the fate of their less prosperous neighbors in the Eastern Caribbean. No less significant is the emigration tradition that over a century has evolved in the Caribbean. Emigration was even formalized as a public policy in Barbados when the government entered into special agreements with British firms to recruit workers willing to emigrate to England. Further, the Barbadian government over the years has provided loans to assist nonsponsored migrants during the initial period of adjustment in destination countries and has instituted special training programs to help its citizens acquire skills qualifying them for selected occupations abroad. These public policies have been justified on the grounds that they help relieve unemployment and high population density and that they result in an increase in the volume of foreign remittances received by Barbados.[24] In short, for years the Barbadian government has actively promoted emigration.

Until the second half of the 1960s, few emigrants left Trinidad and Tobago; the country, instead, was a magnet for migrants from other West Indian territories. The situation began to change as unemployment levels rose because of sizable increases in the labor force and as emigrating to the United States became a viable option following changes in U.S. immigration regulations.[25] Following the 1973 Organization of Petroleum Exporting Countries (OPEC) oil price increases, the national economy boomed. This period coincided with a rise in immigration from neighboring countries and with considerable return migration as the country embarked on an accelerated industrialization program financed with the upsurge in oil revenues. High unemployment levels again reappeared, reaching 13 percent in 1984, as the national economy began to cool off and as capital intensive industries based on the transformation of hydrocarbons failed to generate employment opportunities.

Both countries have encouraged unskilled emigration but have been concerned with the loss of skilled manpower. However, the two countries have been fortunate in having the necessary resources to significantly raise the educational levels of their populations. The limits of their small economies have prevented many of the better educated from fulfilling their aspirations locally, and many have chosen to emigrate. But enough skilled workers have remained, minimizing the ill effects of emigration on the countries' development. This has been achieved partly through the diversification of the national economies and the better employment opportunities more diversified economies provide. Barbados was able to broaden its economic base by expanding the service sector to serve domestic and international needs, by promoting some industrial development, and by encouraging tourism. The emergence of new industrial activities based on the transformation and processing of the country's oil wealth largely accounts for the more broadly based economy of Trinidad and Tobago.

Thus, although emigration rates in recent decades from these two countries have been high, the emigration itself has been less detrimental. These two countries, by following a balanced approach in their development strategies, have been able to overcome some of the limitations inherent in their small size that lead to emigration. Although not able to stem emigration, and in fact encouraging some types, they have been able to reap some of the anticipated gains from emigration (e.g., receiving remittances, relieving unemployment), while minimizing some of the heavier costs associated with it (e.g., brain drain).

It is hoped that other analysts will test the hypotheses presented in this chapter with quantifiable and more rigorous analytical methods. Theoretical formulations employed in these tests should attempt to link development outcomes with the economic and other policies leading to the observed results. Efforts should also be made to take into account the skill composition of emigration outflows. Although these are not simple methodological issues to resolve and the necessary data may not be available, studies along these lines may be designed through a close acquaintance with the political, economic, social, and emigration histories of the countries in question.

In summary, even though emigration is a concommitant result of socioeconomic change in the Caribbean Basin, certain development strategies and outcomes appear capable of limiting the extent of emigration, enhancing some of its benefits, and minimizing some of its costs. The key ingredients of these development approaches are linked to politically accommodating systems that give equal attention to social and economic development objectives while facilitating economic growth.

Notes

Comments by Patricia Pessar, Alejandro Portes, Richard
Feinberg and especially Robert Pastor were useful in
the revision of earlier drafts of this chapter.

1. Francisco Alba, "Mexico's International
Migration as a Manifestation of its Development
Pattern," International Migration Review, Vol. 12
(1978), pp. 502-513.

2. Alejandro Portes, "International Labor
Migration and National Development," in Mary M. Kritz
(Editor), U.S. Immigration and Refugee Policy: Global
and Domestic Issues (Lexington Books, 1982), pp. 71-92.

3. Alan B. Simmons, "Migration and Rural
Development: Conceptual Approaches, Research Findings
and Policy Issues," in United Nations, Department of
International Economic and Social Affairs, Population
Distribution, Migration and Development,
ST/ESA/SER.A/89 (New York, 1984), pp. 156-192.

4. Mark Bogan, "La migracion internacional en
Costa Rica," Instituto de Estudios Sociales en
Poblacion, Universidad Nacional, Informe de Trabajo No.
23 (Heredia, 1980); and Ponciano Torales, Las
migraciones laborales en la frontera de Colombia con
Panama, (Migraciones Laborales No. 2) Bogota, 1979).

5. Many Cuban entries are not included in Table
2.1 This is because Cuban entries are not officially
recorded as immigrants until they adjust their status
from "parolees."

6. Sidney Weintraub, "U.S. Foreign Economic
Policy and Illegal Immigration," Population Research
and Policy Review, Vol. 2 (1983), p. 188.

7. Sergio Diaz-Briquets, "Demographic and Related
Determinants of Recent Cuban Emigration," International
Migration Review, Vol. 17 (1983), pp. 95-119.

8. PREALC, Panama: Estrategia de Necesidades
Basicas y Empleo, Programa Regional del Empleo para
America Latina y el Caribe, Organizacion Internacional
del Trabajo, (mimeo), (Santiago, 1980); Howard J.
Wiarda and Michael J. Kryzanek, The Dominican
Republic: A Caribbean Crucible (Westview Press, 1982);
and Fuat M. Andic, What Price Equity? A Macroeconomic
Evaluation of Government Policies in Costa Rica,
Institute of Caribbean Studies, University of Puerto
Rico (Rio Piedras, 1983).

9. Carmelo Mesa-Lago, The Economy of Socialist Cuba: A Two Decade Appraisal (University of New Mexico Press, 1981).

10. Helio Fallas, Crisis Economica en Costa Rica: Un Analisis Economico de los ultimos 20 Anos, Editorial Nueva Decada (San Jose, 1981); World Bank, Dominican Republic: Its Main Economic Development Problems (Washington, 1978); and Julio Manduley, "Panama: Dependent Capitalism and Beyond," Latin American Perspectives Vol. 7 (1980).

11. World Bank, World Development Report 1984 (Oxford University Press, 1984), pp. 248-249.

12. Gary S. Fields, Poverty, Inequality and Development (Cambridge University Press, 1980); Fallas, Crisis Economica, Supra. fn. #10; and Carmelo Mesa-Lago and Sergio Diaz-Briquets, "Different Strategies, Similar Countries: The Consequences for Growth and Equity in Costa Rica and Cuba," Gustav Papanek (Editor), collection of papers dealing with the comparative performance of free market and centrally planned economies (forthcoming).

13. PREALC, Estrategia de Necesidades Basicas Supra. fn. #8.

14. Andic, What Price Equity? Supra. fn. #8.

15. Jorge Perez-Lopez, "Economic Context," Marcelo Alonso (ed.), Central America in Crisis (Washington Institute for Values in Public Policy, 1984).

16. World Bank, Dominican Republic: Main Economic Problems, Supra. fn. #10.

17. Ibid.

18. Wiarda and Kryzanek, Dominican Republic: Caribbean Crucible, Supra. fn. #8.

19. E.E. Glaessel Brown, "Seasonal Labor Migration in Hispaniola: A Policy of Convenience," J.D. Montgomery et. al., (Editors), Patterns of Policy - Comparative and Longitudinal Studies of Population Events (Transaction Books, 1979).

20. Rosemary Vargas, "Unemployment, Underemployment and labor Imports in the Dominican Republic: A Sketch of Some of the Problems," Ibero

62

Americana Vol. 10 (1981), pp. 39-61.

21. Mesa-Lago, Economy of Socialist Cuba, Supra. fn. #9.

22. It is tempting to ascribe the increase in legal immigration since about 1976 from Costa Rica, Panama and the Dominican Republic to the effects of the international economic recession. However, the increase at least partly if not mainly was produced by the reallocation of immigrant visas earlier assigned to Cuban entrants adjusting their legal status in the U.S The visas had to be reassigned following the Silva legal decision.

23. Mesa-Lago, Economy of Socialist Cuba, Supra. fn. #9 and Andic, What Price Equity?, Supra. fn. #8.

24. G. Edward Ebanks, "Barbados," in Aaron Segal (Editor), Population Policies in the Caribbean (Lexington Books, 1975), pp. 25-47.

25. Jack Harewood, The Population of Trinidad and Tobago (C.I.C.R.E.D., 1975) and Norma Andrews, "Trinidad and Tobago," in Aaron Segal (ed.), Population Policies in the Caribbean (Lexington Books, 1975), pp. 73-87.

3. Political Implications of Migration in a Socio-Cultural Area

Anthony P. Maingot

I. Introduction: A Socio-Cultural Area

It is customary in the study of migration to make a sharp distinction between internal and international migration. The assumption is that the difference is qualitative, that it is fundamentally related to the migrant's degree of stress. It has long been a general assumption in sociology that all migrants experience a steady cycle of "adaptations" that involves "assimilation," "accommodation," "submission," "contention," and finally "revitalization."[1] Today, however, studies in the area of modernization are disputing the assumption that migration is inevitably accompanied by stress and other afflictions to psychic well-being.[2] Such theoretical challenges to the standard sociological assumptions on migration and settlement are supported by the cases of migration to the United States of peoples from the non-Hispanic, ex-colonial Caribbean, i.e., the English-speaking members of what is correctly called the Afro-Caribbean.[3] These West Indians adapted quite successfully to their new U.S. environment virtually from the beginning of the movement. Their early success and the social networks they established allowed others to follow even during periods of strident institutional and social racism.

During the decade 1900 to 1910, 30,000 West Indians arrived; in 1919 and 1920, some 60,000; and during the 1920s some 40,000. By 1930 West Indian blacks were about 1 percent of the U.S. black population and about 25 percent of the population of Harlem.[4] Despite the fact that the migrants were largely working-class people, they must have arrived with the necessary skills and motivation to settle without major trauma and to succeed materially.

Thomas Sowell,[5] for instance, noted that as early as 1901, West Indians owned 20 percent of the black businesses in Manhattan, they were represented beyond

63

their numbers in the professions, and second-generation West Indians had, and still have, higher incomes than U.S. blacks and whites as well as below-average unemployment rates.[6] Sowell related the extraordinary fact that in 1970, the higher ranking blacks in the New York City Police Department and all black federal judges in the city were West Indian. It appears only reasonable to assume that such early and dramatic success has to be explained by factors operating both in the societies they left and in the one in which they settled. In many ways, these West Indians were the "modern ones," entering a peripheral area of U.S. society--black America. Their behavior reflected a combination of skills and attitudes developed back home, the enactment of expectations about what it took to be successful in the United States, and the existence of real material opportunities in their new land. But such a smooth and successful movement required more than personal attitudes and opportunities; it required the background of a fairly high degree of cultural uniformity within the area of movement. The fact that both sending and receiving countries were at different times British gave them similar languages and somewhat similar legal and religious institutions.

Given these facts, it appears plausible as an organizing framework to conceptualize the English-speaking Caribbean and the United States as a socio-cultural area.[7] It is social because, as Alejandro Portes indicated, capitalism operated generally within it and as such migration has taken place between units "articulated into the same system."[8] But the cultural aspect--shared values--helps explain why West Indian migration is more comprehensive than the "fundamentally economic" one described by Portes or why it is not "predictable as to direction and size" as he maintained.[9]

As expected within a socio-cultural area, West Indians have migrated for more reasons than just "to sell their work capacity." For even if the majority did come for jobs, ignoring the other reasons is minimizing the range of skills and attitudes (social, political, economic) that existed from the earliest days of West Indian migration to the United States. It is important to make subtle distinctions in motives if the full range and depth of West Indian perceptions about the United States as a destination are to be understood. The Jamaican, who in the 1920s wished to pursue an artistic career but was blocked by the philistine colonial society, might well work as a laborer upon entry into the United States. However, his original cultural drive tells more about both his reasons for migrating and his mode of incorporation

into the new society than does the mere statistic that
he is a member of the U.S. alien work force.

A premise of our organizing framework, therefore,
is that population movements take place within one
socio-cultural area where differences of social,
economic, and political development encourage and
motivate people to move. In his new environment, faced
with new opportunities and new obstacles, the migrant
often shows the aggressive compensatory behavior
frequently associated with entrepreneurship and
drive. This behavior is not just the result of a
change in social status[10] but the compensation for the
different ranks the individual might at any one time
enjoy. It is well established in sociology that such
"inconsistencies of status"[11] play an important role in
social change. The inconsistencies can operate in the
most complex ways: between social status and political
status or among the former and latter and economic
status. Rather than producing enervating stress, this
inconsistency is a motor of change since the individual
will try to bring his lowest ranking status to the
level of his highest one.

So the Jamaican artist might well have acquired
excellent educational and professional skills back home
but have had his mobility blocked because of his low
social and/or economic status. In the United States
his skills were needed, and he enjoyed occupational and
economic mobility. He will also attempt to be socially
mobile--in the United States and back home. In the
same fashion, blocked political ambitions in the
colonies could, and often did, lead to audacious
political actions in the new society.

By conceptualizing the U.S.-West Indian region, as
a socio-cultural area with a high degree of shared
values and norms and allowing considerable
transferability of skills, one sees the region as
something akin to one social structure with all the
status pressures normal to it. And within this
framework, one has to address the central research
question of this chapter: How does the fact of
migration, actual and potential, in such an area affect
the parameters of political decision-making in the
sending countries? Are West Indian options for
development enhanced or reduced by the size and type of
migration? Some scholars have argued that the options
are dramatically reduced but have given no
specifics.[12] The two cases studied here, Jamaica from
the early twentieth century to 1980 and Grenada from
1979 to 1983, illustrate the dynamics of migration
within this socio-cultural area and help answer this
central research question.

II. The Jamaican Case

Jamaicans, like all West Indians, have a long history of migration. In the mid-nineteenth century they went to Panama, later to the United States, and then to Cuba.[13] The man who led the island into independence left Jamaica as Aleck Clarke and after a long stay in Costa Rica, Cuba, and the United States returned as Alexander Bustamante. To that young man, migration had meant opportunity. As his biographer noted, even though he was socially "heir to an upper-class tradition," his other avenues seemed blocked at home.[14] This was the case of many others. For instance, in Cuba, Bustamante met Marcus Garvey, who, being black and belonging to the artisan class, was much more representative of the Jamaican migrant of the early twentieth century; however, he seemed driven by the same political aspirations.

Marcus Garvey established the United Negro Improvement Association (UNIA) in New York, which eventually became the largest black-based organization in the United States. Several aspects of the Garvey story provide the broad outline by which to illustrate not only British West Indian migration to the United States but also the socio-cultural area and its multidimensional system of status. The essence of the story is well-presented by Robert A. Hill:

> At the simplest level, Marcus Garvey and the UNIA symbolize the historic encounter between two highly developed socio-economic and political traditions: the social consciousness and drive for self-governance of the Caribbean peasantry and the racial consciousness and search for justice of the Afro-American Community. . . . Garvey came to America endowed with this Caribbean ideology.[15]

Leaving aside the psychological aspects of Garvey's struggle to become a personage, we see him as representing a type who, failing to succeed in Jamaica, transfers his energies and ideas to what Hill called "the emerging capital of black achievement in America"-- Harlem. In other words, he went from one set of status inconsistencies to another. The difference was that, not being a colony, the United States provided space for development.

Marcus Garvey indisputably was only one of a type of Caribbean man and so was his pattern of integration into U.S. society. The man who hosted him in the United States and introduced him to prominent established blacks was W.A. Domingo, another

Jamaican. Born of a Spanish father and Jamaican mother, Domingo had collaborated with Garvey in Jamaica in several political projects including publishing political tracts. Domingo's trip to the United States in 1910 was financed by his uncle in Jamaica and his sister who ran a boarding house for Jamaicans in Boston--a typical entry and a typical settling in. No sooner had Domingo arrived in Boston than he organized the Jamaica Club; when he moved to New York in 1917 he organized the British Jamaican Benevolent Association. Domingo's contacts with socialist publishers in New York made possible the publication of Garvey's weekly, Negro World. This was typical of contacts between radical (largely Jewish) sectors and the black community. But it was the migrants' capacity for organization which sustained their efforts. Even though Garvey often said that West Indian Negroes ought to "go back to those islands and teach the doctrine of the association," West Indians instead brought the capacity and propensity to associate with them. And, as Aubrey W. Bonnett noted, this capacity was not a function of social class; the low-status immigrants "aggressively" used rotating credit associations to improve their status.[16] These associations were not only commercial; they were what Bonnett called "structural shields" that helped the immigrant cope generally as well as being directly instrumental in helping him achieve his "dreams"--becoming a professional man, a local leader, a businessman, or a landlord. Such were their drives that immigrants often felt that mobility could be achieved in a decade or two.[17]

This capacity to organize was not limited to Jamaicans nor was it directed solely toward economic ends. The political activities blocked in the colonies seemed to spark new activity in the United States, and many of these new organizers had links with Garvey and the United Negro Improvement Association (UNIA). For instance, Trinidadian Charles Augustus Petioni, was an English-educated doctor whose political aspirations could be fulfilled neither at home nor in England. He migrated to Philadelphia where he immediately established the Trinidad Benevolent Association and later the West Indian Committee in America; the latter was specifically geared to using its U.S. base to fight for West Indian political rights.

Similar men were Eliezer Cadet, a Haitian who first migrated to London where his contacts with black soldiers radicalized him; Arden A. Bryan, originally from Barbados but with a three year interlude in Panama, who, after breaking with Garvey, founded the Negro Nationalist Association; John Sydney de Bourg, who was born in Grenada but immigrated to Trinidad

where he became the leader of the radical wing of
Andrew Cipriani's Trinidad's Working Men Association.
        Along with these political types were also the
artists; by far the most important of which was the
Jamaican, Claude McKay, whom Kenneth Ramchand noted,
"as a Black man, was obliged to emigrate and become a
professional."[18] This was in 1912; since then
virtually every major piece of West Indian fiction has
been written abroad. Whether the status they occupied
was that of professional writer, businessman, or
political or social protestor, their propensity to be
active and their capacity to organize gave them a
special niche. They were excellent at bridging the gap
between the nonconformists and the establishment. Not
surprisingly, the Caribbean blacks created the first
major alliance between the Communist party and the
black community.[19] They tended to be critical of the
status quo in the United States, in part because as
blacks they belonged to a U.S. minority but also
perhaps because they were interested in attacking the
status quo back home. Having achieved success in
various areas in the United States, the West Indian
often attempted to transfer his newly gained political
status in the United States back to the West Indies
where he had none but hoped to create one. If he could
not do this in his home island, he often tried
elsewhere. Such was the case with Garvey who
campaigned throughout the region including Central
America. His sense of political power over the islands
had clearly been enhanced by his New York stay. "I am
going to spend six months more here," he said in 1919,
"and the next six months will be to clean up the entire
West Indian islands."[20]
        He returned to Jamaica where his attempts at
leading a political party failed. After the
Immigration Act of 1932 made migration to the United
States difficult, Garvey, like so many other Jamaicans,
went to England. Others, however, had returned to the
Caribbean to organize. In 1927, for instance, Cyril V.
Briggs went to Trinidad to do political work, and W.A.
Domingo, who had given up his position in the journal
Negro World to another West Indian who migrated because
of literary aspirations, Rick Walrond,[21] never gave up
trying to change Jamaica's political situation. Even
after becoming a reasonably affluent and influential
New York black, he organized the Jamaican Progressive
League (still powerful today), which played an
important role in the labor agitation in Jamaica in the
late 1930s. Domingo was a close adviser to the
People's National Party, one of the two major parties
on the island.
        The salient characteristics of this very early
West Indian migration to the northeast of the United

States are evident: The West Indies had early in the twentieth century reached a stage of social and economic development that generated new political aspirations among new groups. These new groups were educated and socially self-assertive but blocked in their political aspirations by the colonial system. They migrated to many areas; however, their migration to the northeastern United States, which had a long history of advocacy of black rights, provided the context for political activism. That movement did more than just open up one status that had been blocked in the still colonial West Indies--political status--it helped crystallize the socio-cultural area.

Since it is well known that primordial sentiments such as nationalism and ethnicity tend not only to survive but indeed be strengthened by secular trends such as modernization, there was no reason to believe that social and economic success in the United States would still their urge for political advancement back home or, as was the case with Garvey, even in Africa.[22]

As opportunities for political involvement in Jamaica opened up in the late 1940s and especially in the 1950s, some returned. One of these was a future prime minister, Michael Manley. But both those who remained and those who returned to enter politics owed a debt to Marcus Garvey and the generation of the artisan class that migrated in the 1920s and 1930s. Without them, as John Hearne has noted, it would have been hard to imagine the surge in black political and labor organizations of the 1930s and 1940s that eventually led to independent politics.[23] They had set the stage for future political action by Jamaican and other West Indian communities based in the U.S. in favor of independence in the late 1950s and Black Power in the late 1960s and 70s.

In this case, emigration to the United States expanded the parameters of Jamaican politics, providing new options for the black artisan and working class, whose political mobility was blocked back home. Similarly, the rapidity with which U.S. Black Power symbols and aspirations spread to Jamaica and the West Indies says much about expanding aspirations (though in this case not quite options) within a socio-cultural area.

It would be a mistake, however, to interpret the increasingly nationalistic--even radical--tone of Jamaican politics to mean a rejection of two fundamental aspects of the Jamaicans' worldview. First, it did not mean a rejection of migration. After World War II, Jamaicans migrated in large numbers to the United Kingdom; migration to the United States (which had slowed because of the Immigration Act of 1932, the Depression, and World War II) did not pick up

again until after 1962 when Britain began to close its
doors and the United States opened its to skilled
immigrants. The figures in Table 3.1 show that even as
a larger number of Jamaicans returned from the United
Kingdom at the time of the establishment of the West
Indies Federation (1957-58) and at independence (1962),
the numbers emigrating were also increasing.

Table 3.1

Migration to the United Kingdom from Jamaica

	Emigrants Total	Migrants Returning from U.K. Total
1953	2,210	133
1954	8,149	182
1955	17,257	99
1956	17,302	757
1957	13,087	1,376
1958	9,992	1,992
1959	12,796	2,318
1960	32,060	1,791
1961	39,203	1,558
1962	22,779	2,868

Source: G. Tidrick, "Some Aspects of Jamaican Migration to the
United Kingdom, 1953-1962," Social and Economic Studies, vol. 15,
no. 1 (1966), p. 26.

A look at the aspirations of Jamaican youth at the
time gives a clue to this two-way movement. Of a 1955
sample of 2,050 rural youths between the ages of 10 and
15, M. G. Smith found that only 3 percent wished to be

farmers whereas 23.8 percent wished to be professionals
(11.3 percent of these, doctors) and 31.1 percent
electricians, mechanics, or engineers.[24] Obviously
such occupations could be secured in such numbers only
in urban Jamaica and abroad. Smith's contention--that
the formidable gap between reality and desire reveals a
potentially high degree of anomie--has to be accepted
cautiously since his survey never explored migration as
an option that parents fully expected their children to
exercise. In a system where immigration had already
become structural, the fact that the schools presented
"a curriculum. . . . designed for urban population in
industrial countries"[25] cannot be interpreted a priori
as dysfunctional to that population's perceived
needs. In the final analysis, the schools were
contributing to the anticipatory socialization that
partly explains the successful Jamaican adaptation in
the United Kingdom and the United States.

Similarly, it is a mistake to interpret the use of
radical, even anti-U.S., rhetoric among West Indian
spokesmen or political elites as a rejection of the
United States as a desirable country in which to
settle. Although changes in the immigration law in
1952 facilitated entry, it is still very significant
that at the height of the Black Power movement in the
United States, which spread fast to Jamaica and the
other islands, West Indian migration to the United
States rose from 4,000 in 1962 to 20,000 in 1971.[26] An
interesting and early feature of this migration to the
United States is that even though West Indians were
often labeled "agitators" or "subversives" by the U.S.
authorities, these rebellious elites preferred the
United States to virtually any other country of
settlement. Explanations of this preference range from
Garvey's statement that "if there is one country in the
world I love, that country is America"[27] to the
Trotskyite Trinidadian C.L.R. James's plaintive cry--
written on Ellis Island while he awaited deportation--
that his present writing was "a claim before the
American people, the best claim I can put forward, that
my desire to be a citizen is not a selfish nor a
frivolous one."[28] Even though Guyana's Marxist-
Leninist leader, Cheddi Jagan admitted to being first
exposed to racial prejudice in the United States, he
sent his son to be educated there, and he himself
sought U.S. citizenship.[29]

Jamaica became independent in 1962 after a long
period of agitation during which Jamaicans based in the
United States--such as Garvey and Domingo--had made
important contributions to the expansion of popular
participation in Jamaican politics. But in so doing,
they strengthened the forces that made Jamaica part of
a socio-cultural area with the United States--with all

that implied for migration. The political decision-
makers of independent Jamaica would have to contend
with the realities posed by this fact as Michael Manley
discovered after 1976.

Even though an important 1974 study of Jamaican
attitudes concluded that "in Jamaica there is neither a
will to achieve the socialist alternative nor the
necessary political support to sustain it even if such
a will existed,"[30] Manley's massive electoral victory
in the 1976 elections indicated that perhaps he was
correct in believing that he could launch his
"democratic socialism" initiative on an anti-American
note with full support of the masses. Under pressure
from the "radical" wing of his People's National party
(PNP), which showed increased strength, Manley began
radicalizing his rhetoric and that of his party. The
role of Cuba in that rhetoric was noticeable. As early
as July 1975 during a visit to Cuba, his speeches had
not only a strident pro-Cuban and anti-capitalist tone,
but also an anti-United States one. The United States,
Manley told the Cubans, now finds itself "morally
isolated."[31] He appeared to take it for granted that
the bourgeoisie would balk and migrate; he felt free,
therefore, to tell them that three flights a day were
scheduled to Miami. But, alas, Michael Manley should
have known from his study of the Marcus Garvey period
that the bourgeoisie would not be the only group to
leave. Migration to the United States had always been
polyclass and stemmed from a variety of motivations.
The shifting social structure in Jamaica affected
groups and individuals of different social status:
Some were affected economically, others politically,
and others socially or occupationally. Since they have
all become a part of the normative system of the
metropolis, the socio-cultural area, they have all in a
way engaged in a form of anticipatory socialization.
This was all the more a reality since, as one U.S.
social scientist discovered, most of the political,
economic, and professional (medical, judicial,
religious) elites governing since independence had
studied in the United Kingdom or the United States.[32]
These included Manley and his rival, Edward Seaga.
These elites were, and so considered themselves,
equipped to migrate if necessary.

Advocating socialism was one thing; another was
cutting off historical avenues of "escape" or
opportunity. Not surprisingly, a Carl Stone poll of
May 1977[33] indicated that only 14 percent of the sample
opposed seeking aid from Washington or receiving U.S.
or other foreign assistance and foreign investments.
His poll also indicated that a major part of the
radical Left campaign (the discrediting of those who
were migrating to the United States) had little public

appeal. Fully 60 percent of those in Stone's sample
indicated they would go to the United States if the
opportunity presented itself. And, the preference for
the United States cut across class and party lines.
Interestingly, the urban working class appeared more
eager to migrate to the United States than the much
criticized urban middle class--68 percent to 45
percent. In addition, the number willing to migrate
had shown an increase across social class: Those
wanting to migrate to the United States specifically
increased quickly from the early 1970s to 1977--from 58
percent to 68 percent among the Kingston working class
and from 20 percent to 45 percent among the Kingston
middle class. The figure in peasant areas was 68
percent in 1977. These figures should have come as no
surprise. Jamaica's strong orientation toward the West
in general and the United States in particular had
already been documented.[34]

Many of the new emigrants settled in a city,
Miami, that radicals denigrated as laden with southern
racial prejudice and Cuban-exile reactionary
politics. As reflected in a Stone survey in November
1977, Jamaicans viewed their opportunities abroad
differently. (see Table 3.2). In fact Stone found that
62 percent of the Kingston working class and 78 percent
of the peasantry held favorable views toward those who
had migrated to Miami.

Table 3.2

Views on the Jamaicans Who Migrated to Miami

Hostile Views	%	Favorable Views	%
Jeopardise economy	1.5	All have the right to travel	13.3
Selfish	13.5	Must protect interests	14.8
Cowards	6.2	Going to a much better life	8.6
Foolish people	1.5	Wish I could go too, things bad in Jamaica	18.0
Against social change	3.8	Fear of political and class violence	4.4
Total	26.9	Total	59.1

Source: Reprinted with permission of Carl Stone, The Political
Opinions of the Jamaican People (1976-1980) (Kingston: Blackett
Publishers, 1982), p. 64.

What Stone and, before him, Wendell Bell found is
what others who do empirical opinion studies in the
Caribbean have also discovered: In regard to
migration, the working class does not differ much from
the middle class; both hold opinions conditioned by
their self-interest as persons and as members of
groups. In these societies, this perception of
interests, much more than the rhetoric of political
leaders, will govern decisions on whether to migrate or
not. The ultimate consequence of this dynamic to the
central research question will depend on how one
defines politics; here again is the eternal question of
the state versus the citizen. The right and the
freedom to migrate clearly expanded the political
options for Jamaican citizens; however, it just as
clearly reduced the decision-making parameters of
Manley's reformist state during the 1976 to 1980
period. A fundamental question, however, is whether
this dynamic only affects the parameters of "radical"
states. It appears not. It hardly seems realistic,
for instance, that the more conservative Jamaican
Labour Party, which won a landslide victory over
Manley's PNP in 1980, should decide to make the rate of
return migration a measure of its success in national
development. Understandably, any indication of natives
returning home is invariably given much fanfare in the
islands, an indication of the symbolism and sensitivity
to everything related to migration, especially as it
reflects on the regime in power. Naturally, the Seaga
regime has broadcast the fact that the number of people
surrendering their U.S. permanent resident visas
("Green Cards") has steadily increased as follows:[35]

1977	48
1979	50
1980	157
1981	180
1982	220
1983	295

In reality, while 295 Jamaicans returned home in
1983, 43,005 of their fellow countrymen were actively
processed for entry into the United States. Even
though much of this migratory impulse started before
Seaga took power in 1980, no evidence shows that his
more conservative regime has any more of a "hold" on
Jamaicans than did that of his predecessor. The
difference appears to be that Seaga has decided not to
make a political issue out of migration--a wise
decision given the dynamics that have historically
operated in this socio-cultural area.
In Jamaica, as in the other societies analyzed
here, migration appears to be an act that stands apart

from ideology or partisan politics. It is something of a universally held option, and the United States is by far the preferred destination for those who have freedom of choice, i.e., those not explicitly recruited to a job abroad. The propensity among West Indians to migrate to the United States is generalized across social classes even though the capacity to do so varies by class.

The implications of this are important not only to those who attempt to estimate the size and social class of migration waves but also, and perhaps primarily, to those who, like Michael Manley, attempt to modify the parameters of political decision-making in such a way that they appear (or are perceived) to hinder opportunities for advancement at home or abroad. The case of Grenada from 1979 to 1983 illustrates this dramatically.

III. The Grenadian Case

In the late 1970s the Institute of Social and Economic Research in Barbados carried out a survey among people who had spent at least three months abroad (see Table 3.3). The results came as no surprise to those who follow the flow of migration and of remittances from the eastern Caribbean. Even though the new revolutionary government in Grenada did not participate in the survey, a legitimate question is: How different would the Grenada figures have been, and what would those figures have foretold or at least hinted about the policy options realistically open to the new leadership of the People's Revolutionary Government? This question can be answered by placing Grenada in the context of the eastern Caribbean, including Trinidad--as part of the broader socio-cultural area in which migration is one of the dominant socio-cultural patterns.

In his last presentation to his party's annual conference, the late Prime Minister of Trinidad and Tobago, Eric Williams, noted how migration from the West Indies in the 1960s had accelerated. The average annual rates of emigration in relation to the actual increase in population stood at 55 percent for Jamaica, 53 percent for Trinidad and Tobago, 87 percent for Barbados, 53 percent for St. Lucia, 70 percent for St. Vincent, Grenada, and Dominica, and an extraordinary 142 percent for Nevis and 124 percent for Monserrat.[36]

His conclusion was a disconsolate one: "There will soon be no West Indians left in the Caribbean." The origin of his chagrin was not hard to find: In the 1970s, between 60 percent and 70 percent of the emigrants were professionals, managers, and skilled workers. Just in the six years since independence in

Table 3.3

Migration and Remittance Flows From the Eastern Caribbean

	Barbados	St. Kitts	Nevis	St. Vincent	St. Lucia
% with more than 3 months' experience overseas	23.1	50.0	42.3	32.0	33.9
Overseas Location					
United States*	36.8	41.8	36.3	8.5	18.9
United Kingdom	13.0	9.0	18.2	19.1	13.5
Canada	9.6	1.8	-0-	2.1	4.5
English-speaking Caribbean	21.5	14.5	27.3	36.2	26.1
% receiving remittances	45.8	59.3	67.3	56.0	40.5
% sending remittances	15.1	23.7	19.2	21.7	18.5
Choice of overseas residence					
United States*	61.6	40.9	69.3	39.4	41.6
United Kingdom	11.0	9.1	15.4	10.6	11.5
Canada	21.9	18.2	15.4	15.4	13.3
English-speaking Caribbean	2.8	15.0	-0-	24.1	8.0

*Mainland, Puerto Rico and the Virgin Islands

Source: Institute of Social and Economic Research, University of the West Indies (Barbados), "Four Country Questionnaire Survey, 1980," February 1980.

1962, Trinidad had lost 143 doctors and dentists, 170 engineers, 629 nurses, 784 teachers, and 909 other professionals--most of them in the productive twenty to thirty-four year age group.[37]

No West Indian island escaped these general trends though some were affected more than others; this clearly was the case for the ministates of the eastern Caribbean. In these islands the sentiment for independence within some form of federation had always been strong, a reflection of their intrinsic sense of isolation and vulnerability. Yet even when such a federation became a reality in the West Indies Federation (1957-1961), that arrangement did not include freedom of population movement. As a 1960 report to the government of Trinidad and Tobago stated, such an open door would create "formidable and intolerable" pressures on the island.[38] Migration, however, did not stop. In the early 1960s between 5 and 10 percent of the eastern Caribbean population migrated each year;[39] even without an "open door," citizens of the ministates found a way to get to the more urban and industrialized countries such as Trinidad. Between January 1958 and November 1959, for instance, 75 percent of the 10,135 visitors to Trinidad from the eastern Caribbean overstayed their visitors' permits and disappeared into the large resident, illegal population. By 1957 Grenadians represented 6 percent of Trinidad's population and Vincentians, 4.3 percent.[40]

Even though migration was a regionwide phenomenon, none of the islands experienced more critically the effects of migration on its social, political, and economic development than Grenada. Major political watersheds resulted from the government's inability to control, accommodate, or rechannel migration from the island. For instance, the question of the unitary state between Grenada and Trinidad and Tobago was the key issue of the 1962 election. The opposition leader, Herbert Blaize, made this the most important plank of his party's platform against that of the premier, Eric Gairy, who vacillated on the issue.[41] A popular refrain ridiculed "Uncle's" (Gairy's) stance:

But Uncle knows that Trinidad
Is what will make Grenada glad

The Grenadian newspaper The West Indian repeatedly ran headlines proclaiming that some 40,000 Grenadians in Trinidad and Tobago favored the unitary state. Not surprisingly the opposition's theme was that every Grenadian has a relative in Trinidad and let's join them! Blaize won the election, defeating folk hero Eric Gairy strictly on the promise that, as The West

Indian put it the day after the victory, "88,000
Grenadians will soon call themselves Trinidadians . . .
. and the cult of Gairyism will have died a natural
death."

Blaize's party won the election, but the Trinidad
government never acceded to the formation of the
unitary state and Eric Gairy had found a new weapon
against his class enemies--the bourgeoisie of St.
Georges. With Blaize discredited because of the
undelivered promise, Gairy swept the next two elections
and only lost power when the New Jewel movement
overthrew him in March 1979. To a large degree, the
Trinidad government had based its decision on an
estimate of population movements from Grenada
calculated on the following four factors: (1) the
present size of the Grenada population; (2) the history
of emigration and size of past movement; (3) the return
of workers from Aruba, Curacao, and the United Kingdom
and their possible re-emigration to Trinidad, and (4)
the possible change in the age/sex composition of the
new immigration stream.[42] The conclusion of the
special commission set up by the Trinidad government
was that such an emigration would be considerably
beyond Trinidad's capacity to absorb. Points 3 and 4
recognize factors other than employment as causes of
migration (schooling, health, and proximity to
homeland). And the Trinidad authorities also warned
that the expected levels of Grenadian migration would
harm Grenada's agricultural economy by depriving the
estates of workers. Again, it was a case of
institutions--including the state--versus individuals.

Both the unitary state proposal and the short-
lived experiment of federation had a fly in the
ointment: population movements between the islands.
While this issue was establishing the parameters of
power within Grenada, as well as its relations with the
other islands, the United States was lifting its quota
of 100 per year for each West Indian island in favor of
immigration on the basis of needed skills, i.e., on the
Labor Department's certification of U.S. labor needs.
Not unnaturally, Grenadians with the door to the United
Kingdom closing and with resentment against Trinidad,
turned to the United States as the land of hope. This
history is the backdrop against which the Peoples
Revolutionary Government's (PRG) attempts from 1979 to
1983 to challenge the parameters of Grenadian decision-
making have to be seen.

The PRG Prime Minister, Maurice Bishop, grew up on
the island of Aruba where his father worked in the oil
refinery. Eric Gairy, the man he overthrew, had his
start as a labor leader at the same refinery. The man
who succeeded Bishop as prime minister in 1984, the
moderate Herbert Blaize, worked for eight years at the

same refinery. Of the three, only Bishop had the
family means to go to England to study law. Gairy came
from the poor peasantry, and Blaize was one of nine
children whose father had migrated to the United States
in 1919 to work as a laborer; like most Grenadian
immigrants who went to the United States, he settled in
Brooklyn. Not surprisingly, four of Prime Minister
Blaize's six children presently live there; one lives
in London. To Blaize, therefore, migration seemed
quite natural: "The question is not whether to
migrate, but when. It is the normal pattern of
behavior; you don't have to teach it."[43] Like Seaga of
Jamaica, but unlike Michael Manley, he did not intend
to make migration a political issue since he knew that
no Grenadian leader had ever controlled it or indeed
been absent from it himself.

The PRG's Deputy Prime Minister, Bernard Coard,
should have known that. After all, he had two brothers
residing in the United States and had himself gone to
Brandeis University in Massachusetts on a U.S.
scholarship. His grandfather was Barbadian, his
grandmother was from St. Vincent, and his wife was
Jamaican. The family had been a proper middle-class
one, and his father, a civil servant, had done what
many place-bound West Indians do--taken various
correspondence courses from the United Kingdom or the
United States. Bernard Coard's father certainly felt
fully capable of much more than he was "allowed" by the
colonial situation to achieve in his occupation.
Eventually, he would travel to the United States, and,
like so many others, he would write his
autobiography.[44] In this touching story, the father's
blocked status aspirations can be seen to lead to
vivid, vicarious pleasures with the success of his
three sons in the United States. But the youngest son,
Bernard, again like so many others, returned determined
to fill a political position once full political
independence made these available to any son of the
soil with enough gumption to take on Eric Gairy. He
and his colleagues in the New Jewel movement, after a
speedy coup d'etat in March 1979, established a
revolutionary Marxist, decidedly pro-Cuban and pro-
Soviet government.

Since the issue of freedom of population movements
has been part of the context of governmental decision-
making in the area, the PRG's decision to challenge the
existing parameters of politics would also have to deal
head-on with this issue. One would expect any options
to include migration as a variable in the equation.

From a simply logical viewpoint but also one
informed by knowledge of past migratory behavior within
this sociocultural area, the PRG appeared to have two
clear options early in the game. Option 1 was to

recognize the value of the overseas Grenadians as
sources of support, talent, remittances, and lobbyists
within U.S. circles. This option implied an acceptance
of an open door to migration, and freedom of
movement. Option 2 was to restrict freedom of movement
as part of an overall state program of revolutionary
management for change.

By late 1981 the PRG leadership had already
embarked on planning a series of radical internal
reforms, many based on the Cuban model. These included
the proposed creation of a Cuban-style national service
and a labor army. By mid-1982 Grenada's Leninists had
decided to move from the "national democratic" or
"socialist emulation" stage to the "construction of
socialism" stage. The time therefore was not
appropriate for making concessions of a "rightist"
type, which Option 1 signified. Option 2 had to be
seriously considered, and they did this by setting up a
Commission No. 5 to explore the possibilities and
consequences.[45]

That this issue was extremely sensitive and even
volatile is evidenced by the top secret classification
of that report. "The Commission has concluded," the
report began, "that our society is largely petit
bourgeois in mentality as well as socially," and as
such Grenadians would most probably not readily accept
the restrictions necessary to implement the service.
Despite this, the commission wished to go even further
in its sociological analysis, probing the outer
boundaries of Grenada's capacity for change along Cuban
lines. Commission No.5's study of the issue quickly
refers to the fact that when the Cubans implemented the
national service "there was a form of restriction on
people leaving the country."[46] The commission then
asks if Grenada could do the same. The answer was not
long in coming: "Our people, as a tradition, believe
in going overseas to work for more money and there is
at present an unsatisfactory level of patriotism among
the masses. In other words, we have grown up with a
visa mentality. The question we now pose is, can we
apply restrictions to people wanting to leave the
country?"[47]

Again, the commission's response to that all-
important question, the one relevant to the entire
Caribbean Basin, was unequivocal since it immediately
concluded: "Our country is a very open country.
Anyone can turn on to any Radio Station and listen to
all the imperialist propaganda. They can turn on to
look at imperialist television. They can read any
magazine, books, etc. . . , and have access to all the
ways and means in which the imperialist can influence
the mind."

What the report did not mention was that the

Grenadian petit bourgeoisie was already voting with
their feet: The decline in the Grenadian population
caused by migration during the four and one-half years
of the PRG is yet to be empirically established--but is
a well-discussed issue in the eastern Caribbean.[48]
    Exactly when a decision was made to attempt to
cultivate the United States--for both U.S. and
Grenadian citizens--is unclear. Given the visualized
failure of any attempts at controlling emigration, the
decision to take Option 1 was strategically wise,
although, as events would prove, it probably was taken
too late. In any case, by February 1983 the PRG
appeared to have launched a full-scale drive to gain
support within the United States. The New York report
became a feature at Political Bureau meetings. For
instance, the February 23, 1983, report was made by
Commander Liam James after visiting Washington, D.C.,
and New York:[49]

o   met with GRL [Grenadian Revolutionary
        League] and discussed their
        transformation into a mass organization.
        . . ."

o   feature address by Harry Belafonte. . . .

o   held meeting with Tourist Office. . . . a
        renewal of interest in Grenada. . . .

o   re Grenadians abroad, the Party must
        look/develop a perspective on Grenadians
        abroad; seek to organize them wherever
        they go, develop, maintain links with
        them, not to be hostile to them (even
        those who left after the Revolution).

    Such were the ties in New York and fundamentally
with one Miguel of the United States Communist Party
that the PRG's Political Bureau agreed to do the
following in New York: purchase a house and possibly
establish a radio station.
    Another thrust at developing Option 1 came in
April 1983 when PRG Ambassador to the United Nations,
Ian Jacobs toured the United States. He reported to
his government that "our North American networks once
again proved their worth with excellent short notice
organizational efforts."[50] From city to city Jacobs
found great interest and support among U.S. black media
and professional groups (radio, newspapers, lawyers,
etc.) and a multitude of peace and progressive
groups. He recommended:

o   Visits to various points in United
     States. Of particular value would be
     embassy involvement on the campus
     circuit--i.e., regular appearances at
     University campuses for payment of a fee.

o   Close links with important progressive
     movements like the peace movement in
     particular.

o   Regular visits from top PRG officials to
     North America.

But the evidence that Option 1 had been chosen, at
least by the Bishop wing of the PRG, was Bishop's own
visit to the United States from May 31 to June 10,
1983, during which he met not only with large numbers
of Grenadians but also with U.S. government
officials. A rapprochment appeared perhaps to have
been in the offing;[51] it certainly had to be if Option
1 was to pay the expected dividends.

Even though at this point historical analysis
takes on a highly speculative character, logical
deductions are warranted. In a system divided between
those like Bishop who favored Option 1 and the
hardliners who tended toward Option 2, any political
decision had to involve a trade-off. One can
legitimately speculate about what was traded off in
this case, which might well be called the Grenadians-
in-the-U.S. strategy. Thus far, history does not
reveal the internal facts of the trade-off, but it does
record that the Grenadians-in-the-U.S. strategy never
got off the ground since in October 1983 the clash
between the radical wing led by Bernard Coard and the
Bishop faction escalated to the point of murder--those
of Bishop and his most loyal followers.

Again the issues of migration, overseas enclaves,
and being part of a big socio-cultural area played an
important role in West Indian decision-making. One has
to be able to derive both a practical lesson and a
social science principle from this history.

IV. Conclusion

The complex dynamics generating migration in the
Caribbean socio-cultural area have been operating for
some 100 years. Clearly, every West Indian group and
class participates in the culture of migration, and
they all also have the physical capacity to actually
move--as shown by the two case studies presented
here. Does migration in this socio-cultural area help
determine the parameters of political decision-making
in the sending societies? The answer has to be "yes,

but not in any particular direction."

The case of Jamaica showed that migration to the United States before independence increased the parameters of politics in Jamaica by involving new groups in the process. The fact that these groups-- such as Marcus Garvey's UNIA--were based in the United States enhanced their role in Jamaican politics. During Michael Manley's second term (1976-1980), however, the socio-culture area constrained his wish to move more aggressively in a socialist direction. He could have exercised his option only at a high cost, i.e., "encouraging" even greater emigration. Similarly the case of Grenada showed that migration had a dramatic impact on that island's political options. Trinidad's fears of more Grenadian migration led to the collapse of the great dream of a unitary state, reducing the parameters of politics in Grenada and thereby assuring the reintroduction of the highly idiosyncratic rule of Eric Gairy. The PRG, which replaced Gairy, studied the realities of being in this socio-cultural area and despite the ideological preferences of some decided that the best tack would be to recognize the constraints but also the great potential benefits and opportunities presented by the area. Unfortunately, Maurice Bishop was murdered before that option could be selected.

In conclusion, therefore, it is difficult to say with absolute clarity what impact migration has had and continues to have on the parameters of political decision-making in the West Indies. This study does tell us absolutely, however, that migration has had and will most probably continue to have an increasing influence and that this fact cannot be ignored in any planning or policymaking in the West Indies or in the United States. Before decision-makers can turn to questions of economic development or long-range planning in general, they have to come to grips with the political reality of migration. Socialist reformers should understand that this phenomenon is not, and has never been, limited to the bourgeoisie; capitalist reformers should understand that they have no particular long-term claim on that bourgeoisie either.

The socio-political dimension of migration is one of the fundamental characteristics of the area, and no decision--by receiving or sending societies--can be made without addressing it. The costs of ignoring it are too great; the potential benefits from harnessing it for development, too enticing. This can be said about the West Indies and also about much of the rest of the Caribbean--a fact that has very real implications and that can perhaps be summarized in two crucial points.

First, the social and cultural patterns that make this a socio-cultural area will probably be strengthened: The very size of the migration assures this. In 1983 the number of Caribbean people already in the legal immigration pipeline was 438,841 (in all seven "preference categories"). Increasing evidence indicates that other Caribbean people have the proven West Indian ability to assimilate and manage the complexities of U.S. economic and political life and that this skill does not appear to be a function of social class or even language skills as the recent Haitian migration to Miami demonstrates.[52]

Second, it is increasingly evident that the Caribbean migrant to the United States keeps close ties to his homeland. This linkage is not only reflected in the remittances he sends back and his frequent return visits but also in his participation in U.S.-based organizations that deal with issues related to his home island. Many Haitians who, as settlers in the Bahamas, showed little or no organizational abilities and less political agitation skills, did not take long to be organized in either Miami or New York.[53]

Whatever uncertainties might arise about the social and economic implications of these two points, the political implications are clear. Today these implications range from the existence of open groups such as the multiple West Indian associations linked to particular parties back home, to the clandestine groups attempting to overthrow the regimes in Haiti or Nicaragua. So important have the overseas enclaves become that electoral politics in the Caribbean now include New York and Miami as necessary places in which to seek overseas votes and funds. With the rest of the world closing its door to Caribbean migration and with the rising level of movement from the Caribbean, migration to the United States will be an increasingly important part of this socio-cultural area's future and will affect in some way the parameters of decision-making both in the Caribbean and in the United States.

Notes

1. A good statement of the traditional theory is Minaki Kurokawa (ed.), <u>Minority Responses</u> (New York: Random House, 1970).

2. Cf. Alex Inkeles: "It is not the fact of moving but the kind of reward the migrant wins <u>after</u> <u>his move</u>, which determines the presence or absence of psychosomatic symptoms." (<u>Exploring Individual</u> <u>Modernity</u>. New York: Columbia University Press, 1983), p. 272. A good case study which illustrates Inkeles' point is Barry B. Levine, <u>Benjy Lopez: A</u> <u>Picaresque Tale of Emigration and Return</u> (New York: Basic Books, Inc., 1980).

3. Cf. S.W. Mintz, "The Caribbean as a Socio-Cultural Area." <u>Journal of World History</u>, Vol. 9 (1966), Pp. 912-937.

4. Ira De A. Reid, <u>The Negro Immigrant</u>, (New York: AMS Press, 1970), p. 244.

5. Thomas Sowell, <u>Ethnic America</u> (New York: Basic Books, 1981), p. 219.

6. Even those most "invisible" of the West Indian migrants, women, are today being revealed to have had "achievements, abilities and attitudes...quite admirable by American standards." (Cf. Dolores M. Mortimer and Roy S. Bryce-Laporte (eds.), <u>Female</u> <u>Immigrants to the United States: Caribbean, Latin</u> <u>American and African Experiences</u>, (Washington, D.C.: RIIES Occasional Papers No. 2, 1981), p. XIV.

7. Here it is good to keep in mind Melville Herskovitz' warning that the concept of a culture area is a construct, a useful device which "necessitates fixing the eye on the broad lines of similarities and differences between cultures, not on the details seen by those who are too close to a culture. It has the sweep of the mural, not the delicacy of the miniature." (<u>Man and His Works</u> [New York: Alfred A. Knopf, 1952], p. 198). For a discussion on how the Afro-Caribbean and the Afro-North Americans are "becoming more alike," see Sidney W. Mintz, <u>Caribbean</u> <u>Transformations</u> [Baltimore: The Johns Hopkins Press, 1974], Pp. 30-32).

8. A. Portes and J. Walton, <u>Labor, Class and the</u> <u>International System</u> (New York: Academic Press, 1981), p. 21.

9. This emphasis has much to do with the particular cases Portes analyzes for he is keenly aware of the other status-related factors which bring, for instance Argentine MD's to the U.S. His concept of "modernity-in-underdevelopment" is premised on the idea of "the penetration of external standards which become incorporated into normative expectations in contradiction to actual resources and possibilities of perispheral economies." (Cf. Alejandro Portes, "Modernity and Development: A Critique," Studies in Comparative International Development, Vol. 9 (1974), pp. 247-79.

10. As Alex Inkeles notes, most of the literature on modernization believes that individual performance largely reflects the nature of the social system they live in and their particular statuses within the system." ...It is status which determines personality rather than the reverse." (Exploring Individual Modernity [New York: Colombia, 1983], pp. 6-7).

11. Among the first to elaborate on Max Weber's idea that stratification systems were multidimensional was Pitirim Sorokin (Cf. Social Mobility [1927] reprinted as Social and Cultural Mobility [Glencoe: The Free Press, 1959]). Sorokin noted that stratification can be reduced to three fundamental "forms": economic, political and occupational and that the "inter-correlation among the three forms of stratification is far from being perfect..." This is the central idea contained in the contemporary theories of "status inconsistency." (Cf. G. Lensky, Power and Privilege: A Theory of Social Stratification, [New York: McGraw-Hill, 1966]; I. Goffman, "Status Consistency and Preference for Change in Power Distributions," American Sociological Review [22], 1957.

12. Orlando Patterson argues that in Caribbean societies, migration "dominates and defines the social structure" and has created a "modal personality syndrome devoid of trust and seemingly incapable of compromise." As such, migration is an obstacle to good government, with the elite willing and able to "use migration as a weapon against any progressive policy" to correct the conditions which make migration both possible and necessary ("Migration in Caribbean Societies," in William H. McNeill and Ruth S. Adams (eds.), Human Migration [Bloomington: Indiana University Press, 1978], pp. 125 and 138.

13. Cf. George W. Roberts, The Population of Jamaica (Cambridge: Cambridge University Press, 1957), pp. 133-141.

14. George E. Eaton, Alexander Bustamante and Modern Jamaica (Kingston: Kingston Publishers, 1975), p. 13.

15. Robert A. Hill, ed., The Marcus Garvey and Universal Negro Improvement Association Papers (Berkeley: University of California Press, 1983), Vol. I, pp. XXXVI-XXXVII. Henceforth referred to as Garvey Papers, Vol. I or II.

16. Aubrey W. Bonnett, Institutional Adaptation of West Indian Immigrants to America: An Analysis of Rotating Credit Associations (Lanham: University Press of America, 1981), p. 4.

17. R.S. Bryce-Laporte, "Black Immigrants: The Experience of Invisibility and Inequality," Journal of Black Studies, Vol. 3 (September 1972), pp. 29-56.

18. Kenneth Ramchand, The West Indian Novel and its Background (London: Faber and Faber, 1970), p. 241.

19. Cf. Theodore Draper, American Communism and Soviet Russia (New York: Viking Press, 1960), pp. 315-356.

20. The Garvey Papers, I., p. 399.

21. Walrond migrated from British Guiana to Panama and from there to New York. His first collection of short stories, Tropic Death (1926) had plots set in the Caribbean.

22. On the general process see Nathan Glazer and Daniel P. Moynihan (eds.), Ethnicity-Theory and Experience (Cambridge, Mass.: Harvard University Press, 1976); on the Third World case see Cynthia H. Enloe, Ethnic Conflict and Political Development (Boston: Little, Brown, 1973). On how Garvey's success in the U.S. stimulated rather than diminished the urge to return to Africa, an idea born in the 19th century, see Tony Martin, Race First (Westport: Greenwood Press, 1976), pp. 110-150.

23. John Hearne, "Introduction" in his edition of Michael Manley's speeches and writings, The Search for Solutions (Ontario: Maple House, 1976), p. 14.

24. M.G. Smith, The Plural Society in the British West Indies (Los Angeles: University of California Press, 1965), pp. 196-220.

25. Ibid., p. 217.

26. Cf. R.W. Palmer, "A Decade of West Indian Migration to the United States, 1962-1972: An Economic Analysis," Social and Economic Studies, Vol. 23 (September 1974), pp. 571-587.

27. Garvey Papers, I, 506.

28. C.L.R. James, Mariners, Renegades and Castaways (New York, 1953) p. 201.

29. Cheddi Jagan, The West on Trial (London: Michael Joseph, 1966), p. 50. Jagan noticed the status inconsistency of West Indians in the U.S.: "Many West Indians must have felt a psychological compulsion to be different, for at home many had come from families of high social position..." (p. 51). Apparently, he attempted but failed to get U.S. citizenship (Cf. p. 63).

30. Carl Stone, Electoral Behavior and Public Opinion in Jamaica, (Mona: Institute of Social and Economic Research, 1974), p. 96.

31. "Excerpts from Address to Cuban Workers, Alamar, July 12, 1975," in Hearne, ed., The Search for Solutions, op. cit. pp. 205-6. For an example of party rhetoric, see the speech by the Minister of Foreign Affairs, Dudley Thompson, to the Second Socialist International Meeting, Caracas, May 25, 1976.

32. Wendell Bell, Jamaican Leaders (Berkeley: University of California Press, 1964), p. 65.

33. Cf. Carl Stone, The Political Opinions of the Jamaican People (1976-1981), (Kingston: Blackett Publishers, 1982), p. 53.

34. See especially in Bell, op. cit. an analysis of the preference among Jamaican elites across the political ideological spectrum for the U.S. over the Soviet Union.

35. Without any further evidence as to whom these individuals were and the reasons of their action (retirement, forced relinquishment). The Jamaican Gleaner (February 13, 1984) editorialized glowingly about it being a "good sign" for the island. The U.S.

Consul General did report that he thought these counted returnees were only the "tip of the iceberg." (Gleaner, May 2, 1983, p. 31).

36. Forged From the Love of Liberty. Selected Speeches of Dr. Eric Williams. (Port-of-Spain: Longman, 1981), p. 443.

37. Trinidad and Tobago, The Emigration of Professionals, Supervisory, Middle Level and Skilled Man-Power from Trinidad-Tobago, 1962-1968 (Port-of-Spain: Government Printing Office, 1970).

38. Government of Trinidad-Tobago, Economic Development of the Independent West Indies Federation (Port-of-Spain: Office of the Premier, October, 1960), p. 11.

39. David Lowenthal, West Indies Societies (Oxford: Oxford University Press, 1972), p. 217.

40. Trinidad-Tobago, Report of the Caribbean Task Force (Port-of-Spain, February 1974), pp. 90-95. The Task Force called for Caribbean-wide "harmonization" of immigration laws and also recommended such measures as identity cards, and the prosecution of those hiring illegal aliens.

41. The issue of the unitary State is discussed in Archie Singham, The Hero and the Crowd (New Haven: Yale University Press, 1968), pp. 279-288.

42. Trinidad-Tobago, Report of the Economic Commission Appointed to Examine Proposals for Association Within the Framework of a Unitary State (Port-of-Spain, January 1965), pp. 35-40.

43. The Miami Herald, December 16, 1984, p. 24.

44. F.M. Coard, Bitter Sweet and Spice (Ilfracombe: Arthur H. Stockwell, Ltd., 1970).

45. Grenada Documents (hereafter cited as GD), "Top Secret Progress Report of Commission No. 5" (n.d. but apparently early 1982).

46. Ibid.

47. Ibid.

48. It was not the first time that such a politically-motivated migration took place. After Eric Gairy's political victory in the early 1960's a large

number of the island's white petit-bourgeoisie migrated
to Australia. Today there is a solid Grenadian colony
in Brisbane, Queensland (Author's notes, Canberra,
Australia, June 1984).

49. GD, Minutes, PB Meeting, February 23, 1983.

50. GD, Report, April 21, 1983 by Ian Jacobs.

51. Quite accurately the authors of a recent
history of the PRG analyze this visit under the
subheading, "The Risks and Benefits of
Rapprochement." (CF. Anthony Payne, Paul Sutton and
Tony Thorndike, Grenada: Revolution and Invasion [New
York: St. Martin's, 1984], pp. 114-117).

52. Cf. Alex Stepick, "The Haitian business
community has self-consciously attempted to repeat the
earlier successes of the Cuban immigrant
entrepreneurs." ("Haitians Released from Krome: Their
Prospects for Adaptation and Integration in South
Florida," [Dialogues Series No. 24, Latin American and
Caribbean Center, Florida International University,
Miami, Florida, 1984]).

53. Dawn I. Marshall has noted that the dominant
characteristic of the Haitians in the Bahamas was
"isolation" and this despite their large numbers on two
islands, New Providence (Nassau) and Grand Bahama
(Freeport). In Miami they were soon organized into a
vocal pressure group (The Haitian Problem, Mona:
Institute of Social and Economic Research, 1979).
Similar trends are indicated among Haitians in New York
by Nina Glick Schiller, "Ethnic Groups are Made Not
Born: The Haitian Immigrant and American Politics," in
G.L. Hicks and P.E. Leis (eds.), Ethnic Encounters
(Mass., Duxburg Press, 1977), pp. 23-35.

Part 2

The Impact of Emigration on Development:
Case Studies

4. Migration and Development in the Eastern Caribbean

Dawn I. Marshall

The link between international migration and economic development has not yet been made by development planners in the Eastern Caribbean. This is because of the way in which the two phenomena, development and migration, are conceptualized. Economic development is mainly seen as a macro concept, a national concern for which government and its planners are responsible. Although the need for skilled and professional human capital is recognized, this specialized human capital is not regarded as synonymous with "population." Rather, population is seen as the masses who have to be supported and cared for by the nation, who have to be employed by the economy, and whose growth has to be controlled.

Migration, on the other hand, is seen as an individual response to those same limitations of size that constrain the development of the national economy. Opportunities for individual betterment are limited in the nation state, so some individuals seek them outside. Since these opportunities are sought by individuals, the impact of migration is also seen at an individual level. Remittances are sent home for the subsistence of the individual's family. In aggregate, they can be viewed as a national receipt, in much the same way as the emigration of a number of individuals results in reduced population growth. But the connection between individual betterment and the "process whereby the material welfare of a people. . . is improved consistently and substantially over long periods of time" is seldom made.[1]

In this chapter I briefly describe the historical background of the changing meanings of economic development in the Caribbean since the first planning efforts in 1946. I then describe the experience of development planning in St. Vincent to illustrate eastern Caribbean strategies of economic development and to assess the impact of migration on human

91

resources, income, and savings. Finally, based on this assessment, I suggest using migration to foster economic development.

I. Development Planning in the Caribbean: Four Stages

Development planning in the eastern Caribbean began in the 1940s and has passed through four stages. As a result of disturbances that occurred throughout the British West Indies from 1935 to 1938, grants of money were made to the various colonies under the Colonial Development and Welfare Act. One of the stipulations of these grants was that a social and economic development plan should be prepared in each colony, and most of the first development plans for these territories cover the period beginning in 1946. This first stage was based on the concepts of the Moyne Commission that was set up by the Colonial Office to investigate the 1930s disturbances. The second stage was "industrialization by invitation" followed by the pursuit of self-sufficiency and the strategy of integration. These stages are not necessarily separate and discrete.

The Moyne Commission's emphasis was "on welfare rather than on development."[2] To a certain extent this emphasis was a result of prevailing conditions at the time of the Moyne Report. The report saw the crux of the West Indies problem as the coexistence of "a positive demand for the creation of new conditions" with an unfavorable economic trend.[3] It saw the main basis of economic life as agriculture. But at the same time, it recognized that the trend of world conditions had become generally adverse to economic development based on the export of agricultural commodities. The commission did not suggest any solutions to these problems and concluded that there was "no way to avoid expenditure from outside resources on social improvements in the West Indies."[4] Thus the Colonial administrators perceived the Caribbean as completely integrated into the larger colonial system and as incapable of sustaining itself on its own resources even at the low standard of living then prevailing in the West Indies.

Arthur Lewis first submitted his case for rapid industrialization in the British West Indies to the Moyne Commission. He based his case on the fact that the land had reached the limit of its capacity to carry people, on the overpopulation of the islands, and on the dire need to create new opportunities for employment. However, this strategy for development, which became known as "industrialization by invitation," does not seem to have been accepted by Caribbean planners until the 1960s. Up to that time planners saw the economy as based on agriculture. Then in the 1960s, manufacturing was seen as the growth sector of the economies.

In the early 1960s a number of economists came to see economic dependence as the dominant feature of Caribbean economies. They saw the economy as dependent on the rest of the world--for capital, markets, supplies, skills and expertise, and banking and financial services and for the maintenance and growth of internal levels of employment, output, and demand, a natural outcome of previously pursued strategies.[5] The perception of economic dependence was perhaps sharpened when a number of Caribbean countries attained political or constitutional independence at the time, and found the economic prospects still limited. McIntyre saw economic dependence as consisting of two elements:

1. structural dependence: dependence that arises because of the size and structure of the economy and cannot be helped.

2. functional dependence: dependence that arises as a result of the particular policies chosen and can therefore be avoided if alternative policies are pursued.[6]

The view that structural dependence in the Caribbean is conditioned by small size has exerted a powerful influence over economic thought in the region. In this context, regional economic integration became the development model during the mid-1960s. Functional dependence has not achieved an equivalent position but is one component in the most recent development strategy: the need for "structural readjustment."

At all stages in this evolution of development strategies, the integration of the Caribbean into a wider international system was recognized. But this recognition did not extend to migration as an aspect of the interaction between the Caribbean and that system-- at least not to the extent of incorporating it into development planning. This omission was perhaps understandable in the first two stages of evolution. At that time, emigration had virtually ceased and in any case had previously been confined to the Caribbean and Central America. But by the late 1960s, large-scale emigration to the developed countries of the North Atlantic was well under way.

The concept of development in vogue will depend not only on the problems and needs perceived to exist, but also on the extent to which governments and planners perceive the system, as well as themselves, as capable of achieving the concept. Lloyd Best put it succinctly and in terms still relevant for Caribbean planners of today: "Economic development is a problem of management--of timing, sequencing and manipulation in an unending effort to perceive or create, and in any case to exploit a multiplicity of little openings and opportunities."[7]

II. Development Strategies for the Eastern Caribbean: The Case of St. Vincent

How relevant were these concepts to the eastern Caribbean? Demas in his Economics of Development in Small Countries seemed to deny the Eastern Caribbean islands the possibility of development. His 1965 development strategy, although conceived specifically for small, open economies, was based on a minimum size below which the eastern Caribbean fell:

> The Leeward and Windward Islands are so small as to fall into a separate category and, while this factor in itself does not preclude the development of manufacturing industry, it appears to me that their future is much more closely bound up with exports of traditional primary products, the growth in productivity of the domestic food-producing sector and the development of the tourist industry [and] tourism does not develop the capacity to transform to the same extent as manufacturing"[8] (my emphasis).

However, by 1981 Demas had conceded that the agricultural, industrial, and tourism sectors of these islands could grow on a sustained basis at the rates required to give people the level of living to which they could realistically and reasonably aspire.[9]

It is not always clear whether the difficulties of planning for development in the small islands of the eastern Caribbean are fully recognized and appreciated. For this reason, I have included a fairly detailed review of development planning in one of these islands: St. Vincent.

As in the other Caribbean islands, development planning in St. Vincent began in 1945 with the grant of 345,858 British pounds to the island by the Colonial Development and Welfare Act. One of the stipulations of the grant was that a ten-year plan be prepared for the social and economic development of St. Vincent. The general objective of this first development plan was economic expansion, but it also included a discussion of strategies of development.

This first plan noted that the development of new

industries was usually suggested as the key to economic growth, but that this was by no means essential. Rather, economic expansion depended on the efficiency with which available resources were utilized, and efficiency was achieved by the best balance between the various factors of production. The factor most lacking, observed the plan, was managerial/inventive ability. As a result, the process of development, as defined by the plan, "has hardly commenced in St. Vincent."[10]

But this theoretical discussion by Jolly was indeed a luxury. The plan was required by an external agency for the purpose of granting aid. Its main objective, therefore, was for an authoritative survey of financial resources to be carried out to determine (1) just how far the colony could safely and fairly proceed to increase revenue from local taxation and (2) to what extent the colony would need to obtain capital loans in the open market for financing both permanent services and the plan of development.

It concluded that self-reliance was impossible. The colony could barely support its existing services. Import duties, which supplied 38 percent of the government's revenue, were already too "heavy for a country which must rely largely on overseas trade to maintain what standard of living it has already achieved."[11] In fact Jolly rather brutally concluded that the colony's state of economic development was not sufficiently advanced to carry additional taxes and that the expenditure of taxes for other "humane purposes must for the present be callously neglected."[12]

All subsequent development plans have been faced with the same problems. As a result, they have had a number of crucial characteristics in common. First, they have all been prepared by external agencies. This is not to say that the Vincentian government has not had critical inputs into these plans, but they were prepared by external agencies. Second, they were all, with the possible exception of the Institute for Social and Economic Research (ISER) mission, primarily concerned with the perennial problem of balancing a government budget, which had increasing deficits. This second characteristic is particularly important because even capital expenditure on productive investments, and certainly capital expenditure on social services, carries with it inevitable recurrent costs that have to be maintained. Third, again perhaps with the exception of the ISER development mission, most of the agencies engaged in preparing plans, surveys, and projections have either been donor agencies themselves or have been retained by donor agencies. Fourth, all the plans, again with the exception of ISER, have been project oriented; that is, they have been concerned with preparing projects that are either for economically productive enterprises or that will attract donor funds, or preferably both.

And finally none of them has been able to solve what O'Loughlin called the central problem of growth, that is, the attainment of a level of income high enough for savings to be sufficient to sustain growth of national capital from within or with only a modicum of support from outside.[13] With independence, this achievement seemed even further away. Before independence, over 90 percent of capital expenditure came from outside. But if the Vincentian government is no longer likely to receive grants-in-aid to assist in balancing its budget, the little available within St. Vincent will have to be taxed for that purpose or for the purpose of repaying loans, however soft. Balancing the budget, rather than development, is likely to become an even more pressing preoccupation. However, it is unlikely that St. Vincent will be completely abandoned by donor agencies. Resources for capital expenditure will probably still continue to come from external donor agencies.

Apart from this problem, there is fairly general consensus on specific areas in need of development. None of the reports engage in fruitless discussions about which sectors should be the growth areas of the economy--agriculture, tourism, or manufacturing. In microeconomies like that of St. Vincent every possible avenue of growth has to be seized and developed to the fullest extent possible. It is true that the ISER mission was very critical of the still prevailing view that agriculture, almost by a process of elimination, had to be the mainstream of the economy: "It is simply not possible . . . to envisage any form of agriculture, domestic or export, which could form the source for an optimum growth of income at a rate significantly greater than the rate of expansion of population."[14] Constraints on the development of each of these sectors are well recognized, and priority projects have been identified. Still three points need to be reemphasized in the context of Vincentian development.

First, if every possibility for growth has to be pursued, then certainly no sector should be allowed to deteriorate. The contribution of agriculture to gross domestic product (GDP) has declined both absolutely and relatively since 1961. St. Vincent cannot allow such a situation to continue.

Second, a certain degree of infrastructural development is necessary if further growth, in the tourism and manufacturing sectors particularly, is to take place. Electricity and water--crucial utilities to any development in these sectors--have been deteriorating. These utilities constitute public services that should be supplied by government. This area is one in which the conflict between balancing the budget and generating development has to be resolved.

And finally, throughout the reports from 1947 to 1981, the need for innovative and skilled managerial and technical skills is noted, but only briefly. No indication is given about how these skills are to be developed and, more important, maintained in the island. Stringent recurrent budgetary measures by government, especially in the area of civil service salaries, are certainly not the answer. Yet none of the reports nor any of the listed projects address the problem in detail. Yet this is probably the crucial need that has to be fulfilled before self-generated and self-reliant real economic growth can take place in St. Vincent--and in the rest of the Eastern Caribbean.

As developing countries, Eastern Caribbean island states share a number of problems with other Third World countries. Problems such as rapid rates of population growth and high population densities, low agriculture productivity and unequal land distribution, high unemployment and underemployment, high production costs of manufacturing industries, lack of real economic growth, high rates of inflation and relatively large foreign debts have persisted for so long that they are perceived as characteristic of these islands. But these characteristics are symptoms of underdevelopment, not causes. The discussion of development planning in St. Vincent suggests that the important variables to be considered are (1) the attainment of a level of income high enough for savings to be sufficient to sustain growth of national capital from within--O'Loughlin's central problem of growth-- and (2) the lack of innovative and skilled managerial and technical skills to direct or channel these savings for optimum benefit (see Chapter 15 in this book).

III. Impact of Migration on the Eastern Caribbean

As discussed, in the Eastern Caribbean development is seen as a macro concept whereas migration is perceived as an individual strategy. To link these two concepts, any assessment of the impact of migration on the Eastern Caribbean should focus on the two variables identified as crucial to the process of economic development: attainment of a high level of income for savings and the lack of managerial and technical skills. Such an evaluation should attempt a measurement of the extent to which emigration has affected these two variables, thus either facilitating or impeding development. But before this evaluation is attempted, some of the problems involved in assessing the impact of migration are outlined.

Assessing the impact of emigration on the Caribbean is not an easy task. One problem is the poorly developed state of the study of consequences or impacts in migration studies generally. Much more is known about the determinants of migration than about its consequences.[15] This problem is particularly severe in the study of Caribbean migration, which has received little attention from resident Caribbean scholars. In contrast, scholars in the receiving countries, particularly the metropolitan countries, have devoted much more energy to the impact of Caribbean migration on the receiving societies. Thus conceptual frameworks that might assist the assessment are lacking.

Detailed and specific information on Caribbean migration is scarce. The available data are uneven and fragmentary. Nevertheless, in the Caribbean there has always been a general, positive perception of migration. Indeed, this positive perception may have impeded the development of migration studies in the Caribbean since few have seen the need to study a phenomenon that "everyone" knew to be beneficial.

This general perception is mainly the result of two specific perceptions of impact: the control of population growth and the receipt of remittances. Ironically, the two crucial variables identified are actually elements of these two impacts. The original previous observation about savings being a macro concept and remittances a micro impact still holds. But control of population growth and lack of managerial skills are both macro concepts. However, one is positive and the other negative. And because Caribbean emigration has been traditionally a labor migration, only in the last two decades has the lack of managerial skills been partially caused by the loss of these skills via emigration. Jolly, in his analysis of the problems of achieving development in St. Vincent in 1947, could not have said that the lack of managerial skills was the result of emigration.

Human Resources

Since 1844, when the first modern census was conducted in most of the countries of the eastern Caribbean, none of the Leeward Islands or Barbados has even doubled its 1844 population size. The Windward Islands have all tripled their 1844 population size; St. Lucia's has increased fivefold.

The impact of emigration on population growth in the eastern Caribbean has become increasingly important since the 1920s. Fertility rates remained high for all the islands until the 1960s and still remain high for

most of them although family planning is beginning to
have an impact in Barbados. But death rates have
declined dramatically between the periods 1921-1925 and
1951-1953, from about thirty-three per thousand to
fourteen per thousand. As a result, the rates of
natural increase in the islands have soared. Between
1960 and 1970, except for Montserrat and Barbados, none
of the countries had a rate of natural increase under 2
percent, and Dominica, St. Lucia, and St. Vincent had
rates of over 3 percent. These rates have been
substantially reduced by emigration even to negative
population growth rates for Montserrat and St.
Christopher-Nevis.

   Probably because of the high unemployment rates in
the Caribbean, this control of population growth has
also been seen as an alleviation of unemployment.
Migration is believed to relieve unemployment both by
the emigration of the unemployed and by the unemployed
replacing the employed who emigrate. Preliminary data
from the ISER Eastern Caribbean Migration Project
(ECMP) of a sample of 319 current migrants from
Barbados, St. Vincent, St. Lucia, and Grenada to Canada
show a relatively large proportion of unemployed among
those in the labor force. The proportion of the labor
force (N = 221) who were unemployed varied from a low
26 percent in Barbados to 32 percent in St. Vincent and
36 percent in St. Lucia and in Grenada. Moreover,
these unemployment rates can be generalized to the
migrant stream of 1982-1983 since this sample
represented between 62 and 82 percent of the applicants
for visas during this time in all of the islands except
Barbados, where the sample was 17 percent of the
applicants.[16] However, there was also some indication
that some applicants expecting to get visas sometimes
quit their jobs or, if unemployed, stopped looking for
jobs: They were therefore "voluntarily idle." It is
not possible, at this stage of the analysis, to say
what proportion of the unemployed were in this
category.

   Seasonal migration may be more of a relief to
unemployment than permanent migration. In 1980 the
ISER conducted a survey of 129 Vincentian males who
applied to go to Barbados to cut cane. Fifty-three
percent of the survey respondents were unemployed at
the time of the survey, and 27 percent of these had
been unemployed for more than a year. The
questionnaire also asked why the respondent wanted to
go to work in the Barbadian sugar harvest. Twenty-
seven percent wanted to go to obtain work, 18 percent
to obtain money, and 22 percent to obtain both work and
money. Together these three reasons accounted for 67
percent of the responses. If the 11 percent of those
who responded that they wanted to support themselves or

their families is included the proportion increases to 78 percent. When these motives are considered together with the unemployment rate among the respondents, the importance of contract labor, at least at the individual level, to the employment situation in St. Vincent can be appreciated.

A marked difference can be seen between the occupations of those who were employed and the usual occupations of the unemployed. The majority of the unemployed were farm laborers, whereas the majority of the employed were small farmers (see Table 4.1). In fact, only the tradesmen among the unemployed group (16 percent) could be considered own-account or self-employed workers, whereas 74 percent of the employed were self-employed. In other words, those who were employed were employed because they worked for themselves. In developing countries, persons who have difficulty in finding suitable paid employment are often forced into low-income self-employment or employment as unpaid family workers. These usually represent a significant proportion of the labor force and therefore help to disguise unemployment.[17]

Table 4.1

Occupations of Vincentian Applicants to Cut Cane in Barbados

	Employed %	Unemployed %
Small farmers	48.4	--
Farm workers	17.7	53.7
Fishermen	8.1	--
Tradesmen	9.6	16.4
Laborers	14.5	28.4

Source: Institute for Social and Economic Research (Cave Hill, Barbados: University of the West Indies, 1980), Survey of Vincentian Contract Workers.

Comparative data were collected in the ECMP for samples of Barbadian and Vincentian seasonal workers who traveled to Canada and the United States in 1983-84. Preliminary analysis indicates that fourteen out of thirty-six Barbadians (39 percent) and four out of thirteen Vincentians (31 percent) who traveled to Canada and thirty out of sixty-three Barbadians (48 percent) who travelled to Florida were unemployed. Table 4.2, which presents data collected from the farmworkers in Canada, indicates that less than half of the Barbadian farmworkers and about a quarter of the Grenadian and Vincentian farmworkers were certain of jobs when they returned home. One-third of the farmworkers were self-employed.

Table 4.2

What Happens to Job in Home Country
While Farmworker is in Canada

	% from Barbados (n=101)	% from Grenada (n=24)	% from St. Vincent (n=18)
Unemployed	10	13	34
Job lost	9	25	--
Seasonal layoff/cutback	10	4	5
Job kept open	48	25	28
Self-employed	23	33	33

Source: Anne Whyte, "The Experience of New Immigrants and Seasonal Farmworkers from the Eastern Caribbean to Canada," mimeo (University of Toronto, 1984), Table 4.13.

For a number of reasons, statistical data are difficult to obtain to calculate the loss of human resources to the Eastern Caribbean. Data available in the receiving countries are usually based on legal immigration, and estimates of the numbers of illegal immigrants are unreliable. Even when data are available, because of their small size the islands of

the Eastern Caribbean are usually relegated to the
category of "other Caribbean." In the Eastern
Caribbean countries such data are scarce. As a senior
government official in St. Vincent said: "It is
precisely because there is a shortage of skilled
personnel that we have not been able to collect the
data you seek." Thus authors tend to focus on the
larger Caribbean countries of Jamaica and Trinidad.

The main sources of data on the distribution of
occupations in the Eastern Caribbean are the decennial
censuses. Unfortunately data from the 1980 census are
not yet available. In Table 4.3 the professional and
technical, and administrative and managerial
occupations are listed for 1960 and 1970 for some
countries of the Eastern Caribbean. One can infer from
the data that the problem is less one of loss of
professional and technical workers, because for all
islands the proportion employed in this category
increased between 1960 and 1970; rather, it seems to be
one of loss of workers with administrative and
managerial skills. In all the islands, the already low
proportion in this category declined between 1960 and
1970 so that only in Barbados and Montserrat was the
proportion above one percent in 1970.

Table 4.3

Proportions of Professional, Technical, Administrative,
and Managerial Occupations, 1960 and 1970
(As % of Work Force)

Country	Professional & Technical 1960	1970	Admin. & Managerial 1960	1970
Barbados	5.1	9.2	3.1	1.4
St. Lucia	3.6	7.5	2.1	0.9
Grenada	5.1	7.5	3.5	0.6
St. Vincent	5.5	8.5	2.8	0.7
Dominica	4.1	6.9	2.5	0.7
St. Kitts-Nevis	1.3	8.7	3.0	0.9
Montserrat	1.6	9.0	2.4	1.3

Source: Norma Abdulah, The Labour Force in the Commonwealth
Caribbean: A Statistical Analysis, Human Resources Occasional
Papers no. 1, ISER (St. Augustine, 1977).

In Table 4.4, the proportions of those in administrative and managerial, or professional and technical occupations in the labor forces of Eastern Caribbean countries are shown with those in the ECMP (Canada) sample and with those enumerated in New York City Standard Metropolitan Statistical Area (SMSA) counties in the 1980 census. The 1980 U.S. census enumerated a total of 26,847 persons who had been born in Barbados. But the total numbers born in the other Eastern Caribbean islands were much smaller: 7,101 in Grenada, 4,044 in St. Vincent, 3,296 in Dominica, 1,903 in St. Christopher-Nevis, 1,901 in St. Lucia, and 1,212 in Montserrat.[18] For the five islands for which we have data, the numbers enumerated as resident in New York City represented only between 2 and 4 percent of the total enumerated in the United States.

For the islands other than Barbados we can conclude that there is a loss of technical and managerial skills. The proportions in these occupations were much higher in the ECMP sample than those in the national populations (see Table 4.4). In fact the preliminary data from the ECMP (Canada) study suggest that, at least for Canada, those seeking migration from St. Vincent, St. Lucia, and Grenada seem to be of higher "quality" than those from Barbados.[19]

Data are not yet available from the ECMP (U.S.) sample for comparison with the 1980 U.S. census data for New York City. However, in comparison with the national populations, workers with managerial and technical skills appear to be concentrated in New York. This, of course, could be the result of differences in classification schemes. But, if we assume no major differences, then either an accumulation of skills is concentrated in New York, or the loss via migration also includes those who have the potential for filling these occupations and who fulfill this potential after arrival in the United States.

Under the Bishop regime, the government in Grenada was concerned about this problem of loss of skills. It recognized (1) that small states like Grenada with low and slowly growing per capita incomes experienced emigration rates among the highest in the world, (2) that human resources were the key to development, and (3) that skilled and professional workers were particularly mobile and were most likely to migrate permanently. It traced the location of Grenadians who graduated from the regional University of the West Indies (U.W.I.) between 1953 and 1972 and discovered that 81 percent of the 149 graduates were outside Grenada. The situation was particularly bad for medical graduates: "Whereas in general, five Grenadians must be sent to U.W.I. to get one back; to obtain one doctor through that institution, 22 must be

Table 4.4

Proportions of Managerial and Technical Occupations in
National Populations, Current Migration Streams,
and Caribbean Populations Abroad

	1970 Census Pop.[a]		New York City[b] 1980 Census		ECMP (Canada) Sample	
	Tech.	Managerial	Tech.	Managerial	Tech.	Managerial
Barbados	9.2	1.4	42.6	10.4	3.8	1.9
St. Vincent	8.5	0.7	41.6	12.4	11.5	7.1
St. Lucia	7.5	0.9	56.3	2.1	22.2	6.7
Grenada	7.5	0.6	45.4	10.7	13.3	5.7
St. Kitts-Nevis	8.7	0.9	31.4	3.9	-	-
Dominica	6.9	0.7	N.A.	N.A.	-	-
Montserrat	9.0	1.3	N.A.	N.A.	-	-

[a]Percent of Work Force engaged in these occupations in each country.

[b]These percentages refer to those persons with technical and managerial occupations residing in the New York SMSA counties who were born in these Caribbean countries.

Sources: Norma Abdulah, The Labour Force in the Commonwealth Caribbean: A Statistical Analysis, Human Resources Occasional Papers no. 1, ISER (St. Augustine, 1977); Dawn Marshall, ed., Report of the Eastern Caribbean Migration Project, mimeo, ISER (Barbados, 1984).

trained."[20] Most of the other Eastern Caribbean
islands, with the possible exception of Barbados,
probably suffer similar losses of human resources.

Although skilled and professional human resources
are the most crucial and most expensive to replace, the
loss of any individual is a loss to the sending
country--the loss of the money spent raising and
educating that individual to whatever level he has
reached when he emigrates. Very little is available on
this aspect of migration for the Caribbean. A few
studies look at the loss of "high-level manpower" from
Jamaica but, to my knowledge, nothing has been written
for the Eastern Caribbean.

Thus, Table 4.5 has been compiled to give a very
crude estimate of the extent of such losses. The
figures should be viewed with some caution. For
refinement, data are needed at least on the ages and
educational levels of the emigrants and on the costs of
educating the emigrants in their home countries. The
educational value (column 4) was calculated using 1981
public costs of education for Grenada: EC$4,210 for
primary and EC$6,993 for secondary education.[21] The
assumption was made that half the emigrants were
educated to primary level and half to secondary
level. This assumption was based on the educational
levels of the ECMP sample. Both university graduates
and children who had not completed their education,
however, would also be among the emigrants, and these
costs are only educational. The social and medical
costs of raising the emigrants are not included because
attempts to obtain estimates of these costs have been
unsuccessful. Moreover, the value to Canada and the
United States of these immigrants would be greater
because of the higher cost of education in those
countries. Costs in 1968 for Canada were CAN$4,096 for
primary education and CAN$6,144 for secondary
education. Although the figures should be treated with
caution, they do give some idea of the value of the
loss of "low-level manpower" from the eastern
Caribbean.

Seasonal labor migration also involves a loss.
Workers who travel to Florida to work in the sugar
industry are away from the Caribbean for a total of six
months--when their labor is obviously not available in
their home countries. Analysis of data from the
registration cards of 1,390 workers registered with the
Barbados Labour Department showed that 40 percent of
these Barbadian workers had secondary school
education. Moreover, 43 percent of those registered
were skilled workers in such occupations as machine
operators, welders, electricians, carpenters, masons
and plumbers. In 1981, 859 workers traveled from
Barbados to Canada whereas 553 traveled in 1983, so the

Table 4.5

Migrants from the Eastern Caribbean
to the United States and Canada

	Admitted to USA 1971-81	Admitted to Canada 1967-79	Total	Educational Value (EC $ million)
Barbados	23,342	6,372	29,714	166.5
Antigua	7,029	1,430	8,459	47.4
Montserrat	2,130	280	2,410	13.5
St. Christopher-Nevis	7,301	1,095	8,396	47.0
Dominica	5,302	1,007	6,309	35.3
St. Lucia	5,460	897	6,357	35.6
St. Vincent	5,534	2,860	8,394	47.0
Grenada	8,885	2,465	11,350	63.6

Sources: J.P. Guengant, "Recent Caribbean Migration: Negligible or Neglected Factor," presented at IDRC/UNITAR Workshop on International Migration (St. Vincent, 1984), and Robert Cole, "On the Problems of the Reverse Transfer of Technology (Brain Drain) and Human Resources in Grenada," mimeo, n.d., p. 7.

program represents a considerable loss of skilled manpower to Barbados for a substantial part of the year.
        The literature on Caribbean migration suggests that emigration is a survival strategy, a means of obtaining opportunities not available in the Caribbean. This certainly seems to be the case with emigration from the eastern Caribbean. In a four-country questionnaire survey conducted by the ISER in 1980, respondents were asked to state the reasons why they thought people migrated from their home islands. The results are presented in Table 4.6. Migrants clearly are perceived as having mainly economic motives. If the motives of job opportunities, earning money, and attaining a better life are combined as economic motives, the proportion of reasons in this category is not less than 50 percent in any of the islands and rises as high as 70 percent in St. Lucia and 82 percent in St. Vincent. The problem for the small island states of the eastern Caribbean becomes a vicious circle: Human capital is being lost because the economies are not sufficiently developed to generate the opportunities desired, yet the retention

Table 4.6

Why People Emigrate from Eastern Caribbean[a]

	Barbados %	St. Christopher %	Nevis %	St. Vincent %	St. Lucia %
Opportunity	8.1	3.0	14.0	5.2	5.1
Job	18.3	19.8	29.1	22.1	23.5
Education	6.4	7.4	14.9	4.8	12.8
Money	31.7	2.4	18.9	28.9	23.5
Better life	18.7	35.6	7.4	31.0	23.7
Family	2.2	3.0	2.7	0.0	2.3
To see world	7.2	3.0	6.1	3.0	5.1
Other	7.5	4.0	6.7	5.0	4.1
No. of responses	1,383	202	148	461	710

[a]Question 14a: Why do you think so many people from (island) try to get overseas?

Source: Institute for Social and Economic Research (Cave Hill, Barbados, University of the West Indies, 1980), Four Country Questionnaire Survey.

of the skilled and professional human capital is essential to the process of development.

This section has tried to assess the impact of emigration on human resources in the eastern Caribbean. As expected, the results are mixed. Emigration has definitely controlled the growth of population, especially in the last two decades, and this is generally perceived as an advantage to the sending countries. The available evidence seems to suggest that emigration also alleviates unemployment in that unemployment rates among the migrants are higher than those of the national populations. This is particularly true for seasonal migrants: Not only is their unemployment rate high, but a substantial proportion of them are self-employed or unlikely to get jobs when they return home. At the same time the loss of actual and potential administrative and managerial skills is quite high, especially since these were identified as one of the variables essential to the process of economic development. An attempt was also made to quantify the value of the loss of human resources via emigration. The section concludes with the observation that the problem is a vicious circle of loss of essential human capital vital to the process of development.

Income and Savings

In the earlier discussion on development strategies in the eastern Caribbean, the attainment of a level of income high enough for savings to be sufficient to sustain the growth of national capital was identified by O'Loughlin as the central problem of growth.[22] "Private saving is the chief source of finance for capital formation; usually it finances not only the whole of private investment, but (via purchase of government securities) a substantial proportion of government investment as well."[23] Within the context of emigration, this involves remittances.

Some assessment of the magnitude and the use of remittances is essential to judge their impact on development. The receipt of remittances is constantly cited as a benefit of migration, but very few data on remittances in the Eastern Caribbean are available except for the amounts received officially via postal and money orders together with the amounts remitted as "compulsory savings" by seasonal farmworkers who go overseas to work in the sugar camps of Florida or the farms of Ontario. In Table 4.7 the impact of these official remittances can be seen on some aspects of the economies of four of the eastern Caribbean islands: Barbados, St. Vincent, Grenada, and St. Lucia. The impacts in St. Vincent, Grenada, and St. Lucia are very similar; it should be noted that the data for St. Lucia are for 1977 whereas those for St. Vincent and Grenada are for 1979. Receipts for Barbados are much larger than those for the other countries--more than four times as large--although the impact of GDP is less than half that of the other countries. This comparison indicates the different scales of the four economies. But for 1979 the impact on Barbadian imports and exports is very similar to those of the other countries.

Table 4.7

Impact of Remittances on Eastern Caribbean

	Barbados 1982	Barbados 1979	St. Vincent 1979	St. Lucia 1977	Grenada 1979
Total remittances (EC$ 1000)	13,645	19,193	3,399	3,094	3,066
Farmworker savings as % of remittances	8.3	5.9	15.7	14.3	1.9
Remittances as % of GDP	0.8	1.2	3.0	2.0	2.0
Remittances as % of exports	3.8	8.2	9.2	5.6	13.5[a]
Remittances as % of imports	1.2	2.2	2.8	1.9	N.A.

[a]As % of 1980 exports.

Sources: Digests of Statistics, Governments of Barbados, St. Vincent, St. Lucia; Department of Statistics, Grenada, various years.

    In Table 4.7 the contribution of the compulsory savings of farmworkers is shown as a proportion of the total remittances. The proportion in Barbados is about through "official" channels. These seamen are Barbadians who work on ships belonging to various nations and who return home between voyages. They travel by air as far afield as New Zealand and Southeast Asia to join their ships. However, the migration can be considered similar to that of the seasonal farmworker: Labor services are sold abroad for foreign exchange remitted to Barbados.
    A comparison between the data for Barbados for 1979 and 1982 in Table 4.7 indicates that remittances have been declining. This trend has not been general, however. In fact, remittances to Barbados increased from EC$7.516 million in 1961 to almost EC$25 million

in 1981 and have shown a decline only in 1981 and
1982. This trend is also true for the other countries
where remittances have been increasing absolutely, but
their impact, as measured by their contributions to
GDP, imports, and exports, has been declining.
    In St. Vincent the amount remitted via the
Farmworkers' Scheme has been increasing, both
absolutely and as a proportion of total remittances.
The important point here is that the money remitted via
the Farmworkers' Scheme represents only the compulsory
savings deducted from the workers' wages--19 percent of
gross earnings. In 1980, for example, the gross
earnings of 484 Vincentian workers in the United
States, Canada, and Saudi Arabia totaled EC$4.8
million.[24] For comparison, arrowroot--the second-
ranking export crop--earned EC$1.6 million in 1978 and
the manufacturing industry, which employs about 1,500
people, totaled EC$9.6 million also in 1978.[25]
    This trend of the increasing contribution of
farmworker savings is not true for the other
countries. In Barbados the contribution of farmworker
savings has been declining while that of seamen has
been increasing. Unfortunately none of the other
countries gives data on seamen's contributions. In St.
Lucia the picture is not clear. Farmworker
contributions were 30 percent of total remittances in
1954, declined quite sharply to 13 percent in 1956, and
remained at less than 10 percent until 1975 despite the
fact that the Canadian Farm Labour Programme began in
the late 1960s. In 1976 and 1977 the contribution
increased to 13 and 14 percent. Sufficient data are
not available to assess the trend in Grenada, but it
should be noted that Grenadian farmworkers travel only
to Canada. Since the 1960s they have not been included
in the U.S. scheme.
    Data collected from both immigrants and seasonal
farmworkers in Canada during the ECMP facilitate a
comparison between the two in respect to
remittances.[26] In Canada, data were collected from 72
immigrants and from 168 farmworkers. Because of the
small sample size, the data were analyzed by total
sample rather than by island.
    The farmworkers earned an average of EC$6,091
during their average stay of four months in Canada.
For comparison, the per capita GDP at factor cost in
Barbados in 1980 was EC$7,915; in St. Vincent in 1979
it was EC$946; in 1978 it was EC$1,221 in Grenada and
EC$1,618 in St. Lucia. From their earnings, the
farmworkers remitted an average of EC$1,778 during
their stay and took home with them cash and goods worth
an average of EC$1,006 at the end of the season.
Because they would have earned an average of EC$2,618
during the season if they had stayed home and been

employed, the net benefit in the home country was an
average of EC$1,223 for the season. This figure does
not include compulsory savings, only the money remitted
by the farmworker. Compulsory savings actually
received by the farmworker are usually 19 percent of
gross earnings. Therefore, the total benefit in the
home country for each farmworker would be EC$2,380.
However, Whyte warned that these financial data should
be treated cautiously as farmworkers seemed reluctant
to divulge such information accurately.[27] This
statement could be generalized to all ECMP respondents.

In contrast, the immigrant sample remitted an
average of EC$155.50 per month during their first year
in Canada. This amount would be EC$622 for the
equivalent of the four-month farmworker season or
EC$1,866 for the twelve-month season. But only 46
percent of the immigrant sample remitted any money
during the first year.

In the context of economic development,
discussions on remittances tend to imply that migrants
should be making more positive contributions; in
particular that they should be investing
productively. The recipients of the farmworker
remittances in the ECMP were almost all women. The
remittances were intended to support the family on a
day-to-day basis while the farmworker was away. Money
spent in Canada on goods to be taken back home was
mainly used on food and clothing (53 percent for
Barbados, 60 percent for Grenada, and 70 percent for
St. Vincent). The remainder of the purchases tended to
be consumer goods like radios, televisions, and stereos
rather than productive equipment or tools. The money
taken home at the end of the season was used mainly for
the family's general living expenses or for buying or
improving the home. Compulsory savings were more
likely to be saved than spent.[28]

The empirical account of the use of farmworker
remittances suggests that the main use of remittances
is for subsistence--to purchase the basic necessities
of life; little surplus appears to be left over for
investment by either the recipients or the farmworkers
themselves. The question at the beginning of this
section asked whether remittances could be said to
constitute savings. In O'Loughlin's terms they
certainly constitute income and a level of income
higher than would have been earned at home. Some of
this income, the compulsory savings, is saved. But the
contribution to the growth of national capital is more
difficult to ascertain.

Data on domestic savings are available only for
Barbados, and the contribution of remittances to
domestic savings was not concluded. However, in 1980
domestic savings were 25 percent of GDP,[29] and

remittances were 1.3 percent of GDP.[30] These
statistics mean that remittances are the equivalent of
5.2 percent of domestic savings--a not very significant
contribution. But Worrell also noted that, contrary to
expectation, the contribution of domestic savings to
investment spending was lowest during the period when
real investment grew fastest: "The evidence is
consistent with an alternative hypothesis: that the
limits to investment are the resources which can only
be obtained from abroad. In part this is because of
the heavy foreign exchange content of the expanding
sectors. . . . More importantly, foreigners frequently
bring the marketing, technological and organisational
skills on which investment depends."[31]
        From the discussion of remittances, I conclude
that the impact on the Eastern Caribbean economies is
small but useful. However, the impact on domestic
savings does not seem signficant, and in any case the
importance of domestic savings to investment and
economic development seems to have been brought into
question by the experience of the Barbadian economy.
Thus the impact of emigration on development seems to
be mainly apparent in the loss of managerial and
technical human resources--a point reinforced by
Worrell's comment on the importance of foreign manpower
of this nature.

IV. Migration and Development

        The point of assessing the impact of emigration on
development is to enable planners both to use migration
to foster or facilitate development and to minimize
those aspects of emigration that impede development.
Based on our assessment, the most important impact is
the loss of human resources with managerial skills.
This impact seems to be both actual and potential
because not only does a loss of migrants with these
skills take place but a significant proportion of
migrants seem to acquire these skills after they have
migrated.
        The government or planners of an Eastern Caribbean
country can do little to directly affect the out-
migration of skilled human resources. All the
countries are democracies that accept the freedom of
movement of their citizens. Given the tradition and
general positive perception of emigration, any of the
governments would have extreme difficulty in
restricting the emigration of even a small segment of
its population. Action, therefore, has to be indirect.
        The most effective deterrent to emigration must be
the provision at home of the opportunities for which
people migrate. But these opportunities are generated
by the very development that the retention of skills is

intended to foster--the vicious circle that we discussed earlier. Two possibilities therefore exist: (1) providing the skills via the technical assistance of expatriates and (2) attracting skilled nationals from overseas. The first possibility, the traditional one, has not been very effective in the Eastern Caribbean; the second is now being discussed as a feasible alternative.

One of the findings of the ECMP (Canada) study is important in the context of the second possibility. The study found that, in Canada the migration process was selecting persons who had the fewest ties to the home country: The majority of the immigrant sample were unmarried, not in a stable sexual union, had no children, and were not heads of households. The commitment to the home country of migrants with such characteristics would be expected to diminish with time. The attraction offered would therefore have to be great, perhaps by having international agencies "top up" (raise) the salaries of nationals who would return for a period as technical assistants. This suggestion was also made to me by a senior government official in St. Vincent. In a recent article, Trevor Gordon-Somers, resident representative of the UNDP for Barbados and the Eastern Caribbean, recommended that the international community work toward increasing this type of assistance, which is already taking palce in the Eastern Caribbean under the aegis of the United Nations Development Programme (UNDP).[32]

Although I have presented evidence on remittances at the micro or individual level in this chapter, the assessment of their impact was carried out at the macro level. This indicates the pervasiveness of the conceptualization of development as a macro concept. I concluded that remittances had little impact on economic development. But what if, in the spirit of Beckford's definition of consistent and substantial improvement of material welfare, I were to make the assessment at the individual level? Without doubt, seasonal migration has greatly benefited farmworkers and their families. Given their precarious employment situation at home, their material welfare in terms of housing, food, clothing, and consumer durables has definitely improved. I would suggest that the maintenance and increase of such opportunities certainly foster development at the individual level. Assessment at this level is seldom carried out by economists or planners, and, perhaps because of this, the positive contribution of emigration to economic development is underestimated. But this does not mean that it can completely balance the loss of managerial skills that I have determined are crucial to the process of economic development.

Notes

I wish to thank Patricia Pessar and Robert Pastor for their constructive comments on the first draft of this paper.

1. George L. Beckford, "Caribbean Rural Economy," in George L. Beckford (Editor), The Caribbean Economy, Institute for Social and Economic Research (Jamaica, 1975), p. 18.

2. Douglas Hall, "The Ex-Colonial Society in Jamaica," in Emmanuel de Kadt (Editor), Patterns of Foreign Influence in the Caribbean (Oxford University Press, 1972), p. 35.

3. Great Britain, West India Royal Commission (The Moyne Commission) 1938-39, Report H.M.S.O. (London, 1945), p. 8.

4. Ibid., pp. 356-357.

5. Norman Girvan, "The Development of Dependency Economics in the Caribbean and Latin America: Review and Comparisons," Social and Economic Studies Vol. 22 (1973), p. 4.

6. McIntyre, quoted in Ibid., p. 5.

7. Lloyd Best, "Size and Survival," in N. Girvan and O. Jefferson (Editors), Readings in the Political Economy of the Caribbean (New World Group, Jamaica, 1971), p. 30.

8. William G. Demas, The Economics of Development in Small Countries (McGill University Press, 1965), pp. 96 and 60.

9. William G. Demas, "The Viability of the OECS States," in Proceedings of the Eleventh Annual Meeting of the Board of Governors of the Caribbean Development Bank (Antigua, 1981), p. 39.

10. A.L. Jolly, "Preliminary Examination of the Economic and Fiscal Structure of St. Vincent," in Bernard Gibbs (Editor), A Plan for the Development of the Colony of St. Vincent (Trinidad, 1947), p. XVI.

11. Ibid., p. XIV.

12. Ibid., p. XVIII.

13. Carleen O'Loughlin, Economic and Political

Change in the Leeward and Windward Islands, Caribbean Series #10 (Yale University Press, 1968), p. 7.

14. Institute for Social and Economic Research, "The Development Problem in St. Vincent: A Report by a U.W.I. Development Mission, Mimeo (I.S.E.R., Kingston, 1969), p. 58.

15. Alan Simmons, Sergio Diaz-Briquets and Aprodicio A. Lacquian, Social Change and Internal Migration: A Review of Research Findings from Africa, Asia and Latin America, International Development Research Center (Ottawa, 1977).

16. Dawn Marshall (Editor), Report of the Eastern Caribbean Migration Project, mimeo, I.S.E.R. (Barbados, 1984).

17. Norma Abdulah, The Labour Force in the Commonwealth Caribbean: A Statistical Analysis, Human Resources Occasional Papers #1, I.S.E.R. (St. Augustine, 1977), p. 55.

18. Advocate News (October 22, 1984).

19. Marshall, Eastern Caribbean Migration Project, p. 117, Supra. fn. #16.

20. Robert Cole, "On the Problems of the Reverse Transfer of Technology (Brain Drain) and Human Resources in Grenada (mimeo, n.d.), p. 7.

21. The costs for Barbados are much higher. Based on figures for 1983-1984 from the Barbados Ministry of Education, the cost of educating a person at primary level for six years is EC $8,933. If the person completes secondary education up to the age of 16 the total cost is EC $16,844. See Cole, "Problems of the Reverse Transfer," p. 11, Supra. fn. #20.

22. O'Loughlin, Economic and Political Change, Supra. fn. #13.

23. W. Arthur Lewis, Development Planning: The Essentials of Economic Policy (Allen and Unwin, 1966), p. 117.

24. This was a pilot scheme in which 32 Vincentians went to Saudi Arabia for two years to work as unskilled construction labourers.

25. Kingsley Laine, "An Overview of the Vincentian Economy," Bulletin of Eastern Caribbean

Affairs, Vol. 5 (1979), pp. 12-13.

26. Anne Whyte, "The Experience of New Immigrants and Seasonal Farmworkers from the Eastern Caribbean to Canada," mimeo (University of Toronto, 1984).

27. Ibid., p. 4.22.

28. Ibid., Chapter 4.

29. DeLisle Worrell (Editor), The Economy of Barbados 1946-1980, Central Bank of Barbados (Bridgetown, 1982), p. 18.

30. Government of Barbados, Barbados Statistical Digest 1980 (Bridgetown, 1980).

31. Worrell, Economy of Barbados, pp. 18-19, Supra. fn. #29.

32. Trevor Gordon-Somers, Bulletin of the Eastern Caribbean Study, I.S.E.R. (Bridgetown, 1984).

5. Migration and Development in Jamaica

Patricia Y. Anderson

The importance of migration to the understanding of the formation and dynamics of Caribbean societies has been frequently observed by researchers. Like the rest of the British Caribbean, Jamaican society was built on imported labor, and even after this forced mobility was replaced by a voluntary flow, the movement persisted. During the movement to Central America and the United States in the first two decades of this century and the postwar surge to Britain, the pattern of movement was predominantly that of worker migration. When the labor force was successfully established, the migrant chain was subsequently extended and diversified through family reunification. As the movement to the United Kingdom trailed off in the early 1960s and was replaced by North American migration, the pattern repeated itself and reflected the increasing economic linkages of Jamaica with the U.S. economy.

The period of the 1960s was significant because it witnessed the ascent to nationhood for several small Caribbean islands and their increasing concern with the issues of development. In the field of migration research, the latter concern was reflected in attempts to assess the costs and benefits of these outflows to the country of origin, since the growing imbalance between the rapid rate of population growth and the level of job creation made clear the problems of labor force absorption in these tiny states.

As the economies of the host societies contracted during the 1970s and their demand for migrant labor decreased, the perception of this movement also changed. Caribbean migration then became defined as a problem to be explained by researchers and policy analysts in the receiving societies. In response to this perspective, researchers from within the region insisted on the routine character of the movement and

117

on its explanation in terms of the limitations of small size.[1]
The 1970s represent a particularly important period in the migration history of Jamaica, not only in terms of the volume of the outflow but also because of the change in the composition of out-migrants and in their motives for migration. Although the economic motivation remained important for many, for others the decision to migrate was propelled by the determination to escape the social upheaval and political violence that followed the government's decision in 1974 to pursue a socialist path. For these groups, drawn predominantly from the middle and upper classes, migration was a defensive response in their attempt to preserve their way of life, and family migration replaced individual mobility.

This chapter looks at out-migration from Jamaica during the 1970s and offers an assessment of the effects of this movement on the pattern and pace of development in the country. The analysis proceeds from the premise that migration is part of the system of resource flows that occur between countries that pursue a dependent development path and their metropolitan partners. This system includes the movement of capital, goods and services, technology, and ideas. The interdependence of these flows is demonstrated by their feedback relationships, as disruptions in capital flows trigger unplanned movements of population, which in turn discourage further capital inflow, weakening the economic base of the country.

In this chapter I argue that in assessing the costs and benefits to the country of the outflow of population, a distinction must be made between the political and economic effects. Manpower losses may constitute an economic loss if they retard the pace of economic production or social-service provision, but they may also represent a political benefit if they reduce dissonance within the system. During the crisis of the 1970s, the forces generating such dissonance were particularly strong, as production and employment contracted, balance of payments difficulties increased, and inflation soared.

Although several studies have focused on the economic effects of the brain drain, in this chapter I suggest that manpower planning in the Caribbean is still hampered by an inadequate understanding of the causes of the outflow since many of those policies hinge around an implicit and unproved assumption that there is sufficient effective demand for these skills. I make a distinction between social need and effective demand and show that even though Jamaica experienced critical shortages of particular types of skilled manpower, the inability to provide reasonable remuneration levels or to supply the complementary production factors constituted a lack of effective demand. Lack of effective demand is reflected in high labor market mobility and turnover, both within and outside of the country. These labor market features are integrally related to the economic structure of Caribbean countries, but in Jamaica they were thrown into relief during the 1970s when demographic pressures combined with international recession and domestic contraction to create a new context for development planning.

I. Migration and Resource Flows

The demographic history of Jamaica in the post-World War II period cannot be understood without recognizing the major role that migration has played in regulating potentially high rates of population growth. Roberts noted that in the 1943-1960 period the net migration loss was 195,000 persons or nearly one-third of the natural increase in the period. This net outflow increased during the 1960s, reaching a level of 280,000 or 53 percent of natural increase. In the most recent intercensal period, 1970-1982, net migration appears to be on the order of 325,000, or 57 percent of natural increase.[2]

The central contradiction that Caribbean countries face arises from the imbalance between the demographic structure and the limitations of the productive system. This contradiction is expressed in an expanding labor force and increasing joblessness. The high fertility experienced in the postwar period has resulted in a young age-structure, and this, combined with internal migration, creates pressures on the labor market that are reflected in high youth unemployment. In Jamaica, unemployment among persons aged 14 to 24 years increased from 37 percent in April 1973 to 51 percent in 1980. The seriousness of this increase may be appreciated by noting that the youth population (14 to 24 years) represented 29.2 percent of the labor force in 1980, so that 53 percent of all the unemployed belonged to this age group. The expansion of the secondary school system has not been paralleled by similar increases in job creation so that a situation has developed in which the ranks of the unemployed include many graduates of the new secondary schools. This explains the somewhat surprising finding that education levels are higher among the total unemployed than the employed. In April 1980, 30 percent of the unemployed reported having postprimary education compared with 20 percent of the employed.

Although the expansion of migration in the 1970s is essentially a continuation of an earlier pattern, it is distinguished by the relative size of the outflow and the changes in composition. Both of these were related to the increasing pressure of population on resources and to the government's attempt to transform the economy and the resistance that this provoked. For the first time, therefore, migration became a highly politicized issue, on which the middle classes were bitterly divided. Although those who supported the socialist program were strongly critical of the out-migration, those who opposed it responded in differing ways.

On one hand, some people were convinced that their personal and social survival depended on their escape from the island, and they recognized that their movement was the result of social class. This belief was expressed in the popular witticism of the period, "Will the last person leaving the island remember to turn off the lights?"--a metaphor expressing both their recognition that this was the end of their particular society and life-style and their own myopic view that their departure heralded total breakdown for Jamaican society. In contrast, some people reacted with heightened nationalism, refusing to take one of the "five flights to Miami." This response was expressed in the reggae lyrics of Pluto Shervington:

> I man born ya
> I nah go America.

Even though the professional classes that migrated in this period expected that they would become permanent migrants, the business classes found that they had the additional option of maintaining a dual base of operation. This group established manufacturing and import activities within the United States, and by integrating their local and overseas operations they were able to manage their own foreign-exchange supply and to expatriate their profits. They represented a new class of migrants who may be labeled "transnational migrants" because the circularity of their migratory paths was short-term and repetitive. The families of these migrants usually moved to the United States, and their children were popularly labeled "Jamericans," as they lived not between two cultures but on the basis of both. Within Jamaica, the exodus of this class was reflected in a rapid turnover in the social origin and skin color of both the children enrolled in the elite preparatory (primary) schools, and the persons admitted to membership in the private sporting clubs.

Statistics collected by the Planning Institute of Jamaica show that over the 1973-1980 period, professional and managerial workers had the highest rate of emigration, averaging 1,900 annually, or 32 per 1,000 workers. Craftsmen and operatives exhibited the second-highest rate, with an annual average of 2,700 workers, and a rate of 22 per 1,000. In its 1982 special report on migration, the Planning Institute reported that for the period 1970-1980, the combined group of professional, technical, administrative, and managerial workers accounted for 20 percent of all workers with stated occupations. Clerical and sales workers were close to the same level (19 percent), craftsmen and operatives represented one-third of the outflow, and private household and service workers accounted for one-fourth (24 percent).[3]

Although the summary figures for the eleven-year period give an idea of the overall importance of the outflow, they obscure some of the shifts in composition that occurred during the 1970s. During this period and especially after 1975, the occupational composition of North American migrants started to reflect increasing proportions of upper-level white-collar workers, so that by 1980 the combined group of professional and managerial workers represented 27 percent in comparison with 16 percent in 1970. Significantly, within this group administrative and managerial workers more than doubled their representation. The percentage of craftsmen and operatives, though still very important numerically, fell from 38 to 27 percent, whereas that for service and household workers declined from 26 to 18 percent (Table 5.1). The increased concentration of professional and managerial workers shown in these figures is explained by both the change in U.S. immigration policy since 1965 and the accelerated migration of the middle classes during the 1970s.

In discussing the composition of the outflow, the Planning Institute remarked that the loss of the professional and the highly skilled workers had adversely affected the level of development, whereas the departure of domestic workers, general service workers, and laborers had helped to relieve unemployment. The study included an estimate of the cost of training the 35,600 workers who migrated to North America between 1977 and 1980--a figure that amounted to Jam$348 million. This total, which was then equivalent to US$194 million, was considerably higher than the sum of US$26 million that Jamaica had received in the form of grants from the United States and Canada during this period.

Two serious effects of the population outflow during the 1970s were the accompanying flight of capital and the subsequent decrease in the level of recorded remittances. Estimates of the level of outflow vary, but for 1975 it was placed at $300 million by official sources. Most of the continued

Table 5.1

Occupations of Jamaican Migrants
To North America, 1970-1980

Occupational Group	1970-80	1970	1976	1980
Professional, technical administration and managerial	19.8%	15.5%	20.1%	26.7%
Clerical and sales	18.9	18.0	19.5	23.4
Craftsmen and operatives	32.9	38.2	34.1	27.0
Household and service workers	24.3	25.9	23.2	18.2
Laborers	4.0	2.4	3.2	4.8
Total Percent	100	100	100	100
Number	97,167	10,910	7,055	7,364
Total emigrants	214,298	19,692	16,308	17,161

Source: Planning Institute of Jamaica, "Emigration to North
America from Jamaica, 1970-80," special report, Kingston, 1982.

outflow is not recorded, since it occurs through a
variety of means ranging from direct smuggling of cash
to overinvoicing of imports by the manufacturing sector
and informal exchanges. Although the value of
remittances received into the banking system has
increased because of successive devaluations of the
currency, the value in foreign exchange has shown a
marked decline since 1975.[4] Although postal
remittances were equivalent to US$16.26 million in
1975, this figure shrank to US$3.51 by 1983. This
decline was only partially offset by the increased
value of farmworkers' remittances (Table 5.2).

The contraction of investment and the outflow of
capital that occurred during this period serve to
demonstrate the close relationships between the
movement of economic resources and the movement of
population. First, the movement of population is
usually accompanied by the outflow of capital, varying
from personal savings to large-scale capital flight.

Table 5.2

Remittances Received in 1975, 1980, and 1983
($US thousand)

	1975	1980	1983
Postal remittances	$16,263	$14,156	$ 3,507
Farmworkers' remittances	3,865	7,985	9,873
Total	$20,128	$22,141	$13,380

Sources: Bank of Jamaica, Monthly Review (Kingston), 1975, 1980, and 1983.

The extent of these capital flows depends on the motives for migration and the lack of regulation of capital movement. As Palmer suggested, the emigration of professional and managerial workers may serve to discourage the inflow of foreign private capital, as a sizable share of this capital may have been attracted by the stability and competence of this group.[5] Return migration and remittances may restore some of these financial resources to the country, but they are more likely to be utilized to meet the needs of consumption and social investment than for economic production.

Equally important, however, is the fact that unplanned movements of population may be triggered by official attempts to restrict the mobility of capital and goods, as demonstrated by Jamaica's experience during the second half of the 1970s. It is not possible to distinguish how many individual migration decisions resulted from foreign exchange restrictions and the changes in life-style that these threatened to impose on an elite, accustomed to enjoying consumption levels comparable or superior to the levels they would have known overseas.[6] Clearly, however, an integral relationship exists between capital and population movements and a disturbance in one sphere is immediately transmitted to the other.

Although the movement of capital, goods, and technology is essential to the system of dependent capitalism as it serves the goal of profit-realization, the movement of population is not essential to this purpose, although it contributes to the stability of the system in different ways. Migration serves not

only to reduce the pressure of population on resources
but also to moderate social tension by increasing
psycho-cultural identification with the metropole and
by reducing the sense of being trapped within a small
and limited world. Although these benefits are enjoyed
by only a small section of the population--primarily
the elite and middle classes--these groups are
strategically placed to articulate discontent and to
undermine allegiance to the political-economic
system. Their compliance is therefore won at the cost
of further retarding attainment of the development
goals, since their out-migration deprives the country
of needed skills, adding to the familiar lament of the
brain drain.

The access to higher standards of living, which
the working classes achieve through out-migration,
although occurring on a small scale, serves to
reinforce commitment through maintaining the belief
that individual mobility is possible and through the
demonstrable effect of return migration and
remittances. In this way, individual mobility for a
few serves to obscure the recognition of collective
stagnation and decline.[7]

In assessing the overall impact of these migration
flows on Jamaica, it is instructive to ask what would
have happened had the migration boundaries been sealed
and these flows not taken place. Specifically, could
the Jamaican economy under its limited growth
constraints have absorbed the numbers of persons who
entered the labor market at varying skill levels? Some
tentative answers to this question are suggested in the
following section.

II. Manpower Flows and Mobility

Although the loss of skilled manpower during the
1970s undoubtedly hindered Jamaica's capacity to expand
or even maintain production levels and to provide basic
social services, research has tended to focus on this
aspect of the manpower problem without sufficient
examination of the labor market context from which this
outflow comes. The most striking feature of the
Jamaican labor market is the high degree of mobility
and turnover: Workers move in and out of the labor
force, between industries and sectors, and across
national boundaries. This high labor mobility
demonstrates the dilemma that successive governments
face: Although skilled manpower is desperately needed
for economic and social production, the government is
unable to allocate manpower in any rational way because
of its lack of effective demand. This dilemma is most
apparent with regard to the supply of manpower for the
social services, where public investment is expected to

provide the necessary infrastructure and to finance
recurrent expenditure. The high level of social need
in this sector may be appreciated by noting that in
1978 the ratio of doctors to population stood at one
doctor for every 5,900 persons, whereas there was an
average of 24,000 persons to every dentist.[8] Social
need, however, is not easily translated into effective
demand. This lack of effective demand, in terms of the
country's ability to employ these workers at levels of
remuneration that will repay their investment in their
own training, constitutes the manpower planning
dilemma. This dilemma becomes even more apparent in
the current period when rapid increases in the cost of
living, expressed in an anticipated increase in the
cost-of-living index of 40 to 60 percent in 1984, seem
to be triggering another wave of out-migration.

Because of the extreme openness of the economy,
any attempt to restrict the mobility of labor
immediately raises the question of "basic freedoms" and
is translated as a potential threat to the stability
and security of capital flows. Under this system, the
government's role must therefore be quiescent. The
only options that remain open are to continue to
provide on-the-job experience for administrators before
they migrate to the private sector, to continue to
train for export, and to rely on foreign personnel
where remuneration levels for local staff are
unacceptable. These patterns are substantiated by the
data on manpower mobility and turnover that are
presented in the next section.

III. A Manpower Balance Sheet

To demonstrate the extent to which constant
turnover takes place in manpower supply and
composition, it is possible to assemble a manpower
balance sheet for specific occupations, identifying the
sources of increment and decrement in particular
periods. This approach is here attempted for the
supply of professional, technical, and managerial
workers for the years between 1976 and 1980, as shown
in Table 5.3. The sources of increase in labor supply
shown are those increments resulting from the output of
training institutions and from foreign personnel
admitted under work permits. These two sources do not
exhaust all known sources of increase in the supply of
professional workers, since increases in stock can also
be obtained through return migration, occupational
upgrading of workers who may have previously been
classified as clerical or other workers, and through
labor force reentry of persons who are still resident
in the country. At this stage, however, the data are
not available to estimate the size of these other

Table 5.3

Manpower Balance Sheet for Changes in Supply of
Professional and Managerial Workers, 1976-1980

	1976-77	1977-78	1978-79	1979-80
Measure of change of labor force supply[1]				
Labor force at beginning	61,500	68,200	71,000	71,000
Labor force at end	68,200	71,000	71,000	69,800
Net change(D_1)	+6,700	2,800	nil	-1,200
Measure of change based on components of growth				
Increment due to training output[2]	3,300	3,900	4,300	4,200
Increment due to work permits[3]	700	500	400	500
Loss due to legal out-migration[4]	-1,100	-2,300	-2,800	-2,600
Net change (D_2)	+2,900	+2,100	+1,900	+2,100
Difference between measures of net change ($D_1 - D_2$)	+3,800	+ 700	-1,900	-3,300

Sources:

[1]Jamaican Ministry of Labour, Jamaican Labour Force Surveys,
1976-1980.

[2]Government of Jamaica, National Planning Agency, Economic and
Social Surveys of Jamaica, 1975-1979 (Kingston).

[3]Jamaican Ministry of Labour (unpublished figures).

[4]Government of Jamaica, National Planning Agency, Economic and
Social Surveys of Jamaica, 1975-1979 (Kingston).

movements, although it is popularly believed that return migration would be the most significant component.

The sources of decrement in labor supply areidentified as (1) out-migration, (2) retirement, (3) death, (4) labor force withdrawal, and (5) downward occupational mobility. In this balance sheet, only the size of legal migration is known, but the other major source of loss is believed to be unrecorded out-migration.

The purpose of this balance sheet is twofold. First, it allows a quantitative appreciation of the extent to which the Jamaican labor force is constantly exchanging new workers for old, more experienced for less experienced. Between 1976 and 1977, 3,300 professional workers graduated from the training institutions, and 1,100 professional workers migrated legally. By the end of the period, legal migrants included 2,600 professional workers, equivalent to 62 percent of the training output of 4,200 professionals.

The second purpose of the balance sheet is equally important, since it may be used as a crude estimate of unrecorded migration. In the same way that the census is used in combination with vital statistics data to provide a corrected estimate of the volume of net intercensal migration by the balancing equation, similar estimates of occupational flows can be developed by modification of this approach.

This may be expressed schematically as follows:

Original stock   New stock
in occupation X + increments-decrements = in occupation X

By manipulating this equation, it is possible to derive two estimates of changes in labor supply. The first estimate is obtained by finding the difference between the labor force at the beginning and at the end of the period, as measured by successive labor force surveys.[9] The second estimate of change is obtained by finding the net difference between the known sources of increment and decrement. The difference between these two estimates of change, usually known as the error of closure, is an indication of the movements that have not been recorded in the flow statistics and in this case may largely be attributed to unrecorded migration.

In Table 5.3 the two estimates of change in the supply of professional workers show an unexplained increase of 3,800 workers in 1976-77 and 700 workers in 1977-78. On the other hand, an unrecorded decrease of 1,900 and 3,300 professionals occurs in the last two years of the period, respectively. The increase in the earlier years may reflect some return migration, but at present no data are available to substantiate this possibility. The decrease between 1978 and 1980 is more likely to have been caused by unrecorded migration, since the professional class found migration relatively easy through the informal method of a visitor's visa followed by subsequent change of status within the United States. In summary, indirect migration among the professional and managerial class seems almost equal in volume to legal out-migration during the last two years of the decade, and this outflow served to stabilize the size of this occupational group, which within a four-year span (1973-1977) had expanded by 50 percent. Some effects of this outflow may be discerned in the official statistics and studies from this period; one immediate effect is a shift of public-service administrators to the private sector.

Although much of the outflow of professional and managerial workers occurred from the private sector, this flow stimulated movement from the public administration ranks to fill the vacancies thus created in higher-paid jobs. At the beginning of this period, Mills and Robertson (1974) reported that rapid turnover of staff affected 67 percent of the professional, technical, and middle-level grades in the civil service and that posts in the professional categories remained unfilled for more than a year because of the lack of qualified staff.[10] In their study of the civil service in 1983, Green, Gordon, and Jones observed that there appeared to be a problem in the lack of retention of experienced personnel at the height of their capacities, from ages 35 to 44. As a result, the age structure of the civil service showed a bulge in the age group 25 to 34 (42 percent) and a sharp contraction in the older group, 35 to 44 (21 percent). They suggested that even though this turnover may open opportunities to younger, qualified, and more talented personnel, it also robs the service of experienced staff.[11]

IV. The Manpower Planning Dilemma

Assessing the effects of manpower losses through migration is usually related to some perceived need for these occupations in the country. Reference is frequently made to the shortage of managerial skills, particularly within the public sector, and this constitutes a major bottleneck in project implementation as well as general administration. On this premise, lending agencies proceeded to build-in technical assistance components as prerequisites to granting loans, as exemplified by the structural adjustment loan from the World Bank in 1981. Shortages have also been identified in fields like medicine and

engineering, and successive governments have attempted
to attract and retain professionals in these areas
through a variety of means: overseas recruitment, tax
exemptions, inducement allowances, and the bonding of
students.

Although apparently adequate evidence shows that
Jamaica's development efforts are hampered by a lack of
skilled manpower, this shortage of manpower does not
exist in a vacuum but is both related to and created by
the limitations in the other factors of production.
Manpower shortages are not the failure of the training
system but coexist with manpower exports. Although
turnover and mobility are features of the Jamaican
labor market, the identification of manpower needs does
not necessarily imply that jobs for these persons with
scarce skills are available or adequate. On the
contrary, since the existence of a job implies that at
least some other factors of production are available
for execution of the task, it is questionable to view
the Jamaican economy as being stunted by manpower
shortages. This basic question must be addressed by
manpower planning; it is seldom raised under the
traditional approach that projects demand on the basis
of social need, taking as given that the other factors
of production will obligingly fall into place. This
constitutes the manpower planning fallacy in the
Caribbean, since manpower tends to be treated as if it
were a disembodied entity and effective demand is
assumed to exist. The contrary interpretation--that
the Jamaican economy is characterized by a low and
unstable level of job creation--is consistent with
other economic indicators and with the experience of
other countries pursuing the dependent development
path. It is supported by data on job vacancies and
work permit issuances reviewed here.

In the Manpower and Training Needs Survey of large
establishments conducted by the government in 1980,
information was collected on job vacancies.[12] Although
the information was not complete, the survey found
1,672 vacancies in both the private and public sectors
and reported that unoccupied managerial and
administrative posts accounted for 12 percent of these
vacancies (Table 5.4). The occupations next in
importance were health diagnosis and treatment (9.6
percent), stenography, typing, and filing (8.1
percent), and engineering (5.5 percent). The
managerial and administrative vacancies identified in
this survey number only about 200, equivalent to a
small fraction of the recorded outflow of 4,180
administrative and managerial workers to North America
between 1975 and 1979.

The relatively small numbers of job vacancies may
be explained by the fact that some of the empty slots

Table 5.4

Occupations With the Greatest Number of Vacancies

Occupation	Absolute No. of Vacancies	Percentage of All Vacancies
Health diagnosis & treatment	161	9.6
Stenography, typing, and filing	136	8.1
Managers and related (non-government)	101	6.0
Administrative, executive, and related (government)	101	6.0
Engineering	92	5.5
Mechanical repair (excludes electricity)	77	4.6
Accounting	67	4.0
Cashiers and tellers	57	3.4
Drivers of motor vehicles	57	3.4
Office supervision	52	3.1
Librarians and archivists	52	3.1
Architecture and technical assistance	49	2.9
Correspondence clerks	38	2.3
Subtotal	1,040	62.0
Total in survey	1,672	100.0

Source: Planning Institute of Jamaica, Report of the Manpower Planning, Training and Employment Project, 1982 (Kingston, unpublished).

that would have been created by out-migration were
filled by mobility within the occupational system,
including promotions, job changes, and new entrants.
In addition, some of the managerial posts and the
related support service jobs may have simply ceased to
exist once these managers and proprietors had
migrated. The comparison between departures and
vacancies cannot be pushed too far, however, in view of
the incomplete responses to this question in the
survey.

Further insights may be obtained from the
information on work permits issued during the 1970s,
since this period witnessed a conscious attempt by the
government to give priority to the employment of
Jamaican nationals. The objectives of the Foreign
Nationals and Commonwealth Citizens (Employment) Act
(1964) were: (a) to ensure that suitably qualified
Jamaicans are given the opportunity to aspire to and to
hold positions that are held by foreign nationals, and
(b) to ensure the importation of those skills needed by
the economy that are in short supply.

In implementing these objectives and reviewing
applications, the Work Permit Committee is not assisted
by any hard information on manpower demand in the
country but must base its judgment on qualitative
information about the state of the labor markets and
the strength of the case made by prospective
employers. However, the rate of refusals did increase
between 1970 and 1975, indicating that some selectivity
was occurring. In addition to the work permits issued
to the private sector, exemptions are granted to
foreign personnel who work with the government or the
University of the West Indies, or who are related by
marriage to Jamaican nationals. Ministers of religion
and short-term entertainment workers are also granted
exemptions. Although information on exemptions would
also be indicative of manpower shortages, particularly
within the public sector, this series unfortunately
only achieves reliability at the end of the decade in
response to the government's insistence between 1978
and 1979 that letters of exemption must be obtained for
immigration clearance and the approval of foreign
exchange transfers. They cannot therefore be used in
this assessment.

The series of figures on work permit approvals
illustrates graphically the decline in the reliance on
foreign expertise during the 1970s. Between 1970 and
1980, the number of new work permits issued fell
sharply from 3,551 to 700, although in recent years
evidence shows a steady increase (Table 5.5).

The sites of geographic origin of work permit
holders also shifted during the 1970s. At the
beginning of the period, major reliance was placed on

Table 5.5

New Work Permits Issued By Jamaica, 1970-1983

Year	New Work Permits Issued	Year	New Work Permits Issued
1970	3,551	1977	741
1971	3,244	1978	772
1972	2,278	1979	944
1973	2,011	1980	700
1974	1,712	1981	1,096
1975	1,728	1982	1,231
1976	1,078	1983	1,354

Source: Government of Jamaica, Ministry of Labor, Work Permit Division, Kingston, unpublished data.

the United States, the United Kingdom, and Canada; by 1983 these countries accounted for a much smaller proportion of the supply. As the country diversified its linkages, Asia, Europe, and the rest of the Caribbean provided a greater proportion of work permit inflow. This may be demonstrated by noting that in 1972, the United States, the United Kingdom, and Canada accounted for 82 percent of all new work permit holders; by 1983 this number had declined to 57 percent. Most of this decrease was explained by a declining reliance on the United Kingdom.

Although the number of work permits issued is commonly assumed to reflect manpower shortages within the country, an examination of the occupational composition of this inflow suggests that the more important explanatory factor may be the dependent linkages of the economy and the policy of management of foreign investment by foreign personnel. This is apparent not only in the large proportion of directors, managers, and working proprietors among the work permit inflow, but also in the fact that foreign expertise is concentrated at the top management levels in such sectors as bauxite and alumina, banking and insurance, and tourism. Since these workers are concerned with the management of foreign assets, their presence cannot be equated with manpower shortages; Jamaican manpower, even if available, would not be used at the highest levels of decision-making in foreign investment. Below this apex are accountants, auditors, and training officers who are often employed by the head company overseas to undertake site visits to the local subsidiary.

Besides this group of managers, administrators, and working proprietors whose inflow must be related primarily to the movement of capital, a large group of professional workers are employed in the development and maintenance of physical plant and infrastructure. These include engineers, surveyors, and architects, whose utilization is often temporary unless they are involved in management or supervision as occurs in the bauxite industry. The only other group of significance is that of teachers and lecturers at tertiary institutions. The assignment of many of these teachers to rural schools indicates the importance in reducing the regional imbalance.

The occupational composition of work permits is shown in Table 5.6 for selected years. The series shows that the proportion of directors, managers, and working proprietors declined during the 1970s from its share of 27.7 percent in 1970, but that this level was restored by 1983. Foreign architects, engineers, and surveyors contributed significant proportions over the period, and accountants and auditors represented a fairly stable proportion of between 7 and 10 percent since 1978. The only other group of significant size was that of teachers and lecturers.

Table 5.6

Occupations of Recipients of New and Extended Work Permits
(percentages)

	1970	1978	1980	1983
Directors, managers and working proprietors	27.7	14.9	17.5	27.1
Architects, engineers, and surveyors	30.3	10.4	8.2	11.0
Accountants and auditors	3.3	8.7	7.3	7.7
Teachers and lecturers	12.5	35.3	20.9	18.5
Physicians, surgeons, and dentists	1.0	2.4	1.7	2.4
Nurses	1.8	0.8	2.0	1.0
Other	23.4	27.6	42.5	32.4
Total Number	3,967	1,110	966	1,729

Source: Government of Jamaica, Ministry of Labour, Work Permit Division, Annual Reports.

134

To summarize the main impressions conveyed by the
data on vacancies and work permits, there does not seem
to be any extensive unutilized capacity. Put simply,
Jamaica's manpower problems do not appear to be that of
jobs looking for people. This interpretation does not
deny that the economic need exists for increased
production and that there is a critical social need for
additional teachers and medical personnel. However,
the other factors of production--physical facilities
and other capital needs--clearly are not lying idle in
the country, waiting for manpower to become
available. On the contrary, the migration outflow
would suggest that the absence of these other factors
of production leads to domestic underutilization of
manpower and ultimately to migration. The inflow of
managers, directors, accountants, and engineers is very
largely determined by the flow of capital, as their
role is primarily to manage, implement, or service
foreign investment. Without this capital inflow, the
management inflow ceases or is reversed.

Our dissatisfaction, therefore, with the
traditional cost-benefit approach to assessing manpower
losses results from its assumption that effective
demand exists: There is little reason to believe that
most manpower lost through out-migration would have
added to net employment rather than unemployment by the
calculation of potential unemployment rates. Unless
the 2,100 professional and managerial persons who
migrated to North America during 1977 had been self-
employed, their continued participation in the labor
force could have increased the unemployment rate for
this occupational group. This rate would have reached
a level of 11.2 percent instead of the recorded rate of
8.5 percent. Similarly, clerical and sales workers
would have reported an unemployment rate of 29.3
percent instead of 26.7 percent, and craftsmen and
operatives would have experienced 24.2 percent
unemployment instead of the actual level of 22.5
percent.

Although these hypothetical figures are dependent
on many other assumptions, they serve to dramatize the
fact that the employment structure of the country was
not capable of the high degree of expansion necessary
to absorb the available labor supply under the
conditions that existed during the 1970s. From this
perspective, migration presents no puzzle to be
explained.

V. Conclusion

The central argument of this chapter has been that
the dependent structure of the Jamaican economy, with
its heavy reliance on foreign capital, requires the

flow of capital, goods, and technology between Jamaica
and its metropolitan partners. The migration of labor
is at times part of this flow, setting in motion other
kinds of resource flows in the form of capital, goods
and services, technology, and ideas. The limitations
of the productive system result in an insufficient
effective demand for certain categories of manpower:
The country is unable to provide the complementary
factors of production for their effective utilization
or to supply adequate economic returns. The
traditional approach to manpower planning has therefore
been criticized on the grounds that it focuses largely
on social need without planning for effective demand.
In this situation, the inevitable outcome of the
manpower training system will be training for export.

The argument has also been advanced that in
assessing the impact of out-migration, a distinction
must be made between economic and political effects.
Even though the outflow of labor may have economic
costs, it nevertheless serves to reduce some of the
tensions and contradictions generated by the system.
Because different types of migration flows may have
opposing effects on the total political-economic
system, the management of that system and the
development of a migration policy becomes a trade-off
between conflicting goals.

In the development of migration policy, receiving
societies openly acknowledge that migrant labor is
simply the factor of production that must be brought
into balance with domestic investment capital and
manpower needs. The approach to this situation within
sending societies such as Jamaica is considerably more
obtuse. This is reflective both of the government's
implicit recognition that it is the passive partner in
the relationship and of its acknowledgment that it
cannot provide sufficient employment, even for all the
persons who have been trained at public expense.

From the perspective of this chapter, therefore,
the major policy recommendation that must be put
forward for countries like Jamaica, which adhere to the
dependent development path, is that migration must be
recognized as a major regulatory force within the
system of relationships and that its continuation must
be ensured. If a mutual commitment exists between
Jamaica and its major partners to maintain the present
system of political-economic relationships, this
commitment must also be translated into an agreement to
maintain migration at levels acceptable to both
countries. Within this agreement, and despite the
limitations this outflow must necessarily impose on the
attainment of economic and social transformation, the
country can work out certain ameliorative measures that

will produce the best trade-off in terms of the
deployment of resources.

Such a migration policy would therefore first
acknowledge the importance of migration and seek to
obtain a firm commitment, at least from the United
States to maintain present levels of migration.
Second, the program would be designed to increase the
outflow of lower-skill workers, if necessary through
the extension of contract work programs but under
conditions that would reduce the degree of worker
exploitation possible under present programs. Third,
such contract work programs could be diversified to
include white-collar workers and so to ensure a greater
return of resources to the country. Temporary-worker
schemes for professionals would allow this group to
accumulate savings or to upgrade their skills through
on-the-job exposure without incurring the greater
losses of permanent migration. Such a program would be
particularly attractive to midlevel professionals, such
as teachers and nurses, who may have strong family and
emotional ties to their homeland but who are totally
beleaguered by the cost of living.

Although these proposals are essentially limited
and conservative, they may be regarded as short-term
strategies to ease some of the social pressures created
by population growth and economic constraints. A
longer-term strategy, however, must address those
economic structures that generate excessive labor
market mobility and turnover, thus stimulating
migration. Without these changes, persisting economic
imbalances will continue to fuel the migration flow,
and Jamaicans will continue to "go a foreign."

Notes

Acknowledgements are made for the extensive assistance
and critical comments provided by Omar Davies,
University of the West Indies, in preparation of this
paper. The comments made by Richard Bernal, Patricia
Pessar, Nick Carter, Alejandro Portes and Robert Pastor
were particularly useful in the revision of the
paper. Thanks are also extended to Patricia Northover
and Peter Espeut for research assistance, and to the
Institute of Statistics and the Ministry of Labour for
access to data. Part of this analysis was conducted
under a post-doctoral fellowship from the Center for
Afro-American Studies, UCLA, while later work was
supported by a research grant from IDRC, Canada, to the
University of the West Indies.

1.   Dawn Marshall "Toward an Understanding of
Caribbean Migration," in U.S. Immigration and Refugee
Policy, edited by Mary Kritz (Lexington, Mass.:
Lexington Books, 1983; Elizabeth Thomas-Hope "Off the
Island: Population Mobility Among the Caribbean Middle
Class," in White Collar Migrants in the Americas and
the Caribbean, edited by Arnaud Marks and Vessuri
(Hebe, Netherlands: Department of Caribbean Studies,
Royal Institute of Linguistics and Anthropology, 1983).

2.   These estimates, which are derived on the
basis of census totals and vital statistics data by
means of the balancing equation, serve as a corrective
to the annual net migration figures which are obtained
by subtraction of departure and arrival immigration
cards. While the Institute of Statistics (of the
Government of Jamaica) suggests that there may be some
undercounting of deaths, it seems that the major source
of error lies in the annual migration estimates, and
that this undercount was more pronounced during the
first half of the seventies. The findings from the
1982 Census are now being used to adjust population
estimates downwards for the seventies.

3.   Planning Institute of Jamaica, 1981. Manpower
Information Bulletin (Kingston, 1981), and "Emigration
to North America from Jamaica, 1970-1980," Special
Report (Kingston, 1982).

4.   It should be acknowledged that the amount of
money remitted through the postal system is only part
of the value of total remittances. The transfer of
commodities has also become increasingly important
during the seventies as a result of the shortage and
high prices of particular consumer goods on the local
market. In addition, there are money remittances which

are transferred directly in the form of cash, and when
turned into the Central Bank, are recorded in the
national accounts under the category of private
unrequited transfers. However, it is not advisable to
use this category of transfers as the basis of
assessments on remittances as they include a very large
and increasing proportion of foreign exchange which is
obtained directly as a result of the trade in ganja.

5.   Ransford Palmer,"Emigration and the Economic
Decline of Jamaica," in White Collar Migrants in the
Americas and the Caribbean, edited by Marks, Arnaud,
and Vessuri (Hebe, Netherlands: Department of
Caribbean Studies, Royal Institute of Linguistics and
Anthropology, 1983).

6.   Portes suggests that the threat to the
consumption levels of the middle classes is one of the
most significant factors propelling migration,
particularly in Latin America. (Commentary at
Conference on Migration and Development in the
Caribbean, Wye Plantation, Sept. 14-16, 1984).

7.   A similar observation has been made by
Charles Stahl who notes that the maximization of
individual private objectives is not necessarily
consistent with the maximization of the broader
objectives of society. He points out that the
divergence created by labor migration between private
and social costs and benefits raises a fundamental
socio-political question: To what extent should a
society impose constraints on the individual to ensure
that the outcome of his decisions is consistent with
broader social objectives? (Charles W. Stahl, "Labour
Emigration and Economic Development," International
Migration Review, 16, No. 4, 1982: 869-899.)

8.   Government of Jamaica, National Planning
Agency, Economic and Social Survey, 1978 (Kingston,
1979).

9.   Estimates of occupational supply at the
beginning and end of the period are available from the
series of labor force surveys conducted in April and
October of each year by the Statistical Institute of
Jamaica. The April survey is used as the basis of this
exercise. Although the labor force surveys which are
used in this analysis have not yet been adjusted
downwards on the basis of the 1982 Census findings, it
is nonetheless possible to work with the series since
the methodology utilizes the net change in the labor
force size, and the analysis is limited to the period,
1976-80, during which net migration estimates seem most

reliable. Adopting this precaution, it should be possible to rule out fluctuations in labor force size which are the result of faulty population estimates arising from errors in the annual net migration figures.

10. G.E. Mills and Paul Robertson, "The Attitude and Behavior of the Senior Civil Service in Jamaica," Social and Economic Studies, Vol. 23, No. 2, 1974.

11. Phyllis Green, Derek Gordon, and Edwin Jones, "Employee Morale in the Civil Service," Administrative Staff College, Ministry of the Public Service (Kingston, 1983).

12. The Manpower and Training Needs Survey was part of a larger project, the Manpower Planning, Training and Employment Project, funded jointly by the Government of Jamaica and the United States Agency for International Development. The project was designed to establish an adequate basis for manpower planning and was coordinated by the National Planning Agency (now the Planning Institute of Jamaica).

6. Migration and Development in Hispaniola

Ernest H. Preeg

I. Introduction

The island of Hispaniola is divided between the sovereign states of Haiti and the Dominican Republic, each containing between five and six million people. Beyond this similarity in size of population, however, comparisons of the two countries usually stress the sharp contrasts that are fundamental to each national identity. Haiti occupies the western one-third of the island, mostly mountainous with limited arable land, and the Dominican Republic occupies the more fertile two-thirds in the east. Haiti's population is overwhelmingly black, with deep African roots and a unique cultural, linguistic, and religious heritage; the Dominican Republic's culture follows the Old World/criollo patterns of former Spanish colonies. Haiti is the poorest country in the hemisphere with up to 80 percent of the population below the poverty line, whereas the Dominican Republic is considerably more advanced, with a per capita gross national product (GNP) three times that of its neighbor. Haiti has an autocratic government under a president-for-life; the Dominican Republic, on the other hand, boasts a functioning democracy of growing strength and self-confidence.

Superimposed on this setting of sharp contrasts is a history of internal and external migration that has a profound impact on the development of both countries and that has, moreover, certain similarities that are less frequently noted than the differences. Since 1960, both countries have built up "diasporas" on the order of 300,000 to 500,000 emigrants in the United States, which have resulted in large dollar remittances and greatly expanded personal contact and communication between Hispaniola and the large neighbor to the north. Both countries are also experiencing the internal rural/urban migration common to many

developing countries, with urban populations growing 5
to 6 percent per year compared to 1 percent or less
growth in the countryside. The Dominican Republic is
more advanced in this process of internal migration,
with over half the population now urban, but Haitian
rural population has dropped from over 90 percent to
almost 70 percent in the past quarter century, and this
trend shows no signs of abating. A final similarity of
significance for future development on the island is
that the opportunities for external migration, the
"safety valve" for population growth, are being reduced
as a result of U.S. immigration policy and other
factors, especially in the case of Haiti.

The principal nexus between the two countries also
relates to migration. During the almost two centuries
since Haitian independence in 1801 relations between
the two nations that share this relatively small island
have been difficult and at times bloody. Two early
occupations of the Dominican portion by Haiti and later
invasion threats have made Dominicans wary of their
neighbor to the west. The brutal slaughter of an
estimated 15,000 to 20,000 Haitian migrants in 1937 by
Rafael Trujillo's armed forces is an enduring stigma
for the proud Haitian nation. In recent years, the
30,000 or so Haitians who come to cut sugarcane in the
Dominican Republic on a seasonal basis have been the
subject of harsh criticism by human rights groups
abroad, including the Anti-Slavery League in London.
And always lurking in the background is the specter of
the gradual encroachment of Haitians spilling over the
border into the Dominican Republic as population growth
and poverty at home become more intense. The shutting
off of outward migration and the dynamics of the
rural/urban flow within Haiti appear to be increasing
such pressures.

This chapter examines some of these issues in more
detail. Relatively greater attention is given to
conditions within Haiti since the more acute issues of
migration and development policies stem from
circumstances there. Sections II and III deal with the
long history of Haitian external migration and the more
recent experience of internal Haitian migration.
Section IV examines the impact of migration on
Dominican development, both external and internal, with
respect to Haitian workers. The final section (V)
discusses a possible strategy for Haitian development
to cope with growing migration pressures.

II.   External Haitian Migration

The practice of migration by sea is deeply
embedded in Haitian history and mentality. Importation
of African slaves into the burgeoning French colony of

Saint Dominique occurred largely in the fifty-year
period prior to independence. It is estimated that
two-thirds of the slaves on the island when revolution
broke out in 1789 had been born in Africa. The
terrible sea voyage was fresh in the minds of the
leaders of the new republic, and memories of Africa
evolved into a rich folklore and religious practice.

During and after the long, bloody war for
independence (1789-1801) one enduring form of outward
migration took shape, namely the fleeing into exile of
political activists on the losing side of internal
struggles. Political instability and insurrection were
frequent during the first century of independence, and
many talented and influential Haitians were forced to
take up residence in Europe, the United States, or
neighboring Caribbean islands, awaiting the opportunity
to return home when political circumstances turned
favorable. This form of out-migration had two
principal effects. First, it deprived the country of
sorely needed professional and administrative talent,
especially since Haiti had severed its colonial ties
very early and thus did not develop the cadres of
trained administrators that evolved in other colonial
relationships. And second, the political exiles
usually became particularly severe critics of the
regime back home, publicizing their own cause and
writing many of the best known tracts and books that
make up Haitian literature. In other words, attitudes
about Haiti abroad were greatly influenced by resident
Haitian exiles who were less than objective in their
political views.

This outward migration of the educated elite
reached its most dramatic proportions during the recent
presidency of Francois Duvalier (1957-1971), when tens
of thousands of middle- and upper-class Haitians fled
the violence and disruption of the Duvalier black
populist revolution. The loss of professional and
managerial talent was a major cause of the economic
decline in Haiti during the 1960s, and exile groups
from New York and Chicago to Montreal and Paris remain
today a forceful political voice of unremitting attack
against the government of Jean Claude Duvalier, the
son.

A second form of out-migration from Haiti is that
of poor, illiterate, creole-speaking Haitians seeking a
better life abroad and willing to perform the most
arduous work in countries that receive them. This form
of migration became prominent in the second and third
decades of the twentieth century when large numbers of
Haitians went to Cuba and the Dominican Republic to cut
sugarcane. Another surge occurred in the 1960s to the
Bahamas and other Caribbean islands: Economic
conditions worsened in Haiti, whereas elsewhere in the

region tourism and other new industries were growing, requiring more low-wage, unskilled labor. By the mid-1970s, these traditional outlets for poor Haitian migrants had become saturated. Considerable political pressure was exerted in countries like the Bahamas and the Dominican Republic to reduce the Haitian presence, whereas in Haiti the "push" factors of growing population, declining arable land because of soil erosion, and unemployment continued to increase.

These circumstances led to the "boat people" phenomenon in which many thousands of Haitians undertook the dangerous voyage from Haiti to southern Florida, often via Cuba or the Bahamas, to search for a better economic life. Initially they came in crowded sailboats, and no record exists of how many perished en route. Toward the end of the decade, organized traffickers, using small steamers with hidden compartments, developed a lucrative trade, by charging $500 to $2,000 per head for the clandestine voyage. By mid-1981, as many as 1,500 Haitian boat people per month were landing on the beaches of southern Florida.

The arrival of illegal Haitian migrants by boat created a legal issue in the United States that has still not been fully resolved. The Justice Department under both the Carter and Reagan administrations has contended that almost all boat people are seeking a better economic life, not fleeing political persecution, and are thus excludable and should be sent back to Haiti. Lawyers for the Haitian migrants, in contrast, claim that the boat people are political refugees, and they have challenged the fairness of the judicial process. In the face of prolonged litigation and inconclusive court decisions, most Haitians, once in the United States, have been able to stay indefinitely, although many have spent long periods in federal detention centers.

Political sentiment in the United States in 1981 was split over how to treat Haitians already in the country--whether to let them stay or to send them back to Haiti--but was in broad agreement that the illegal trafficking in boat people had to be stopped. In spring 1981 Congress took the initiative through an amendment to the foreign assistance legislation sponsored by Congressman Dan Mica (D-Fla.) and strongly supported by the Florida delegation and the congressional Black Caucus. The Mica amendment made all aid to Haiti conditional on the full cooperation of the Haitian government to stop illegal migration and supported increased aid to Haiti if this and other conditions were met. The Reagan administration, in line with its policy of cracking down on illegal migration, concluded the bilateral so-called "interdiction agreement" with the government of Haiti

in September 1981. The agreement permitted the U.S.
Coast Guard to patrol in international waters off the
coast of Haiti, board Haitian flag vessels, and return
to Haiti those persons intending to migrate illegally
for economic reasons. The interdiction program in the
strategically located Windward Passage was immediately
successful in causing the organized traffickers to
cease operations. A few open sailboats still try
occasionally to get through, but as of early 1984, only
one is confirmed to have arrived successfully in
Florida. The number of Haitians known to have arrived
illegally in the southeastern United States dropped
dramatically from 15,094 in 1980 to 134 in 1982 and 350
in 1983.

The current situation is thus one of abrupt
decline in the pattern of substantial out-migration
from Haiti that had been going on for decades. For the
period 1950-1980, population growth within Haiti was
reduced through migration from 2.0 percent to 1.5-1.75
percent per year.[1] Currently, with migration curtailed
to the United States, the Bahamas, the Dominican
Republic, and elsewhere, the effect on population
growth may be on the order of 0.1 to 0.2 percent.[2]

III. Internal Haitian Migration

The origins of large-scale rural/urban migration
within Haiti are more recent, dating essentially from
the late 1950s to early 1960s. They include both push
and pull factors, familiar to many developing
countries, but they have taken on special force in
Haiti. Largely as a result of the war for
independence, Haiti became a country of small farmers,
with land generally subdivided between sons from
generation to generation. Arable land was always
limited and in this century has been steadily declining
in absolute terms as a result of soil erosion. Peasant
farmers have cut down the trees on hillsides either to
sell them as firewood, the main fuel for cooking, or to
clear land for corn and other food crops. Without
trees, the topsoil cover washes away within a few rainy
seasons, leaving large bald areas of countryside
visible from airplanes. As a result of this pattern of
erosion and population growth, the ratio of population
per hectare of arable land has increased substantially,
giving Haiti one of the highest population/arable land
ratios in the world. Together with general neglect by
the government, the Haitian agricultural sector is
today characterized by low productivity and widespread
underdevelopment, resulting in pervasive poverty and
malnutrition. Urban areas do not have to offer very
large economic improvements to tempt the rural peasant
to migrate.

The pull factors of rural/urban migration into the Port-au-Prince area took on momentum in the late 1950s to early 1960s with the development of light industry, including the manufacture of such products for export as textiles and baseballs. The traditional elite business community was the target of much violence and extortion in the early Francois Duvalier years, and many left the country. Many others stayed, however, and made their peace with the regime, and in the later years Duvalier became more favorably disposed to encourage new investment, indigenous and foreign, and business prospered. In fact, despite the extremely low level of overall development, conditions for labor-intensive industry in Haiti are favorable: low costs, hardworking labor force, relatively sophisticated and self-confident business community drawn largely from the mulatto elite and substantial Arabic-origin community, and a government that generally encourages private-sector development.

The major impulse for industrial development has come during the presidency of Jean Claude Duvalier (1971-present). After fourteen years of political strife and economic neglect, Jean Claude adopted an initial development strategy centered on building the nation's economic infrastructure so as to encourage industry, create jobs, and earn export revenues. He appealed for external assistance and received a favorable response: Total foreign assistance increased from $9 million in 1970 to $106 million in 1979, of which the U.S. share went from $2 million to $25 million. During the 1970s, a paved highway system was constructed between major cities and a secondary road system to open up agricultural communities was begun. Modern container port and air cargo facilities were built in Port-au-Prince. Electric power and telephone service were expanded more or less apace with industrial growth. Two industrial parks were constructed in Port-au-Prince, and a third is planned.

The results of the infrastructure program are striking. More than 200 companies are now engaged in a wide range of production, mainly for export, including textiles, shoes, electronics, automotive components, toys, and sporting goods. Export earnings from light assembly industry have increased from $2 million in 1972 to $55 million in 1982, and only leveled off but not declined during the recent recession. Some 60,000 workers are now employed in this industry, and taking account of an estimated four dependents supported by each factory worker's salary, nearly one-third of the Port-au-Prince population is directly dependent on manufacturing industry, and many more indirectly through service industry and construction.

Thus far almost all industry is located in Port-

au-Prince, whose population has grown to almost a
million people. The second largest city, Cape Haitien,
is less than one-tenth the size of the capitol. Over
the last few years, however, the infrastructure
program--port facilities, electricity, communications--
has been extended to provincial cities, and several
could well develop into additional centers of light
industry during the late 1980s.

These developments are rapidly transforming Haiti
and creating predictable social and economic problems
in urban areas. Congestion in Port-au-Prince is
intense. Overwhelming needs exist for housing, potable
water, and waste disposal. Infant mortality is higher
in the Port-au-Prince slums than in rural villages.
Part of the solution is to try to redirect some of the
migration to the provincial cities. More fundamental
is the need to improve the economic conditions in the
countryside to moderate the incentive to migrate to
urban areas. During the past several years, a growing
share of foreign assistance and the government budget
have been devoted to rural development, but the
challenge is staggering. Thousands of peasant
villages, most of which are located in difficult
terrain with poor access, need schools, health
facilities, technical assistance, and agricultural
credit. In most areas the absence of clearly
established title to land greatly inhibits investment
or improved land utilization. The necessary first step
for rural development is to build access roads, a
process underway. Unless vehicle access is available
to the principal towns, the other components of rural
development cannot be advanced. However, the opening
of roads can initially have an adverse effect of
accelerating rural/urban migration. Heretofore,
peasants spent their entire lives in isolated native
village; now, with road access and greater personal
contact with city dwellers, migration is more tempting
and certainly more feasible. Often the more ambitious
and able take up the challenge of a new life in the
cities to the detriment of the villages they leave
behind.

The process of Haitian external and internal
migration has important interrelationships. The boat
people period of 1980-81 in particular had a
significant and probably lasting impact on rural
attitudes about mobility and change. In most peasant
families today, at least one neighbor or relative has
left for the United States, and stories about the
voyage and the new life abroad have taken on their own
legendary form. Although statistics are sketchy, it
appears that most boat people were not from the poorest
stratum of society, but were rather those with some
skills and work experience, and migration abroad was

often preceded by migration to cities within Haiti. In
fact, a prevalent concern of Haitian businessmen during
1981 was that some of their best workers and most
skilled people would leave any day for Florida. In
fact, the public mentality in Haiti in that period was
focusing more and more on how and when to make the trip
north rather than on how to cope best with the limited
prospects for life within Haiti. This attitude has
been dampened considerably by the U.S. Coast Guard
interdiction program, but has not entirely
disappeared. The continuing rural/urban migration and
longer term hope of joining friends and relatives in
the United States are weakening the traditional
stability and static circumstances of Haitian peasant
life. A gradual economic and political wakening of the
mass of poor Haitians has important implications for
the future of the country that are not yet well
perceived.

One beneficial aspect of the interaction between
external and internal Haitian migration is a
significant reflow of trained and professional Haitians
back from the United States, particularly to the
rapidly growing industrial sector. Most light industry
is Haitian owned, and many businessmen have not only
been trained in the United States, but have learned
marketing and developed business contacts there as
well. Several daily flights between Port-au-Prince and
Miami and New York are usually fully booked in both
directions; the large majority of passengers are
Haitians, many engaged in business and commerce. A
common occurrence is for younger generation Haitians in
family-owned firms to return from residence in the
United States and to assume management responsibilities
in a flourishing manufacturing business or even to
start a new operation. General Telephone and
Electronics (GTE) one of the few large U.S. companies
with a wholly owned subsidiary in Haiti, started in
1977, has grown to employ over 1,000 workers and has
full quality control for its various assembly
operations. Almost all professional and technical
personnel are Haitians, in large part recruited in New
York and other U.S. cities.

An important factor regarding Haitian migration is
the deeper cultural and historic roots of Haitians
compared with most other Caribbean migrant groups.
Haitians abroad invariably long for the feel and smell
of the Haitian countryside, the sound of the creole
language, the music, the intense personal contact and
banter that make up national life. In some cases
economic and political circumstances at home may
prevent return, but given reasonable opportunity and
hope, the homeward pull of the oldest black republic
runs very deep. For the large majority of Haitians

abroad, such opportunity and hope would require long-term, successful economic development within Haiti, but for some key segments of the diaspora, such as businessmen and professionals, the prospects for homeward pull are more immediate.

IV. Migration and Development in the Dominican Republic

The two major issues of migration that influence development in the Dominican Republic are the substantial emigration of Dominicans to the United States, which began in the 1960s, and the longstanding question of Haitian workers in the Dominican Republic. According to the 1980 U.S. census, the number of Dominicans who took up residence in the United States rose dramatically from 7,000 persons during the 1950s to 63,000 during the 1960s and to 96,000 during the 1970s. Estimates of the total number of Dominicans currently residing in the United States generally range from 300,000 to 500,000, or roughly 6 to 10 percent of the population.[3] Recent studies indicate some general characteristics of this wave of migration, although authors do not fully agree on all points. Most migrants leave urban rather than rural habitats, but many of these urban dwellers have rural origins, indicating a two-stage pattern of rural/urban and later external migration. The migrants tend to be either middle-class or at least experienced workers motivated to improve their economic circumstances. The main reasons for migration are economic; one study sample indicated that the principal motivations are higher income (30 percent), unemployment at home (30 percent), education (18 percent), and joining relatives (14 percent).[4] A fairly large proportion of migrants (39 percent in the same study) return to the Dominican Republic, of which 25 percent indicate completion of studies as the reason for return. The poorer migrants are the least likely to return.

The impact of this wave of migration on Dominican development has both positive and negative aspects. Remittances, estimated at 10 percent of foreign exchange earnings, are an important plus for the balance of payments and dependent families at home. Dominicans that return with better education or savings to invest in a home or business also make a net contribution. The impact on unemployment is less clear. If, in fact, the majority of migrants are high-achieving middle-class or upwardly mobile working-class members of the community, their departure could have a negative effect on the dynamics of new investment and job creation in the Dominican Republic. A negative social aspect is the separation of families when the breadwinner goes abroad.

On balance, the general view appears to be that the large Dominican migration to the United States since the 1960s has had a positive effect on Dominican development. In any event the Dominican government has not taken significant measures to impede such migration. The constraining factor is U.S. immigration policy, which has been tightened for illegal migration over the past few years. This constraint should put greater emphasis for future migration on people qualifying for immigrant visas--principally those with family ties as delineated in the preference categories and students.

The situation with respect to Haitian migration into the Dominican Republic is less well defined. The total number of Haitians in the Dominican Republic is generally estimated to be between 200,000 and 400,000, substantially greater than estimates for earlier years.[5] The most prominent role of Haitians in the Dominican economy is in cutting sugarcane. Ninety percent or more of the roughly 50,000 cane cutters are Haitian, of which some 30,000 are seasonal workers. The exploitation of these Haitians has received wide publicity, and some steps have been taken by the two governments to improve the situation. The future course of sugar production in the Dominican Republic is uncertain. The low and declining real wage rate of Haitian cutters over the years has discouraged capital investment. As a result, worker productivity is very low: only one to one and a half tons of sugarcane cut per worker per day compared with five to seven tons in such countries as Jamaica, Mexico, and Peru. Although considerable talk is going around about mechanizing the cane cutting process and thus excluding Haitian cutters, it is not clear whether the machinery involved would be cost competitive with Haitian workers and could be adapted to much of the terrain under cultivation. Meanwhile, Haitian workers perform an essential function for the principal Dominican export industry.

What is even less clear is the prospect for Haitians other than cane cutters in the Dominican Republic; these make up the large majority of resident Haitians. They do various forms of work, usually less desirable tasks at lower wages than those acceptable to Dominicans. One study describing the recent influx of Haitians into the Dominican coffee industry stated that they numbered 29 percent of the salaried work force during the 1980 harvest.[6]

Concern in the Dominican Republic, often played up emotionally in the press, is widespread that the surplus population in Haiti may encroach upon, if not innundate, the country. At the same time, vested

economic interests have become dependent on low-cost,
hard-working Haitians who would be difficult to replace
with native Dominicans. The situation at this point is
relatively stable and calm, with recognition of the
contribution Haitian workers make to the Dominican
economy. But the nightmare for many Dominicans is a
situation of political turmoil and economic collapse in
Haiti, in which large numbers of Haitians pour across
the unsecurable border seeking refuge and a new life in
the Dominican Republic.

V. A Development-Migration Strategy for Haiti

The key to resolving the interrelated issues of
migration and development in Hispaniola is a balanced
program of economic, social, and political development
in Haiti. The current situation of containing Haitian
migration pressures through U.S. Coast Guard
surveillance at sea and Dominican border patrols by
land provides a practical solution for curtailing
illegal Haitian migration in the short run. However,
it could serve merely to bottle up growing problems of
poverty and unemployment in Haiti, leading to even
greater, perhaps uncontainable pressures for out-
migration at some future point, unless coupled with a
forceful program to improve conditions within the
country.
        A successful development strategy for Haiti will
require firm and substantial commitments by the
government of Haiti and the international community.
The recent record of the Duvalier government in
promoting national development has been disappointing
in a number of respects, but it is not as bad or
hopeless as often portrayed by critics abroad. The
infrastructure program of the 1970s and the resulting
growth of labor-intensive industry have already been
noted. Since 1981, a cooperative framework between the
government of Haiti and the international community has
been established, consisting of three related
components.
        1. IMF financial stabilization program. After
lengthy consultations with the International Monetary
Fund, Haiti implemented a financial austerity program
in May 1982 and remained in general compliance with the
program during the subsequent two years. By mid-1984,
the government borrowing requirement was down to 1
percent of GNP, inflation was 10 percent or less, and
the national currency was within a few percent of
convertibility.
        2. World Bank-supported medium-term development
strategy. In June 1982, Haiti became a full
participant in the World Bank-chaired Caribbean
Consultative Group, a mechanism to coordinate foreign

assistance through an agreed medium-term strategy.
Consultations within this framework have pointed up the
enormous development needs within Haiti and have also
helped the World Bank expand its program in Haiti.

3. U.S. bilateral support within the Caribbean
Basin Initiative. U.S. economic assistance to Haiti
has increased from $31 million in fiscal year 1980 to
$45 million in fiscal year 1984, while in the process
becoming more explicitly contingent on change within
Haiti and on economic performance by the government of
Haiti in particular. The Mica amendment, in addition
to stipulating cooperation to stop illegal migration,
made increased economic assistance conditional on
improved aid project implementation and a satisfactory
record on human rights. A revised amendment in 1983,
this time sponsored by Congressman Robert Garcia of New
York, went a step further and linked bilateral aid to
political reform within Haiti, including progress
toward the formation of political parties, free
elections, and a free press. This expanded and more
intense aid relationship has taken place within the
context of the Caribbean Basin Initiative, wherein the
one-way free-trade arrangement and investment
incentives can be especially supportive to the Haitian
private sector.

This improved framework for support of Haitian
development does not mean the task will be easy. On
the contrary, the challenge of creating productive
employment, better living conditions, and a more just
society for the large majority of poverty-striken
Haitians is formidable, certainly the most demanding in
the Caribbean region. Such an undertaking would have
two central economic objectives, assuming the political
will and resources are available.

The first would be to redirect the rural/urban
migration toward the provincial cities. The incentives
for more balanced urban growth are partly in place but
so far have not succeeded in attracting light
industries to cities other than Port-au-Prince.
Further development of infrastructure is part of the
solution. Tax credits for investment are more generous
in the provinces, but these may not be enough to
overcome the resistance of businessmen to locating
outside the capital. Differentials in electricity and
minimum wage levels, on the grounds that the cost of
living is lower in provincial cities, have been
discussed but have not attracted much support.

The second objective would be to increase
productivity in the agricultural sector. The flow of
migrants from the rural areas is inevitable; the only
issues for public policy are whether it will be a
moderate flow or a flood and whether agriculture will
be left more or less productive. This is the greatest

challenge for Haitian development and essential to
moderating the rapid rural/urban migration. Yields for
most crops are very low compared to cultivation in
neighboring countries, but improvement will require not
only financial resources but technical competence in
the countryside, which is not readily available. The
road system is well advanced. A network of rural
health clinics, including facilities for malaria
control and family planning, is underway. Progress in
reforestation has been made over the past few years,
especially through a USAID-sponsored project utilizing
several nongovernmental organizations. Gaps, are still
present, however, particularly with respect to
providing peasant farmers with technical services and
credit. Moreover, large segments of the rural
population remain outside the scope of all support
programs. In 1985, the United States signed a new
agreement with the government of Haiti, under P.L. 480
Title III, that would enable an integrated approach to
development in two or more targeted watershed
subregions. If such a concentrated effort were to
produce solid results over the next few years, it could
serve as a model for expanded efforts elsewhere as
resources become available.

Such a development strategy within Haiti could
benefit from complementary actions in migration
policies abroad, although the prospects for such action
are probably quite limited compared with the
development challenge within Haiti. Special incentives
for highly skilled or professional expatriate Haitians
to return and work for national development could help
increase the reflow, particularly to the private
sector. Participation by Haitians in seasonal worker
programs in the United States could provide work and
income for needy Haitian families. However, such an
arrangement has not been effected for two principal
reasons. The first is the lack of clear court
decisions on the political status of Haitians entering
the United States; as long as a claim for political
refugee status by almost any Haitian can result in an
indefinite stay, it is unlikely that poor, seasonal
workers from Haiti would be allowed in. And the second
is that decisions on who is chosen for seasonal work
under the existing H-2 program are made by private-
sector employers, who have not been interested in
creole-speaking Haitians. An expanded seasonal worker
program, as envisaged by the Simpson-Mazzoli bill,
could require guidelines on the national origin of
seasonal workers, and a case could be made that it is
in the U.S. interest to include a modest number of
Haitian workers in such a program.

A higher level of permanent legal migration of
Haitians to the United States would also help alleviate

unemployment in Haiti and increase remittances, but if anything the relatively low level of immigrant visas issued to Haitians in recent years of 6,000 to 7,000 per year is declining. Almost all such visas are issued on the basis of preference categories, based on family ties, subject to a global quota. There is a growing backlog of qualified applicants in some preference categories, particularly the one for people with brothers or sisters already in the United States. In fact, fewer Haitians are able to establish such family relationships than Jamaicans or Dominicans, for example.[7] Adoption of legislation legalizing the status of Haitians already in the United States before a given date could help in establishing family relationships and might lead to some increase in legal Haitian migration. A radical change in U.S. immigration policy, away from global quotas based on preference categories and toward country quotas, could result in a higher level for Haitians, but such a change in U.S. immigration policy is extremely unlikely.

One area of migration policy that has not produced significant results has been to seek other developing countries willing to receive Haitians for permanent residence. A recent proposal for such a program in Belize has not moved forward, in large part because it would be very costly for relocating a relatively small number of Haitians.

With respect to the Dominican Republic, the tendency has been to further restrict rather than to encourage Haitian migration. In fact, relatively little trade and investment exist between the two countries that share the island of Hispaniola, although considerable Dominican contraband has entered the Haitian market over the past few years as a result of a relatively strong gourde and the difficulties of policing the border. The historic wariness between the two neighbors and the threat of large-scale eastward migration of Haitians have tended to discourage economic integration on the island, and road connections are extremely difficult, probably by design. The gains from orienting exports toward the United States market are another factor inhibiting intraisland trade.

In conclusion, problems of migration and development are closely linked in the island of Hispaniola, particularly in the more acute current circumstances in Haiti. This chapter does not try to assess the viability or costs of a successful development program in Haiti over coming years, which in any event would have to take account of the pace of social and political change as well as economic progress. The experience since 1981 and new economic incentives provided by the Caribbean Basin Initiative give some grounds for hope, under certain conditions, but many observers remain deeply pessimistic about the outcome.[8] Major pressures are building up within Haiti, in which migration and development closely interact, and for which a constructive and sustained response is important not only to Haitians and the government of Haiti, but to other nations in the region as well, particularly the Dominican Republic and the United States.

Notes

    1. Aaron Segal, "Demographic Factors in Haitian Development," in Charles Foster and Albert Valdman (Editors), Haiti: Interdisciplinary Perspectives (University Press of America, 1984).

    2. This is a crude estimate. In the early 1980s, about 6-7,000 Haitians per year were receiving immigrant visas to the United States each year, although many were already resident. Illegal migration has been reduced but undoubtedly still occurs, particularly through overstaying a tourist visa. The Bahamas repatriated some Haitians in 1983. The 0.1-0.2 figure translates into about 5,500-11,000 Haitians per year.

    3. The figures in this section, unless otherwise specified, come from Antonio Ugalde, et.al., "International Migration from the Dominican Republic: Findings from a National Survey," International Migration Review, Vol. 13 (1979); Sherri Grasmuck, "Migration within the Periphery: Haitian Labor in the Dominican Sugar and Coffee Industries," International Migration Review, Vol. 16 (1982); and Thomas K. Morrison and Richard Sinkin, "International Migration in the Dominican Republic: Implications for Developing Countries," International Migration Review, Vol. 16 (1982).

    4. Ugalde et.al., "Migration from the Dominican Republic" Supra. fn. #3.

    5. A consistently based comparison is not available. Grasmuck, "Migration Within the Periphery," Supra. fn. #3, presents figures from the Dominican census of 19,000 Haitians in 1950 and 24,000 in 1960; a figure from the Dominican migration department for 1970 shows 87,000 Haitians, of which 42,000 registered and 45,000 undocumented.

    6. Grasmuck, Ibid.

    7. In 1983, the American consulate in Port-au-Prince undertook a detailed investigation of factors within Haiti that might impede the issuance of immigrant visas, including the availability of birth certificates and other documents, the cost of processing, and the illiterate creole speaking status of many potential applicants. No significant impediments were found, which confirmed the view that the problem was principally in establishing clear

family relationships with residents in the United States.

    8. For an elaboration of the author's views, see Haiti and the CBI: A Time of Change and Opportunity (North/South Center, The University of Miami, February 1985).

Part 3

The Impact of Different Types of Migration on Development

7. Return Migration and Its Implications for Caribbean Development

Elizabeth M. Thomas-Hope

Some Caribbean migrants remain for a lifetime overseas and never return; most return periodically or regularly or to stay. Caribbean migrants return to their homelands for a number of reasons; in some cases for little other than changes in their domestic circumstances; in other cases because they perceive that their migration goals have been accomplished. In returning, their original intention is realized and the migration circuit completed.[1]

Many migrants are obliged to return because of their immigration status and their terms of contract in the host country. Others never see their sojourn or frequent visits abroad as anything other than part of their work pattern. For example, vendors move between islands and to the United States to sell and purchase goods; laborers cut cane in neighboring islands as well as in the United States; business people travel to other Caribbean and mainland countries in the normal performance of their affairs; students from middle-class families (given the financial resources) naturally go to North America to study, selecting colleges and universities as though they were not separated by national boundaries. Working-class men and women leave their families to seek work overseas in order to supplement the family income at home, and invariably they remain permanent circulators. What, then, is return migration in the Caribbean case?

For the implications of the return migration phenomenon to be fully assessed, the term must be used in its widest sense--to refer to all the "homeward" flows associated with the circular nature of population mobility. Far from being a simple component of the migration process, return migration is a compound and complex one: It includes not a single flow but a series of returns, sometimes over a long period of time. Furthermore, it involves not only numbers, but people, with specific orientations, views, skills,

ideas, and the ability to readjust, who must fit back
into the existing structural framework of the
Caribbean. To varying degrees, these people accept the
status quo or become agents of change.

The absence of comprehensive data on return
migration is not surprising given the great complexity
of the movement. Empirical studies have tended to be
limited in scope, referring in each case to just one
small sample that invariably omits many of the relevant
types of return. With the exception of farm contract
workers who are recruited by the Ministry of Labor in
the respective islands, virtually no official data
exist on the return movements of nationals. This lack
partly reflects the logistical difficulties of
monitoring the return and partly the relative
disinterest in the movement at the official level.

I. Historical Background

All major international migrations of Caribbean
people have been characterized by significant
counterflows. The phenomenon of the return is
therefore not new. The first free movements of
Caribbean people took place from one part of the region
to another, especially within the Eastern Caribbean.
Other spontaneous movements occurred to the Caribbean
coast of Central America as early as the 1840s and
1850s when labor was sought for railway construction
and later for fruit plantations and the building of the
Panama Canal. Migrants typically shifted from one
destination to another, returning in some cases to
their countries of origin and then perhaps remigrating
to the same or a new destination.[2]

By the beginning of the twentieth century,
numerous new interregional flows of Caribbean people
were taking place. Large numbers of migrants from the
Eastern Caribbean were going to the oil refineries of
Curacao, Aruba, and Venezuela, whereas others were
going to Trinidad. The sugar plantations of the
Dominican Republic and Cuba were attracting English-
speaking West Indians to provide laborers well
experienced in sugar production. Without exception,
these outward flows of people from their home
territories were associated with significant return
flows. For example, in the year 1886-1887, 7,100
Jamaicans are reported to have returned home from
Panama whereas 10,400 left for Panama in the same
year.[3] The trend continued throughout the migration
period of the early twentieth century. From 1907 to
1915 never fewer than 3,500 persons were returning in
any one year, and in most years the figure was between
6,000 and 8,000 persons.[4] The numbers of migrants
returning to Jamaica from Cuba were even more dramatic

in certain years. For example, in 1920, 22,659 persons
were reported to have returned home, and in 1921,
13,317. There were very few years during the peak of
the migration to Cuba from 1907 to 1933 when the number
of returnees was below 1,000.[5]
     Caribbean interregional migrations continued
throughout the twentieth century, and, especially after
World War II, additional movements to Europe and North
America occurred outside the region. Colonial subjects
went in large numbers to their metropolises: the
British West Indians to Great Britain, the Dutch West
Indians to the Netherlands, the French West Indians to
France, and the Hispanic Caribbean islanders, by then
directly within the U.S. sphere of influence, to the
United States, along with Haitians and British West
Indians. By the mid-1960s British West Indians and
Haitians were also going in significant numbers to
Canada.

II. The Return Orientation

     The migration pattern that evolved in the
Caribbean and became well established was not usually
seen as a means of severing relationships with the
homeland and family, but rather as extending island
opportunities and circumventing the constraints to
upward mobility Imposed by the system at home. The
precise purpose of migration and the benefits derived
from it differed with occupation and social class as
well as with the purpose of going overseas and the
frequency and duration of visits. But migration has
mostly been seen as an acknowledged avenue of self-
advancement and upward mobility and a means of
improving the individual's and family's situation back
home.
     The return has undoubtedly remained an integral
component of the Caribbean migration circuit. Even in
those cases where migrants have settled overseas,
except when a political reason has prevented return to
the home country, a significant return orientation has
persisted.[6] Whether the return represents a real or
simply an imagined future prospect, while it remains
the intention, money is remitted to the homeland and
contacts maintained through correspondence and return
trips. The phenomenon of the return, therefore, is an
institutionalized aspect of the migration process,
rooted in an ideology that includes the expectation of
the better life or simply nostalgia for home.

III. Characteristics of the Return Flows

     The return of people and the associated transfers
of capital and goods vary with the characteristics of

the migration. The periodicity of the return varies widely, as does the country or countries from which the migrant returns. The stages in the life cycle at which the primary migration takes place and that during which the return phase occurs, differ from one another, as do the social and political activities and occupation in which the migrant engages before and during the return. All these aspects influence the orientation, skills, and "cultural baggage" of the returnee.

In this section the main types of circular migrants are described, based on the time variable that distinguishes long-stay from short-stay migrants; migrant activity and purpose of migration serve as subdivisions of these two categories. It must be pointed out that individual migrants may engage in more than one type of migration in their lifetime.

Long-Term Migrants

Settlers. Settlers are those persons who for varying time periods established their households overseas. A stay of twenty or thirty years was not uncommon in the Jamaican samples studied by Thomas-Hope,[7] and Gmelch found in his Barbadian study that the average period spent overseas was thirteen years.[8]

Although it is impossible to give an estimate of the number of long-stay migrants who return to any of the Caribbean countries, some indication may be derived from sample studies. For example, in both the rural and urban studies in Jamaica conducted by Thomas-Hope, never more than 5 percent of the population of any community or district were returned long-term migrants.[9] In Nutter's study of the manufacturing sector of Kingston, only 52 of the 372 firms in the sample employed long-stay migrants who had returned. These 52 firms together employed sixty-three returnees.[10]

Most of the existing studies on Caribbean return migration focus upon this group, and information and stereotypes about returning migrants tend to be based on the experience of these long-term overseas settlers who eventually return intending to live permanently in their country of birth. Yet because of the length of stay overseas they differ from other migrants in many important respects.

The problem of readjustment to the home society is understandably greatest for those who have lived for several years in a very different social and economic environment. Furthermore, these migrants are predominantly those whose occupations overseas were related to the labor demands of industrialized countries, and they thus acquired few if any skills relevant to the work opportunities in their homeland.

Despite the relative isolation imposed by distance, long-stay migrants who finally return permanently to the Caribbean are always those who have maintained close contacts with home. All such persons in the Jamaican studies had made previous visits home for vacations and business, and in all cases they had invested in land or housing during their period overseas.[11] A similar situation has been found in other studies; Rubenstein points out that migrants continue to send home remittances for as long as they intend to return.[12]

Although a small number of long-stay migrants return home after retirement and continue to receive pensions and social security payments from overseas, the great majority return to continue working. Their greatest financial contribution to the home country, therefore, occurs prior to and at the time of their return. For example, Gmelch found that some 85 percent of the returnees in his Barbadian study returned with the intention of working, suggesting that their cash remittances had probably ceased, and their investments made while abroad were not sufficient to sustain them for long after their return.[13] Those migrants returning to rural areas were primarily found to be engaged in agriculture or as owner-operators of a business, invariably a retail shop.[14] The urban returnees were employed in a wide range of occupations, but the white collar workers were mainly concentrated in management positions or self-employed in the retail and transport sectors.[15]

Students and Other Young Persons. A number of persons go overseas to study and often stay for several years before returning home permanently or semi-permanently. Those who do not return fairly soon after the completion of their studies are seldom among the permanent returnees. The great majority of young persons who go overseas become settlers and are among those who remit little or nothing to their homeland. With their overseas education they become established in their new country and invariably make it their permanent home. These people are often professionals, such as nurses or teachers, or paraprofessionals.

Those persons who have returned after studying or training overseas are ideally situated to contribute significantly to the home society. However, societal constraints, whether real or perceived, frequently prevented their potential from being developed.[16] Within this group are found the most politically active returnees; many of the most radical Caribbean politicians have been returnees who studied overseas or went abroad to live for a few years while young. Taylor discussed such ideas with specific reference to Marcus Garvey, Alexander Bustamante, and Norman Manley of Jamaica.[17] To these may be added a large number of other Caribbean leaders who had studied overseas.

Whether the overseas experience was critical in determining the subsequent roles played by these individuals in their home society can never be proved. However, while abroad they certainly became acutely aware of the extent and nature of the difference between their own country and that of their temporary residence in North America or Europe. Further, for the first time they personally experienced the sense of alienation that accompanies the reality of being part of a minority--and in most instances a less-privileged minority--in society. The impressionable stage in their lives at which this occurred, coupled with their relative advantage in Caribbean society on their return, led to many such persons making their contribution in a range of leadership roles which has been highly significant in the pattern of change in Caribbean societies.

Long-Term Circulators. Long term circulators are those individuals who repeatedly go overseas, usually to the same country, reentering the job market each time and becoming a permanent resident of that country or even a citizen. Because of their high rate of mobility and long periods spent away from the Caribbean, these persons are not well represented in sample surveys carried out in the region; nevertheless some have been included in the rural and urban studies conducted in Jamaica.[18]

Long-term circular migration from the Caribbean chiefly involves women going to the United States or men to other regional locations, such as to the U.S. Virgin Islands from the Leeward Islands. In most cases the individual effectively remains part of his or her household in the Caribbean, living in a more temporary setting in the overseas country despite the fact that the person spends more time in that country than "at home." At first, the family remains in the Caribbean, and then through citizenship or residency privileges, the dependents of the migrant often obtain residency rights. The children either attend schools in the United States, or they attend school in the Caribbean and spend their vacations in the United States.

The perpetual circulators generally regard the Caribbean as home and the foreign country as the work place. The family of the migrant is predominantly Caribbean-based, and the spouse invariably retains his or her job and manages the household in the home island while the other circulates one or more times a year. In the early years of long-term circulation the frequency of the return is limited, partly because the worker has not yet obtained citizenship or residency rights and partly for economic reasons.

This group of migrants comprises persons without highly specialized skills who chiefly work in private domestic or nursing capacities in the United States or Canada. In the U.S. Virgin Islands the circular migrants from other islands usually work in construction and other unskilled jobs. They do not typically reenter the job market back home, because they have repeatedly obtained work overseas with no great difficulty. Not surprisingly, those who have reduced or ceased this pattern of mobility are elderly and retired.

With regard to remittances, these migrants transfer large quantities of consumer goods, especially household equipment and clothing. Furthermore, they remit substantial sums of money, both during their working life from their income and, upon retirement, from their state and other pensions. The main reason that they transfer large amounts of capital and goods is not because their gross incomes are large but because almost all their expenditures and investments have a homeward orientation. Their money is principally invested in housing; its other uses include the education of children, supplementation of family income, and expenses incurred in further travel. The remittances have a considerable impact on the standard of living of the families involved in this circular mobility. Moreover, through the financing of education the future success of the children is promoted.

Transients

The numbers of people involved in the three major types of long-term migration are matched by those who go overseas as transients in one or another capacity. For the transient group, the return is a built-in component of their migration pattern not only in terms of their own personal intentions but also due to the visa regulations by which they are constrained. There is, of course, an attrition rate whether legally or illegally, but the overall pattern is one of short periods spent overseas followed by a return. Several groups of persons are involved in this aspect of the migration process; they share the fact that they travel between relatively close locations.

International Vendors. The circulation of vendors is predominantly a female activity and essentially represents an international aspect of the female role as a higgler in the Caribbean. In the small islands of the Eastern Caribbean higglering is an old practice and involves both the buying and the selling of goods while outside the home country. For example, from St. Lucia, St. Vincent, or Grenada, agricultural produce is taken to other islands such as Trinidad and Barbados; in

turn, the vendor returns home with household items and
clothing. A similar pattern occurs in the Windward
Island group where a considerable circulation of people
takes place from St. Kitts, Nevis, Antigua, and other
places to the Virgin Islands of St. Thomas, St. Croix,
and St. Martin.

In the Jamaican case, the recent practice of
higglers (now termed "informal commercial importers")
going overseas to purchase goods for sale in the
informal retail sector back home is a highly organized
pattern of international circulation by small
traders. The number of persons engaged in this
activity is not known and has proved difficult to
determine in sample studies because many higglers
participate only irregularly and have not received
government licenses for imports. However, the large
volume of the movement is indicated by the separate
customs area established at the Norman Manley
International Airport to handle the inspection of
imports accompanying passengers. It had been reported
in the press that the vendors "jammed the passenger
arrival lounge at the Airports with goods in large
quantities which should have been handled as
freight."[19] Certainly, the official recognition
afforded to vendors since 1983 has regularized the
trade, and thus controlled the taxation of imported
goods and the contribution made by the vendors to
government revenue.[20]

A similar pattern of international circulation
occurs in Haiti but without the formalities of the
Jamaican case. Unlike their Eastern Caribbean
counterparts, both the Jamaicans and Haitians travel by
plane, not boat, and remain at their destinations for
several days. In general, the Haitians go to the
Bahamas and Puerto Rico to purchase goods, and return
to sell them in Haiti. From Jamaica, the movement is
to Haiti as well as to Cayman, Panama, and Miami.

To overcome the restrictions on the conversion of
the Jamaican dollar and the difficulties in obtaining
foreign currency in the island, many Jamaican vendors
take fresh fruit and vegetables to Cayman on the first
leg of their journey, and sell them for U.S. dollars.
The vendors then continue to Miami and with their
dollars purchase clothing and other consumer goods for
sale back home.

This migratory activity has permitted the rise of
successful entrepreneurial groups in the lower echelons
of most Caribbean societies and particularly in
Jamaica. They operate informally both at home and
abroad; the home country obtains revenue from them
through import duties levied on the goods
transferred. They establish their own commercial
contacts, foreign currency accumulation, and, on

return, distribution and marketing. This process has
allowed capital accumulation and the potential for
upward mobility in an otherwise essentially rigid
system controlled by the traditional groups of
entrepreneurs.

Contract Workers. Contract workers constitute
another important group of circular migrants. They are
usually agricultural or construction laborers, domestic
workers, or waiters, who obtain visas for specified
periods and for the specific purpose defined by the
contract. As in the case of vendors, several regional
destinations are involved in this movement as well as
those in the United States and Canada. For example,
thousands of Haitians are contracted each year to work
as laborers on the sugar estates of the Dominican
Republic[21] and Vincentians in Barbados.[22] Barbadians
and others from the Eastern Caribbean go to various
parts of the United States and Canada to engage in
agricultural jobs, principally those associated with
the annual harvesting.

Contract workers do not characteristically upgrade
their skills overseas, and on return their migratory
experience appears to make virtually no difference to
their occupational activity. The great benefit derived
by contract workers is the relatively large sums of
money that they send and take home. Total earnings for
Jamaican workers throughout the United States in 1983
exceeded US$47 million, and for Jamaican workers in
Canada in the same year, the earnings were over C$7.5
million.[23] The number of workers involved were 9,946
and 2,608, respectively.[24]

In the case of farm workers on contract in the
United States, the agreement stipulates that 23 percent
of the workers' bimonthly pay is automatically
transferred to a bank account in the home island. In
addition to this amount the workers send and take home
substantial sums. For example, McCoy estimated that
for the 1980-81 sugarcane season in Florida nearly
US$19 million were earned by Caribbean contract
workers, of which $7,764,000 were remitted in the
mandatory savings plan, $6,669,000 were otherwise
remitted, and the rest was spent in the United
States.[25] The money remitted was chiefly spent on
housing: Some 60 percent of the Caribbean sugar
workers in Florida (in 1980-81) invested in housing
back home. Other areas of substantial investment
included livestock and farming (47.8 percent of the
workers) and other businesses (4.4 percent).[26]

The farm contract workers also take back a large
quantity of goods, predominantly consumer items--
chiefly clothing and entertainment equipment--and to a
lesser extent producer goods, such as agricultural
equipment and tools. McCoy's study showed that 97.4

percent of the workers purchased clothes and other personal items, 59.4 percent purchased entertainment equipment, and only 2.6 percent purchased tools.[27]

Other Itinerant Labor Migrants. Other itinerant labor migrants are principally men and include casual farm and construction workers who travel seasonally to nearby islands to seek work but without specific contractual arrangements. They return home after some weeks. Dominicans migrate in this manner to Guadeloupe to work in the banana industry; Haitians go to the Bahamas where they work as casual laborers;[28] others travel annually to a number of destinations within the region. The individual's chief benefit from these migrations is the money earned, which, although small in cash terms, is usually remitted to provide the main economic base of the migrant's household.[29]

International Business Commuters. In most islands, a middle-class variation of the circulating workers is the person traveling within the region or to North America on a regular basis to engage in business.[30] Those who move within the Caribbean region usually maintain their households in the home island and stay in temporary accommodations while away. In many cases, however, especially where the movement is to the United States or Canada, the commuter effectively lives in two households. In some instances the family remains resident in the Caribbean household, and business is conducted by one or more members overseas; in other cases the reverse situation occurs. For example, a small but significant minority of middle-class Jamaicans who since the 1970s have transferred their families to North America, have resumed or continued their businesses in the home country, making return trips on a regular basis. People in this category are reluctant to give details about their mobility so that it is difficult to assess the numbers involved.

The pattern of capital and goods transfer is complex, but in general, a considerable amount of foreign exchange is either lost or foregone to the home island in the Caribbean. On the other side of the balance, viable businesses are sustained and some of the money generated is reinvested or spent in the home island whether for real estate, productive activities, services, or simply personal consumption.

IV. The Developmental Impact of the Return

As the above discussion demonstrates, the return involves a wide variety of persons who differ in class, education, skills, purpose in migrating, and patterns of return. The migration may be periodic or a single move, but in all cases it is associated with a complex

number of ancillary flows of goods and capital, and
with the socio-cultural characteristics of the
individuals and families themselves--namely, their
goals and attitudes, life-styles, and patterns of
consumption. The linkages maintained do not relate
solely to personal communication and goods, but also to
items for production or retail. The return is
therefore complex; hence the impact on the home
countries will also necessarily be complex.

As in outward movements, the impact of return
flows cannot be measured simply in terms of the
magnitude of flow. Although the full significance of
such movements is determined partly by the displacement
and replacement of people, the characteristics of the
people involved--their acquired education, skills,
ideas, and economic behavior--are more critical than
mere numbers.

These aspects of the return are relevant to the
process of development in the Caribbean, and they can
be identified fairly accurately in any specific case.
However, an additional factor is that the linkages
between the return flows of the migration process and
the process of development in the home country cannot
be easily evaluated. Such an evaluation is largely
determined by the expectations people have of
returnees, and thus the reference against which their
contribution to the local system is measured. An
important question is whether they are expected to act
differently from non-migrants. Are the returnees
expected to spend their money differently, more wisely,
and less selfishly than the non-migrants, concentrating
on national development goals rather than on personal
consumption? These objectives would certainly be
counter to current perceptions held by returning
migrants of the purpose of their migration.

Much has been written or said about the loss of
skills through migration. Concern over the net loss of
human resources at the professional and managerial
level was the basis of an address given by Prime
Minister Edward Seaga to the Governing Council of the
United Nations Development Programme (UNDP) in Geneva,
in 1984. He said that an estimated 60 percent of the
Jamaicans who graduated as professionals or skilled
workers left their homeland from 1977 to 1980; this
out-migration resulted in a loss of approximately
US$194 million, the estimated cost of training those
migrants.[31] Seaga indicated that the loss of high-
level manpower from Third World countries was a
commensurate gain to the industrialized countries. On
the other hand, little is known about the acquisition
of skills while the migrant is abroad and the
utilization of those skills or education on the
return. Are the skills of return migrants those most

needed by the home society at any particular time? Again, this relation cannot be totally evaluated by an equation of financial losses and gains estimated for training. Would the educated migrant have had the opportunity to be as productive at home as abroad? The feeling among most return migrants interviewed was that they would not have done as well had they never been abroad.

A further issue in assessing the developmental impact of return migration is the interpretation of development. Development cannot simply be regarded in terms of national economic growth unless it promotes the establishment of a self-reliant, buoyant society characterized by an increasing equalization of opportunity. Neither in terms of economic growth nor societal change will any individual migrant make a noticeable contribution--other than in exceptional cases. The question to be assessed is whether the contribution of the returnee is oriented consciously or unconsciously toward these goals.

In summary, the contribution or potential contribution of return migration is determined by the associated flows of human resources, and the capital transferred and the goods remitted to the home country from the migration destinations. The scope of this chapter does not permit a detailed assessment of any of these, nor do the available data provide as many answers as they do questions. At the same time, the existing studies go some way toward indicating some of the trends in the return migration process and their implications for development.

Skills and the Occupational Contribution of Returning Migrants

Spatial mobility is closely associated with occupational change. However, little upgrading of skills or educational standards is apparent for most migrant groups, except for the student group. Indeed, those who go overseas to study and later return home make their greatest contribution to the home society through their acquired skills and experience.

A study of return migration to Kingston, Jamaica, and San Juan, Puerto Rico, showed that 48 percent of the returnees, were categorized as professional, technical, administrative, and managerial workers in the Jamaican case and 21.6 percent in the Puerto Rican sample.[32] These percentages would have been even higher if they were calculated only in terms of the numbers in the labor force; however, the majority of professionals and managers among the return population had already been in an educational category before their migration that would have ensured their white collar status. Likewise, in a study conducted in Nevis, little skill improvement was demonstrated among return migrants.[33] Like other unskilled migrants or artisans who migrated, they were predominantly employed as casual laborers or in unskilled jobs overseas, thus gaining no skill training.

The loss of useful skills in the Caribbean is a feature of long-term migration when professionals, technicians, and managerial personnel settle permanently abroad. Students and young migrants take with them skills that are lost to the countries they leave. What is not always appreciated is that a significant number return, but many, as Gmelch found in his Barbadian study, feel constrained in implementing any changes in the workplace because such actions could engender resentment among non-migrant colleagues.[34]

Blue collar migrant workers who settled abroad were found to return with skills unsuited to the local situation. For example, migrants who settled in England typically worked in manufacturing industries, and acquired skills unsuited to use in the Caribbean situation on their return. They chiefly moved into own account work requiring some capital outlay but no specialized skill. At the same time an overconcentration in some occupations is typical of returning migrants. The number of entrepreneurs and retailers, in particular, exceeds local or national requirements in many areas.[35]

In the total equation, one factor is not immediately obvious: Although many return migrants do not engage in occupations in short supply locally, nevertheless migrants who establish their own businesses operate on a much larger scale and with better equipment than they otherwise could. The capital and goods which the migrants remit facilitate the achievement of this higher level of operation.

Return migration certainly appears to create an imbalance in skills, manpower requirements, and supplies. Structural factors in the Caribbean reduce the overall impact that return migrants could make, and, in addition, some groups of professionals are poorly represented among the returnees, discouraged from returning by salaries and working conditions much poorer than they experienced overseas. Given the constraints, it is difficult to envisage any short-term measures that would successfully enhance the positive impact that returning white collar migrants could make to national development.[36]

Capital Transfers

In both an ideological and a practical sense, remittances are an integral part of the return. The

impact of the capital transfers on development is
determined largely by two factors: the amount of
capital transferred to the sending countries and the
uses to which it is put.

Absolute figures regarding the return flow of
capital are understandably difficult to ascertain, and
the official figures mask the additional sums received
unofficially. However, several studies have
demonstrated that such sums are substantial and provide
the major source of income for many households. An
even larger proportion of households depends in part on
the money sent or brought by migrants. The returnees
who have retired overseas before returning regularly
receive a state or work pension that in most cases is
their major source of income. Dirks cited the case of
the island of Tortola where some 45 percent of the
income of the average household comes from
overseas.[37] Philpott found that remittances provided
the main source of foreign capital transfers in the
case of Montserrat.[38] Frucht reported the same for
Nevis,[39] as was also found in a recent study by
Liburd.[40] Hill described a similar situation for
Carriacou,[41] Brana-Shute for the Eastern Caribbean,[42]
Richardson for St. Kitts and Nevis,[43] and Thomas-Hope
for Puerto Rico and Jamaica.[44]

All groups of return migrants, whether long-term
or transient, are involved in capital transfers. The
groups contributing least are students and vendors;
they make their contributions in other ways. The rest
make a signficant impact: Long-term circulators,
contract workers, and commuting business people
transfer large sums of money overall. In this regard,
the returning national compares very favorably with the
short-stay immigrant. Invariably short-stay
professional immigrants, often on contract, contribute
their professional expertise, but usually do not
locally invest the capital transferred in salary
payments; instead, they either spend it or repatriate
it at the end of the contract.

For most groups of migrants the obligation of
remitting money is institutionalized, for all groups it
is in a social and economic sense an essential
concomitant of the return. The critical issue is
whether the capital transferred at various stages of
the migration process is utilized in ways that maximize
its contribution to national development.

No doubt the capital transfers that form part of
the migration circuit are essential to the economic
viability of a significant number of Caribbean
households and communities. Such capital makes a major
positive contribution to development, since without
economically viable households, populations would not
exist above minimal survival levels. The empirical

studies on this theme all confirm that buying land and housing is a returning migrant's priority, with very much less emphasis on substantial investment in other areas. Specific cases were found of large investments being made in businesses, which in turn employ other workers. Likewise, in rural areas livestock is an important means of smaller scale investment. However, in general, no evidence has been found to suggest that return migrants are larger investors than non-migrants or that they invest in operations that have wider ranging multiplier effects than others.

A difficult question to answer in the present context is whether the infusions of capital from overseas have created a persisting dependency on external sources of funds that has in the long run exacerbated the process of underdevelopment. The extent to which this is the case is the extent to which the capital transfers are a negative factor in Caribbean development. On the positive side, in so far as the capital is providing income to Caribbean people and thus assisting in the financing of nutrition and education, shelter, and clothing, it is inevitably an investment in the human resources of the region. This investment must be seen as being as important, if not more so, than those in infrastructure and productive capacity. The caution is simply that this issue has long-run and short-run dimensions. The vital question is whether the short-run positive impact of capital associated with return migration is contributing to the desired long-run effects.

Transfer of Goods

Caribbean people undoubtedly associate migration with a consumer bonanza. Improvements in living standards have resulted from this process: Clothing, food, household items, and electronic equipment have been imported directly to Caribbean households from overseas. Inevitably, the transfer of such goods has served to create and widen the gap between those households affected by migration and those not. A further negative aspect is the effect that the transfer of goods has on the expectations and value systems of the societies in general.

Goods for productive purposes are also remitted by returning migrants. Whether this practice should be encouraged depends once again on whether Caribbean countries should in the long run further entrench their structural dependence upon outside countries for their very productive and export capacities. In the short term, the issue is simply whether the trade-off between the outgoing foreign exchange (or potential incoming foreign exchange foregone) on the one hand and the enhancement of production on the other is beneficial.

Goods transferred for commercial purposes by circulating vendors form another variant in the overall pattern of goods remitted as part of the circular mobility of Caribbean people. As already suggested, the positive implications of this activity lie in the opportunities it affords for the local development of a new entrepreneurial group with a potential for substantial upward mobility. As in the matter of capital transfers associated with migration, for the transfer of goods the positive impact in the Caribbean is indisputable in terms of short-run economic benefit. However, it is highly questionable in terms of long-run development.

V. Conclusion

The return flows of circular migration form a major potential resource for Caribbean societies when they include the flows of goods and capital as well as the ideas, attitudes, and skills of the migrants themselves. In assessing the impact of these flows upon development, the major point of divergence is between their implications for short-run benefit principally to the returnees and their dependents on the one hand and to long-run societal development on the other.

In terms of short-run personal advantage, the return flows of circular migration appear to have a positive effect. This is not to say that individual returnees or all aspects of the return make a positive contribution to the economy or that the capital and skills that are transferred are optimally utilized. What it implies is that living standards and levels of subsistence, housing stock, and entrepreneurial activity, among other factors, are improved by the capital and goods remitted.

The careful evaluation of national developmental goals is necessary if policies relating to the maximization of return flows are to have the desired long-term effects. At present, the return of skills, capital, goods, and ideas is apparently contributing to prolonged and more widely diffused dependence upon the outside world for life-styles, patterns of consumption, and the basis for productive capacity. As a consequence, the costs in foreign capital of consumption and production continually increase. Migration itself is perpetuated, and the material gap between the migrant and non-migrant household widens. The dangers are that in the short run, the return flows associated with the migration process could continue to mask many of the fundamental structural weaknesses in Caribbean economies, and that in the long run,

consumerism on levels that domestic economies cannot
support could continue to be confused with development.
     Carefully formulated and implemented policies
could increase migrant contributions to national
economic priorities and at the same time benefit the
return migrants themselves. Schemes tried in Europe
include the use of migrants' savings for creating jobs
and specific long-term investment programs.[45] These
have met with varying success, depending primarily on
whether the programs assist migrants to participate in
ways consistent with their pre-existing goals.
Likewise, in the Caribbean with its deeply rooted
return migration culture, only those policies that fit
the dynamics of the existing migration system and the
ideology that surrounds it are likely to succeed.

Notes

1. This is discussed more fully in Elizabeth M. Thomas-Hope, "Hopes and Reality in the West Indian Migration to Britain" Oral History: The Journal of Oral History Society, vol. 8 (1980), pp. 35-42.

2. See Elizabeth M. Thomas-Hope, "The Establishment of a Migration Tradition: British West Indian Movements to the Hispanic Caribbean in the Century after Emancipation" in Colin G. Clarke (ed.) Caribbean Social Relations (Liverpool, 1978), pp. 66-81; Elizabeth M. Thomas-Hope, Population Mobility in the West Indies: The Role of Perceptual and Environmental Differentials (1977), D. Phil. thesis, University of Oxford, pp. 15-23.

3. Figures cited in George W. Roberts, The Population of Jamaica (Cambridge, 1957), p. 133.

4. Figures cited in Malcolm J. Proudfoot, Population Movements in the Caribbean (Port of Spain, Trinidad, 1950), pp. 77-78.

5. Ibid.

6. The return orientation is discussed more fully by Hymie Rubenstein, "Return Migration to the English-speaking Caribbean: Review and Commentary" in William F. Stinner, Klaus de Albuquerque and Roy S. Bryce-Laporte (eds.) Return Migration and Remittances: Developing A Caribbean Perspective (Washington, D.C., 1982), pp. 20-27. See also Elizabeth M. Thomas-Hope, "Hopes and Reality in the West Indian Migration to Britain" Supra. fn. #1.

7. Elizabeth M. Thomas-Hope, "The International Migration of Caribbean Peoples: Circular Movement and Development Policy" (research project, the Ford Foundation, 1982).

8. George Gmelch, "From London to Bridgetown: The Motives and Readjustment of Return Migrants in Barbados," (unpublished paper, 1984). See also George Gmelch, "Work, Innovation and Investment: The Impact of Return Migration in an Eastern Caribbean Society," (unpublished paper, 1984).

9. Thomas-Hope, "The International Migration of Caribbean Peoples" Supra. fn. #7.

10. R.D. Nutter, "The Employment of Return Migrants from the United Kingdom in the Manufacturing

Sector of Kingston, Jamaica" (Institute of British Geographers conference paper, 1985).

11. Thomas-Hope, "The International Migration of Caribbean Peoples" Supra. fn. #7.

12. Rubenstein, "Return Migration to the English-speaking Caribbean," Supra. fn. #6.

13. Gmelch, "From London to Bridgetown" p. 15, Supra. fn. #8.

14. See, for example, Hymie Rubenstein, "Migration and underdevelopment: The Caribbean" Cultural Survival Quarterly vol. 7, No. 4, (1983) pp. 30-32; see also Elizabeth M. Thomas-Hope, "Population Mobility and Rural Development" (research project, Overseas Development Institute, London, 1984).

15. See Nutter, "The Employment of Return Migrants from the United Kingdom in the Manufacturing Sector of Kingston, Jamaica" Supra. fn. #10. Gmelch, "From London to Bridgetown" Supra. fn. #8.

16. See Gmelch, "From London to Bridgetown" Supra. fn. #8,

17. Edward Taylor, "The Social Adjustment of Returned Migrants to Jamaica" in Frances Henry (ed.), Ethnicity in the Americas (The Hague, 1976), p. 217-220.

18. Thomas-Hope, "Population Mobility and Rural Development Supra. fn. #14. "The International Migration of Caribbean Peoples" Supra. fn. #7.

19. The Daily Gleaner, September 10, 1983.

20. The Daily Gleaner, April 15, 1983; January 24, 1984.

21. Martin Murphy, "Haitian Workers in the Dominican Republic's Sugar Industry" (conference paper, Migration and Culture Contacts in the Caribbean, Barbados, 1984); Paul R. Latortue, "Haitian Migration to Santo Domingo" (conference paper, Migration and Culture Contacts in the Caribbean Barbados, 1984).

22. Dawn Marshall, "Vincentian Contract Labour to Barbados: Satisfaction of Mutual Needs" (unpublished paper, 1980).

23. Figures obtained from the Ministry of Labour, Kingston, Jamaica.

24. Ibid.

25. Terry L. McCoy, Chapter 8 in this book.

26. Ibid., p. 22.

27. Ibid., p. 20.

28. Dawn Marshall, The Haitian Problem: Illegal Migration to the Bahamas (Kingston, Jamaica, 1979), pp. 141-194.

29. This is discussed in Linda Basch, Population Movements Within the English-Speaking Caribbean: An Overview (unpublished paper, 1982), pp. 48-53.

30. Elizabeth M. Thomas-Hope, "Off the Island: Population Mobility Among the Caribbean Middle Class" in Arnaud F. Marks and Hebe M.C. Vessuri (eds.), White Collar Migrants in the Americas and the Caribbean (Leiden, 1983), pp. 39-58.

31. Address by the Rt. Hon. Edward Seaga to the Governing Council of the UNDP Geneva, 12 June 1984, Jamaica Information Service news release 1080/84, 5.

32. Thomas-Hope, "The International Migration of Caribbean Peoples" Supra. ft. #7.

33. Carolyn Liburd, "Migration from Nevis Since 1950" (B.A. thesis, University of the West Indies, Mona, 1984).

34. Gmelch, "From London to Bridgetown" Supra. fn. #8.

35. Generalizations about the unsuitability of the skills of return migrants may be misleading since this varies from one area to another with clustering of occupations associated with the least successful return migrants. For example, Hernandez Alvarez reported for Puerto Rico that the least successful migrants returned to rural areas whereas the most successful went to San Juan. Jose Hernandez Alvarez Return Migration to Puerto Rico, (Westport, Connecticut, 1976).

36. Martin J. Boodhoo and Ahamad Baksh, The Impact of Brain Drain on Development: A Case-Study of Guyana, (Georgetown, Guyana, 1981).

37. Robert Dirks, "Network Groups and Adaptation in an Afro-Caribbean Community" Man vol. 7., no. 4 (1972), p. 572.

38. Stuart Philpott, West Indian Migration: The Montserrat Case (London, 1973), pp. 141-196.

39. Richard Frucht, "Emigration, Remittances and Social Change: Aspects of the Social Field of Nevis, West Indies," Anthropoligica vol. 10, no. 2 (1968), p. 202.

40. Liburd, "Migration from Nevis," p. 52 Supra. fn. #33.

41. Donald R. Hill, "The Impact of Migration on the Metropolitan and Folk Society of Carriacou, Grenada" in Anthropological Papers of the American Museum of Natural History (New York, 1977), p. 230.

42. Gary and Rosemarie Brana-Shute, "The Magnitude and Impact of Remittances in the Eastern Caribbean: A Research Note" in Stinner, Alberquerque and Bryce-Laporte (eds.), pp. 273-281, Supra fn. 6.

43. Bonham C. Richardson, Caribbean Migrants: Environment and Human Survival on St. Kitts and Nevis, (Knoxville, Tennessee, 1983), pp. 47-51.

44. Thomas-Hope, "The International Migration of Caribbean Peoples" Supra. fn. #7.

45. Rosemarie Rogers, "Incentives to Return: Patterns of Policies and Migrants' Responses" in Mary M, Kritz, Charles B. Keely and Silvano M. Tomasi (eds.), Global Trends in Migration: Theory and Research on International Population Movements (New York, 1981), pp. 338-364. See also Robert Pastor and Rosemarie Rogers, Chapter 15 in this book. Jose Ignacio Cases Mendez and Octavio Cabezas Moro, "The Relation between Migration Policy and Economic Development and the Promotion of New Employment Possibilities for Returnees (Foreign Investment and Migrant Remittances): International Migration, vol. 14, (1976), pp. 134-162.

8. The Impact of U.S. Temporary Worker Programs on Caribbean Development: Evidence from H-2 Workers in Florida Sugar

Terry L. McCoy

I. Introduction

In examining the impact of migration on development, Simmons reminded us that the developmental context and character of the migration are important variables.[1] According to his taxonomy, most Caribbean migration occurs in labor-surplus plantation economies in which the impact of remittances can logically be expected to differ from that in rapidly industrializing economies or those with dynamic rural sectors. Within the Caribbean and its individual countries, different types of migration take place simultaneously -- rural to urban, island to island, long-term island to developed country and temporary island to developed country. Each has a distinctive impact on the sending society. In this chapter, I shall consider the developmental implications for the Caribbean of one kind of migration: temporary labor migration to the United States.[2]

Temporary Worker Programs

Although legal temporary labor migration to the United States currently accounts for only a small percentage of all Caribbean migrants, examining it is important for several reasons. First, because such migration is legal, the data concerning it are easier to analyze than those for other types of migrants, and the analyses' results are more likely to be reliable. In contrast to the larger flow of illegal migration, the composition and characteristics of this stream are known or are knowable. Second, current U.S. temporary worker policy is almost exclusively aimed at the Caribbean. Every year since 1943 the Florida sugar industry has imported workers from the English-speaking Caribbean to harvest its cane. This program is the largest and oldest continuous temporary worker program

in the United States. Third, recent attempts to reform
U.S. immigration policy have included an expansion of
temporary foreign worker programs. If adopted, the new
policy promises to increase temporary Caribbean workers
in the U.S. labor market.

When compared to other forms of migration,
temporary worker migration is attractive to less-
developed countries like those of the Caribbean. It
virtually guarantees the workers' return, and evidence
indicates that they regularly remit to their homeland
larger amounts of their overseas earnings than do
permanent migrants.[3] Because they have legal status,
temporary migrants are afforded more protection in the
country of employment. Within developed receiving
societies, foreign workers are not universally
welcomed; nevertheless, the advantages that their
hiring affords employers assure that there will always
be pressure to adopt temporary worker programs.

Contemporary temporary worker policy in the U.S.
dates from the Second World War, when the country
turned to foreign workers to help alleviate war-related
labor shortages. The largest such effort was the
Bracero program, in which millions of Mexicans were
imported for temporary employment, largely for
agricultural work in the southwestern United States
(see Table 8.1). A smaller but similar program allowed
growers in the southeastern United States to import
workers from the British West Indies and the
Bahamas.[4] Following the war, demand for foreign labor
continued, suggesting that employers preferred it, even
when U.S. workers were again available. In response to
the labor shortage caused by the Korean War, the U.S.
Congress passed legislation (P.L. 78), and the United
States and Mexico signed a bilateral agreement
reauthorizing the Bracero program. Mexico insisted on
a government-to-government arrangement in order to
protect its workers in the United States from
discrimination and exploitation. The Bracero program
reached its peak in 1959, when the number of Mexicans
entering for seasonal work was over 430,000. The
number then declined until the act was repealed in
1964.[5] It succumbed to a determined attack by
organized labor (which charged that it took jobs away
from U.S. citizens) and a sympathetic Democratic
administration.

With the elimination of Bracero labor (as Table
8.1 demonstrates, it took several years to phase the
program out), the only way temporary foreign workers
could enter the United States was through a provision
in the Immigration and Nationality Act of 1952. The
smaller Caribbean temporary workers program, operating
under this provision, managed to avoid attracting the
ire of those opposed to the Bracero program by keeping

Table 8.1

Foreign Workers Admitted for Temporary Employment
in U.S. Agriculture
(1942-1972)

Year	Total	Mexican	British West Indian	Bahamian	Canadian	Other
1942	4,203	4,203	0	0	NA	0
1943	65,624	52,098	8,828	4,698	NA	0
1944	84,419	62,170	16,574	3,048	1,414	1,213
1945	73,422	49,454	17,291	2,100	4,055	522
1946	51,347	32,043	11,081	2,690	5,533	0
1947	30,775	19,632	1,017	2,705	7,421	0
1948	44,916	35,345	2,421	1,250	5,900	0
1949	112,765	107,000	1,715	1,050	3,000	0
1950	76,525	67,500	4,425	1,800	2,800	0
1951	203,640	192,000	6,540	2,500	2,600	0
1953	215,321	201,380	4,802	2,939	6,200	0
1954	320,737	309,033	2,159	2,545	7,000	0
1955	412,166	398,850	3,651	2,965	6,700	0
1956	459,850	445,197	4,369	3,194	6,700	390
1957	452,205	436,049	5,707	2,464	7,300	685
1958	447,513	432,857	5,204	2,237	6,900	315
1959	455,420	437,643	6,622	2,150	8,600	405
1960	334,729	315,846	8,150	1,670	8,200	863
1961	310,375	291,420	8,875	1,440	8,600	40
1962	217,010	194,978	11,729	1,199	8,700	404
1963	209,218	186,865	11,856	1,074	8,500	923
1964	200,022	177,736	14,361	0	7,900	25
1965	35,871	20,284	10,917	0	4,670	0
1966	23,524	8,647	11,194	0	3,683	0
1967	23,603	6,125	13,578	0	3,900	0
1968	13,323	0	10,723	0	2,600	0
1969	15,830	0	13,530	0	2,300	0
1970	17,474	0	15,470	0	2,004	0
1971	13,684	0	12,143	0	1,541	0
1972	12,526	0	11,419	0	1,107	0

Sources: 1942-1964: U.S. Senate, Committee on the Judiciary, the Select Commission on Immigration and Refugee Policy, "Temporary Worker Programs: Background and Issues," A report prepared by the Congressional Research Service, Library of Congress, 96th Congress, Second Session, February 1980, p. 36; 1965-1972: U.S. Senate, Committee on the Judiciary, Subcommittee on Immigration, "The West Indies (BWI) Temporary Alien Labor Program: 1943-1977," 95th Session, Second Session, 1978, p. 27.

a low profile, although it survives today only in the [6]
Florida sugar and East Coast apple industries. [6]
Current reform efforts are directed at again expanding
this source of temporary workers.

H-2 Regulations

The recruitment of foreign labor for employment in
the United States is currently authorized by Section
1101(a)(15)(H)(ii) of the 1952 Immigration and
Nationality Act. Although an explicit intent of the
law is to reserve U.S. jobs for U.S. workers, section
H-2 allows the entrance of nonimmigrant aliens into the
United States to perform temporary services or labor,
if unemployed persons capable of performing such
service or labor cannot be found in this country.
The responsibility of administrating the H-2
program is shared by the Departments of Labor and
Justice. The former, in response to petitions from
employers, must certify that "qualified persons in the
U.S. are not available" and that the employment of
nonimmigrant aliens would not "adversely affect" the
wages and working conditions of U.S. workers similarly
employed. To ensure that no domestic workers are
available for the jobs in question, Department of Labor
regulations require that the petitioning employer
actively recruit through state employment services. To
protect U.S. workers "similarly employed" from unfair
foreign competition, the department has established the
"adverse effect wage rate," the job-specific minimum
wage that must be offered foreign workers. Domestic
workers cannot be paid below this rate either. The
Department of Labor thereafter advises the Immigration
and Naturalization Service of the Department of Justice
about approvals and denials of petitions for
certification. The service may then accept or reject [7]
this advice. [7]
Senator Alan Simpson (R-Wyo.) and Congressman
Romano Mazzoli (D-Ky.) sponsored a comprehensive
Immigration Reform and Control Act in 1982 and again in
1984. The act's major purpose was to address the
problem of illegal aliens, but it also included a minor
provision that would have turned the administrative
regulations on temporary workers into law. This
provision provided an opening for those who wished to
expand legal access to temporary foreign workers. As
the Simpson-Mazzoli bill worked its way through the
legislative process in 1984, provisions were added that
would have authorized a substantially enlarged
temporary worker program. Although the Simpson-Mazzoli
bill failed to win final approval, considerable support
continues to exist for easier access to foreign
workers. [8] In evaluating the implications of a

liberalized temporary worker program for Caribbean development, the history of H-2 labor in the Florida sugar industry is instructive.

The H-2 Program in the Florida Sugar Industry

Florida sugarcane is grown on some 370,000 areas of fertile muck soil on the southern shores of Lake Okeechobee. Two large corporations (U.S. Sugar and Gulf and Western) control over one-half of the acreage.[9] The Florida sugar industry emerged from modest proportions in the early 1960s when the Cuban sugar quota was partially reassigned to domestic producers, and today Florida is a leading sugar-producing state. Its 1982-83 harvest yielded a record crop of 1.3 million tons of raw sugar.[10] The domestic cane producers in Florida are unique in their use of manual labor for harvesting. This dependence is a function of ecological and technical constraints that render mechanical harvesting of the region's recumbent cane less efficient than hand harvesting. The profitability of Florida sugar, to an important extent, thus rests on access to a large, relatively inexpensive seasonal labor force.

The labor force currently comes from five islands: Jamaica (which provides approximately 80 percent), Barbados, St. Vincent, St. Lucia, and Dominica. What originated as a war-related labor shortage has been certified to exist by the Department of Labor ever since. In spite of wages in excess (the adverse-effect wage rate for the 1980-81 season was $4.09 an hour) of those paid other agricultural workers, free room, subsidized board and transportation, and a "positive recruitment" effort, the industry does not attract domestic workers in sufficient numbers. Although the reasons for this are disputed, once a shortage of domestic workers is certified, the practice of the Immigration and Naturalization Service has been to issue permits for a fixed number of workers (usually between 8,000 and 9,000) for the specific task of harvesting sugarcane in Florida for a period not to exceed eight months. The subsequent recruitment of offshore labor is governed by a private contract, annually renewed, between organizations representing the employers and the West Indian Regional Labour Board, representing both the island governments and the workers.

Because the supply of workers greatly exceeds the demand for their services, a fundamental conflict of interest exists between the employers and the governments of the sending islands. The former would prefer to have complete control over labor recruitment. This would enable them to preselect all workers from one season to the next on the basis of their past productivity. However, were the Regional Labour Board to accede to this desire, the island governments and local politicians would lose an important source of patronage. Consequently the contract stipulates that employers may only predesignate up to 60 percent of a season's work force. The remaining "nonpreferred" workers are selected by industry recruiters from pools generated on each of the islands. This arrangement that does not guarantee employment from one year to the next--a source of uncertainty for individual workers and their families.

Each worker signs an individual employment contract with a specific grower. It guarantees those completing 50 percent of the contract period free transportation, free room, subsidized board, and medical care. Changing employers during the season is discouraged. If a worker leaves the cane fields to seek other work, he is subject to immediate deportation. All H-2s are bonded to discourage job abandonment and visa abuse. The workers are housed on the sugar estates in barracks, which vary considerably in their configuration and accommodations. On arrival, they are given an eight-day training/trial period during which they are paid the hourly adverse-effect wage. To be hired for the season, applicants must demonstrate the ability to cut cane at a piece-rate equal to the hourly adverse-effect wage. Most domestic applicants either fail this test or voluntarily drop out. Once the season begins, actual earnings are determined by a formula combining the adverse-effect wage rate as a guaranteed minimum with a complex piece-rate formula that rewards the workers who exceed the daily quota. Industry records show, for example, that average hourly earnings for the 1980-81 season were $5.10, or 24 percent above the adverse-effect wage rate of $4.09 [11]

The contract guarantees pay for three-fourths of the contract period (36 hours per week), even if weather does not permit work in the fields. The required work week is 40 hours, but most H-2 workers work Saturdays and Sundays to maximize earnings. Field and camp supervisors are predominantly West Indians, also on H-2 contracts; the Regional Labour Board's administrative arm, the British West Indies Central Labour Organisation (BWICLO), maintains liaison officers in the region to assist workers. The workers are paid once every two weeks; on payday they go to town to make purchases and mail money back to the islands. From each worker's biweekly pay 23 percent is deducted and sent back to a non-interest-bearing account on the home island that can only be redeemed on returning home. The pay is not subject to either U.S. taxes or Social Security payments.

In recent years the Department of Labor has been certifying approximately 18,000 foreign workers for seasonal employment in U.S. agriculture. One-half of these workers have come from the Caribbean to cut cane in Florida.[12] As the largest existing temporary labor program, the Florida H-2 arrangement can tell a great deal about the probable impact of an expanded H-2 program on Caribbean development. After briefly reviewing other relevant studies on the developmental effects of temporary employment, I shall summarize the results of a study of the Florida experience.

II. Existing Evidence

The body of literature dealing with the impact of migration on Third World development is increasing in quality and quantity. It is helpful to think of it in terms of levels, moving from the general to the specific. At the most abstract level, there are two general theoretical treatments of the subject. Derived from neo-classical economics, the equilibrium model posits a development-fostering role for migration. In moving from low-income, labor-surplus countries to high-income, labor-scarce developed countries, the migrant not only increases his or her own standard of living, but by remitting earnings contributes to the development of the sending society. Furthermore, migrants return home with new skills and aspirations, and in their absence local wages are bid up. The competing historical-structural view, derived from the Marxist tradition, stresses that migration tends to perpetuate the underdevelopment of the sending societies. Overseas wages are too low to generate savings and investment in expanded production at home. On the contrary, remittances are diverted into consumption and speculative activities. Because they are employed abroad in menial tasks, migrants do not acquire new skills, nor does their absence improve the local job market.[13] For the purposes of this chapter, this literature is intrinsically flawed to the extent it specifies neither the developmental context nor nature of migration.

At a second level, there exist empirical studies of the relationship between migration and development. Here are some studies dealing specifically with labor migration and others with migration and development in the Caribbean. The former are largely based on guestworkers in Western Europe.[14] A cursory review of this literature suggests that the developmental impact of guestworker migration

on the sending societies is quite limited. However,
one must exercise care in generalizing such conclusions
to the Caribbean, most importantly because the sending
societies are not the same but also because the kind of
labor migration varies significantly. European
guestworkers were contracted for industrial employment
for periods extending for several years. In contrast,
the labor migration currently permitted under section
H-2, and contemplated under the Simpson-Mazzoli bill,
is seasonal and agricultural.

In a recent review of studies of migration and
development in the English-speaking Caribbean,
Rubenstein concluded that "remittances, and perhaps the
entire migratory system as presently constituted, are
detrimental to the long-term prospects for economic
improvement in the societies."[15] This view concurs
with findings from studies of the Hispanic
Caribbean.[16] All are limited, however, by the fact
that they deal with long-term emigrants, both legal to
Great Britain and Canada and illegal to the United
States.

Elsewhere we have observed that it is reasonable
to expect that workers who enter the United States for
temporary seasonal employment are likely to behave
differently than long-term residents abroad.[17]
Unfortunately very little literature speaks directly to
such behavior. Marshall and Whyte are completing a
study of seasonal labor migration from the Eastern
Caribbean to Canadian agriculture. Since their
preliminary findings provide useful comparisons with
this work, they will be frequently cited in this
chapter.[18] The largest experiment in temporary worker
policy, the Bracero program, apparently generated no
empirical evidence regarding the impact of such
migration on development in Mexico. Cornelius, Wiest
and Reichert have studied the effects of contemporary
Mexican migration to the United States.[19] Since much
of it is seasonal, their findings are relevant to our
interests here. In his study comparing legal (Green
card) and illegal migrants and nonmigrants in a rural
community of Michoacan, Reichert found that the
community as a whole was heavily dependent on seasonal
migration to the United States and that the three
groups differed substantially. Although the community
has been able to capture some migrant earnings through
a graduated public works assessment, he found no
evidence that migrants voluntarily invest in
development-fostering activities. Local investments
are too risky and their yield is too low to replace
migration to the United States. "In effect, money
earned in the United States has enabled migrants to
raise their standard of living to a level that can only
be maintained through recurrent migration."[20]

Although the existing literature does not offer much hope regarding the contribution of temporary labor migration to Caribbean development, it does not deal directly with temporary labor migration from the Caribbean. I will now turn to the findings of a study of the H-2 program in the Florida sugar industry, which fulfills the strict criteria needed to evaluate the impact of temporary labor migration on Caribbean development and serves as a prototype for future temporary worker policy.

III. The Case of Seasonal Employment in the Florida Sugar Industry

This section summarizes the relevant findings of a survey administered, at the end of the 1980-81 season, to a sample of the Caribbean work force seasonally employed by the Florida sugar industry.[21] Before turning to the relationship between migration and development, the sociodemographic profile of the workers presented in Table 8.2 is discussed.

Profile of the Work Force

The data summarized in Table 8.2 merit some elaboration. First, although not captured in the table, the distinctive character of the workers from Barbados needs to be underlined: They are better educated (100 percent had some elementary education), more mobile, more urban, and better off economically than workers from the four other islands. This characterization is in keeping with Barbados' standing as the most developed of the sending countries. Second, the educational attainment of the cane cutters is low. For example, according to the 1970 Jamaican census, average schooling for males between the ages of 15 and 64 on that island was 6.1 years, or more than two years greater than the H-2s.[22] It is also interesting to note that the Florida cane cutters have significantly less formal education that the Caribbean farmworkers Marshall and Whyte studied in Canada.[23] The sample's figure for mean years of schooling declines as the number of seasons worked increases, indicating that the younger workers are better educated. Third, consistent with the multiple occupations characteristic of the West Indies, most respondents reported having more than one job; construction-related activities were the second most frequent category.[24] Nevertheless, the importance of farming to the group (again excepting the Barbadians) is unmistakable; this fact also contrasts with Whyte's findings.[25] Fourth, the small amount of land cultivated indicates the marginal nature of the farming in which they engage. Finally, the large household size and high proportion of dependent members suggest that the seasonal laborers directly support a substantial number of people back in the islands. In addition, most have dependents (children) outside the household of residence.

Table 8.2

Summary Characteristics of H-2 Work Force
In Florida Sugar Industry

Characteristic	Value
Educational Attainment	
No schooling	13.0%
Average years primary schooling of remainder	3.9 years
Some secondary schooling	4.4%
Geographic Mobility	
Currently residing in country of birth	97.3%
Currently residing in parish of birth	66.2%
Occupation	
Farming principal occupation	63.8%
Farming second occupation	37.1%
Did some farming in previous year	88.4%
Average size of plot	2.2 acres
Household Composition	
Average household size	6.3 persons
Average dependents under age 15	3.0 persons
Members (including respondent) with jobs	1.6 persons

Source: McCoy/Wood Survey, Supra. fn. #21.

Composition of the labor force is hardly
coincidental. Industry representatives deliberately
recruit from the semiprolitarianized peasantry of the
sending islands.[26] Dependent on both wage labor and
small-scale agricultural production for subsistence,
this social stratum is accustomed to arduous physical
labor and characterized by high rates of
unemployment. For every opening in the labor force,
several eager candidates are available. This means
that employers have the pick of the lot in selecting
members for the 40 percent not already predesignated.
Whether this practice results in the most skilled and
motivated workers being skimmed off to the detriment of
the sending society can only be conjectured, although
it seems less likely than in the case of permanent
emigration.

The structural characteristics of the work force
have two other consequences relevant here. Being self-
sufficient small farmers, the workers are capable of
maintaining themselves and their households in the off-
season, or in the event that they are not selected to
cut cane in Florida. This gives the H-2 workers a
considerable cost advantage over domestic workers,
since neither their employers nor the host community
assume any responsibility for supporting them in the
off-seasons.[27] Second, those workers chosen for the
cane harvest would seem to have the means for
generating significantly higher earnings than
nonmigrants and, thereby, for contributing to both
their own advancement and their community's
development. To test this hypothesis with the study's
data, which are not longitudinal, in some of the
remaining analysis the sample is divided into
categories according to the number of seasons
previously worked (none: 65 workers or 25.7 percent;
one to three: 68 workers or 27.0 percent; four to
six: 70 workers or 28.0 percent; and more than six
seasons: 48 workers or 19.3 percent).[28]

This step is taken on the assumption that the
repeat workers are more likely to engage in
developmental fostering behavior for two reasons: (1)
Previous seasons have allowed them to take care of
basic survival and consumer needs (i.e., after the
initial purchase of consumer durables, the demand in
each household declines), and (2) each season builds
the assurance of subsequent participation and the
income thereby generated. By controlling for possible
confounding variables, such as island of residence,
age, and education, we should be able to determine if
repeated labor migration does produce effects that are
conceivably developmental in their impact.

Overseas Earnings

Advocates of both the equilibrium and historical-structural perspectives agree that, within socioeconomic strata, migrants earn more than nonmigrants as a result of migrating. Data on the earnings of H-2 workers in the Florida sugar industry do not challenge this consensus.

Respondents in the sample reported average gross and net biweekly wages for the 1980-81 season of $420 and $245, respectively. After subtracting various deductions, including the 23 percent mandatory savings that is returned home and extrapolating across the entire season, the seasonal income from cutting cane in Florida was estimated to be $3,990.[29] Given that per capita GNP is $2,010 in Barbados, $1,352 in Jamaica, and well under $1,000 in the three small islands, the opportunity to cut cane would appear to be financially rewarding.[30] In fact, when asked why they wanted to cut cane, the workers' most frequent answer was to earn more income. The second most frequent response was to be able to purchase items not available locally. In interpreting the relative magnitude of earnings, it is important to remember that, on the one hand, the cane cutter comes from the poorest segment of West Indian society; on the other, more than six persons are dependent on his overseas earnings.

The multiple classification analysis of earnings reported in Table 8.3 reveals that after controlling for island of residence, age, and education, veteran workers earn substantially more than novices. The average net biweekly wage of workers with the most experience is almost $96 greater than that of the novice workers. This 48 percent wage differential constitutes proof that men who are repeat participants in the migrant labor stream do indeed have higher incomes than novice migrants. It also demonstrates the value of experienced workers to their employers since total wages are closely linked to individual productivity through the piecerate system.

Table 8.3

Multiple Classification Analysis of the Biweekly Earnings
By Seasons Worked (U.S. dollars)

Grand Mean of Net Biweekly Wages	Independent Variables Seasons Worked	N[1]	Deviation from Mean Unadjusted	Adjusted[2]	Adjusted Mean Biweekly Wages
$247.8[3]	0	42	-38.6	-47.0	$200.8
	1-3	63	- 8.3	-11.9	$235.9
	4-6	64	3.7	6.9	$254.7
	6+	47	40.8	48.9	$296.7

[1]Number of cases; excludes those with any missing data.
[2]Controlling island of residence, age, and education.
[3]Net pay for fortnight prior to the interview.

Remittances

The next step in determining the developmental
impact of seasonal labor migration is to trace income
earned cutting cane back to the islands. The first way
this occurs is through the mandatory savings plan by
which 23 percent of the gross biweekly wages of each
worker is deducted and deposited in a non-interest-
bearing account back home. The plan not only acts as
an inducement for the worker to return, but it also
generates hard currency for his island. Money
accumulated in this account is redeemed in local
currency to the worker on his return. Extrapolating
from the sample to the entire work force gives an
estimate of $7.7 million being remitted to the islands
through this channel during the 1980-81 season.

The second way earnings are transferred is through
mailed remittances. Substantial amounts of money per
worker are remitted in this fashion, primarily to
members of his immediate household. For example, over
90 percent of those workers interviewed reported
regularly sending an average of $71 to one recipient
back home, most frequently a wife (53.0 percent) or
girlfriend (23.8 percent). Many less frequently sent
funds to other recipients. When asked how this money
was used, 76 percent of the sample replied that it was
for daily household living expenses. By multiplying
the average amount sent by the frequency of the
remittance, an indication of the total remitted to the
leading recipient during the season is derived. If
island of residence, age, and education are controlled
for, analysis shows that workers with at least three
seasons of experience sent $266 more per season than
their counterparts with three years or less. Given
such a large difference, one might expect to find
distinct patterns of utilization of the funds
remitted. Thus far, however, the evidence demonstrates
that the Caribbean cane cutters give top priority to
household-related expenses. This pattern conforms
closely to that of the Canadian farmworkers and that
uncovered in other studies.[31]

Items purchased in the United States for use at
home constitute the third path through which resources
are transferred. In analyzing the developmental impact
of migration, the most important distinction in this
category would be between consumer items and small-
scale capital purchases that could be used to expand
the workers' and the islands' productive capacities.
No evidence was found that the workers invest a
significant amount of their earnings in the latter type
of purchase. Even recognizing that the exact
classification of items is difficult, the fact that
only 2.6 percent of the respondents had purchased tools

reveals a clear preference (for a variety of perfectly valid reasons) for consumer over capital items. Once again this preference is confirmed by other remittance studies.[32]

The final way H-2 workers transfer resources from the United States to the Caribbean is through the cash they take home at the end of the season. This survey generated a mean figure of $407, which, although not as large as might be expected, constitutes a particularly strategic resource since it is hard currency in the worker's possession. It undoubtedly reflects the end-of-season bonus customarily awarded by the growers.[33]

Table 8.4 presents a summary of the estimated flow of resources by category from Florida to the five sending islands for the 1980-81 harvest season. Overall the H-2 program generated nearly $19 million, a figure equal to 56.2 percent of total seasonal earnings and 9.1 percent of all development assistance received by the five islands during 1981.[34] The most important source of remittances, the mandatory savings plan, is also the one most directly controlled by local authorities. Whether these resources are invested in development-fostering activities, at either the individual or societal levels, is addressed in the following section.

Table 8.4

Estimated Total Value of Remittances for Entire
H-2 Work Force for 1980-81 Season
(U.S. dollars)

Mandatory savings plan	$ 7,764,000
Mailed remittances	4,774,000
Value of foods purchased in U.S.	4,551,000
Cash in hand on return	1,895,000
Total	$18,984,000

Utilization of Overseas Earnings

Two agents control the $19 million earned harvesting Florida sugar cane and remitted to the West Indies: the migrants and the island governments. Given the position of the former in the local economy, if they are to contribute to development, they would logically do so through investing in small-scale agriculture or off-farm businesses. Concretely this means using their overseas earnings to purchase land, equipment, and other production inputs and to hire local workers. The island governments have the discretion to invest the hard currency generated by the mandatory savings plan in a wider range of development projects. Of course, either agent may choose not to invest but rather to use the funds for maintenance and consumptive purposes.

The high percentage of mailed remittances dedicated to household living expenses and the predominance of consumer items in migrant purchases are preliminary evidence that the resources transferred to productive activities are secondary. When asked how they intended to use the cash with which they returned home with and the savings awaiting them in the islands, 60 percent of the sample answered that they would be used for housing related expenditures. The fact that livestock and farming expenditures were the next leading categories (27.9 and 19.9 percent, respectively) does offer some evidence of development fostering investment strategies. When veteran and novice workers are compared to determine differences that might provide additional support for this tendency, the findings are mixed.[35] Overall the incidence of developmentally oriented investment activities is rather low.

Before proceeding, it is appropriate to elaborate on expenditures for schooling in view of the importance universally assigned to upgrading human capital in the development process. Only 6 percent of the sample reported that it would devote overseas earnings to education of dependents. This indicator probably underestimates actual investment, however, since portions of the mailed remittances also pay for schooling. At the same time, only 13 percent of the work force reported taking advantage of the free high school equivalency night course offered in Florida by the employers. Therefore, it must be concluded that the impact of the H-2 program on the education of the workers and their children is mixed at best.

Because the workers come overwhelmingly from a class of peasant farmers, one direct path for them to expand their own productive capacities and to contribute to the development of the islands is to buy

and/or bring more land under cultivation. Although the
average plot size cultivated is small (Table 8.2), one
would expect to find that veteran migrants have
accumulated and farm more land than those workers with
less time in the program. Controlling for residence,
education, and life-cycle, we find that the difference
in land owned between the two groups is small (2.44
acres for those with four seasons or more versus 2.15
for those with less than four). The cumulative
overseas earnings of a worker who has repeatedly
migrated do not apparently go into the purchase of
land. Nor do they lead to increased land under
cultivation, according to Table 8.5. Partially
offsetting this is the finding that the proportion of
the work force owning land (regardless of the amount)
does correlate with the number of seasons worked,
rising from 20 to 40 percent.

Table 8.5

Multiple Classification Analysis of Land Cultivated
By Seasons Worked
(acres)

Grand Mean of Acres Cultivated	Independent Variables Seasons Worked	N[1]	Deviation from Mean Unadjusted	Deviation from Mean Adjusted[2]	Adjusted Mean Acres
2.27	0	41	-0.17	-0.21	2.06
	1-3	55	-0,11	-0.09	2.18
	4-6	57			2.44
	6+	41			2.44

[1]Number of cases excludes those with missing data.

[2]Controlling for island of residence, age, and education.

Similar analyses of assets such as livestock failed to detect significant differences in investment behavior according to seasons worked.[36] Furthermore, in a follow-up field study conducted in central Jamaica, Griffith found few differences between small farmers who seasonally migrated to Florida and those who did not along the dimensions of land use, crop production, and marketing and ownership of livestock and transportation vehicles.[37]

Another development-fostering mechanism posited for out-migration from rural areas by the equilibrium model is increased income for the nonmigrants through new employment opportunities and higher wages. The departing migrants increase the relative scarcity of labor and bid up wages.[38] Overseas remittances may be used to hire workers to tend the absent migrant's farm or to create new enterprises employing local workers. Even though we have no data relevant to the first effect, it would seem unlikely to stimulate wages in labor surplus situations like the Caribbean. As for hired labor, less than 10 percent of the sample reported that their farms were tended by hired workers while they were in Florida. Griffith found that those left in charge of the farm did hire day labor, but this practice amounted to only 1,024 full-time job equivalents, or 0.1 percent of the labor force, in rural central Jamaica.[39]

If the small farmers who annually migrate to Florida to cut sugarcane do not invest their earnings in expanded agricultural production, how do they use their overseas earnings? Aside from the money that goes for their daily living expenses and those of their dependents, the data leave little doubt that the accumulated earnings of seasonal migration to Florida go disproportionately into buying, building, furnishing, and expanding housing. Sixty percent of the sample listed housing as the most important investment category. The data in Table 8.6 demonstrate that the more seasons a worker migrates, the more likely he is to live in a house and, more importantly, to own the house in which he lives. This pattern is quite consistent with the findings of other migration studies.

Thus far this case study of Caribbean workers in the Florida sugar industry has demonstrated that, although temporary labor migration provides the migrant and his household with increased income and an elevated standard of living, it does not lead to savings and investment behavior that might strengthen his productive capabilities at home and assist in the development of his community. The same pattern holds at the macroeconomic level. H-2 labor in the Florida sugar industry provides the five sending islands

Table 8.6

Housing Arrangements by Seasons Worked
(percent)

Housing Variable	Seasons Worked	
	0-3	3+
Type of Residence		
House	79.2%	83.6%
Flat	11.7%	10.0%
Room	9.1%	6.4%
Type of Occupancy		
Own	37.3%	67.3%
Rent	26.5%	16.0%
Live with Parents	21.2%	8.2%
Family Property	13.0%	5.4%
Other	2.0%	3.0%

substantial benefits. In exchanging a resource in abundance locally (labor) for one that is scarce (foreign currency), the program helps alleviate rural poverty and unemployment, on the one hand, and chronic balance-of-payments deficits and low hard-currency reserves, on the other. The financial contribution is crucial to the political stability of the Caribbean in periods like the present when regimes in the region are grappling with declining terms of trade and growing foreign debts. Although not denying the significance of the H-2 programs to the islands' immediate economic and political well-being, we could find no evidence that local authorities target the resources transferred through it for developmental purposes. Rather they are comingled in the general pool of foreign exchange, which is primarily used to meet current obligations.[40]

IV. Summary

For more than four decades thousands of workers from the English-speaking Caribbean have annually travelled to south Florida to cut sugarcane. A survey administered to a sample of the 1980-81 work force

demonstrates that this temporary labor program benefits
the participants with employment remunerated at a rate
considerably in excess of wage rates on the islands.
Substantial proportions of the overseas earnings are
remitted home to the worker's dependents and island
economies. There is little question that the H-2 labor
program in the Florida sugar industry sustains a higher
quality of life than that enjoyed by nonparticipants
through the increased income and access to a broader
range of consumer items it affords the seasonal
migrants. A major advantage is that it provides
participants with the resources for improving their
housing.

The study of H-2 labor gives no indication that
either the workers or their governments systemically
invest the resources transferred from the United States
in development-fostering activities. The significance
of such a conclusion is twofold. First, it
corroborates the conclusions of studies of other types
of migration and development in the Caribbean and labor
migration and development in other regions of the
world. Legal temporary-worker programs, as currently
constituted, are no more supportive of Caribbean
development than are European guestworker programs of
Mediterranean development or other types of migration
of Caribbean development. The Marshall-Whyte study of
temporary Caribbean workers in Canada reinforces such
pessimistic conclusions.[41]

Second, the failure of seasonal employment to
generate Caribbean development means that migrants are
dependent on migration to maintain their standard of
living. This leads to a conclusion similar to that
reached by Reichert in a study of a Mexican
community: "Decades of out-migration have fostered the
attitude among townspeople that U.S. wage labor is the
key to prosperity and success. . . ."[42] Because the
small farmers of the five sending islands can only
sustain a higher life style through repeated migration,
Florida sugar growers are guaranteed a motivated,
experienced and highly productive labor force, one that
they have fought hard to keep.[43]

V. Policy Implications

Given the above findings, should the Caribbean
seek greater participation in the U.S. temporary labor
market, in the event that U.S. agricultural interests
eventually succeed in easing restrictions on foreign
workers? Are there changes that would "reduce the
costs and multiply the benefits" (to use Pastor's
phrase) of seasonal labor migration to Caribbean
development?

Although I have dealt elsewhere with the questions

of whether foreign workers are needed and what are
their costs and benefits to the United States, it is
appropriate to review the issue here since it puts into
perspective their function and status.[44] The debate
over foreign workers in the United States is based
almost entirely on the perception of whether there is a
domestic labor shortage or not. Supporters of an
affirmative answer argue that there are insufficient
domestic applicants for various jobs in agriculture.
But are these temporary or recurring seasonal shortages
that exist every year? If U.S. workers will not take
certain jobs, one answer might be to improve wages and
working conditions to make them more attractive. An
alternative would be to seek permanent immigrants to
fill permanent shortages. However, immigrants will
leave farm labor as soon as the opportunity presents
itself. As currently constituted, it is no more
attractive to them than to long-term residents.
Therefore, only foreigners from low-income countries,
who are admitted to the United States for the sole
purpose of cutting sugarcane and are deported if they
cease cutting, will do such work.

From this perspective, nonimmigrant labor policy
converts nationality to a labor control mechanism.
Does the availability of foreign workers obviate the
need to make the work more attractive and perpetuate
industries based on "arduous and badly paid jobs," as
Castells charged?[45] How is it decided which employers
have access to such a labor force? These questions
were raised in the United States in the recent debate
over the Simpson-Mazzoli bill. Their significance here
is that they make clear that Caribbean workers are
being asked to take jobs that are unacceptable to U.S.
workers and assume second-class status while employed
on a nonimmigrant basis in the United States.

Once the special nature of temporary employment in
the United States is recognized, Caribbean nations do
have valid reasons to pursue expanded participation in
the U.S. labor market. These include the strong
tradition of labor migration that exists in the
Caribbean, the undeniable fact that it provides the
migrants and their dependents with a higher standard of
living, and the widespread belief that it relieves the
sending societies of overpopulation, unemployment, and
insufficient foreign exchange.

In view of the pressures for participation in
temporary labor programs, what policy measures--
unilateral, bilateral, or multilateral--could be
adopted that would (1) induce the migrants to
voluntarily divert more of their overseas earnings into
agricultural production and off-farm businesses and (2)
better utilize the foreign exchange generated?
Although no one can deny the preeminence of the

developmental context and the secondary role of labor
migration, this study does suggest certain policy
changes that might strengthen the developmental impact
of temporary worker programs.

Changes in U.S. immigration policy that could
contribute to Caribbean development include (1)
recognizing statutorily the developmental consequences
for sending Third World countries of U.S. immigration
policy and authority for the federal government to
promote them; (2) lengthening the maximum period that
temporary migrants may work in the United States (up to
two years) and discouraging them from repeat migration
on the assumption that a longer, one-time-only
opportunity would act as a stronger incentive to save
for investment in income generating activities back
home (on the negative side, it could increase the
incidence of not returning home when the contract is up
and deny U.S. employers the skilled repeat worker); and
(3) removing any distinction between foreign and
domestic workers for employment purposes. This last
measure would serve to minimize the cost advantages to
employers of the former while at the same time
extending greater protection to them.[46] The federal
income taxes and Social Security payments deducted
might be rebated to the worker and his island in
special development-enhancing schemes.

This study has not analyzed why the small farmers
who cut cane in Florida do not invest in agricultural
production back home. Nor has it examined why the
foreign exchange generated is not better utilized for
development purposes. Both issues fall well outside
its purview. Nevertheless, even conceding that failure
of development-fostering behavior by the migrants and
their home governments is rooted in the structure of
Caribbean agriculture and exigencies of international
finance, the current arrangement could be improved to
provide incentives for individual investment and
institutions for development. The mandatory savings
plan operating in the Florida sugar program is
inequitable and counterproductive for development. If
the home governments are going to appropriate the
workers' overseas earnings, even if only on a temporary
basis, they ought to funnel them into development
projects of perceived benefit to the contributors. The
Mexican migrants studied by Reichert were at least able
to see the public works constructed in their village
from their special assessments.[47] Could not the island
governments likewise invest the interest earned from
the mandatory savings in labor-intensive projects in
the communities where the migrants reside? As it is,
they have no idea what the government does with the 23
percent deducted from their pay.

Beyond this, the island governments might join

with the United States to create a Caribbean remittance
bank or banks of the type suggested by Pastor. Such an
institution would not only direct funds earned overseas
into development projects of relevance to the workers;
it would also treat workers' remittances as deposits,
subject to both interest and withdrawal. As a
development bank, it would carefully evaluate
investment opportunities. The bank's lending power
could be augmented by matching loans and grants from
the United States under the Caribbean Basin Initiative
and the remitted income tax and Social Security
deductions withheld from the migrants. Representatives
of the migrants should be included on the bank's board
of directors. Working together, the U.S. Agency for
International Development, Caribbean governments and
employers could develop training programs for the
workers while they are in the United States, which
could be linked to development projects and employment
opportunities at home. In this way seasonal migration
would help strengthen the human capital of the sending
countries.

Should it be decided that more foreign workers are
needed in the United States, there is currently no
policy mechanism for deciding how many should come from
where. There is no assurance that the Caribbean
countries would share in the expanded labor market.
The H-2 program in the Florida sugar industry is
regulated by a private arrangement with the
employers. Once certified, they are free to recruit
workers anywhere. In the past they have not been above
playing the sending countries off against each
other.[48] To prevent inter-island competition, not
unlike that which occurred over the U.S. sugar quota,
and to protect Caribbean interests in the face of
strong pressure from Mexico, it is essential that
sending countries in the region coordinate their
efforts. This suggests that the procedure for
recruiting and selecting temporary workers be
established through an official agreement between the
United States and a Caribbean regional organization.

For the small, labor-exporting countries of the
Caribbean, the issues of who gets to work in the United
States and under what terms are crucial. They touch
not only on matters of equity and justice but of
national development. Although recognizing that
migration is important for a variety of reasons and
that its developmental impact will always be limited,
ways still exist in which policy might be altered to
strengthen the contribution of temporary labor
migration to Caribbean development. Chief among them
are incentives to participants for development-
fostering behavior and the need for the nations in the
region to present a united front in seeking expanded

access to the U.S. labor market. For its part, the government of the United States needs to minimize the differences between domestic and foreign workers and use its foreign assistance to reinforce the developmental activities of temporary workers from the Caribbean.

Notes

1. Alan B. Simmons, "Migration and Rural Development: Conceptual Approaches, Research Findings and Policy Issues," paper prepared for the Expert Group Meeting on Population Distribution, Migration and Development organized by the United Nations Population Division, Tunis, March, 1982.

2. The study on which this paper is based was financed by a grant from the National Institute for Child and Human Development (RO1-HD-14277-01). The Center for Latin American Studies and the Division of Sponsored Research at the University of Florida supported additional field work in Florida and the West Indies. The project was a joint undertaking with Charles Wood. Although his assistance on this paper is greatly appreciated, I alone am responsible for the interpretations and errors found in it. The comments of Robert Pastor, Alan Simmons and Oded Stark on the conference draft were also helpful.

3. Simmons, "Migration and Rural Development" Supra. fn. #1, pp. 10-11.

4. Terry L. McCoy and Charles H. Wood, "Caribbean Workers in the Florida Sugar Cane Industry," Occasional Paper No. 2, Caribbean Migration Program, Center for Latin American Studies, University of Florida, Gainesville, December, 1982, pp. 6-7.

5. U.S. Congress, Senate, Committee on the Judiciary, Subcommittee on Immigration, "The West Indies (BWI) Temporary Alien Labor Program, 1943-1977: A Study," 95th Congress, Second Session (1978), pp. 16-18.

6. McCoy and Wood, "Caribbean Workers in the Florida Sugar Cane Industry" Supra. fn. #4, pp. 6-7.

7. DOL Regulations as printed in the Federal Register, 43, 1-0313 (May 10, 1978).

8. The January 27, 1985 edition of the New York Times reported (p. 1) that "The Immigration and Naturalization Service is preparing new rules that would make it much easier for farmers to bring foreign workers into the United States temporarily to pick fruit and vegetables."

9. In June 1984 Gulf and Western announced that it was selling its sugar division, which operated in Florida and the Dominican Republic ("Business Monday,"

The Miami Herald, June 25, 1984, p. 5). The corporation grew sugar on 90,000 acres and employed 3,500 workers in season and 600 year-round in Florida. In the Dominican Republic it owned 240,000 acres and employed 300,000, many of them seasonal cane cutters from Haiti. Although the company found a buyer in October, who promised to maintain production in Florida, sugar production throughout the world has become increasingly problematic in recent years (see Terry L. McCoy, "U.S. Sugar Policy and its Effects on the Caribbean," paper presented at the IX Annual Conference of the Caribbean Studies Association, St. Kitts, May 30-June 2, 1984).

10. "Business Monday," The Miami Herald, May 16, 1983, p. 18.

11. George F. Sorn and James Terrill, "Testimony of the Florida Fruit and Vegetable Association Before House Subcommittee on Labor Standards (Presented on behalf of the Florida Sugar Cane Employers of H-2 Workers)," April 11, 1983, Belle Glade, Florida, p. 54.

12. U.S., Employment Service, Division of Labor Certification, "Labor Certifications Granted for Temporary Foreign Workers (H-2's) in Agriculture and Logging Occupations," January 29, 1982, and U.S., Senate, Committee on the Judiciary, Subcommittee on Immigration, "The West Indies (BWI) Temporary Alien Labor Program: 1943-1977," Supra. fmn. #5, p. 27.

13. For a fuller discussion of both models, see Edwin P. Reubens, "Interpreting Migration: Current Models and a New Integration," Occasional Paper No. 29, New York Research Program in Inter-American Affairs, New York University (1981) and Charles H. Wood, "Equilibrium and Historical-Structural Perspectives on Migration," International Migration Review, 16, No. 2 (1982), pp. 298-319.

14. See Chapter 15 in this volume and Philip L. Martin and Mark J. Miller, "Guestworkers: Lessons from Western Europe," Industrial and Labor Relations Review, 33, No. 3 (April, 1980), pp. 315-333.

15. Hymie Rubenstein, "Remittances and Rural Underdevelopment in the English-Speaking Caribbean," Human Organization, 42, No. 4 (Winter, 1983), p. 304.

16. Sherri Grasmuck, "The Impact of Emigration on National Development: Three Sending Communities in the Dominican Republic," Development and Change, forthcoming.

17. Charles H. Wood and Terry L. McCoy, "Seasonal Migration, Remittances and Development: A Study of Caribbean Cane Cutters in Florida," International Migration Review, Summer 1985, p. 4.

18. Anne V. Whyte, "Preliminary Results of a 1983 Survey of East Caribbean Seasonal Farmworkers to Ontario, Canada," Institute of Environmental Studies, University of Toronto, 1984.

19. Wayne Cornelius, Mexican Migration to the United States: The View from Rural Sending Communities, Migration and Development Study Group Monograph c/76-12 (Cambridge, Mass.: Massachusetts Institute of Technology, Center for International Studies, 1976); Raymond E. Wiest, "Implications for International Labor Migration for Mexican Rural Development" in Fernando Camara and Robert Van Kemper (eds.), Migration Across Frontiers: Mexico and the United States (Albany, New York: State University of New York at Albany, 1979); Joshua S. Reichert, "The Migrant Syndrome: Seasonal U.S. Wage Labor and Rural Development in Central Mexico," Human Organization, 40, No. 1 (1981), pp. 56-66.

20. Reichert, "The Migrant Syndrome," Supra. fn. #19, p. 63.

21. The survey was administered by the principal investigators and a team of interviewers in March 1981. During 1980-81, 8,460 Caribbean workers were employed in the sugar fields of south Florida. Since the distribution of this labor force by place of origin was known from industry records (82.2 percent from Jamaica, 6.0 from Barbados, 4.6 from St. Lucia, 6.7 from St. Vincent and 0.5 from Dominica), a quota system was used so that the number sampled from the five islands was proportional to each island's weight in the total mid-March population of H-2 workers. On the suspicion that there might be systematic differences associated with camp size and company, the quota method was also used to obtain a representative sample by size of living quarters and employer. About 17 percent of the sample was drawn from small camps (less than 200 workers); 49 percent from medium-size camps (201-599); and 34 percent from large ones (600 and larger). At each site, the country and camp quotas were met by randomly selecting individuals from the camp roster. Using these procedures, we obtained a sample of 251 cases representing the labor force as a whole. In order to permit inter-island comparisons, an additional 51 non-Jamaicans were interviewed. When the results

are presented by place of origin, we use the total sample of 302, collapsing St. Lucia, St. Vincent and Dominica into the single category: "small islands."

22. McCoy and Wood, "Caribbean Workers in the Florida Sugar Cane Industry," Supra. fn. #4, p. 21.

23. Whyte, "Preliminary Results..." Supra. fn. #18, pp. 4-5.

24. Gary Brana-Shute and Rosemary Brana-Shute in "The Unemployed of the Eastern Caribbean: Attitudes and Aspirations," unpublished research report, discuss the phenomenon of occupational multiplicity.

25. Whyte, "Preliminary Results..." Supra. fn. #18, pp. 5-6.

26. McCoy and Wood, "Caribbean Workers in the Florida Sugar Cane Industry," Supra. fn. #4, p. 11.

27. Terry L. McCoy, "The Ambiguities of U.S. Temporary Foreign Worker Policy," Population Research and Policy Review, 4(1985), pp. 31-49.

28. Although the contract between the growers and the Regional Labour Board limits the number of workers whom can be requested to 60 percent of a season's labor force, it does not prevent experienced workers who are not requested from entering the pool for the remaining 40 percent.

29. For a discussion of how the income data were generated and the steps taken to minimize errors and distortion, Charles H. Wood and Terry L. McCoy, "Caribbean Cane Cutters in Florida: Implications for the New International Division of Labor," in Steven Sanderson (ed.), The Americas in the New International Division of Labor (New York: Holmes and Meier, 1985), pp. 125-144.

30. Caribbean/Central American Action, C/CAA's Caribbean Databook, (Washington, D.C.: C/CAA, 1981).

31. Whyte, "Preliminary Results..." Supra. fn. #18, p. 13.

32. See, for example, Charles W. Stahl, "Labor Emigration and Economic Development," International Migration Review, 16 (Winter, 1982), pp. 872-876.

33. McCoy and Wood, "Caribbean Workers in the Florida Sugar Cane Industry," Supra. fn. #4, note 19 on p. 72.

34. We estimate total wages for the 1980-81 season to be $33.8 million. Of the amount not remitted (43.8 percent), 22.8 were accounted for by deductions for meals, clothing and the BWICLO assessment and 21.0 percent for other. Dividing the last item among all members of the labor force leads to the estimate that the average worker spent only $838 on himself (Wood and McCoy, "Seasonal Migration, Remittances and Development," Supra. fn. 17, p. 14 and tables 4 and 5).

35. Terry L. McCoy, "The Impact of Seasonal Labor Migration on Caribbean Development: A Case Study," paper presented at the annual meeting of the American Political Association, Chicago, September 1983, p. 10.

36. Wood and McCoy, "Seasonal Migration, Remittances and Development," Supra. fn. 17, p. 19.

37. David Craig Griffith, The Promise of a Country: The Impact of Seasonal U.S. Migration on the Jamaican Peasantry, Ph.D. dissertation, University of Florida, 1983, Chapter 4.

38. Keith Griffith, "On the Emigration of the Peasantry," World Development, 4, No. 5 (1976).

39. Griffith, The Promise of a Country, Supra. fn. #37, p. 127.

40. Although Jamaica, which had a current accounts deficit of $337 million in 1981, had guidelines for the allocation of foreign exchange, the first two priorities -- non-volitional (debt servicing) and government budget consumed most of the foreign exchange licensed by the government and sold at favorable rates. All other foreign exchange had to be purchased on the parallel market, over which there was less government control. Public officials have even less control over the allocation of foreign exchange in the four other islands (McCoy, "The Ambiguities of U.S. Temporary Foreign Worker Policy," Supra. fn. #27, p. 44).

41. Whyte, "Preliminary Results..." Supra. fn. #18.

42. Reichert, "The Migrant Syndrome," Supra. fn. #19, p. 64.

43. In comparing experienced workers with novices, we found that the former are not only more productive, as measured by earnings (workers with seven seasons or more earned 48 percent more than beginners), but that they were less prone to illness and sickness than the latter (Wood and McCoy, "Seasonal Migration, Remittances and Development" Supra. fn. #17, pp. 22-23). Therefore, the high percentage of repeat workers in the labor force maximizes its productivity.

44. McCoy, "The Ambiguities of U.S. Temporary Foreign Worker Policy," Supra. fn. #27.

45. Manuel Castells, "Immigration of Worker and Class Struggles in Advanced Capitalism: The Western European Experience," Politics and Society, (Spring, 1975), p. 54.

46. McCoy, "The Ambiguities of U.S. Temporary Foreign Worker Policy," Supra. fn. #27, pp. 46.

47. Reichert, "The Migrant Syndrome," Supra. fn. #20, p. 58.

48. McCoy and Wood, "Caribbean Workers in the Florida Sugar Cane Industry," Supra. fn. #4, pp. 8-12.

9. Illegal Caribbean Migration to the United States and Caribbean Development

Demetrios G. Papademetriou

I. Introduction

During the past decade, few issues have attracted more widespread and persistent attention among U.S. elites and the mass public than illegal immigration. The problem has become exacerbated by another factor: In terms of responsiveness to state intervention, few phenomena have proved as elusive and intractable as the control of unauthorized international migration. Yet, as this book's primary interest is in examining the impact of migration on the sending countries of the Caribbean, in this chapter I will attempt to assess the impact of illegal migration by relying on evidence collected in field studies about the socioeconomic and demographic profiles of those undocumented immigrants in the United States who originate in Caribbean countries. Among the key questions to be explored are whether that impact is positive, negative, or neutral, and whether it is likely to be very much different from that of legal, and presumably more permanent, migration.

One of the most ubiquitous and enduring axioms about international migration is that it is positively related to development. Assuming for a moment that, in terms of how each type of migration affects the sending society, the distinction between legal and illegal immigration might be largely moot, adherence to this axiom would also require that one look favorably toward its frequent corollary: that in the context of substantial emigration, Caribbean countries could reasonably expect to grow economically and gradually reach a dynamic milieu that offers both socio-cultural and psychological disincentives for external migration and offers socio-economic and, in certain instances, political incentives to return.

Although the data reported in this chapter do not always enable us to speak directly and authoritatively

on the precise nature of the relationship between
illegal international migration and development in the
Caribbean, they do allow us to draw a number of limited
conclusions. The limitations of these data are many
and serious and inherent in the nature of the research
problem: Illegal aliens are in the United States
clandestinely and are extremely difficult to identify
and locate--and even more difficult to interview.
Furthermore, very significant regional variations are
present in both the composition of such flows and the
manner in which illegal migrants become inserted into
local labor markets and local communities. In this
chapter, I will try to sift through some of these data
and compare some of the findings of studies on illegal
aliens from Caribbean countries with the results of a
still ongoing research project on illegal aliens in the
New York metropolitan area.

II. Caribbean Immigration to the United States

In few regions has international migration played
as pivotal a role as in the Caribbean Basin. In fact,
most political entities in the region owe their very
existence, as well as their specific sociodemographic,
linguistic, cultural, and economic configuration to the
migration of Europeans, Africans, and Asians. Although
these early migrations occurred during the age of
classical imperialism, more recent regional flows have
responded to the capital and labor needs of the
advanced industrial societies (especially the United
States) that have played, and continue to play, a
dominant role in the economy of the region.[1]
Caribbean immigration to the U.S. mainland takes
place along both immigrant and nonimmigrant lines. The
former peaked during the 1911-1920 period, when nearly
124,000 such immigrants entered the United States[2] and
began to pick up steam again in the 1950s, when it
reached a size comparable to forty years earlier. That
flow nearly quadrupled during the 1960s, to 470,000
immigrants, and increased by an additional 63 percent
in the 1970s -- to 741,000 people. Although virtually
all Caribbean nations were significant contributors to
this flow, six countries have been clearly dominant and
routinely account for between 90 and 95 percent of all
Caribbean immigration to the United States.[3]
These increases occurred within the context of
changes introduced by the 1965 Immigration and
Nationality Act, which abolished discriminatory quotas
based on national origin in favor of hemispheric
numerical limits.[4] Although the largest beneficiaries
of these changes were Asians (who saw their
representation rise in excess of 800 percent between
1965 and 1980), immigration from the Americas

maintained its privileged position under the new law in
spite of the numerical limits set for the Western
Hemisphere. In fact, the hemispheric proportion of
total immigration increased from about one-third in the
1950s to about 45 percent in the last two decades.
Within the same period, additional substantial long-
term changes are also evident. For instance, in the
1960s, Canada relinquished to Mexico its long-held
position as the principal regional source of
immigration to the United States. Mexico's ascendance
has reflected that of the region as a whole. Yet, the
most substantial gains have been registered by
immigrants from a group of countries denoted in U.S.
immigration statistics by the name of "West Indies."
Their numbers during the past fifteen years have nearly
doubled, and the share of such countries as Jamaica and
Trinidad and Tobago has increased at almost geometric
rates. Most of these immigrants are found in New York,
Florida, and New Jersey.[5]

Nonimmigrant admissions from the Caribbean to the
United States, however, have far outpaced immigrant
admissions. Among the former are visitors for business
or pleasure--by far the largest nonimmigrant category[6]-
-as well as students, diplomatic personnel, and other
official and quasi-official representatives of foreign
governments and multinational corporations. Of the
nearly 12 million nonimmigrants admitted to the United
States in 1981, 614,000 came from the Caribbean.[7]
Among these are many individuals of particular concern
to this paper: those who seek and obtain employment in
the United States in violation of the terms of their
visas.

In addition to these entrants, a number of
Caribbean-origin persons enter and work in the United
States under several nonimmigrant labor programs.[8]
Among those are the participants in not only the
Temporary Farm Worker program with Mexico (1917-1922)
and the subsequent Bracero program (1942-1964)[9] but
also in such other de jure but lesser known labor
programs as the border commuters,[10] the special
programs for the British West Indies (BWI)[11] and the
U.S. Virgin Islands,[12] and the H provisions[13] of the
Immigration and Nationality Act.

Finally, one "program" that is of paramount
importance for both source and destination countries is
illegal immigration. Although illegal immigrants are
in the United States formally in violation of the
country's immigration statutes, they can be regarded as
part of a massive de facto quasi-nonimmigrant
policy.[14] The often deliberate failure of the U.S.
immigration authorities to enforce the law and the
equivocal legislation with regard to such matters as
the hiring of undocumented workers acquiesces and in

effect encourages further illegal immigration. The existence of ethnic networks with their well-established pathways to the United States--and the ability of these networks to provide a number of essential services to newcomers--further reduces the many risks attendant to the decision to immigrate nd facilitate the newcomers' cultural and economic insertion into the receiving society.[15]

III. Caribbean Migration and Development

Caribbean immigration has been finely attuned to the needs and opportunities of its neighbors to the north.[16] This section will set the stage for evaluating whether this process has allowed substantial benefits to accrue to the countries of immigrant worker origin in the Caribbean. Two broad schools of thought will be briefly identified in an attempt to demonstrate how sharply contrasting theoretical and philosophical traditions combine with the inherent analytic and methodological complexity of the subject to feed the flames of contention and equivocation on the relationship between Caribbean emigration and development. One of the ancillary objectives of this chapter will be to test these perspectives against the evidence from field studies.

For the student of international migration, the question of properly anchoring the study on a particular school of thought is important in that it often influences the outcome of the research[17] and the character of the ensuing recommendations. For instance, those whose basic premises adhere to the tenets of the classical liberal school are likely to applaud the entire process: Through individual initiative, sending countries are expected to experience considerable relief in unemployment, reduction in aggregate demand for both internally produced (but scarce) and imported consumer goods,[18] a lessening of the social welfare burden, an appreciable contribution to their foreign exchange reserves (through remittances), and a concomitant reduction in their substantial trade deficits. Last, but certainly not least, these societies are offered the considerable luxury to effect change gradually by siphoning off many individuals who might provide the critical mass for vocal and uncompromising demands for immediate structural changes.

In another large body of scholarship, however, authors are much more critical of the migration process. Adopting a historical-structural perspective, this group views emigration as a result of the incorporation of less-developed countries into more-advanced ones. The process of incorporation compounds the inequality among such countries and makes emigration an integral component of the capital accumulation process. In effect, then, emigration becomes an instrument in the "progressive subordination" of the weaker regions to the stronger ones and serves as a means of additional surplus extraction by the core (receiving) state.[19] In other words, emigration might be expected to worsen, rather than improve, the condition of the sending socieites vis-a-vis that of the receiving societies.

IV. Illegal Caribbean Migrants in New York: A Profile

The information reported in this section has been culled from a research project I directed in the New York metropolitan area. More specifically, it reports on three samples of unapprehended, undocumented aliens who sought the assistance of migration counselors of the Catholic Community Services (CCS) of the Archdiocese of Newark for matters ranging from regularization of status to employment placement and overall counseling. The migration offices of CCS are located in several cities in northern New Jersey. In sample I, information is reported from 856 of the organization's intake forms for the last quarter of 1980 through the end of 1981. Beginning with 1982, the organization began to use a new intake form for new clients on which I inserted about thirty questions of particular interest to the research project. As a result, the data from sample II (n=778) are considerably richer than those from sample I (n=856). Sample III (n=60) reports on a random sample drawn from sample II. During the first six months of 1984, these respondents were administered a questionnaire composed of 363 questions on such subjects as their socioeconomic background, their motivations for coming to the United States, details about their settlement in the United States and their incorporation into the U.S. labor market, and their plans for the future.

The questionnaire collects data of relevance to both sending and receiving communities. It affords both a microscopic and a macroscopic view. It looks at the goals and motivations of the family unit and the individual while permitting a glimpse of the structural causes and consequences of international migration. Social, economic, and political conditions at home and destination are examined. Finally, it sheds some light on the complex relationship between emigration, remittances, return, and development, by yielding hard evidence on the principal components of the arguments repeatedly heard during the ongoing debate on the proposed Immigration Reform and Control Act.

Whenever possible, the data from this study will

be compared and contrasted with data reported by a
number of other studies in this research area. Of
particular relevance will be research results that
focus on Caribbean-origin immigrants in the New York
area--regardless of legal status. At the same time
whenever possible comparisons will be drawn with the
results of studies that attempt to paint national
pictures of illegal immigration to the United States
from countries in the Western Hemisphere and pictures
of illegal aliens from Mexico. Before the empirical
evidence is presented, however, certain caveats about
the data must be made explicit: With the qualified
exception of the CENIET Mexican study[20] and the Gurak
study in New York,[21] all other studies, including the
one reported here, have used samples that are neither
replicable nor representative in a statistically valid
sense. Many of them rely on "snowball" techniques;
samples I and II in this chapter are self-selected
samples of persons who voluntarily sought the
assistance of Catholic Community Service
organizations. Sample III, on the other hand, is a
nonstratified simple random sample of sample II with a
response rate of nearly 80 percent.

Even in the two studies that appear to be more
statistically rigorous, the Gurak survey concentrated
only in areas known to be dominated by Colombians
(Queens) and Dominicans (Manhattan), and the CENIET
study focused on a sample of return migrants to Mexico
who were older than fifteen years of age and had worked
or had looked for work in the United States during the
previous five years. Thus, the results of the CENIET
survey will not convey any insights about people who
did not return to Mexico during the time of the survey
in 1978-1979. In fact, this survey is most useful in
comparisons between the characteristics of regular
commuters to the United States (almost half of whom
have legal residence and/or work status in the United
States) with those of noncommuters (almost all of whom
are illegal and are defined in the study as those who
entered the United States less than six times during
1978). Hence, as a result of the different timing--
ranging from the mid-1970s for some of the Mexican
studies and the North-Houston study[22] to 1984 for the
New York CCS study--and the different objectives,
priorities, and methodologies of these studies, the
comparability of these data sets is diminished. These
caveats should be kept in mind.

Nearly 94 percent of the respondents in sample III
(n=60) were from countries in the Western Hemisphere
and 77 percent of them originated in Central America
and the Caribbean. Table 9.1 gives the distribution of
all three samples by sex and country of origin. As can
be seen, Colombia, Haiti, El Salvador, and the

Table 9.1

Distribution For Three Survey Samples By
Principal Countries of Origin[1]

Country of	I N	I %	II N	II %	II Male	II Female	III N	III %	III Male	III Female
Argentina	8	1.0	13	1.7	11	2	1	1.7	1	-
Austria							1	1.7	1	-
Bolivia	3	0.4	6	0.8	4	2				
Chile	15	1.9	9	1.2	5	4	1	1.7	1	-
Colombia	101	13.1	105	13.5	55	50	6	10.0	4	2
Costa Rica	11	1.4	6	0.8	4	2				
Dominican Republic	24	3.1	33	4.2	22	11	6	10.0	4	2
Ecuador	42	5.5	37	4.8	20	17	2	3.3	2	-
Egypt	54	7.0	18	2.3	16	2				
El Salvador	96	12.5	210	27.0	136	73	18	30.0	9	9
Guatemala	18	2.3	12	1.5	7	5	1	1.7	1	-
Haiti	110	14.3	85	10.9	94	41	14	23.0	7	7
Honduras	14	1.8	12	1.5	9	3	1	1.7	-	1
Italy	3	0.4	7	0.9	6	1				
Jamaica	6	0.8	10	1.3	2	8	1	1.7	-	1
Mexico	15	1.9	32	4.1	20	12	1	1.7	1	-
Nicaragua	10	1.3	15	1.9	6	9	1	1.7	-	1
Peru	35	4.5	30	3.9	16	14	3	5.0	2	1
Poland	39	5.2	57	7.3	34	23				
Portugal	35	4.5	6	0.8	3	3	1	1.7	-	1
Spain							1	1.7	1	-
Trinidad & Tobago	3	0.4	7	0.9	2	5				
Uruguay	7	0.9	10	1.3	1	9				
Zaire							1	1.7	1	-
Other	121	15.7	58	7.4	-	-	-	-	-	-
Total	770	99.9	778	99.9	460 (59%)	316 (41%)	60	100	35 (58%)	25 (42%)

[1] An arbitrary cutoff of three subjects per country for sample I and five subjects per country for sample II has been employed.

Dominican Republic are heavily represented in all three
samples. Sex and age information on samples II and
III, when such information is available, indicates that
slightly less than 60 percent of the respondents are
males and similar proportions of respondents fall
between the ages of 21 and 44 years of age. The
average age for sample II respondents is almost 32
years whereas that for sample III subjects is slightly
under 35 years.

Although the age data for the proportion of the
samples that falls within the prime ages of economic
activity are comparable to those of most other studies
on illegals, the average values for age are somewhat
higher than the norm. For instance, North and Houston
reported an average age of less than 29 years;
Bustamante[23] less than 28 years; van Arsdol[24] slightly
less than 31; and the CENIET study, slightly more than
31 for noncommuters and nearly 39 years of age for
commuters.

Of the respondents in sample III, 58 percent were
married. The average size of the respondents'
households was 4.1 members, of whom 1.6 members were
minors (n=92). About 30 percent of these children were
born in the United States, and 35 percent were
attending school in the United States. Fifty-six
percent of all children lived with the respondents
whereas 8 percent were on their own but not in the
United States, and the remainder were living with
relatives abroad.

Table 9.2 provides an educational profile of
respondents in all three samples. The data indicate
that the respondents are quite well-educated: A
substantial group has had postsecondary education, and
mean and median values for samples II and III are about
ten years of formal schooling. This finding confirms
the information obtained in several other studies of
Caribbean immigrants, such as Pessar's sample of
Dominicans in New York[25] and Gurak's 1981 New York City
survey of Colombians and Dominicans,[26] as well as those
of an earlier National Survey of Emigration from the
Dominican Republic,[27] two samples of Costa Ricans and
Salvadorans,[28] and a sample of Haitians drawn in
1977.[29] The average distribution of the educational
levels of the samples in this study also coincides with
that of legal immigrants from the region reported
annually by the Immigration and Naturalization Service
(INS). These same data, however, sharply contrast with
most of the data reported for Mexican illegal aliens.
For instance, although approximately 60 percent of the
respondents in samples II and III had more than nine
years of formal education, the comparable figures for
the North-Houston sample were less than 30 percent; for
Maram's Hispanic legal and illegal garment and
restaurant workers in Los Angeles, 10 and 3.7 percent,

Table 9.2

Educational Profile of Three Survey Samples

Years of Education[1]	I		II		III	
	N	%	N	%	N	%
0-8	250	29.2	268	34.4	23	38.3
9-12	313	36.5	335	43.1	23	38.3
13-16	121	14.1	100	12.9	11	18.4
More than 16	25	2.9	18	2.3	3	5.0
Unascertained	147	17.2	57	7.3	-	-
Total	856	99.9	778	100.0	60	100.0
Mean	8.04		10.00		9.76	
Median	7.69		10.33		10.10	

[1]Data collection procedures for years of education were different in sample I where information was collected in grouped form.

respectively;[30] for van Arsdol's sample of illegals in Los Angeles slightly under 21 percent and for the illegal noncommuter respondents to the CENIET survey, the average education reported was 4.2 years.[31]

Before I report briefly on labor market matters, a final datum of interest is the subjects' duration of stay in the United States. In sample II the reported average stay was 37.9 months whereas the length of stay in sample III was 59 months. Much of the difference is a function of the relationship between the two samples and of the time when the question was asked: in 1982-83 for sample II and in 1984 for sample III. Although tentative, these data suggest that much of the new illegal immigration is of relatively recent origin and that the respondents have been in the United States much longer than those surveyed in the West Coast (mostly of Mexican origin).

The labor market status and participation of the subjects are also of particular interest to this chapter. In Table 9.3 the employment rates of the three samples are shown; they range from a little over 40 percent for sample I to nearly 77 percent for sample III. One should be careful not to assume here that illegal immigrants have high rates of unemployment, however. Instead, the rates are uneven because the person interviewed in every instance was the person who

approached the agency for a service. At times that
service was job placement--hence the high rate of
unemployment. However, because of the time-consuming
nature of obtaining a service, the spouse without
employment at the time was more likely to undertake
this task.

Table 9.3

Labor Market Status for Three Survey Samples

	I		II		III	
Status	N	%	N	%	N	%
Employed	355	41.4	447	57.4	46	76.6
Unemployed	307	35.8	204	26.2	12	20.0
No U.S. Employment	8	.9	59	7.5	2	3.3
In School	30	3.5	18	2.3	-	-
Other	-	-	42	5.3	-	-
Missing Information	156	18.2	8	1.0	-	-
Total	856	99.8	778	99.7	60	99.9

Of those employed, the vast majority earned more
than the minimum wage[32] (see Table 9.4). Only 16
percent of sample I earned less than the minimum wage,
a figure similar to that for the current jobs held by
sample III respondents (15 percent) and substantially
lower than that for either the jobs held by sample II
respondents at the time of the interview (22.5 percent)
or the previous jobs held by subjects of both samples
II and III (ranging between 42 and 59 percent). The
average wage for those employed from sample I was $3.65
per hour; that for sample II was $4.62 for their
present job and $4.02 for their previous job. Finally,
the average hourly earnings for sample III respondents
for their first job in the United States were $3.25;
for the job previous to their current one, $4.28; and
for their current job, $4.81 per hour. Again, the
figures are comparable with the $4.36 hourly wage
reported by Pessar's informants in 1982. Furthermore,
the average hourly wage earnings of our sample III are
also similar to those reported by Poitras for his Costa
Rican subjects (but not for his Salvadoran ones who
earned about 17 percent less). Again, however, a very

appreciable gap is apparent between earnings by
Mexicans and other illegal immigrants originating in
the Caribbean and elsewhere. For instance, in spite of
the problem with comparability across time, North and
Houston found that Mexican illegal immigrants earned
between one-quarter and 43 percent less than other
identifiable groupings of apprehended illegal
immigrants (such as whites, Eastern Hemisphere aliens,
and visa abusers), and CENIET subjects who worked in
the United States illegally in 1978 earned an average
wage of $23.00 per day for work concentrated heavily in
agriculture.

Table 9.4

Hourly Wages for Three Survey Samples

Hourly Wage (U.S. dollars)	I N	I %	II Present N	II Present %	II Last N	II Last %	III Present N	III Present %	III Previous N	III Previous %	III First N	III First %
3.35 and under	68	16.2	100	22.5	94	41.8	7	15.2	12	46.2	25	59.5
3.36 to 4.99	276	65.3	204	45.8	96	42.7	19	41.3	9	34.6	15	35.7
5.00 to 6.99	51	12.1	96	21.6	26	11.6	12	26.1	2	7.7	2	4.8
7.00 to 8.99	16	3.8	32	7.2	7	3.1	4	8.7	1	3.8	-	-
9.00 and above	11	2.6	13	2.9	2	0.9	4	8.7	2	7.7	-	-
Subtotal N	421	100.0	445	100.0	225	100.1	46	100.0	26	100.0	42	100.0
Missing cases	435		333		553		-		-		-	
Total N	856		778		778		60		60		60	
Average wage	3.56		4.62		4.02		4.81		4.28		3.25	

In Table 9.5 annual salary information for samples
II and III is given. In Sample II a mean annual salary
of $9,873 was reported for the job held at the time of
the interview--an increase of $1,300 over the average
annual salary for the job held previously. Comparable

Table 9.5

Annual Salary Information for Samples II and III
(U.S. dollars)

Mean	II		III			
	Present	Past	Present	Past	First	Gross Family Income
N	$9,873	$8,535	$12,614	$10,296	$8,181	$18,549

Annual Salary By Hemisphere for Sample II

Annual Salary (U.S. dollars)	Western Hemisphere		Eastern Hemisphere	
	N	%	N	%
Less than $6,968	65	19.9	10	20.0
6,969-8,736	97	29.7	12	24.0
8,737-12,459	104	31.8	13	26.0
12,460-16,619	39	11.9	10	20.0
More than 16,619	22	6.7	5	10.0
Total	327	100.0	50	100.0

Average Hourly Wage $4.77 $5.09

Annual Salary by Marital Status
and Hemisphere for Sample II

Marital Status	Western Hemisphere		Eastern Hemisphere	
	N	Salary	N	Salary
Single	113	$ 8,740	15	$ 9,159
Married	181	10,523	33	11,367
Other	33	8,979	2	10,878

figures for the current job in sample III were $12,614
mean annual salary, an increase of $2,328 over the
previously held job and of $4,433 over the first job
the subject held after arriving in the United States.
For this sample, household income was also ascertained
and registered a mean value of $18,549. As usual for
immigrant households, several members pool their income
so that the household earns an amount substantial
enough not only to allow it to enjoy an economic status
dramatically higher than it could in its home country

but also to build some equity in the United States.
The remaining data reported on this table are also of
interest. Subjects from sample II who originated in
the Eastern Hemisphere make a substantially better
showing in terms of both annual salary and average
hourly wage than those from the Western Hemisphere.
Furthermore, when controlling for marital status, the
hemispheric difference continues to hold: Married
respondents show substantially higher earnings than
single ones.

A different way of looking at employment and wage
data for sample II is displayed in Table 9.6, which
lists earnings according to type of employment and
sex. The vast majority of the 375 jobs on which
detailed information was available were in the
manufacturing sector where 70 percent of the male
respondents and 63 percent of the female respondents
were employed. The annual wages paid for those jobs
ranged from $9,138 to $12,928 for men and from $8,042
to $8,977 for women. The only other significant
concentrations of jobs were found in hotel and
restaurant services (where 10 percent of the men and 5
percent of the women were employed) and in domestic
service for women (13 percent). The wage differential
in annual salary between men and women for the same
type of hotel and restaurant jobs was $1,621 whereas
for the same category of manufacturing activity it
ranged from 12 percent in unskilled positions to 33
percent for supervisory and technical manufacturing
positions. Besides the typical and widespread wage
discrimination according to sex that these data
confirm, the table also shows the job categories in
which virtually all Caribbean immigrants in the
Northeastern United States--regardless of legal status--
are found: secondary-sector manufacturing jobs and
low-level service occupations. In the southwestern
United States, however, substantial proportions of
illegal Mexican immigrants work in agricultural
occupations. For instance, between 40 and 50 percent
of those subjects studied by Cornelius[33] in the mid-
1970s were employed in that sector; the figures for the
CENIET subjects were nearly 50 percent; and those for
the North-Houston study were 18.8 percent for the
entire sample and 24.1 percent for the Mexican
subsample.

When the wage data for this study are juxtaposed
with data on earnings for Hispanics in New Jersey (as
tabulated in the 1980 census, see Table 9.7), it
becomes clear that although the two sets of data are
not fully comparable, this study's respondents compare
well. For instance, New Jersey Hispanics are found in
all income categories, but this study's respondents are
virtually nonexistent in income categories over $20,000

Table 9.6

Job Category and Annual Salary for Undocumented Aliens
by Sex for Sample II

Job Category	Male Annual Average Wage (U.S. dollars)	N	%	Female Annual Average Wage (U.S. dollars)	N	%
Manufacturing (unskilled)	$9,138	53	21	$8,042	28	23
Manufacturing (skilled)	10,399	91	36	8,977	43	36
Manufacturing Technician	12,928	34	13	8,632	5	4
Utilities	18,720	1	-	-	0	-
Construction	12,411	8	3	7,280	1	-
Service, Hotel	9,318	25	10	7,697	6	5
Transportation	13,273	12	5	6,968	1	-
Service, Finance	12,064	1	-	-	0	-
Service, Pers.	11,098	4	2	7,992	2	2
Other	9,605	22	9	8,179	17	14
Domestic	-	0	-	7,917	16	13
Self-Employed	14,829	4	-	6,968	1	1
Total		255	99		120	98

[1] Sex distribution of those employed is 68% male and 32% female.

per year (over 25 percent of Hispanics in New Jersey
earn more than that figure). At the same time,
however, none of this study's samples had any
respondents in the category of less than $2.00 per
hour, whereas 18 percent of the New Jersey Hispanic
residents fall into this group. This favorable
comparison holds further when median family incomes are
compared between total Hispanic households and sample
III. In fact, sample III respondents score nearly
$1,500 better than New Jersey Hispanics in this
category--a function of multiple jobholders per
household, typical of survival strategies of recent and
illegal immigrants. These figures also holds well when
compared to the median income for white and black
households for New Jersey ($21,900 and $12,670,
respectively) -- in spite of the two-to-three-year time
lag between the two data sets.

Table 9.7

Income Distribution of Spanish-Origin Persons in New Jersey
According to 1980 Census
Compared to Income Levels of Subjects to New Jersey CCS Study

Income(U.S. dollars) Hourly	Annual	% of Total Population	% of Combined Samples I and II Annual Income
Less than $2.00	Less than $5,000	18.07	0.8
2.41-4.80	5,000-9,999	17.12	71.2
4.81-7.21	10,000-14,999	15.98	20.4
7.22-9.61	15,000-19,999	15.37	5.5
9.63-12.01	20,000-24,999	12.06	2.7
-	25,000-34,997	13.03	-
-	35,000-49,999	.06	-
-	More than 50,000	.02	-

Additional Income Data

	New Jersey Study	Sample II(n=46)
Median income	$14,597	$16,032
% below poverty level	26.4%	6%
Median family income, 1980 White Black	$21,900 12,670	

Source: 1980 U.S. Census data compared to income levels of New Jersey
in subjects in Catholic Community Services Study.

On the other hand, respondents to this study fare
less well when their earnings are juxtaposed with other
average gross economic indicators for New Jersey
metropolitan areas. In particular, the concentration
of subjects in low-paying manufacturing and service
jobs and their junior status in these jobs (the average
hourly wage for all manufacturing jobs in New Jersey in
1982 was $8.71) prevent them from making an even better
economic showing in the per capita income category;
they lag nearly 25 to 35 percent behind the average for
the New Jersey sample (data not shown). In spite of
this evidence and in line with my comments on the
vitality of the multiple income households, a
significantly lower proportion of the households in
this study falls below thepoverty level for New Jersey
than do Hispanics as a group. In fact, only 17 percent
and 5 percent of the respondents for samples II and
III, respectively, fall below the poverty level when
size of household is a controlled variable. The
comparable figure for Hispanics in New Jersey in 1980
was 26.4 percent.

The data on the socio-demographic and economic
background of this study's respondents support other
surveys that indicate that the prior residences of
illegal immigrants in the northeastern United States
are mostly urban; that such immigrants are typically
employed prior to emigration (77 percent of sample
III); that they elude the immigration authorities with
relative ease; that they are frequently repeat
immigrants (one-third of sample III respondents had
been in the United States more than once); that they
came to the United States primarily to advance their
economic status (although nearly one-fourth cited
political reasons as the main cause); that they are
economically rather successful (including experiencing
substantial upward economic mobility with each job
change); and that they are traveling along well-
established and smoothly functioning ethnic pathways
and networks, which assist them repeatedly and
substantively during the course of the immigrant
experience.[34] Significantly, the respondents reported
almost as frequently receiving assistance from friends
(nearly 50 percent of those who reported that they
received some assistance) as from family.

The depth and relative success of the economic and
social incorporation of the respondents in the United
States are reflected in their reluctance to consider
returning to an environment over which they can
exercise little control. In fact, 96 percent of those
who reported a change in plans about the likely length
of their stay indicated that it would be substantially
longer than they expected when they arrived, and 80
percent indicated that it was either "probable" or

"very probable" that they would still be in the United States ten years after the interview.

The question of intended length of stay is a difficult one to address because it is often inextricably intertwined with an enduring and elusive concept: the almost universal expression of the intention to return. When probed, however, the respondents expressed rather clear intentions that, to a large degree, expose the often mythical nature of this concept. Although a plurality of respondents was "not sure" about how long they expected to stay in the United States when they first came to the New York metropolitan area, only about one-fifth said that they expected to stay as long as five years. Five years later (the average length of stay of the respondents in sample III, from which these and all subsequent data have been culled, was 59 months), almost all subjects admitted to a change in plans in favor of a longer stay, and 88 percent now expect to stay in the United States for a minimum of an additional five years.

When asked why they have continued to stay in the United States beyond their original projections, five conditions seem to be of particular relevance (although none attracted more than 15 percent of the sample): Two responses revolve around family matters--starting a family here and reunifying the family in the United States; two responses revolve around the continuing economic and political uncertainty at home; the final answer involves an explicit economic reason--success in adapting to the United States. The importance of economic considerations -- perhaps not as clear in the above five answers -- becomes starkly evident when those respondents who indicated that they now expected to be in the United States ten years from now (80 percent of the total) and fifteen years from now (75 percent of the total) were asked why they now planned on such lengthy stays. Forty-six percent identified "economic opportunities in the U.S.," followed by "plans for their children" (26 percent), "restrictive political conditions at home" (24 percent), and the superior "quality of life" in the United States (22 percent).

The resolve of the respondents to remain in the United States and the depth of their incorporation into their adopted community are corroborated further when a remarkable 72 percent of the sample reported that they would not return to their home country if offered jobs of comparable status and pay. This finding seems to support Piore's thesis that (temporary) immigrants are willing to take jobs in their new country that they would be unwilling to take in their home country, and conceivably, that they would be unwilling to return to their home country even if they could be guaranteed the

same job.[35] At the same time, the data seem to support
Pessar's finding about the reluctance of immigrant
households to return to their home country. However,
the analysis is not sufficiently advanced to test
Pessar's finding that those women performing wage labor
outside the household are most reluctant to return.[36]

Another area of concern to this chapter is the
remittance behavior of the sample of undocumented
aliens (sample III). The importance of the remittance
question lies not only in its possible direct and
indirect effect on the development of the home country,
but also in its potential relationship to the
permanence question. A frequent and/or high rate of
remittance might reflect a close identification with
the home country and a propensity to return home to
enjoy the fruits of one's labor. Conversely, an
infrequent and/or low rate of remittance might be a
good predictor of an intention to settle permanently
abroad.

Table 9.8 indicates that in 76 percent of the
cases (n=60) either the respondent or a member of
his/her household in the United States remitted some
funds to the home country during the previous twelve
months. The average annual amount remitted was $1,086,
and the average amount of each remittance was $159--
very substantial figures when considering the average
household's annual income reported earlier. In fact,
these remittances average more than 7 percent of the
gross annual average family income. Of those sending
regularly, 73 percent reported remitting a constant
amount. Seventy percent of those reporting a change in
the amount remitted reported an increase (data not
shown).

These data compare favorably with the findings
from the few studies in which such data are reported.
For instance, Poitras reports $3,173 average total
remittances over the full length of the trip for Costa
Ricans (average length of stay of over twenty-five
months) and $1,622 for Salvadorans (average length of
stay of a little over seventeen months). The amounts
reported by those studies dealing with illegal Mexican
aliens are considerably lower (North-Houstoun, $169 per
trip for Mexican respondents; CENIET, $115 per month in
trips that averaged only a little over four months
each).[37] The explanation certainly lies with the
frequency and brief duration of trips by Mexicans and
the frequency of their apprehension, as well as their
lower earnings and, as a result, their reduced ability
to save substantial sums.

Of particular interest are the persons who receive
the remittances and their relationship to the
remitter. Spouses and children of this study's
respondents were the sole beneficiaries in only 35

Table 9.8

Remittance Information for Undocumented Aliens

Remitted during past year	N	%
Yes	46	76
No	14	24
Total	60	100

Receiver of remittance		
Spouses and children only	16	35
Other family members	28	60
Others	2	5
Total	46	100

Amount of support provided		
Less than half	25	54
About half	12	27
More than half	8	17
All	1	2
Total	46	100

Need for support		
Very necessary	32	69
Helpful, not critical	3	7
Marginally useful	1	2
A gift, not support	10	22
Total	46	100

	Total Amt. Remitted (Per Year)	Amt. Each Remittance	Duration of Remittance (months)
Mean	$1,086	$159	49.2

percent of all the cases whereas the extended family (principally parents) received assistance in 60 percent of all cases. When considering that most respondents in sample III had their spouses and children with them (respectively, 71 and 61 percent), the size and distribution of the remittances are easier to understand. On the average, 4.1 persons were assisted by each remitter, but the respondents estimated that the amount sent usually provided less than half of each recipient family's needs. In line with this finding, nearly 70 percent of the remitting respondents considered the support as "very necessary" for the well-being of their families in the home country but could not state precisely how the funds were expended.[38]

Before I attempt to recapitulate and discuss the significance of the data in this chapter, I should emphasize again that almost regardless of immigration status, there is an apparent convergence in the socioeconomic experiences of recent immigrants from the Caribbean area. In fact, in comparing sample III with a sample of legal immigrants assisted by CCS counselors and with a sample of over 500 apprehended aliens in the custody of the Newark Immigration and Naturalization Service (INS) authorities during the first ten months of 1984, I noticed some not entirely unexpected differences but even more similarities. Legal CCS immigrant clients reported a less than 5 percent wage advantage over illegal immigrant clients--although both groups did substantially better than those in the custody of the INS. The explanation for the small wage difference between legal and illegal immigrants who are CCS clients is rather simple: Both groups perform similar functions in the labor market. Those apprehended and in custody, however, report less hourly income because of their less complete incorporation into the local labor market--they obtained jobs in factories that are repeatedly targets of INS enforcement teams. These differences aside, however, the three samples report similar country of origin, sex, age, and ethnic characteristics.

V. Conclusion

This study's data, when taken in the larger context of the emerging empirical picture of recent legal and illegal immigration from the Caribbean, point to an extremely complex process that, as a result, has often contradictory impacts. With the possible exception of Mexican illegal immigrants, Caribbean legal and illegal immigrants exhibit socio-demographic characteristics that seem to support the position of those who are skeptical about the entire emigration

process and may even see it as a net loss for the
sending societies.[39] Furthermore, it should be obvious
from the other chapters that although individuals are
the actors in this process, the process itself is part
of a long-term complex set of interconnections that
unites the United States with its neighbors to the
south. This larger process--of which immigration is
only a small part--appears to be disproportionately
sensitive to the needs of the United States. In spite
of the debate concerning the precise impact of legal
and illegal international migration on the United
States, the evidence warrants the questioning of the
argument that individual initiatives to emigrate are
necessarily compatible with society-wide benefits.

The incompatibility manifests itself in a number
of ways. For instance, if emigrants represent a net
human capital loss to the home country and they become
in effect a subsidy to the receiving society--both in
terms of their educational and demographic
characteristics--and opportunity costs and
sociopolitical considerations are put aside, how might
international migration become a net societal asset to
the sending society? Remittances and selective return
migration offer opportunities for increasing benefits
to the sending countries. Yet, as the authors in this
book forcefully point out, neither avenue can bear
fruit without thoughtful public intervention. In the
absence of such intervention, remittances might
continue to be used in ways that offer only marginal
intersectoral linkages and other societywide multiplier
effects[40] or perhaps be used to import foreign-made
luxury items and stimulate aggregate demand that often
cannot be met by domestic supply. These uses would
only lead to a deteriorating balance of payments and
severe inflationary pressures.

Because both the Poitras and CENIET studies
reported relatively high average transfers of savings
for their subjects, and recalling that respondents for
this study indicated that their remittances are used
principally to upgrade the quality of the
beneficiaries' lives, one might wonder whether socially
and economically useful investments might not be more
likely to take place only when emigrant households
return and only if they return with a substantial
nestegg. If subsequent studies bear this speculative
conclusion out, authors might need to reevaluate many
of the assumptions about emigration and focus much more
on return.

In spite of the fact that this study now joins an
expanding list of studies that indicate that immigrants
from the Caribbean region to the New York area are
likely to stay in the United States far longer than
they initially expected, substantial minorities of

legal and illegal immigrants undeniably do
repatriate. The often unarticulated assumption by
countries in the labor-exporting universe--that the
skills of returning migrants will be largely compatible
with the home countries' economic requirements for
making a sustained transition to enhanced development
status--also needs reassessing. Certainly, the data on
the occupational structure of the sample indicate that
this assumption might not be true.[41]

At least two major reasons indicate why the
occupational qualifications of most returnees--and
certainly of the subjects who have been the focus of
this and other similar field studies--often fail to
match the skills needed by their countries. First, the
migrant's role in the migration process is not
necessarily to acquire skills. Self-investment in
human capital is usually not part of the migrant's goal
structure, and the receivers' labor market is usually
not interested in helping him enhance his skills.
Second, the failure to match skills with needs reflects
an understandable gap in sending-country planning.
However, both problems may be amenable at least to some
ameliorative action involving the admittedly difficult
cooperation between sending countries and the U.S.
public and private sectors--and Pastor and Rogers
outline some of these possibilities in Chapter 15.

In principle at least, the cooperation of U.S
business might be elicited on grounds of equity--for
that sector is the greatest beneficiary of the
migration process. Of course, any such cooperation
would only be possible within the context of major
changes in U.S. immigration laws, accmpanied by the
creation of bilateral commissions designed to address
this problem by treating migration in a regional
context, as a key component in a regional labor policy
sensitive to the needs of actors at both ends of the
migration flow. The cooperation of the U.S. government
can be sought on grounds of self-interest, particularly
in light of the increasing perception in many sectors
in the United States that immigration, and particularly
illegal immigration, might be a long-term social,
economic, and political liability.

Although the need to develop such bilateral and
regional responses to the problem of unauthorized
international migration is repeatedly recognized,[42]
systematic pursuit of these avenues should not be
expected in the near future. Hence, one may anticipate
illegal immigration from the Caribbean region to
continue unabated. One might further expect that if
legalization and employer sanctions were jointly to
become legislative reality, and if we could assume that
these initiatives would work as expected, the medium-
and long-term economic impact on most Caribbean

countries -- with the notable exception of Mexico --
might be marginal. For, barring any concomitant
dramatic changes in U.S. immigration law regarding
family reunification, the legalization of the illegal
citizens of Caribbean countries would guarantee the
continuation of a steady immigration flow with impacts
not unlike the present ones.

Notes

1. For instance, island migrants built several area rail systems and the Panama Canal. Furthermore, U.S. agricultural and commercial interests in Cuba and elsewhere also employed large numbers of islanders. See D. McCullough, The Path Between the Seas: The Creation of the Panama Canal, 1870-1914 (Simon and Schuster, 1977); and E. Petras, "Caribbean Labor Migrations in a Global Perspective." Mimeo, 1982.

2. See Annual Report: Immigration and Naturalization Service, various years; see also M.M. Kritz, "International Migration Patterns in the Caribbean Basin: An Overview," in M.M. Kritz, C.B. Keely and S.M. Tomasi, Global Trends in Migration (Center for Migration Studies, 1981), pp. 208-33.

3. In descending order of annual legal immigration to the United States, the six countries are Cuba, Dominican Republic, Jamaica, Haiti, Trinidad/Tobago, and Barbados. See Annual Report, 1960 through 1981.

4. The 1965 Act did not come into force until 1968. For the details of how the Act affected immigration from the Barbados, Grenada, St. Lucia, Dominica, Antigua and Barbuda, St. Kitts/Nevis, St. Vincent and the Grenadines, and Belize, see the excellent recent PRB Occasional Series: The Caribbean (Population Reference Bureau, 1984).

5. See Annual Reports, 1979, Tables 12a-e. Also see the data culled from the Immigration and Naturalization Service's "alien address registration" system and the 1970 and 1980 census in D.G. Papademetriou, New Immigrants to Brooklyn and Queens: Policy Implications Especially with Regard to Housing (Center for Migration Studies, 1982), Tables 7 and 30.

6. From the total number of nonimmigrant visas issued in 1981 to citizens of Caribbean nations over 85 percent were for "temporary visitors for pleasure." See Annual Report, 1981. Presumably, and in spite of the extreme care taken by U.S. State Department officials in issuing such visas, a large proportion of illegal immigrants come from the ranks of "visitors." For instance, one-third of our sample III respondents entered the U.S. as visitors. For a disucssion fo the sample, see text, pp. 4-5.

7. See Table 64, Annual Report, 1981.

8. The Alien Contract Labor Law of 1885, as amended in 1887 and 1888, had actually prohibited employers from assisting or encouraging the immigration of aliens under terms of a contract or agreement. See J. Higham, Strangers in the Land: Patterns of American Nativism 1860-1925 (Atheneum, 1969); also see D.G. Papademetriou and M. Miller, "U.S. Immigration Policy: International Context, Theoretical Parameters and Research Priorities," in D.G. Papademetriou and M. Miller, The Unavoidable Issue: U.S. Immigration Policy in the 1980s (Institute for the Study of Human Issues, 1983), pp. 1-41.

9. Nearly 77,000 Mexican workers were admitted to the U.S. during the 1917-1922 program, while as many as half-a-million Mexicans a year were working in the U.S. during the height of the Bracero program. Less than half of the participants in the first program returned to Mexico while unknown numbers of braceros remained in the U.S. Both programs proved to be controversial and the U.S. resorted to mass roundups and deportations both times. See V.M. Briggs, "Nonimmigrant Labor Policy: Future Trend or Aberration?" in Papademetriou and Miller, The Unavoidable Issue, pp. 93-122; and D.S. North, Nonimmigrant Workers in the U.S. (New Transcentury Foundation, 1980).

10. Border Commuters live in Mexico but work in the U.S. On the basis of a 1929 Supreme Court decision (Karnuth v. Albro, 279 U.S. 231 (1929)), which equated employment with residence, they have been classified as "immigrants" -- in spite of the 1965 legislation which actually seems to prohibit such practice. The Court reaffirmed the classification in Saxbe v. Bustos, 419 U.S. 65 (1974). See Briggs, "Nonimmigrant Policy," p. 99.

11. The BWI program has existed since 1943 and seeks to facilitate the entry of citizens of the British West Indies and the Bahamas to work in agricultural occupations in eleven East Coast states. The authorized industries include the sugar cane industry in Florida, the apple industry in the Northeast, the woodcutting industry in Maine, and the sheepherding industry in the West.

12. The reference is to the easing of the restrictions in converting from "nonimmigrant" to "immigrant" the status of the many Caribbean workers who had lived and worked in the U.S. Virgin Islands since WWII. See Briggs, "Nonimmigrant Policy," pp. 107-10.

13. The 1952 Immigration and Nationality Act substantially expanded the classes of nonimmigrant visas and introduced the "H" program for temporary workers. This program includes both an agricultural group (H-2), which comprises between one-third and one-half of the annual admissions, and another group composed of workers, entertainers, athletes and white-collar and skilled workers. The professional standing of this latter group is lower than that of those of "distinguished merit and ability" categories of H-1.

14. In view of the frequent propensity of illegal immigrants to remain in the U.S. indefinitely, one could also consider illegal immigration as a de facto immigration program.

15. Such services range from short-term accommodations and labor market placement to the provision of informal but critical buffers against sociocultural alienation, temporary socio-economic displacement and a variety of similar "safety nets." See P.R. Pessar, "The Role of Households in International Migration and the Case of U.S.-Bound Migration from the Dominican Republic," International Migration Review, Vol. 16 (1982), pp. 342-64; Pessar, "Kinship Relations of Production in the Migration Process: The Case of Dominican Emigration to the U.S." New York University, Center for Latin American and Caribbean Studies, Occasional Paper No. 27, 1982; M.M. Kritz and D.T. Gurak, "Kinship Assistance in the Settlement Process: Dominican and Colombian Cases," Mimeo, 1984; and C.H. Wood, "Equilibrium and Historical-Structural Perspectives on Migration," International Migration Review, Vol. 16 (1982), pp. 298-319.

16. For the structural nature of the need of advanced industrial societies for "temporary" foreign labor, see D.G. Papademetriou, "Rethinking International Migration," Comparative Political Studies, Vol. 15 (1983), pp. 469-98; and Papademetriou, International Migration in Western Europe and North America: Trends and Consequences (Population Associates International, 1983), Chapter 1.

17. At a minimum, by the questions one chooses to investigate.

18. The situation usually reverses itself, however, as remittances are often used to purchase consumer goods many of which are produced abroad.

19. See especially A. Portes and J. Walton, Labor, Class, and the International System (Academic Press, 1981), Chapter 2; see also R.L. Bach, "Emigration from the Spanish-Speaking Caribbean," in M.M. Kritz, U.S. Immigration and Refugee Policy (Lexington, 1983), pp. 133-53.

20. See C. Zazueta, "Mexican Workers in the United States: Some Initial Results and Methodological Considerations of the National Household Survey of Emigration." Mimeo. 1980. The study reports on the results of the Encuesta Nacional de Emigracion a la Frontera Norte del Pais y a los Estados Unidos. The analysis was done by the Centro Nacional de Informacion y Estadisticas del Trabajo (CENIET) of the Mexican Secretariat for Labor and Social Services. Incomplete results of the study are also reported in S. Ranney and S. Kossoudji, "Profiles of Temporary Mexican Labor Migrants to the United States," Population and Development Review, Vol. 9 (1983), pp. 475-93; and S. Forbes, "The Half-Open Door: Illegal Migration to the United States," in U.S. Immigration Policy and the National Interest (Staff Report of the Select Commission on Immigration and Refugee Policy, April, 1981), pp. 457-558.

21. Kritz and Gurak, "Kinship Assistance," Supra. fn. #15.

22. See D. North and M. Houstoun, "The Characteristics and Role of Illegal Aliens in the U.S. Labor Market: An Exploratory Study." Report prepared for the Employment and Training Administration of the U.S. Department of Labor, 1976. The authors interviewed 793 illegal aliens in the custody of the Immigration authorities of whom 481 (61 percent) were Mexicans and an additional 34 percent were from other countries in the Western Hemisphere. Sixty percent of the entire sample was in custody in the states of Texas, Arizona and California. In view of these distributions, and of the selection of the sample and the location of the interviews, the study must be used with care.

23. See J. Bustamante, "Undocumented Migration from Mexico: Research Report," International Migration Review, Vol. 11 (1977), PP. 149-77. The author interviewed undocumented Mexicans deported by U.S. immigration authorities in a number of Mexican border towns.

24. M. van Arsdol, J. Moore, D. Heer, and S. Haynie, "Non-Apprehended and Apprehended Undocumented

Residents in the Los Angeles Labor Market: An
Exploratory Study." Population Research Laboratory,
University of Southern California, Mimeo, 1979. The
authors examined the social adjustment, labor force
status, and earning patterns of a sample of the records
of the clients of a social agency in Los Angeles, the
One Stop Immigration Center. The records were for the
period of 1972 to 1975.

25. See "The Linkage Between the Household and
Workplace in the experience of Dominican Immigrant
Women in the U.S." Georgetown University, Center for
Immigration Policy and Refugee Assistance, 1984.
Pessar's informants were members of both legal and
illegal households.

26. See Supra. fn. #21.

27. A. Ugalde and T.C. Langham, "International
Return Migration: Socio-Demographic Determinants of
Return Migration to the Dominican Republic," in W.F.
Stinner, K. de Alburquerque and R.S. Bryce-Laporte,
Return Migration and Remittances: Developing a
Caribbean Perspective (Smithsonian Institution, 1982),
pp. 73-95; and A. Ugalde, F.D. Bean and G. Cardenas,
"International Migration from the Dominican Republic:
Findings from a National Survey," International
Migration Review, 13 (1979), pp. 235-54.

28. See G. Poitras, "International Migration to
the United States from Costa Rica and El Salvador."
Trinity University, Border Research Institute, April,
1980; also, Poitras, "The United States Experience of
Return Migrants from Costa Rica and El Salvador,"
Border Research Institute, August, 1980.

29. See C. Keely, P. Elwell, A. Fragomen, and S.
Tomasi, "Profiles of Undocumented Aliens in New York
City: Haitians and Dominicans," Center for Migration
Studies, Occasinal Papers and Documentation, 1978. The
authors interviewed 54 Haitians and 17 Dominicans in
New York in a number of social service settings in 1976
and 1977.

30. S. Maram, "Hispanic Workers in the Garment
and Restaurant Industries in Los Angeles County."
Program in U.S.-Mexican Studies, University of
California, San Diego, Working Papers in U.S.-Mexican
Studies, No. 12, 1980. The author analyzed the
findings of a sample of 862 Hispanic workers in the Los
Angeles restaurant and garment industries interviewed
by the State's Concentrated Enforcement Program of the

Department of Industrial Relations. Ninety-six percent of these workers were found to be illegals.

31. The data do not allow one-to-one comparison here. By the same measure of average years of education, the CCS sample III scored 9.8 years of education. See Ranney and Kossoudji, "Profiles," p. 490-491. For an excellent review of the problems with comparability see "Illegal Aliens: Analysis and Background," report prepared by the Education and Public Welfare Division, Congressional Research Service, Library of Congress, for the Committee on the Judiciary, U.S. House of Representatives, June, 1977.

32. The minimum wage may be less relevant as a measure of wage discrimination against undocumented aliens since it has not been augmented for several years and many starting wages for low-level jobs now voluntarily exceed it.

33. W. Cornelius, "Mexican Migration to the U.S.: The View from Rural Sending Communities," Migration and Development Study Group Monograph, No. 76-12, MIT, 1976. The study reported on subjects interviewed in a major Mexican sending region, Jalisco.

34. Over 40 percent of our sample III respondents reported various concurrent types of assistance by relatives--ranging from assistance with the cost of the trip (33 percent), to such post-immigration help as housing and employment search. The role of the family in the migration process has been explored in considerable depth by Patricia Pessar who, however, cautions against use of the concept as a "collective strategy, adjusting the unit to external changes in the productivity system... [i.e., as] a black box." Instead, she seeks to reintroduce to it "...the complexity of activities and social relations, as these are guided by gender and seniority." See her "The Constraints Upon and Release of Female Labor Power: Dominican Migration to the United States," Georgetown University, Center for Immigration Policy and Refugee Assistance, 1984, p. 1. See also R.L. Bach, and L.S. Schraml, "Migration Crisis and Theoretical Conflict," International Migration Review, 16 (1982), pp. 320-41.

35. See M.J. Piore, Birds of Passage: Migrant Labor in Industrial Societies (Cambridge, 1979), Chapter 3.

36. See her "When the Birds of Passage Want to Roost: An Exploration of the Role of Gender in Dominican Settlement in the United States." Georgetown

University, Center for Immigration Policy and Refugee Assistance, 1984.

37. This figure represents averaged total repatriated savings and, as a result, it is higher than expected. Roughly, a comparable figure for our own sample would have to include the savings of our subjects.

38. See also R. Brana-Shute and G. Brana-Shute, "The Magnitude and Impact of Remittances in the Eastern Caribbean: A Research Note," in Stinner, et. al., Return Migration, pp. 267-89; H. Rubinstein, "The Impact of Remittances in the Rural English-Speaking Caribbean: Notes on the Literature," in Stinner, et. al., Return Migration, pp. 237-66; and W.F. Stinner and K. de Alburquerque, "Introductory Essay: The Dynamics of Caribbean Return Migration," in Stinner, et. al., Return Migration, pp. xxxvii-lxvii.

39. Of course, one must consider a number of issues before a final assessment can be made. For instance, social and political considerations must be balanced against economic ones; and all of them must be evaluated in terms of short, medium, and long-term consequences.

40. See A. O. Hirschman's intersectoral linkage model in The Strategy of Economic Development (Yale, 1958). For a discussion on its application in the migration context, see D.G. Papademetriou, "Emigration and Return in the Mediterranean Littoral," Comparative Politics, forthcoming, 1985.

41. There is, however, a well-stocked reservoir of high-level manpower of Caribbean origin in the U.S. and elsewhere which must receive attention before any comprehensive initiatives for Caribbean development are proposed. Several of the authors in this book discuss precisely these immigrants.

42. Both the Final Report of the Select Commission on Immigration and Refugee Policy and the Hispanic Caucus Bill in the 98th Congress seem to place a premium on such cooperation. The "Simpson/Mazzoli" Bill, however, was much less interested in this approach. For a discussion of this legislation, see D. Papademetriou, "Immigration Reform, American Style," International Migration, Vol. 22 (1984), pp. 265-79.

10. The Impact of Immigration on Caribbean Development

Trevor J. Hope

North American and Caribbean peoples tend to view their nations' background in rather different ways, which condition their perceptions of themselves and their relationships with the outside world.[1] North Americans talk with some pride of their ethnic origins and of their society as an "immigrant society." Even before the publication of John F. Kennedy's A Nation of Immigrants, the term had gained wide currency, and it has become even more popular since. Both the United States and the Caribbean states have colonial and immigrant backgrounds, but the culture of the former stresses the immigrant whereas that of the latter stresses the colonial impact. U.S. politicians make a virtue of their immigrant origins; Caribbean politicians tend to conceal theirs.

The reasons are not hard to find. The United States began as a settler colony which threw off colonial authority at an early date, whereas until recently, the Caribbean states were plantation colonies. The whole impact of colonial domination was therefore different. At the same time, the majority of immigrants into the Caribbean suffered the trauma of the Middle Passage, and even later immigrants--contract laborers from Africa, China, and India--often came less than willingly. The immigrants landing on North America's shores did so with the feeling that a new light had dawned and that their lives would be better. Those landing in the Caribbean did so more often than not with trepidation and a heavy heart, or with the idea of working their contracts out, earning some money, and getting back to their native land. Even those who had no hope of returning home still dreamed of the prospect, passing on their unfulfilled aspirations to succeeding generations.

These differences are reflected in both popular and official attitudes toward migration. North America's obsessions are with immigration; the

Caribbean's are with the outward process. This contrast is reflected in the migration literature; in a recently published bibliographical review of studies on Caribbean migration, only a handful relate to the process of immigration into the region.[2] The relative paucity of literature on this aspect reflects overriding local and metropolitan interest in the reverse process.

The fact remains that the two processes are intimately connected. The Caribbean emigrant is the descendant of the relatively recent Caribbean immigrant, and the migration impulse is deeply implanted in the national psychology of the Caribbean people. As the late Eric Williams once proclaimed of Trinidad and Tobago, "We are not a nation but a bunch of transients."[3] Immigrants into the Caribbean islands have bequeathed a legacy of restlessness to the small island societies, none of which have adequately come to terms with the problems that this has posed for the long-term development of the region.

Political imperatives in the Caribbean have also worked to disguise or blunt considerations and studies of select ethnic groups. No Caribbean politician draws attention to ethnicity for fear of stirring racial antagonism. In the Caribbean, to talk of ethnicity is to talk about color, which is to "pick a way through thorns while walking on eggshell."[4] Governments hide the ethnic divisions behind euphemistic slogans: Guyana, formerly the "Land of Six Peoples," now proclaims it is "One People, One Nation;" Jamaica's coat of arms is "Out of Many One People;" Trinidad and Tobago's slogan is "Together We Aspire, Together We Achieve;" the ruling People's National Movement (PNM) slogan is "All o'we is one."[5] The realities are somewhat different.

Although the slave system and plantation economy dominated all considerations of Caribbean societies, rarely have the direct descendents of African slaves become the dominant political or economic segments of society. A local furor arose in July 1984 when a prominent Jamaican People's National Party (PNP) politician said it was time black men ruled the country.[6] The press and other politicians angrily denounced such sentiments as racist, but everyone knew what he meant. Few Caribbean societies are homogeneous, without distinctions of color and class. Lowenthal identified only Carriacou, the Caicos Islands, Barbuda, St. Barthelemy, Marie Galante, Ile de la Gonave, Ile de la Tortue, Tortola, and Virgin Gorda as having such societies; together these islands had a population estimated in the 1960s at about one-quarter of a million out of a total of 11.25 million people.[7]

I. Historical Overview

After the abolition of the British slave trade (1807) and then slavery itself in the British colonies (1834), the immigration of contract labor was organized as a substitute for the slave labor on which the West Indies' sugar industry depended. The importation of contract labor began at this time and was to last in one form or another for more than half a century.[8] Periods of acute labor shortage followed the economic troughs in the sugar market throughout the nineteenth century and into the twentieth. In the 1850s and 1860s indentured immigration to Guadeloupe, Martinique, British Guiana, and Trinidad halted, if not reversed, their economic decline and brought about a substantial degree of prosperity by the 1870s as sugar production increased. (Between 1850 and 1870 British Guiana's sugar crop trebled.) There was a direct correlation between imported labor and the rise in sugar production in these colonies. As William Green remarked, "Immigration saved the sugar economy in Trinidad and British Guiana."[9]

Two areas in particular provided the bulk of these new immigrants--India and China. The total numbers of indentured Indians imported into the British West Indies until the termination of the system in 1917 were as follows:[10]

British Guiana	238,909	Grenada	3,200
Trinidad	143,939	St. Vincent	2,472
Jamaica	36,412	St. Lucia	4,354

In the smaller islands where sugar cultivation played a much less significant part in the economy, the role played by immigrant labor was less important. As sugar production in the smaller islands declined, indentured labor was discontinued--St. Vincent (1880), Grenada (1885) and St. Lucia (1893). In the larger colonies, the planters' constant desire to expand their cultivation, which they tried to do whenever prices were favorable, as well as to keep wages low, led them to persist in their clamor for immigrant labor. Given the fact that one-quarter to one-third of the indentured Indian laborers took up their option to return home at the end of their contract, such demands may have had some justification; yet by the early 1880s it was apparent that immigration had become a means of cheapening labor rather than a necessity for the maintenance of the sugar industry.[11]

Nor was Indian immigrant labor only imported into the British colonies. The emancipation of slaves in the French colonies in 1848 led to planters there following the British example of the importation of

Europeans, Indians, Africans, and Chinese. Sugar planters in Guadeloupe feared total ruin as a result of the severe labor shortage, and by the early 1850s contracts were signed for the importation of Africans and Asians.[12] French Guiana also sought immigrant labor as its former slaves took to new occupations. Although some 16,000 Africans were recruited to Martinique and Guadeloupe between 1850 and 1861, by far the most easily available source was the East Indies. Between 1853 and 1885 about 80,000 Indians were brought to the French possessions, mostly from Pondicherry and Calcutta.[13]

The labor shortages of the 1850s had their impact in the Dutch colonies too, even before the emancipation of their slaves in 1863. Efforts to import labor from the Dutch East Indies date from 1853. Between 1873 and 1917 when Indian indentured immigration ceased, some 34,304 Indians were brought to Suriname.[14] Throughout the Caribbean, therefore, with the exceptions of Cuba, Haiti, Puerto Rico and the Dominican Republic, Indian immigrants proved the most numerous and the most important, and Indian immigration determined the general characteristics of the whole system of contract or indentured labor. Whether in Suriname, Guadeloupe, or Jamaica, the importation of Indian contract labor saved an ailing sugar industry. The presence of the descendants of those immigrants is powerfully asserted in Guyana and Trinidad, and no small number of them is still to be found in agricultural pursuits--even in the sugar industry--to this day.

Since 1835 Caribbean planters had been demanding access to Africa to recruit free laborers; they focused their attention on the liberated Africans established in Sierra Leone by the British government.[15] British reticence about such schemes and an unenthusiastic response on the part of liberated Africans themselves resulted in only 36,120 Africans being conveyed to the Caribbean between 1841 and 1867, the years of officially sponsored African emigration. Of those, at least one-half were seized south of the equator, freed at St. Helena, and then removed to the Caribbean.[16]

The importation of Chinese contract laborers was first tried by the Cubans who brought a party from Amoy in 1847. Between 1853 and 1874 a considerable traffic developed, resulting in the importation of 150,000 Chinese laborers into Cuba.[17] By 1852-1853 Trinidad obtained almost 1,000 Chinese immigrants and British Guiana, 647. The following year Jamaica imported one shipload directly from Hong Kong and also received in 1853 the remainder of the 800 Chinese recruits (less than 200) who went to Panama to work for the Panama Railroad Company.[18] In 1855 the first shipload of Chinese reached Guadeloupe, and over the next few years a few hundred others arrived, with about 500 Indo-Chinese. About 1,000 Chinese were brought to Martinique and others to Trinidad, but the high cost of such immigrants was a major obstacle to further recruitment.[19]

During the 1860s some 2,000 Chinese immigrants entered Surinam. Following the Anglo-French occupation of Canton in 1859, Chinese emigration to the Caribbean accelerated to the point where, by 1866, British Guiana had received 11,282 Chinese and Trinidad, 1,557. However, because of the costs numbers never reached those of the East Indian indentured laborers. Though the Cubans prized the Chinese as hard workers, the planters who recruited them in the other islands found they had little experience as agricultural laborers and only wanted to redeem their indentures as quickly as possible and turn to shopkeeping, huckstering, or market gardening.

By the late nineteenth century the Dutch were looking to their own East Indian colonies for labor and in the 1890s began importing Javanese workers. Over the next half century this practice resulted in the introduction into Suriname of almost 33,000 Javanese.[20]

A measure of the relative unattractiveness of the Caribbean islands to nineteenth century Europeans is that, with the exception of workers for the Spanish colonies of Cuba, Santo Domingo, and Puerto Rico, European labor was never procured to any really significant degree. In 1834 the first Portuguese immigrants arrived in Trinidad, and British and German groups came to Jamaica in response to the island's bounty system.[21] But in four years Jamaica received about 3,000 British, Portuguese, and German immigrants, whereas British Guiana and Trinidad secured only a few hundred Portuguese, mainly from Madeira. Even where Madeirans were secured on contract, as in the case of Guadeloupe, most soon deserted field labor for commerce.[22]

One further group of immigrants, which although numerically small has had an important impact upon the Caribbean, is the Levantines--Syrians, Lebanese and Palestinians--who came to the region after the 1880s. These were not contract laborers but migrants in search of a more prosperous and secure future than could be found in the Ottoman-dominated Middle East. But the role they created for themselves has made them a key element in the economic life of the region. The manner of their arrival in the Caribbean and the way in which they have developed as an elite group set them apart from most other immigrants.

For the purposes of this chapter the two case studies which follow will examine in greater detail the

242

roles of the Levantine and Chinese immigrants in
Caribbean society.

II. The Levantines

The Lebanese, Syrian, and Palestinian immigrants
to the Caribbean--here referred to collectively as the
Levantines--were neither solicited nor welcomed. They
came to the Caribbean of their own volition, often
because they were forced out of their homeland by
religious persecution and political antagonism.[23]
Contrary to popular belief, they were not primarily
traders but agriculturalists by background--olive
growers and sheep farmers, or their sons. They did not
bring commercial skills with them usually, but acquired
them in the Caribbean. Writing of the class structure
in Dominica, the Marxist historian, Bill Riviere said:

> The commercial sector is dominated by Syrians, led
> by Astaphan with ownership of a supermarket, a
> construction company, a hotel . . . and five
> premises specialising in electrical appliances . .
> . plumbing material. Next, Nassief owns a
> supermarket, a hardware store and an electrical
> centre; in the non-commercial sphere, he owns
> Belfast plantation, a rum distillery, and a factory
> producing oil soap from coconuts. [Until recently
> he also owned Geneva Estate and] a big clothing
> store. . . . Their class equals include Syrians
> Gabriel, Ibrahim and Raffaoul.[24]

What Riviere describes of the Levantines' role in
Dominica could apply equally to many other Caribbean
islands.
Most of the Levantines who arrived in the
Caribbean in the late nineteenth century were from a
small-landholder or tenant-farmer background, though
they also included those with some educational
attainment--schoolteachers and small businessmen. Like
other immigrant groups in the Caribbean a large
proportion were young, unmarried males, although many
soon brought other relatives and obtained Levantine
wives.[25] On arrival, some like Abdulla Younis in
Jamaica and Miguel Cury in the Dominican Republic went
into farming. Others like Elias Issa, who arrived in
Jamaica in 1894, went into the dry goods business as
itinerant pedlars. (It has been claimed that the first
Levantines in Kingston came for the Jamaica Exhibition
in 1891.)[26] From pedlaring they moved into shopkeeping
and from retail commerce into the import-export trade.
In Suriname, the Levantines concentrated their
business activity in textiles and haberdashery,
following the lead of the legendary Karkabe and--the

most successful of all--J. Bersaoui Nassief. Many
started as pedlars and market vendors and by 1940
occupied a commanding position in the textile trade,
owning some 45 percent of registered drapery
businesses. By 1956 29 textile establishments in
Paramaribo were owned by Levantines; this number had
risen to 38 in 1967 and to 43 by 1975.[27] In Cuba, too,
the Levantines founded garment factories and exported
their products to Arab merchants throughout the
Caribbean.

The scattered nature of the Levantines' settlement
throughout the Caribbean facilitated this type of
exchange. As David Nicholls pointed out, a notable
feature of the Arab migration is the way in which
families have cut across national boundaries and they
way that international links have been extended through
marriage. Thus, he went on:

> The Handals are found in Jamaica and Haiti as well
> as Honduras and Brazil and are related by marriage
> to the Daccarett, Deek, Hasboun, Cassus, Talams,
> Zaround, Boulos and Jaar families. The Jamaican
> Llama family is related to those in the Dominican
> Republic who in turn are related to the Issas of
> Jamaica who are related to Abellas, Habeebs,
> Ganems, Gadala, Marias, Shoucairs, Ghisays and
> Selehs. The Hannas in Jamaica are related to the
> Deeb and Boulos families in Haiti, to the Laquis in
> Trinidad and to the Brimos, Zaggas, Fatta, Karrams
> and Ziadies in Jamaica itself.[28]

Such strong family links have often facilitated
commercial links and allowed the Levantines to move
fairly easily from one country to another. This great
mobility was made possible in the early years by lack
of restrictive immigration laws. During times of
persecution and official campaigns against them in
Haiti in 1903, 1905, and 1911, Levantines migrated to
Jamaica and other islands. Their pattern of migration
was the classic chain-link variety, with relatives and
friends often following the initial migrant. In
Jamaica, therefore, a large number of Lebanese families
all came from the village of Schweifat just outside
Beirut, and all belonged to the Greek Orthodox
Church. In the Dominican Republic many of the leading
Levantine families came from the Maronite community in
Gazhir. The Syrians in Port-au-Prince are largely from
the Greek Orthodox community in Tartous. Most of the
large Palestinian families in the Caribbean--the
Handals, Marzouca, Jaars, Mourras, Lamas, Talamas, and
Issas--all originated from the Latin parish in
Bethlehem.[29] In Suriname the Lebanese came mainly from
Bazhoun, a Maronite village near Tripolis-El Mina.

Emigrants from Bazhoun also went to Cayenne, Antigua,
Dominica, and St. Kitts; indeed the Lebanese migration
to Surinam developed relatively late and usually went
via Cayenne and St. Kitts.[30]

Strong family and business connections with both
the rest of the Caribbean and the outside world might
account for the great success that the Levantines have
undoubtedly had in commercial activities. However,
their high mobility and readiness to move in response
to unfavourable political and economic circumstances
have given them a certain reputation. As Leonard Broom
put it, "Stong kin and commercial ties affect the
operation of Syrian enterprises, and their association
with other Syrian communities in the Western hemisphere
and beyond tends to mute their commitment to Jamaican
society."[31] When Jamaican Prime Minister Edward Seaga
was questioned about the possible handicap of his
Lebanese background in Jamaican politics, he replied
that in one sense being of Lebanese descent was an
advantage for he did not have to prove his
competence. In another respect, however, it was a
disadvantage for he did have to demonstrate his good
faith and genuine identification with the interests and
aspirations of the Jamaican people.[32]

The decline in the number of Levantines in Jamaica
from 1,354 in the 1960 census to 1,007 in the 1970
census (and perhaps less than that figure today) bears
out the point. During the government of Michael Manley
in the 1970s, Levantines, like so many other
businessmen, took "one of the five flights to Miami."
Others, however, facing the choice of going into
manufacturing or quitting business altogether, because
of the restrictions placed on imported goods, decided
to manufacture those foods that had previously been
imported as, for example, did the Ammar-Azan
partnership.[33]

Although Levantine migrants have married into
local society, the majority have not married or
cohabited as much as might have been expected with the
blacks or creoles, though this varies from one part of
the Caribbean to the other. They have maintained their
ethnic separateness which has also carried over to
their business activities; most Levantine businesses
remain family and private concerns. How much of their
wealth is repatriated remains a closely guarded secret,
although it is safe to assume that those remaining for
three generations or more have invested a considerable
amount in the local economy. Although Levantine
families have generally been accepted by other ethnic
groups, many maintain strong links with the Middle East
and perpetuate Arab customs in their family life.
Others return and live for long periods in the Levant--
as the Azans did in 1946; this dual attachment has led

to ambiguities over their patriotism and commitment to
the Caribbean nations in which they have settled.

Nicholls remarked that in Haiti the Levantines
have kept out of politics, but this statement needs
qualification. Even in 1912 at the time of President
Leconte's assassination, Arabs had been accused of
conspiring with the opposition. Elias Cassis and
Victor Saliba are close allies of the Duvaliers, the
former even being an alleged member of the old Tonton
Macoutes, whereas Antoine Khoury, who was murdered
during Carnival in 1981, was allegedly involved in
anti-Duvalier politics. Younger members of the
Levantine minority have also been involved in
opposition politics, and the mysterious fire that
destroyed the home and killed several members of the
prominent Jaar family has been variously ascribed to
political motives, though whether local or
international is not clear. Accusations about the role
of the wealthy Levantines on Cap-Haitien in drug
trafficking are likewise hard to prove for obvious
reasons.

As a prominent minority, the Levantines have been
a useful whipping boy for Haitian politicians,
especially in the early decades of the twentieth
century. Riots against them and the destruction of
their property and businesses took place in Haiti in
1912. More recently, however, they have been accepted
into political circles, occasionally reaching
ministerial rank, as in the case of Carlo Boulos and
Rindel Assad; another--Jean Deeb--became mayor of Port-
au-Prince.[34] In the Dominican Republic, Jottin Khoury,
Rafael Kasse Acta, General Elias Wessin-y-Wessin,
Jacobo Majluta Azar, Hugo Tolentino Dipp, and Narciso
Isa Conde--all of Levantine background--play a
prominent role in politics.[35] But in the Dominican
Republic, as in Haiti, the Levantines have been
assimilated into society far more meaningfully than
elsewhere, although in Jamaica Levantines have found it
possible to attain the offices of prime minister and
chief justice.

The Levantines have been less discriminated
against in Jamaica where the presence of the larger
Chinese community--which could serve as a scapegoat--
enabled the Levantines to gain high status while
arousing relatively little animosity. But Levantines,
like other minorities, have excited their share of
hostility in other parts of the Caribbean. Newspapers
in Guadeloupe periodically denounce the "foreign"
(i.e., Levantine) monopoly of business and threaten
them with creole takeovers; creole businessmen in
Martinique call for Levantine abdication of property.
Nevertheless, from Haiti to Surinam, from Jamaica to
St. Kitts, the Levantines dominate the import trade and

the dry goods business, rivaled only by the Portuguese in Guyana and the Jews in Jamaica.[36] They own the largest department stores in Jamaica, St. Kitts, and Dominica. Levantines operate a high proportion of Caribbean hotels and cafes, cinemas and soft drink plants, and figure prominently on local tourist boards, chambers of commerce, and other public bodies.

III. The Chinese

The Chinese represent another minority in the Caribbean who, under rather different circumstances from those of the Levantines, managed to establish themselves in economic niches and find a role in contemporary Caribbean society. Although arriving as contract laborers in virtually all territories in which they are found, they quickly moved out of the agricultural sector as soon as they found the time and money to do so.

Since emigration was generally frowned upon by the Chinese and discouraged by their government, most of those who did migrate initially were the poor, destitute and social outcasts. Contemporaries often alleged that many were confirmed opium addicts, but this statement may well have been exaggerated by prejudice against the new arrivals. Notwithstanding this unpromising background, the Chinese did adapt to working their contracts and were praised by the planters for their workmanship and tidy habits. They attempted to desert the plantations whenever opportunities arose, however, and were generally more prone to do so than the East Indians, though statistics on this point are unreliable.

Of the 12,500 Chinese who migrated to British Guiana between 1853 and 1873, many had to submit to renewed contracts when the original ones expired, if only because of the virtual monopoly maintained by the Portuguese over the retail trade and professions.[37] Nevertheless, as Brian Moore has shown, by the 1870s some Chinese had begun to infiltrate the licensed service sector such as retail huckstering, shopkeeping, and transportation, and within 25 years were posing a considerable threat to the Portuguese traders and shopkeepers. By the 1890s, the Chinese had established vibrant commercial centers in the two principal towns of British Guiana--New Amsterdam and Georgetown.[38]

The pattern of Chinese settlement in Guiana as elsewhere showed a marked tendency toward ethnic separation. This was a two-way process: (1) Hostility existed on the part of those already in British Guiana who saw the immigration of Chinese as a threat to their wages and ultimately their jobs, and (2) their own natural inclination was to stick together as part of an

ethnic group so distinct in every way from the existing
population and in a hostile environment.[39] Even in
their law-breaking activities the Chinese operated in
groups. Their habit of descending on plantations and
village properties in armed nocturnal gang raids caused
serious concern to the authorities. It was not only an
echo of the triad secret societies that operated in
Fukien and Kwangtung Provinces where most of the
Chinese had originated but also a way of mobilizing the
arrivals as a cohesive force to strike against the sort
of harassment to which they were subjected in a
racially hostile system.[40]

The immigration of the Chinese into Jamaica,
although on a smaller scale, exhibited similar
characteristics. The argument has been made that they
arrived in the island with commercial skills that were
in short supply and by the turn of the century had
secured a commanding place for themselves in the retail
grocery trade, which extended by vertical development
to the wholesale food trade and food products
industry.[41] This point is debatable. As Lee Tom Yin
remarked, many of the original Chinese immigrants to
Jamaica were peasant farmers or the sons of
farmers.[42] They, like their compatriots in other parts
of the Caribbean, had been recruited from village
communities in the rural areas of Kwangtung Province
for the express purpose of filling Jamaica's deficit of
agricultural labor. Although a proportion of the new
immigrants clearly had skills other than agricultural
ones, most of them were rural smallholders. Yet within
a short time, the position was reversed, and by the
turn of the century the majority had become
shopkeepers.

Although some writers have tried to show that the
Hakka rather than the Punti predominated among the
Chinese immigrants--the Hakka being more noted as
successful traders--the point has not been proved.
Apart from their facility to use the abacus, nothing in
the background of the Chinese immigrants sets their
skills clearly above those of the creole and negro
storekeepers. Even the hypothesis advanced by Andrew
Lind of the relationship of alien status and trade,
attractive though it may seem, is undemonstrated.[43]

More important seems their recognition that
participation in trade was an economically desirable
goal. Emigration was frowned upon by Chinese society
and until 1894 carried harsh legal penalties.[44] Those
who did migrate, therefore, did so mainly in the
expectation of a financially rewarding excursion that
would make themselves and their families secure on
their return. Their residence abroad was viewed as
temporary, and the acquisition of land and property was
discouraged by frends and relatives at home who feared

that it might lead to the migrants remaining overseas permanently. To eradicate the stigma of having migrated in the first place, it was essential to acquire wealth; failure to do so could amount to permanent exile.[45] Since the quickest monetary return came from commerce and the least from agricultural labor, the Chinese immigrant like the Levantine seemed to have few options.

What clinched their entry into the grocery trade in Jamaica, according to Jacqueline Levy, were the current socio-economic conditions prevailing at that time. The grocery trade had been poorly developed, and the archaic system of plantation stores was ill-adapted to independent purchases by urban populations. They were not the only observers to take advantage of this opening. Creole and Indian shopkeepers also participated in the trade that coincided with the breakdown of merchant control over the import trade. The Chinese extended their activity through a network of communal and kinship bonds, first in the often repeated pattern of the recruitment of immigrants and subsequently through sponsoring and training them. In this fashion the network of kinship was integrated with reciprocal economic obligations. Under such conditions, voluntary associations further strengthened ethnic solidarity. As Broom stated: "The Chinese cut a niche for themselves in the Jamaican economy and enlarged it into a social nest."[46]

In 1908 the Collector General's department produced the following statistics for persons engaged in the retail trade by ethnic origin:[47]

CHINAMEN:	834	or	13.2%
COOLIES:	444	or	7.1%
SYRIANS:	88	or	1.4%
ALL OTHERS:	4,933	or	78.4%

The significance of these figures can be readily appreciated when they are placed against the total number of Chinese in Jamaica, which in 1911 amounted to 2,111 or 0.3 percent of the island's population.

By March 1925 the number of trade licenses held by the Chinese in Jamaica increased to 1,805 or 28.2 percent of the total number of such licenses issued during the previous financial year. By then the Chinese population had risen to 3,696, an increase of approximately 75 percent over the Chinese population in 1911, whereas the number of trade licences had increased by 116 percent. One in every two Chinese was therefore employed in the grocery retail trade in the 1920s.[48] Figures extrapolated by Colin Clarke show that even in 1960 almost half the Chinese wage earners were in trade.[49]

Whether the entrepreneurship exhibited by the Levantines and Chinese can be linked to economic progress and development in the Caribbean is a complex question. Clearly the Chinese and Levantines have succeeded in establishing ethnic enclaves. Not only have they moved into the middle classes, but some have become extremely wealthy. Their financial contribution to the countries in which they have settled, through taxation and benevolence or as providers of employment, can be variously assessed. Their contribution to local culture and the arts has likewise been positively remarked: "The number of Chinese painters and their full-time dedication to art distinguishes them in Trinidad; painting is valued most, but for a younger Chinese to become a painter is also a form of creolization."[50] Entrepreneurial success puts the Chinese among the richest as well as the best educated of West Indian ethnic groups. The average Chinese income was almost five times that of blacks and three times that of colored Jamaicans in 1960, and the Chinese of Trinidad and Surinam prosper similarly.[51] Well-to-do younger Chinese have moved into upper class neighborhoods in the suburbs of Port-of-Spain, Georgetown, Kingston, and Paramaribo. In British Guiana, rice cultivation, usually associated with Indian farmers, was done by the Chinese even before the Indian immigrants became involved on a large scale.[52]

But their ethnic identification also marks the Chinese out for envy and hatred. In Jamaica, alleged Chinese mistreatment of a negro employee in 1965 sparked a riot in Kingston in which many Chinese stores were burned and looted.[53] Decisions by Chinese West Indian umpires in England-West Indies cricket test matches have sparked mass riots in Guyana (1953-1954), Trinidad (1959-1960), and Jamaica (1968). The ordinary Jamaican saw the game as a replica of the society, symbolized "in the person of the Chinese umpire . . . a racial type inevitably associated with the dominant class in the West Indies."[54] Yet despite this, Guyana selected a Chinese as its first president (Arthur Chung), and Trinidad's first native-born governor (Solomon Hochoy) was also Chinese.[55]

IV. Contributions of Immigrants

Arguments based on European experience of immigrant groups have been summarized by Alejandro Portes as follows:

(a) Labor migration tends to exercise a downward movement on working class wages and job security;

(b)   Labor migration tends to upgrade health and the general work fitness of the labor force;

(c)   The dominant classes in the receiving countries collectively save the cost of reproducing a section of their labor force. Similarly, unemployment, illness and old age produce a reverse flow as migrants seek the support of their primary networks in regions of origin;

(d)   Labor migration tends to fragment the solidarity of the working class as natives blame a deteriorating economic condition on the migrants; racist ideologies and discrimination obscure common economic interests.[56]

In most instances, the Caribbean experience of East Indian, Portuguese, and Chinese immigrants supports these general theses. Initially, the immigration flows depressed wages but prompted the territories to create effective medical systems on the estates. British Guiana led the way with properly equipped and serviced estate hospitals; Trinidad, Jamaica, St.Vincent, and Surinam followed suit. Elsewhere arrangements were made for immigrants to be treated in the public hospitals, and Jamaica changed over to such a system in 1879. The system of estate hospitals was also employed in the French colonies. In the 1870s the estate doctors in Trinidad and British Guiana were transformed into government medical officers, whose services were then available to the whole population.[57]

The migration of these groups undoubtedly did fragment working class solidarity, and the dominant class--the planters--avoided some of the costs of raising and educating a native labor force. But the costs of immigration were high, both to the planters and to the colonial administrations. How much was remitted back to China, Madeira, or the Middle East is impossible to calculate, beyond the fact that it would be appreciably more in the case of the Chinese than the Levantines and over a much longer period. The influx of East Indians and Chinese certainly had the effect of depressing wages. In British Guiana, Trinidad, and Martinique wages fell continuously over a number of years as a direct result of immigration. By 1870 the British Guiana Commission felt that immigration should be restricted to prevent any further lowering of wages.[58]

It is harder to make a case for a reverse flow of migrants to their primary networks in the event of

unemployment, sickness, or old age. Even among the
Levantines, the group mainly regarded at least
initially as "sojourners," there was an intention of
returning to the Middle East, although this has usually
not been honored to any significant degree. Even with
the Chinese, the question of a return to China or even
Hong Kong is scarcely ever realized. The most that
might be attained is the dispatch of offspring to Hong
Kong for their education.

   Finally, the existence of sizeable minorities has
resulted in racial attacks in times of hardship or
political turmoil. Guyana's racial politics are
proverbial, and Trinidad too has had to struggle to
preserve a delicate balance. Elsewhere, riots and
physical assault have accompanied the ethnic minorities
from time to time throughout the region.

V. Immigration Policies

   Except in the days of severe labor shortage, most
Caribbean governments in recent times have placed
restrictions on immigration. Since the Second World
War and particularly in the postindependence era, all
governments have instituted barriers to the point that
free and unrestricted immigration does not exist in the
Caribbean. In 1984 Trinidad and Tobago went so far as
to demand visas from Grenadians traveling to Trinidad.

   Warnings are constantly being given by the island
governments against illegal immigrants. Trinidad and
St. Lucia have been the latest to show alarm at the
recent wave of illegal immigrants--mainly from
Guyana. As the tables in Malcolm Proudfoot's study
show, such restrictions have a history stretching back
to the earlier part of the century and the legislative
enactments have increased dramatically since the
1960s.[59] In the case of some countries--Barbados is
one--even return migration by those born in the
territory is discouraged, although this may be changed
in the review of Barbadian immigration policy currently
underway. Immigration restrictions are most severe
against those trying to enter the islands from within
the region, but everywhere they are highly
restrictive. As a general rule, those entering for
periods of more than three months are people on
contract who have been recruited for specific tasks--
medical personnel, teachers, managerial and technical
staff, and the like.

   Given the current world economic situation it is
unlikely that Caribbean governments will loosen their
restrictive immigration legislation--much of which is
bilateral or reciprocal anyway. Selective immigration
of skilled manpower, which is in short supply, and
policies geared towards encouraging the return migrant

are different matters. Here constructive suggestions
can be made, chiefly along the lines already being
adopted by some Caribbean missions abroad, of offering
greater incentives to those with much-needed skills to
come to the Caribbean. The whole point is that
entrepreneurial and technological talents, managerial
skills, and specialist know-how are the chief
requirements, not the unskilled labor that would almost
certainly take advantage of an open-door immigration
policy.

The Need for Entrepreneurs

Thirty years ago Simon Rottenberg of the
University of Chicago wrote about the need for a class
of entrepreneurs--men with creative minds--who would
not be bound by tradition, who would be shrewd and
ruthless in the pursuit of calculated self-advantage,
who would be willing to sacrifice much in the present
for gain in the future. Referring to Jamaica, he asked
where such a class might be found. They might, he
wrote, be brought from the outside, if Jamaica were
willing to administer a policy of immigration.
However, this he rejected, for in the complex
nationality situation pervading the world, such a
policy would be labeled "exploitation" or as "taking
our jobs" and would therefore be unacceptable. He
dismissed the Jamaican whites as being too wedded to
the conservation of the old order--change would be too
hazardous to their vested interest in the status quo.
Innovation could not be expected from that quarter. The
creoles he dismissed as "social risers" who were too
closely linked to metropolitan values and too conscious
of their "property" to be willing to take risks and
invest. The blacks he saw as the wage earners or
independent peasants for whom the immediate future
seemed to offer no reservoir of entrepreneurship.[60]
Instead, Rottenberg pointed to what he called the
"socially marginal men"--the Levantines, the East
Indians, the Portuguese, and the Chinese--who had no
roots in Caribbean tradition. They were not plagued by
principles of fair play. They could drive competition
to the wall or make sharp bargains or seize the
advantage of temporary monopoly. There was no
community whose standards compelled them to withdraw
from these tactics. They were shrewd enough to be
considered somewhat disreputable:

> The Levantines and Chinese are people willing to
> forego consumption. They are capital
> accumulators. Some Jamaicans will tell you that
> they are grubby descendants of pack pedlars, that
> they pursue profit too much, that they are shabby

and that they are not well mannered and polished.
This leaves them unaffected precisely because they
are marginal in the community and they persist in
operating on western entrepreneurially-oriented
premises.[61]

The Value of Entrepreneurs

In his 1983 paper, Peter Kilby of Wesleyan
University underscored some of the advantages that the
immigrant entrepreneur has over the native population--
a superior initial endowment of capital, market, and
technical knowledge and acquired traditions. External
environmental parameters--limited occupational choice,
the intensifying effect of the never-distant threat of
expulsion, greater freedom to undertake extralegal
arrangements--tend to strengthen entrepreneurial
performance. Last, enforced cooperation with fellow
aliens as the sole path to survival builds up over time
networks of trust that provide access to scarce
information, to various risk-spreading arrangements, to
credit on favorable terms, to influential people, and
to a larger pool of individuals to whom portions of
managerial responsibility can be safely delegated.[62]
    Kilby went on to state that although domestic
entrepreneurs could not replicate the advantages of the
alien, they could learn the management practices
directly by working for, or in collaboration with,
minority businessmen. Apprenticeship with aliens, he
claimed, had been a far more important seedbed for
medium-scale domestic firms than association with
multinational corporations.
    He also expressed the view that two types of
policy changes were needed to release the full
potential of the alien's contribution: (1) the removal
of de facto discrimination against these minorities
with respect to licensure, enforcement of government
regulations, and access to development assistance
programs; and (2) policy changes designed to encourage
rather than inhibit the formation of private joint
ventures. Full disclosures, monitored sharing of
managerial responsibilities, and provision for a buy-
out at appraised market value after ten years were some
of his ingredients for a successful "transfer of
technology."

Manpower Resources Fund Proposal

Thoughts such as those expressed by Rottenberg and
Kilby might well pass through the minds of Caribbean
leaders but for them to publicly advance policies
favoring the minorities would be ruinous politically,
as well as ruinous to the group they might seek to

help. Instead, Jamaica's prime minister has put forward ideas about the supply of the technocrats and entrepreneurs required by developing Caribbean nations. In speeches in the United States in 1984, and in Geneva to the United Nations Development Programme (UNDP), Edward Seaga propounded his ideas for the creation of an international fund for manpower resources.[63]

He referred to the brain-drain problem of Third World countries and the fact that between 1977 and 1980 alone, Jamaica lost to North America the equivalent of 60 percent of those who graduated as professional or skilled workers during the same period. Seaga advocated the establishment of an International Manpower Bank that would finance the recruitment of skilled manpower on a medium-term basis with whatever concessions may be affordable from the use of grants, operational projects, or any other concessional resources available to the parties. Such an organization would be administered by an existing UN agency, the UNDP being the most obvious one. Moreover, it would involve universities and foundations and would act as a clearing house, a registration center and an international directory of skills.

Such an idea undoubtedly has its attractions, given the complexities of contemporary Caribbean societies. But whether it affords anything more than temporary relief to the problems of technological advance and entrepreneurial innovation remains open to question. A closer examination of the roles of the minorities in the Caribbean might well reveal options or variants that Caribbean governments might do well to consider, even though finding the risk-takers is only the first step in the battle to induce economic growth.

VI. Conclusion

The history of immigration into the Caribbean shows the outstanding way in which immigrants have contributed to their own and society's development. The contemporary Caribbean would simply be a different place without the racial and cultural varieties and variations that mark those islands. But had the East Indians, the Chinese, and the Levantines not come when they did, would the economic problems that plague the region be any more or less than they are today? Had the Chinese not moved into the grocery trade, others doubtless would have. Had the Levantines not moved into the textile and dry goods business, others would surely have done so. They may have conducted themselves and their businesses differently, but people would still have established marketing patterns that would have fed the population, and people would still

have been clothed and provided with imported goods.
The interesting point about developments in
Jamaica in the 1970s is that as top-level businessmen
fled the worsening economic climate, others rose to
take their places. At the lower level, the higglers
made their operations international and organized
themselves to take flights to Haiti, Panama, and Miami,
to seek out goods in short supply at home and import
them for resale at great profit. So successful did
they become that they now are given the official title
of informal commercial importers (ICIs). When leading
Kingston businessmen met recently with the prime
minister to voice complaints over the unfair way in
which higglers were importing banned items and selling
them on market stalls or on the pavement right outside
the very shops of those same businessmen, the prime
minister silenced them by reminding them of how most of
their businesses had started. The ICIs are an
interesting example of native entrepreneurship, and
they are not confined to Jamaica but span the entire
Caribbean.

Similarly, the economic openings available to the
Chinese and Levantines in the early part of the
twentieth century are not the same as the openings now
in need of filling. Shopkeepers and dry goods
importers are not in demand. Manufacturers of light
industrial products, agricultural technologists,
engineers, computer programmers, and those with
teaching, medical, and managerial skills are the people
now required to gear Caribbean economies to the
requirements of the twenty-first century. True, the
entrepreneurial spirit is needed to motivate such
people to maximize their opportunities and harness
their skills to promote economic growth, but the
climate in which such an entrepreneurial spirit may
thrive depends as much on the actions of Caribbean
governments as on outside forces or the will of the
individuals themselves. A selective immigration policy
for the importation of much-needed manpower skills is
certainly one of the imperatives for Caribbean
governments, given the fact that the brain-drain of
professionals from the region is not going to be
stemmed in the immediate future and may even accelerate
if the promise of better economic prospects for the
Caribbean does not materialize.

256

Notes

1. Elizabeth M. Thomas-Hope (ed.), _Perspectives on Caribbean Regional Identity_ (Liverpool: Centre for Latin American Studies, Monograph Series no. 11, University of Liverpool, 1984), pp. 1-4.

2. Rosemary Brana-Shute (ed.), _A Bibliography of Caribbean Migration_ (Gainesville, University of Florida Libraries, Bibliographic Series No. 3, 1983).

3. Quote from _The Trinidad Express_ 5 July 1970.

4. A.P. Thornton, "Aspects of West Indian Society," _International Journal_ vol. 15 (1960) p. 113, quoted in David Lowenthal, _West Indian Societies_ (London, 1972), pp. 261-262.

5. _Ibid._, Lowenthal, p. 18.

6. _The Daily Gleaner_ 2 August 1984.

7. Lowenthal, _West Indian Societies_ p. 78, _Supra._ _fn._ #4.

8. W.E. Riviere, "Labour shortage in the British West Indies after Emancipation," _Journal of Caribbean History_ Vol. 4 (1972) pp. 1-30.

9. W.A. Green, _British Slave Emancipation: The Sugar Colonies and the Great Experiment 1830-1865_ (London, 1976) p. 261.

10. K.O. Laurence, _Immigration into the West Indies in the 19th Century_ (Aylesbury, Buckinghamshire, 1971), p. 26. See also G.W. Roberts and J. Byrne, "Summary statistics on indenture and associated migration affecting the West Indies," _Population Studies_ Vol. 20, no. 1 (1966) pp. 125-134.

11. Laurence, _Immigration into the West Indies_ pp. 66-67 _Supra._ fn. #10; Edgar L. Erickson. "The Introduction of East Indian Coolies into the British West Indies" _Journal of Modern History_ Vol. 6 (1934) pp. 127-146.

12. P. Guiral, _L'immigration reglementee aux Antilles francaises et la Reunion_ (Paris, 1911) p. 85.

13. Laurence, _Immigration into the West Indies,_ p. 42, _Supra._ fn. #10. See also E. Revert, _La Martinique, etude geographique et humaine_ (Paris, 1949), p. 241.

14. C.J.M. de Klerk, De Immigratie der Hindustanen in Suriname (Amsterdam, 1953), pp. 72-73; Pieter Emmer, "The Importation of British Indians into Suriname (Dutch Guiana) 1873-1916" in Shula Marks and Peter Richardson (eds.) International Labour Migration; Historical Perspectives (London, 1984) pp. 90-111.

15. George W. Roberts, "The Immigration of Africans into the British Caribbean," Population Studies Vol. 7, no. 3 (1954) pp. 235-262. See also: Mary Thomas, Jamaica and Voluntary Laborers from Africa 1840-1865 (Gainesville, 1974) and Monica Schuler "Alas, Alas, Kongo": A Social History of Indentured African Immigration into Jamaica 1841-1865 (Baltimore, 1980).

16. Green, British Slave Emancipation, p. 273, Supra. fn. #9.

17. Laurence, Immigration into the West Indies, p. 30, Supra. fn. #10; D.C. Corbitt, "Immigration in Cuba" Hispanic American Historical Review Vol. 22 (1942) pp. 293-302.

18. Olive Senior, "The Chinese Who Came from Panama," Jamaica Journal Vol. 44, (1979), pp. 78-79; Jacqueline Levy, "Chinese Indentured Immigration to Jamaica During the Latter Part of the Nineteenth Century" unpublished paper for the Fourth Conference of the Association of Caribbean Historians, U.W.I., Mona, Jamaica, 9-14 April, 1972.

19. Laurence, Immigration into the West Indies, p. 41, Supra. fn. #10. B.W. Higman, "The Chinese in Trinidad 1806-1838," Caribbean Studies, Vol. 12, no. 3 (1972), pp. 21-44.

20. A. de Waal Malefijt, The Javanese of Suriname: Segment of a Plural Society (Assen, 1969), pp. 72-73.

21. See: K.O. Laurence, "The Establishment of the Portuguese Community in British Guiana," Jamaican Historical Review, Vol. 5 (1965), pp. 52-56; Robert Ciske, "The Vincentian Portuguese: A Study in Ethnic Group Adaptation" unpublished Ph.D. thesis, University of Massachusetts, 1975; Carl Senior, "German Immigrants in Jamaica," Journal of Caribbean History, Vol. 10-11 (1978) pp. 25-53. Carl Senior, "Bountied European Immigration into Jamaica, 1834-1842," unpublished Ph.D. thesis, University of the West Indies, Mona, 1977; Carl Senior, "The Robert Kerr Emigrants of 1840: 'Irish

Slaves' for Jamaica," Jamaica Journal Vol. 42 (1978) pp. 104-116.

22. Brian L. Moore, "The Social Impact of Portuguese Immigration into British Guiana after Emancipation," Boletin de Estudios Latinoamericanos y del Caribe, Vol. 19 (1975), pp. 3-15.

23. W.K. Crowley, "The Levantine Arabs: Diaspora in the New World" Proceedings of the Association of American Geographers, Vol. 6 (1974) pp. 137-142; E. Safa, L'emigration Libanese (Beirut, 1960).

24. Bill Riviere, "Contemporary Class Structure in Dominica," in Susan Craig (ed.), Contemporary Caribbean: A Sociological Reader (Port of Spain, 1981), Vol. 1, p. 277.

25. Nellie Ammar, "They Came from the Middle East" Jamaica Journal, Vol. 4, no. 1 (1970), pp. 2-6.

26. Colin G. Clarke, Kingston, Jamaica: Urban Growth and Social Change 1692-1962 (Berkeley, 1975) p. 34.

27. G.A. de Bruijne, "The Lebanese in Suriname," Boletin de Estudios Latinoamericanos y del Caribe, Vol. 26 (1976) pp. 15-37.

28. David Nicholls, "Arabs of the Greater Antilles," Paper presented at the Conference on Migration and Culture Contacts in the Caribbean. University of the West Indies, Cave Hill, Barbados, 4-7 April 1984.

29. Ibid., pp. 9-11.

30. de Bruijne, "Lebanese in Suriname," p. 19, Supra. fn. #27.

31. Leonard Broom, "Urbanization and the Plural Society" Annals of the New York Academy of Sciences, Vol. 83 (1960), p. 882.

32. Nicholls, "Arabs of the Greater Antilles," p. 20, Supra. fn. #28.

33. David Nicholls, "No Hawkers and Pedlars: Levantines in the Caribbean," Ethnic and Racial Studies, Vol. 4, no. 4 (1981), 415-431.

34. Nicholls, "Arabs of the Greater Antilles," Supra. fn. #28.

35. Ibid., pp. 31-32. See also: Harry Hoetink, "The Dominican Republic in the Nineteenth Century: Some Notes on Stratification, Immigration and Race" in Magnus Morner (ed.), Race and Class in Latin America (New York, 1970), pp. 96-121.

36. Nicholls, "Arabs of the Greater Antilles," p. 38, Supra. fn. #28.

37. M.H. Fried, "Some Observations on the Chinese in British Guiana," Social and Economic Studies, Vol. 5, no. 1 (1956), pp. 61-62.

38. Report of the Immigration Agent General 1899-1900, cited in B.L. Moore, "Chinese Immigrants in Nineteenth Century Guiana: Socio-cultural Adaptation in an Alien Environment," paper presented at the Conference on Migration and Culture Contacts in the Caribbean, University of the West Indies, Cave Hill, Barbados, 4-7 April 1984, p. 20.

39. Ibid., p. 19.

40. Ibid., p. 16.

41. Broom, "Urbanization and the Plural Society," p. 882, Supra. fn. #31.

42. Lee Tom Yin, The Chinese in Jamaica (Kingston, 1963), p. 55.

43. Andrew W. Lind, "Adjustment Patterns Among the Jamaican Chinese" Social and Economic Studies vol. 7, no. 2 (1958), pp. 144-164.

44. H.F. McNair, The Chinese Abroad (London, 1926) p.2

45. Jacqueline Levy, "The Economic Role of the Chinese in Jamaica: The Grocery Retail Trade" unpublished seminar paper, U.W.I. History Department (Mona, 1967), p. 4.

46. Broom "Urbanization and the Plural Society," p. 882, Supra. fn. #31.

47. Cited in Levy, "Economic Role of the Chinese in Jamaica," p. 14, Supra. fn. #45.

48. Ibid., pp. 15-16.

49. Broom, "Urbanization and the Plural Society," p. 882, Supra. fn. #31; Lowenthal West Indian Societies, p. 203 quoting Colin Clarke, Supra. fn. #4.

50. Lowenthal, West Indian Societies, p. 205, Supra. fn. #4.

51. Ibid., p. 204.

52. Moore, "Social Impact of Portuguese Immigration," p. 39, Supra. fn. #22.

53. Lowenthal, West Indian Societies, p. 209, Supra. fn. #4. Also, Terry Lacey, Violence and Politics in Jamaica 1960-1970 (Manchester, 1977) pp. 85-87.

54. H. Orlando Patterson, "The Ritual of Cricket" Jamaica Journal vol. 3, no. 1 (1969) 23-25, quoted in Lowenthal, West Indian Society, p. 207 Supra. fn. #4.

55. Lowenthal, West Indian Society, p. 208, Supra. fn. #4.

56. Alejandro Portes, "Modes of Structural Incorporation and Present Theories of Labor Immigration" in Mary M. Kritz and Charles B. Keeley (eds.) Global Trends in Migration: Theory and Research on International Population Movements (New York, 1981), pp. 281-282.

57. Laurence, Immigration into the West Indies, p. 50, Supra. fn. #10.

58. Ibid., p. 68.

59. Malcolm. J. Proudfoot, Population Movements in the Caribbean (New York, 1950), pp. 119-147.

60. Simon Rottenberg, "Entrepreneurship and Economic Progress in Jamaica" Inter-American Economic Affairs vol. 7., no. 2 (1953), pp. 74-79.

61. Ibid., p. 78.

62. Peter Kilby, "The Role of Alien Entrepreneurs in Economic Development: An Entrepreneurial Problem" American Economic Association Papers and Proceedings, May 1983, pp. 107-122. See also C.S. Holzberg, "Race, Ethnicity and the Political Economy of National Entrepreneurial Elites in Jamaica," unpublished Ph.D. thesis, (Boston University, 1977).

63.   Address by Rt. Hon. Edward Seaga to the
Governing Council of the UNDP Geneva, 12 June 1984
J.I.S. news release 1080/84, Kingston, Jamaica.

Part 4

Migration and Development:
Caribbean Policies

11. Factors in the Development of a Migration Policy for the Caribbean

Courtney N. Blackman

Migration has been an integral part of the Caribbean experience since the first settlers came to North America across the Siberian land bridge. Migration remains such a fundamental part of the region's personality that governments have been reluctant even to consider policies on the subject. To develop a migration policy for the Caribbean, one must understand first the history of the Caribbean experience with migration and second the islands' uniquely open economic development model. In this chapter I will discuss the economic theory of migration as it applies to the Caribbean and offer a critique of the dependency perspective that is sometimes used. Finally, I will propose some principles that should undergird a Caribbean migration policy and make recommendations for such a policy.

I. Four Phases of Caribbean Migration

Phase One

Migration from the smaller colonies to the larger ones and immigration of contract workers from Europe and Asia characterized the first phase of Caribbean migration from the 1830s through the 1880s. After emancipation, plantations in Trinidad and Tobago, Guyana, and Jamaica faced labor shortages as large numbers of former slaves were lured away by the promise of establishing their own farms on nearby unoccupied crown land. To meet the demand for plantation labor, government bounties encouraged migration from neighboring territories, particularly Barbados.[1] But the need was so acute that additional workers were sought from outside the region. Fleeing the famine of 1846-47, arrivals from Madeira, Portugal, to Trinidad, Grenada, St. Kitts, Nevis, Antigua, Dominica, and St. Vincent prepared the stage for large-scale contractual migration that eventually would bring almost 500,000 laborers from India before migration to the Caribbean was abolished by the Indian government in 1917.[2]

Phase Two

Severe unemployment brought on by the collapse of sugar prices in the 1880s and the ensuing economic depression reduced the flow of labor migration within the Caribbean and introduced a new outward movement that lasted until the end of World War I. The years 1890 to 1920 were a time of substantial emigration from the British West Indies to Cuba, the United Kingdom, and various countries of Central and South America, particularly Panama.

The ready availability of employment in Panama's Canal Zone provided a welcome escape from depressed conditions in the Caribbean; over 23,000 migrant workers were employed there between 1904 and 1914 alone.[3] The abolition of slavery in Cuba (1886) encouraged the flow of immigrants, which gathered momentum with the boom in the sugar industry after World War I. Substantial migration to Costa Rica began in 1885 for railroad construction, and immigrants stayed on to work on the banana plantations. Migrants also went to Haiti, Brazil, Honduras, the Dominican Republic, and Colombia. In addition, the start of World War I provided an outlet for migration to the United Kingdom to join the fighting forces and provide labor for the war effort.

Phase Three

The third phase of Caribbean migration, which spanned the years between the two world wars, was marked by the gradual reduction in opportunities for emigrants and by the return of a large number of migrants who swelled the ranks of the unemployed in the 1930s.[4] The slump in the sugar industry in the 1920s ended migration to Cuba, and the general economic depression severly curtailed migration to other countries, as many governments enacted legislation restricting the number of new entrants. Despite some new opportunities for intraregional migration, prompted, for example, by the abolition of contractual labor from India and the opening of oilfields in Trinidad, the employment situation deteriorated in most countries. After the crash of 1929, large numbers of Caribbean migrants returned home just at the time when the need to "escape" was most pressing.

Phase Four

The outbreak of World War II provided new avenues for outward migration. Some emigrants left to join the fighting forces of Britain and other countries.[5] Others went to Trinidad as mechanics and bus drivers, or migrated to work on the U.S. naval bases being constructed in the region or on the oil refineries of Curacao, Aruba, and Trinidad, which were being expanded to meet wartime needs.

During World War II the shortage of industrial and agricultural labor in the United States was met by the recruitment of contract workers from Jamaica and other Caribbean islands (as well as from Mexico). For almost a decade following the war, the severe shortage of labor for reconstruction offered almost unrestricted permanent entry into the United Kingdom. A similar arrangement, especially for domestic helpers and seasonal workers, facilitated emigration to Canada. Although the United Kingdom subsequently closed its borders, the United States retained its arrangement for contractual seasonal farm labor,[6] and a similar system was set up between Jamaica and Canada in 1967. Permanent migration to the United States increased dramatically after 1965 when the United States dropped its national quota system.[7]

The postwar years also have witnessed a strong undercurrent of agricultural migration into Barbados from St. Vincent and St. Lucia and into Trinidad and Tobago from Grenada. The policy of both receiving countries has generally been to turn a blind eye and from time to time grant amnesty to the many seasonal workers who stay on illegally.

II. Economic Theories of Migration: Open System Versus Dependence

All first-term economics students in West Indian Universities learn that their countries are "open economies" par excellence by reason of their small size, limited natural resources, and extensive cultural, political, and commercial links with other countries. It is therefore remarkable that Caribbean economists have been so slow to invoke the theory of open systems in their analyses of regional economies.

Instead, the conventional wisdom of the 1970s focused on "dependence," blaming the region's underdevelopment on its dependent relationship with former imperial powers. This dependence is characterized by the institution of the plantation and perpetuated by existing multinational corporations that exploit mineral and agricultural resources and control terms of trade between the dependent Caribbean and the dominant metropolis. Dominance is further exerted through a variety of financial, social, and cultural relationships that ensure that major decisions affecting the region are made in the metropolis and in the interest of the metropolis.

As an antidote to dependence, the common prescription of economists has been to recommend reducing interaction with the former imperial powers and maximizing self-reliance. But the more the Caribbean countries have tried to close their economies, the more disastrous have been the results. Closed systems are like machines that work predictably without inputs from their outside environments and tend increasingly toward total disorder. Open systems, on the other hand, have the potential for growth and, through the continuous elaboration and differentiation of their internal organs, can develop the capacity to process inputs from the outside for the welfare of the overall system.

The implication of the open systems theory for the Caribbean countries is that the continous interchange of goods, information, technology, capital, and people is essential to the process of economic development. Migration is an important vehicle for such an interchange.

III. Costs and Benefits of Migration

The theories of comparative advantage and factor price equalization are particularly relevant to formulating a cost-benefit analysis of Caribbean migration. The theory of comparative advantage supposes that trade takes place between two countries because each wishes to exchange commodities that use more of its relatively abundant factor of production for other commodities that use more of its relatively scarce factor. Migration, whether seasonal or permanent, is the manifestation of such trade in the labor market. Where no restrictions are placed on movements, factor prices will tend to equalize between the two countries.[8] The existence of comparative advantage and the tendency for factor prices to equalize combine to create conditions of Pareto optimality, benefiting both sending and receiving countries.

In some Caribbean countries, Barbados in particular, labor surpluses tended to be endemic. Other countries were plagued with an almost continuous shortage of labor. When sugar prices were high, the emigration of labor from Barbados created modest pressure for wage hikes in that country. In the receiving countries, the availability of immigrant surplus labor gave planters an opportunity to balance

the wages of native labor against those of migrant
workers.
Migration also allowed workers to accumulate
savings. Contractual migration to the Caribbean was
seen in India as an escape valve for labor displaced by
the introduction of factories. It also provided an
escape for the peasants who, because of a comprehensive
inheritance system, were forced over the years to farm
smaller and increasingly suboptimal plots of land.
Following World War II, the migration of large
numbers of skilled and unskilled workers from the
Caribbean to the United Kingdom, the United States, and
Canada was actively encouraged by the governments of
receiving and sending countries alike. The Caribbean
had both an excess of unskilled labor and a comparative
advantage in the production of intermediate workers
such as nurses, electricians, and mechanics who were
encouraged to emigrate to Canada and the United
States. Barbados is currently producing a surplus of
high school and college liberal-arts graduates, a
situation that should encourage both Barbados and the
United States to view migration to the United States as
a socially and economically sound policy.
Another element of the analytical framework
involves international commodity trade and the creation
of captive markets abroad for "ethnic" products. Large
West Indian communities in the United Kingdom, the
United States, and Canada have created export markets
for such ethnic products as West Indian rum and flying
fish. Over the years, substantial West Indian markets
have been developed in such immigrant centers as
Shepherd's Bush in London, Flatbush in Brooklyn, New
York, and Kensington in Toronto. The next step in
export stimulation would be to expand marketing efforts
to extend demand for these products beyond the
immigrant community.
The tourist industry in the Caribbean has also
benefited from emigration. In most countries,
emigration has created a tourist market consisting of
nonresident nationals and their children. Migrants and
their families tend to return to the Caribbean for such
festivals as Christmas, Carnival (in Trinidad and
Tobago), or Crop Over (in Barbados) and to attend
cricket matches, especially when the West Indies are
hosting English or Australian teams. As families are
established in the host countries, succeeding
generations often return to the home country in search
of their roots.

The Transfer of Human Capital

In further assessing the costs and benefits of
migration, one can turn to development economics and

the theories of human capital and the transfer of
resources. Although emigration can and, under certain
circumstances, will remove skills that society needs
for its development, a brain drain need not necessarily
occur. One might as easily argue that the less
talented migrate since the more talented succeed at
home as to argue that only the intelligent and
enterprising members of society respond to the stimulus
to move abroad.[9]

The situations that <u>do</u> prompt a brain drain are
serious political or economic disturbances, as occurred
in Cuba in the 1960s and more recently in Jamaica and
Guyana. Although some experts believe that Jamaican
emigration during the 1960s represented a significant
transfer of human capital from the Third World to the
industrialized countries,[10] one might liken emigration
during this period to a blood donation compared to the
hemorrhage that occurred in the 1970s when large-scale
emigration from both Jamaica and Guyana was triggered
by the economic decline and drastic deterioration in
the quality of life stemming from local experimentation
with socialism. In both countries earlier emigration
coincided with economic prosperity. More recent
movements, however, involve the helter-skelter flight
of technical and professional personnel which, for
example reduced the number of doctors in Jamaica by a
third in just two years during the mid-1970s.[11] In the
industrial sector, the emigration of local capitalists
has closed down or reduced the scale of numerous
businesses.[12]

Another aspect that must be included in the
analysis of migratory flows is the return to the
Caribbean of skilled labor. Some talented individuals,
who may have remained trapped in mid-level positions
had they not moved abroad, have returned to the
Caribbean to make significant contributions to the
development effort in the professions of banking,
management, engineering, and computer science. Results
of a Barbados study show that the influence of
returning migrants on colleagues who never migrated has
generally been positive, leading to improvements in
office standards and routines.[13] Migrants, whether
returning nationals or recruited laborers, have brought
new skills to the Caribbean. Rice cultivation in
Guyana and Trinidad, for example, was introduced by
contract workers from India.

Financial Capital Flows

Foreign exchange flows have also been affected by
migration. From the earliest phase, emigrants have
sent back cash remittances to support and educate
children, maintain dependent relatives, and improve

housing conditions. Remittances in kind have also been
substantial, especially during periods of foreign
exchange difficulties when imported goods are difficult
to obtain. Remittances were a significant item in the
current accounts of all Caribbean countries during the
1950s and 1960s. Transfer payments rose from less than
10 percent of Guyana's current balance in 1960 to over
25 percent between 1964 and 1967. Since then,
remittances have gradually declined, both in absolute
and relative terms, as Guyana's economic conditions
have worsened. In the case of Barbados and Jamaica,
remittances have grown in value but have declined
proportionally.

With the rise of politically motivated emigration,
a flight of capital has taken place from Jamaica and
Guyana, and the inflow of remittances has fallen off.
The outflow of capital is difficult to trace, but
persistent deficits and movement in the errors and
omissions column of balance of payments accounts give
some indication of the extent of the problem. The
errors and omissions figures in the balance-of-payments
of both Jamaica and Guyana tended to be positive and
large, indicating unaccounted inflows of capital during
the period of economic growth and political normalcy.
In Guyana, the errors and omissions figure has been
positive on only four occasions since 1974, despite
large inflows of borrowed money.[14] In Jamaica it has
been positive only three times during the same period.

Not surprisingly, migration, both inward and
outward, has been a very important feature in Caribbean
countries as it is in all small socieites. Throughout
history, small societies, such as the American Indians
or Australian Aborigines, have paid dearly for their
isolation. The rate of economic development in the
Caribbean depends on the progressive improvement of
efficiency in the country's political, legal, social,
and other management systems. Migration is an
important vehicle through which small societies, like
those of the Caribbean, can receive the inputs of
information, capital, technology, and new talent so
necessary for their survival and growth. An open
economy, rather than a closed one, offers the best
possibilities for correcting the problems stemming from
economic dependence and underdevelopment.

IV. Migration Principles and Policies:
Recommendations

In addition to its role as a catalyst for economic
modernization, migration serves as an escape valve for
surplus workers during times of rapid labor force
growth when opportunities for employment are limited at
home. Migration from labor-surplus to labor-short

societies is beneficial to both countries. Migration from developing countries to more-developed countries is not limited to unskilled laborers but may include relatively skilled personnel, such as nurses, if the sending country has developed a comparative advantage in providing certain types of training. In a few instances, persons of extraordinary talent in areas like science, medicine, sports, and the performing arts find it necessary to leave smaller countries to reach their highest potential.

Migration is an important vehicle for the transfer of technology from the developed world to the Caribbean. Immigrants from the developed countries and returning emigrants who have obtained education and experience abroad are important carriers of new technologies and attitudes. On the other hand, emigration induced by economic or political disorder at home is likely to signal a significant loss of both human and financial capital. The flight of middle-class professionals and skilled workers usually precipitates balance-of-payments crises as these emigrants liquidate as many of their assets as possible. If links with the home country are completely severed, there is the loss of possible future remittances and investments.

Mindful of the potential benefits of migration, Caribbean governments should liberalize their national policies with respect to the movement of people, especially skilled workers within the region. Restrictions on the movement of professionals, technicians, managers, and entrepreneurs should be removed by mutual agreement between countries. To facilitate this, exchange control restrictions on the transfer of funds within the region and on nonresident borrowing in various territories might also be removed. Caribbean nationals abroad should be exempted from any exchange control or other restrictions imposed on non-nationals or non-residents. The immigration of skilled labor into the Caribbean region might also be extensively liberalized.

It is important that migration be regulated whenever possible to avoid disruptions in the labor markets of either sending or receiving countries. Where permanent settlement may present problems to the receiving country, seasonal migration might be arranged. To ease the burden of administrative costs, a modest tax could be levied on the seasonal or permanent migrant. Deductions might also be made from the income of seasonal migrants to ensure the financial security of any dependents left behind in home countries.

Governments should pursue policies that encourage Caribbean migrants to return their skills to the region. For example, vacancies for technical or professional posts could be advertised in foreign cities with heavy concentrations of West Indians. To pave the way for Caribbean nations returning permanently to their home countries, governments may wish to grant concessions on household goods or automobiles. The punitive levels of personal income tax prevailing in the Caribbean must also be reduced if the region is to attract an adequate number of its skilled nationals from foreign countries.

Deliberate measures could be taken to help Caribbean migrants in the developed countries strengthen their ties to their countries of origin. Consular missions should maintain close links with overseas Caribbean communities and promote their welfare whenever possible. This would facilitate expansion of export markets for "ethnic" goods and motivate migrants to make investments in their home countries. Cultivating the loyalty of Caribbean migrants would also place their political lobbying power at the service of the region.

Finally, Caribbean governments should bear in mind that the outcome of economic and political disorder is often the flight of both skilled workers and capital-- two essential elements of development and modernization. The cultivation of a political, social, and economic climate that keeps educated and skilled individuals at home includes the guarantee of civil rights and protection against personal harm as well as provisions to prevent the sharp deterioration of living conditions.

Notes

1. Dawn I. Marshall, "Migration Within the Eastern Caribbean, 1835-1980," Mimeo (Institute of Social and Economic Research, 1984), p. 14.

2. K.O. Lawrence, Immigration into the West Indies in the Nineteenth Century (Ginn and Co., 1977).

3. V.E. Newton, West Indian Labour Migration to Panama 1850-1914: The Silver Man, (Cave Hill, Barbados: Institute of Social and Economic Research, 1984).

4. I. Dookhan, A Post Emancipation History of the West Indies (Collins Press, 1978).

5. Ibid.

6. H.F. Edwards, "The West Indies Programme for Supplemental Farm Labour," Mimeo (West Indies Central Labour Organization, 1977).

7. R.W. Palmer, "A Decade of West Indian Migration to the United States, 1962-1972: An Economic Analysis," Social and Economic Studies, Vol. 23, No. 4(1974). In 1977 the U.S. established an immigration limit of 20,000 persons from each sending country within an overall annual ceiling.

8. M.O. Clement, R.L. Pfister and K.J. Rothwell, Theoretical Issues in International Economics (Houghton Mifflin Co., 1967).

9. W. Peterson, "Migration--Social Aspects," International Encyclopedia of the Social Sciences, Vol. 10 (The MacMillan Company and the Free Press, 1968).

10. R.K. Girling, "The Migration of Human Capital from the Third World: The Implications and some Data on the Jamaican Case," Social and Economic Studies, Vol. 23, No. 1 (1974); Palmer, "A Decade of West Indian Migration," Supra fn. #8.

11. R.W. Palmer, "Emigration and the Economic Decline of Jamaica," Mimeo, Department of Caribbean Studies, Royal Institute of Linguistics and Anthropology (Netherlands, 1983).

12. Palmer, "A Decade of West Indian Migration," p. 70, Supra. fn. #7.

13. G. Gmelch, "Return Migration to Barbados," Mimeo, Department of Sociology and Anthropology, Union College (Schenectady, 1984).

14. International Monetary Fund, Balance of Payments Statistics 1983, Vol. 34 (Washington, 1984).

12. Migration, Manpower, and Underdevelopment of the Commonwealth Caribbean

Ralph Henry
Kim Johnson

The thesis of this chapter is that although higher wages and opportunities for individual advancement undoubtedly influence the flow of migrants to North America, the major impetus for emigration lies in the structure and functioning of the Caribbean economies. Our historical review of Commonwealth Caribbean migration relies on the Dependency Theory of Underdevelopment in which Caribbean economies are viewed as appendages of the North Atlantic metropolitan countries.[1] As such, the peripheral Caribbean countries remain mired in dependent underdevelopment. In the era of plantation slavery and indentureship, the Caribbean colonies specialized in the production of agricultural staples for their metropolitan center, Great Britain. Great Britain, in turn, provided for the demands of the colonies in the form of economic goods, capital, and technology and in so doing fueled its own industrial transformation.

While continuing to produce primary goods, minerals, and agricultural produce for the metropolis, the ex-colonies have diversified in recent times, as assembly-type industry has been established. However, the introduction of multinational industries seeking the advantage of cheap labor has brought with it a new form of dependence.[2] The failure of the Caribbean countries to adapt and to apply creative policies vis-a-vis multinationals has resulted in the region being far less developed than it could be in terms of diversification and of economic resiliency, compared to countries like Singapore that retained local leverage over the use of foreign capital and broke the historic vertical division of labor between the more advanced and developing countries.

Our approach has much in common with a new theory of international migration, which eschews the assumptions of value neutrality of neoclassical scholarship and explores the effects of structural

273

relations on the process of international migration,
without discounting the push-pull explanation of
migration provided by the neoclassical framework.[3]
Some scholars, especially those whose views are shaped
by conservative traditions, tend to decry the
application of the dependency model since it offers no
prescriptions sui generis. The fact that this is
undoubtedly true does not contradict the model's great
contribution to understanding historical and existing
realities, however. Indeed, approaches that discount
the relevance of insights provided by the dependency
model invariably fail to prescribe anything more than
mere palliatives, since they fail to address underlying
structural problems. At the policy level, few
decision-makers contemplate the possibility of
encouraging return migration. Yet it is time for
attention to be focused on attracting skilled nationals
back to the home country, since human resources are so
vitally important to countries with relatively small
populations and limited land area.[4] The work of Ebanks
et al. represents one of the few attempts to quantify
return migration, but so far no known attempts have
been made to integrate return migration into the
overall planning framework of the region.[5]

In this chapter we will attempt to rectify some of
these omissions and suggest policy proposals that take
into account the goal of severing the dependency
relationship that has precluded the development of
Commonwealth Caribbean economies. We will trace both
the continuity and the changes in the economic
structure of these economies as well as in their
manpower policies, noting that some efforts at
transformation have exacerbated the outflow of
people. We will conclude with some recommendations
that use the limited terrain available to policymakers.

I. Labor Under the Colonial System

In the first phase of the colonial period,
Europeans satisfied their work force requirements by
the forcible movement of African labor to the West
Indies. Colonial policy was geared to ensuring an
"adequate" (meaning excess) supply of labor to the
plantation system through coercive measures, despite
unemployment and underemployment in the local labor
class. Subsequently, slavery gave way to "free" labor
and Indian indentureship. The availability of unused
land permitted many ex-slaves an escape to self-
sufficient subsistence agriculture. However, the
plantation system, by retaining control of virtually
all but the most infertile land and by dominating both
the political and social systems of the Caribbean
countries, kept the mass of West Indians in conditions

hardly better than those imposed on them under the earlier policies of slavery and indentured labor.

Citizenship rights had, at least, allowed Caribbean workers freedom of movement, and many migrated at the turn of the century to the banana plantations of Central America, canal construction in Panama, and the sugar plantations of Cuba, as well as to the United States and Britain.

The Great Depression constricted these outlets to jobs overseas, and the effect was soon manifested in the precipitous decline of already poor living conditions in Commonwealth Caribbean countries. The social conflagration of the 1930s, 100 years after emancipation, was inevitable. The Moyne Commission, established by the British Government to examine the cause of the riots, produced an analysis that was an absolute, if unintentional, indictment of the colonial order. It catalogued a litany of social and economic problems in the British West Indies: unemployment, poverty, malnutrition, poor public health facilities, high infant mortality, bad housing, fractious industrial relations, and limited prospects for the small-scale agriculture in which large numbers of people were engaged. Yet the commission's recommendations epitomized the dependency relationship that was officially regarded as inexorable for the colonies of the Caribbean. With its sole concern the continued supply of cheap plantation labor, the commission failed to recommend any restructuring of the economy and rejected schemes for industrial development. Instead it suggested that the solution to the crisis might be found in encouraging a large and prosperous peasant class--a naive proposal given that the responsibility for implementing it would fall into the hands of local assemblies that were dominated by plantation interests.

As basic freedoms were granted, the working classes began to demand the expansion of educational opportunities. Although opposed by the plantation interests, the gradual expansion of liberal arts schooling provided some natives with an escape from the plantation or subsistence farm and an entrance into the lower ranks of the colonial bureaucracy or school system. Thus a school system heavily biased toward the liberal arts was firmly established as was the bias toward a literary education among the people of the Commonwealth Caribbean.

In sum, the dependency status of the British West Indies not only determined the nature and scope of early migratory movements, but it also influenced the labor utilization system and the structure and functioning of the educational and training systems. The early demographic history of the Commonwealth

Caribbean countries was functionally related to the effect of the sociopolitical structures of slavery, indentureship, and colonialism. The task of economic planners in the postcolonial period was to transform the Caribbean economies through the optimal utilization of local resources and labor.

II. Decolonization and Labor Utilization

After the Second World War, the newly elected assemblies of the Caribbean decreed that the former colonies should be more than producers of primary products for the British market. They were encouraged toward the possibility of industrial development by the import substitution experience of the war years. Arthur Lewis, flying in the face of the Moyne Commission, provided intellectual artillery for industrialization with his then radical thesis suggesting that the British West Indian economy suffered from overpopulation or "unlimited supplies of labor" and that the agricultural sector could provide decent living conditions only to a much reduced labor force.[6] What was required, he said, was the growth of an industrial sector (with the active support of the state) that would absorb surplus labor. Lewis estimated that the Commonwealth Caribbean needed to create over 100,000 jobs over a ten-year period. The deus ex machina of this transformation was "a considerable inflow of foreign capital and capitalists." Foreign capital provided the initial investment and expertise, foreign markets offered the arena of demand, and, apart from "wooing and fawning upon such people," the locals supplied cheap labor. Eventually, this "modern" sector would expand as profits were ploughed back into productive investment, jobs would be created, locals would gain experience to take over the enterprises, and the need for capital could be satisfied from internal sources.

The labor strategy supporting the Lewis model addressed itself to the following issues: (1) the maintenance of low wages to retain comparative advantage, (2) the inculcation of industrial discipline in the working class, (3) the development or expansion of vocational education and technical training, and (4) the transfer of technology through the training of local managers and technicians.

On paper, this strategy appears interventionist. In practice, however, it can be swayed by social demand and biases inherited from the colonial period.

The first component of Lewis's model was negated by the fact of political democracy and the right to collective bargaining it accorded to workers. It was unrealistic to assume that West Indian trade unions born in the furnace of the 1930s would have passively accepted what they considered a less than decent standard of living for their members when they could see other highly visible groups in society prospering.[7]

Early development programs seemed to honor the spirit of the Lewis strategy by proposing the rapid expansion of vocational and technical training for a nascent industrial sector. However, deep-seated tradition worked against the reorientation of the educational system away from the liberal arts toward new economic demands. In the experience of Trinidad and Tobago, which was replicated to some degree in many Caribbean countries, the government introduced new "modern" secondary schools in the 1950s with a curriculum that emphasized the vocational arts. However, by the mid-1960s, all these new schools were pursuing the same curricula as the traditional prestige schools. On reviewing the situation in the English-speaking Caribbean, Carrington found that efforts to modify the curriculum of the academic-style schools were only "minimally successful."[8] Finally, as unemployment rose, the school system was used to delay the entry of young people into the labor market. Training was deliberately extended, often despite the saturation of graduates in particular fields.[9]

Although a strict benefit-cost analysis would have yielded a high premium on technical skills and training for the economy as a whole, the high individual returns arising from a traditional liberal arts education reinforced the bias against nonprofessional technical and craft training. Henry found rates of return for technicians and others with critical skills substantially below those for traditional arts majors.[10] Ironically, the technicians and skilled workers found easy entry into the North American labor market in the late 1960s and early 1970s. Unrewarded and even exploited at home, these workers were able to multiply their earnings in the same occupations abroad.

The general approach to labor planning mirrored the laissez-faire stance of government vis-a-vis direct productive activity and long-range planning. The education and training systems were expected to adjust to new economic requirements without the benefit of state intervention. Development plans were not supported by educational or labor planning. Nor was there any examination of the impact of development planning on migration, despite official concerns in that area.

By 1951, most territories in the British West Indies had begun inviting foreign capital for industrialization. Incentive legislation was enacted in Antigua, Barbados, Belize, Grenada, Guyana, Jamaica, Monsterrat, St. Lucia, and Trinidad and Tobago.

Concessions were offered in the form of tax holidays, accelerated depreciation allowances, subsidized factory space, duty-free raw material imports, and the right to repatriate unlimited profits.

Large flows of foreign capital entered the West Indian economies, but the social and economic effects were disappointing. After the initial period of investment, capital outflows vastly exceeded capital inflows.[11] Profits were repatriated, either directly or by transfer pricing, and the region became a net capital exporter. If, as Lewis argued, the economic development of the region required an infusion of capital, industrialization by invitation made development even less possible because of the subsequent repatriation of capital.

Moreover, Carrington, Girvan, and others have shown that the introduction of subsidiaries and branch plants created only the veneer of industrialization.[12] Many of the plants set up in response to fiscal incentives were geared to provide for local and regional demand rather than for extra-regional export markets. With the incentive structure weighted in favor of imported capital and other inputs, production was relatively capital intensive, offering few opportunities for backward linkages and employment creation, even in such areas as food processing. As a result, the modern sectors of the Commonwealth Caribbean economies proved incapable of creating employment sufficient to cope with the increase in population and labor force.

In Table 12.1 data are presented on manufacturing workers compiled by Abdullah for the census years 1960 and 1970.[13] Even though the absolute numbers of manufacturing workers increased, the percentage of the total labor force employed in manufacturing declined in virtually every country. Certainly the manufacturing sector failed to live up to the expectations of the Lewis strategy.

Table 12.1

Proportion of Working Population in Manufacturing
in Commonwealth Caribbean Countries, 1960 and 1970

	1960	1970
Jamaica	15.0	14.2
Trinidad & Tobago	16.6	14.4
Guyana	16.3	15.3
Barbados	15.2	13.6
Belize	15.2	15.2
St. Lucia	12.1	8.3
Grenada	10.3	8.5
St. Vincent	11.7	8.0
Dominica	11.3	7.9
St. Kitts-Nevis	10.9	10.7
Montserrat	8.3	5.6

Source: N. Abdullah, The Labour Force in the Commonwealth Caribbean (St. Augustine, 1977), Tables 23 and 24.

Meanwhile, unions threatened to increase wages dramatically. In 1965, the government of Trinidad and Tobago found it necessary to pass the Industrial Stabilization Act, which restrained the use of industrial action by employers and employees, thus blunting the strike weapon. The wider objective of the legislation was to control the rate of increase in the price of labor, which was seen as the cutting edge of comparative advantage and the major attraction to direct foreign investment.

At the same time, however, the gap between the rich and poor widened. In Trinidad and Tobago between 1957-58 and 1971-72 the poorest 20 percent of the population saw their share of total income fall from 3.4 percent to 2.2 percent whereas the richest 10 percent increased their share from 33.3 percent to 37.8 percent.[14] If the argument of Harewood and Henry is correct--that this growing household income disparity is caused by increased unemployment--then a similar tendency would have applied throughout the Commonwealth Caribbean.[15]

After pursuing development programs that exacerbated an increasingly desperate unemployment and underemployment situation, the governments of the Commonwealth Caribbean countries resorted to measures to influence demographic patterns. Temporary and permanent emigration and fertility control were to become part of economic strategy--succeeding where labor policies had failed. Unskilled workers were encouraged to emigrate to Britain in the 1950s and early 1960s, until British restrictions were imposed. The liberalization of immigration laws in the United States and Canada permitted the reorientation of migration to North America, and Caribbean governments encouraged emigration to those two countries during the 1960s and 1970s. Segal summarized the reasoning behind this approach: "It was the means whereby unemployment would be reduced, remittances [should be] received to provide for the young and old left behind, the school dropout would be kept from becoming politically volatile, and new families and initial child bearing would occur elsewhere. Since such emigration was spontaneous, popular governments could not be accused of deporting their own people. . . ."[16]

The other implicit component of labor policy--fertility control--was met with initial opposition in countries with large Roman Catholic populations. By 1974, however, nearly all Commonwealth Caribbean governments were involved in some form of family-planning program and even turned a blind eye to abortion practiced by medical doctors.

III. Post-Lewis Experiments

The experience of the three largest and one of the smallest Commonwealth Caribbean countries in the 1970s and early 1980s demonstrates the intractability of problems associated with structural dependence. In each case, the government abandoned the Lewis contention that its role be restricted to providing infrastructure and limited control over private-sector investment, income flows, and employment. Minimal objectives, in the redefined role of the state, included: (1) direct creation of employment by government, (2) participation, ownership, or total control over the main sectors of the economy, (3) redistribution of income and wealth to correct for gross inequality, and (4) comprehensive economic planning.

The government of Jamaica adopted the philosophy of "Democratic Socialism," while Guyana announced itself the first "Cooperative Socialist Republic" and embarked on a new economic model with the cooperative and state sectors forming the axis of transformation. Trinidad and Tobago embarked less stridently on a "mixed economy" path. Although the economy remained largely under private control in Grenada, the government acquired ownership of agro-processing industries and sought a large state cooperative sector.

In Guyana, the ruling party nationalized the bauxite and sugar industries that contributed approximately 90 percent of the country's export earnings and 33 percent of its gross domestic product and that employed a majority of its work force. By the mid-1970s, the government controlled some 80 percent of economic activity and, by establishing a state planning commission, was on its way toward breaking the shackles of underdevelopment and foreign domination. Guyana embarked on a major exercise to restructure its training program, especially with respect to vocational, agricultural, and cooperative studies and tertiary education.

However, the ultimate objectives of Guyana's development strategy were not fulfilled for reasons having to do, in part, with the supply of labor. The bauxite and sugar markets were poor in the 1970s, and there was not enough down-stream development among traditional export industries, nor enough generation of new industries for external markets. As foreign exchange earnings dwindled, the increased price for fuel, capital equipment, and other imports put a severe strain on the Guyanese balance of payments, forcing the government to impose draconian foreign currency regulations and strict controls over wages, salaries, and other employee benefits.

Basic needs suffered. Persistent strife created a climate that was not conducive to economic advancement. Private foreign investment was not forthcoming and the state could only attract limited official investment flows from friendly eastern bloc countries.

The deteriorating economy created a stampede of talent from Guyana. Skilled and unskilled workers alike sought refuge in neighboring Suriname, Barbados, and Trinidad and Tobago, while higher level managers and professionals found employment in North America.

Thus, although the government of Guyana expended tremendous resources on education and training, it was unable to provide the conditions necessary to achieve adequate returns on those investments, despite various schemes to recruit graduates into the public service. Guyana is perhaps the classic example of a country where individuals view education and training as a passport to geographical as well as social mobility. As a result, the country is a net exporter of human capital, even though it is one of the most progressive of the Caribbean countries in terms of reorienting its educational and training system to suit the developmental needs of a Third World society.

During the 1970s, Jamaica introduced a literacy program, training schemes, and free secondary and university education, all with a view toward providing an appropriate labor base for the structural transformation of the economy. But the government raced into early headwinds as it took up the challenge of social redistribution and economic reorganization at the very moment when resources were declining. The sugar market collapsed after 1974; bauxite demand tapered off, and the tourist industry plummeted with the oil crisis. Shrinking foreign exchange reserves could no longer be expected to pay for both higher priced oil imports and economic development. The absence of a diversified economic structure exposed the vulnerability of Jamaica's dependent economy. The Manley government's inability to stimulate new sources of growth eventually put it at the mercy of the International Monetary Fund's adjustment policies and, in time, led to its downfall.[17]

Massive emigration began in the 1970s. Jamaica's efforts to integrate training with development strategies turned out to benefit the U.S. economy as skilled workers took flight to North America. Because Jamaica's economic planners could do nothing to reduce the labor outflow, the country found itself increasingly dependent on technical assistance from Cuba and other friendly governments to provide basic services.

Trinidad and Tobago was fortunate in that the

country's major export--petroleum--benefited from the post-1973 escalation in oil prices. The government utilized "petrodollars" to expand the state sector and to adopt a resource-based strategy dependent on such industries as urea, methanol, fertilizer, and steel. Oil revenues afforded the government an opportunity to advance its objectives of universal secondary education and improved on-the-job training.

Despite its financial resources, the government refrained from integrating its myriad activities into an overall plan and adopted instead a project-by-project approach that created havoc in the labor market, upsetting wage structures and engendering unrealistic expectations even among the unskilled and unemployed. The country's frenzied efforts to expand its infrastructure and to establish resource-based industries intensified the demand for labor, as did the booming oil and construction industries. This led to return migration and the importation of workers, especially at the skilled and professional levels, who demanded astronomical wages and other benefits.

The recent collapse of oil prices, however, has exposed the inherent vulnerability of the Trinidad and Tobago economy as a specialized, dependent exporter. The country's so-called "new" industries, all based on mature technologies, face stiff competition on the open market. Its vertical incorporation into the North Atlantic economy and the narrowness of its export base keep Trinidad and Tobago as dependent as before, and its labor utilization and migration patterns will continue to be influenced by that fact. The current problems of Trinidad and Tobago are no different from those in the early 1970s. Already there is evidence of high-level labor outflows that could increase with economic recovery in the North Atlantic. In the absence of a transformation to a less-dependent and truly diversified economic base, the country is once again at risk of losing (through migration) much of the human capital attracted over the last ten years.

In the case of Grenada, only in 1979 did a new government begin to pursue policies to improve the human-resource base of the country. Given the government's socialist posture, foreign training was limited for Grenadians, except in socialist bloc countries, but substantial improvements in the work force were in the making before the foreign intervention of 1983. Agricultural diversification, agroindustrial development, cooperatives, and state control constituted the major planks of economic transformation.[18] Severe unemployment, inherited from the previous administration, had been substantially reduced by 1983, in part by the exodus of nationals opposed to the new government. Behind the rhetoric,

the government adopted realistic strategies to
diversify the agricultural sector to satisfy local food
requirements, provide basic needs in housing and
health, and create new export markets through
industrialization. Priority was given to agricultural
training, cooperative education, and the improvement of
vocational skills.

Yet the stuttering of economic growth in 1983 was
undoubtedly caused in part by poor technical training,
lack of worker support, and the emigration of skilled
workers. Grenada never addressed itself to the task of
attracting return migration, although it was concerned
with the brain drain. Instead it depended on the
ideological commitment to its socialist transformation
policy to entice back some of those who had fled during
the previous government. In addition, a number of
left-leaning Commonwealth Caribbean nationals were
attracted to the government's program and took up high-
level positions in the state bureaucracy.

The fact that the Caribbean countries embraced
regional economic cooperation, first through the
Caribbean Free Trade Association (CARIFTA) and then
through the Caribbean Common Market (CARICOM), did not
affect the basic structural relations that prompted a
high rate of emigration from the region as a whole. In
the final analysis, internal conflicts were to retard
the process of Caribbean integration and thus stymie
any beneficial efforts it might have had in labor
utilization.

We have examined the experience of those countries
that took the greatest initiatives at social and
economic transformation, with the state playing the
major role. The weakness and vulnerability of these
dependent economies were demonstrated. Increased
emigration served as a good index of the failure of
their attempts at economic restructuring.

In Barbados and the smaller territories,
governments seemed only to respond to whatever
strategies were advocated by the international lending
agencies in their support of education and training
programs. More recently, however, a discrete change
has taken place in Barbados' approach as evinced in its
concern over new technologies and the upgrading of
technical training. Indeed, Barbados seems better
prepared than many of the region's countries to embark
on the development of skill-intensive industries.
Although Barbados has demonstrated a growing
aggressiveness toward the transfer of skills and
knowledge from non-nationals to nationals, it is still
too early to pass judgment on the efficacy of this
approach in reversing emigration, particularly in the
absence of complementary physical investment and
capital formation.

IV. Conclusions and Recommendations

In the absence of genuine economic transformation, labor strategies have proved to be cosmetic, if not actually harmful. The mismatch between the educational system and the local economy has translated a great deal of investment into an involuntary gift to the North Atlantic countries. The emigration of skilled, professional people represents one of the features of structural dependence. What may pass for human-resource development may be little more than the provision of passports for emigration or, at best, passive incorporation into the restructuring of the North Atlantic economies, as the latter slough off their sunset industries.

The experience of the last three decades invites questioning of the presumed benefits of trade arrangements between the Commonwealth Caribbean and North Atlantic countries. The Lome Accords and the Caribbean Basin Initiative have been characterized as milestones in the new economic arrangements between developed and developing countries and have even been advanced as possible solutions to the problem of emigration from the Commonwealth Caribbean. Although these treaties no doubt contain important benefits for the region, unless they are creatively interpreted from a Caribbean perspective, they could merely guarantee the continuation of the old order.

The newly industrialized countries of Southeast Asia have been cited as classic examples of the successful application of the Lewis strategy. What has brought success to these countries is an active policy to "skill up" from labor-intensive to skill-intensive and finally to knowledge-intensive industries. If this experience could be replicated in the Caribbean region, the tide of migration would be stemmed, and both North and South would prosper. The following recommendations address this goal.

Cooperative Research Projects

There is a need for "joint-venture" approaches to the analysis of the problems of the region. One example is tropical agriculture, where there is a dearth of information on food strains appropriate to the region's needs and tastes. Even though much land is tied up in uneconomic export agriculture, the region's dependence on imported food increases and rural-to-urban migration mounts. Cooperative research could bring skills and information (particularly in the area of biogenetics) from the metropole to the region. This approach could be replicated in other high-tech fields. Private U.S. firms could be granted

concessions under bilateral government agreements to
promote research in universities and joint-venture
corporations in the region.

A New Basis for Trade

If trade is to liberate the Commonwealth Caribbean
from underdevelopment and labor emigration, an entirely
new basis for trade must be promoted. Instead of
relying on labor-intensive products, the focus should
shift to dynamic new growth industries requiring
skilled workers, which the region can provide with some
comparative advantage. This shift would allow the
region to approach more quickly the best features of
the East Asian economies and promote genuine
interdependence. Arrangements like the Caribbean Basin
Initiative would need to be modified considerably to
weight incentives in the direction of new higher
technology products.

A Large-Scale Scholarship Program

The United States needs to assist the Commonwealth
Caribbean in upgrading its work force especially in the
scientific and technical fields. A training program
should anticipate future growth industries and mirror
the requirements deriving from our second
recommendation. Students would receive scholarships to
attend universities, technical schools, and community
colleges in the United States and would be bonded by
their governments to return and serve their countries
for a specific period on completion of their course of
study.

Labor Training Strategies

The Caribbean countries need to define more
carefully their labor and training objectives. In the
final analysis, economic competitiveness in resource-
poor countries will depend on the capacity,
flexibility, and resilience of the work force.
Educational and training programs must accommodate a
rapidly changing technological environment. Thus it is
important to provide a broad level of education on
which training and retraining programs can be mounted
during the course of working life. (Since the
comparative advantage of the Commonwealth Caribbean
lies in its human-resource potential, an emphasis on
training for the growth industries could attract future
investment to the region.)

286

Return Migration

All these proposals seek to increase the attractiveness of employment at home. However, some migration from the region to the United States and elsewhere will continue to occur, especially among those seeking higher education not found in the region. There is an unfortunate tendency in the Commonwealth Caribbean to ignore the needs of students who sponsor their own studies abroad. A program is needed to inform migrant students of job prospects at home and to entice back some of those who have acquired extensive training and experience abroad.

The above recommendations are basic but do not exhaust the approaches relevant to genuine transformation of dependent underdeveloped economies into countries achieving interdependent development. The full utilization of the human resource base of the region is a major plank of the new structure and vital to the elimination of the problems of emigration. The region finally has to develop the integrated framework that will allow it to retain its most important resource--its people.

Notes

1. While the Latin American structuralists are credited with the dependency thesis, the "plantation school" developed similar notions first. See L. Best, "A Model of Pure Plantation Economy" Social and Economic Studies, Vol. 17 (1968). This work stands in the middle of a Caribbean tradition established by E. Williams. Rodney's work is the most recent expression. See also E. Williams, Capitalism and Slavery (London, 1964) and W. Rodney, How Europe Underdeveloped Africa (Dar es Salaam, 1972).

2. An excellent exposition of this thesis is S. Sassan-Kooh, "The Internationalization of the Labour Force," Studies in Comparative International Development Vol. 15 (1980).

3. See H. A. Watson, "Theoretical and Methodological Problems in Commonwealth Caribbean Migration Research: Conditions and Causality," Social and Economic Studies, Vol. 3 (1982).

4. In a recent analysis, the issue of small size has been addressed in terms of the "Economics of Rocks". The smaller the physical size of the country the lower the probability that there would exist a range of high valued natural resources and the greater the need to depend on the creative utilisation of human resources. See R.M. Henry, "Human Resources in Trinidad and Tobago: A One Factor Problem?" ASSET, Vol. 3 (1984).

5. See G. Ebanks, P. George and L. Noble, "Emigration from Barbados, 1951-1970," Social and Economic Studies Vol. 28 (1979).

6. W.A. Lewis, "Industrialisation of the British West Indies," Caribbean Economic Review, Vol. 7 (1950).

7. Ibid.

8. L. Carrington, Education and Development in the English Speaking Caribbean: A Contemporary Survey (ECLA, Port-of-Spain, 1978).

9. In the late 1960s, students of the largest Technical Institute in Trinidad often applied to the U.S. Embassy to emigrate on graduation.

10. R. Henry, The Basic Situation in Manpower Planning in Caribbean Countries, CDCC/PWG: M/81/3(ECLA, Port-of-Spain, 1981).

11. A. McIntyre and B. Watson, Studies in Foreign Investment in the Commonwealth Caribbean (Mona, 1974), McIntyre and Watson undertook their study using the framework inspired by the dependency model. For an analysis of the Jamaican experience, see N. Girvan, Foreign Capital and Economic Underdevelopment in Jamaica (Mona, 1971).

12. See E. Carrington, "Industrialisation by Invitation in Trinidad and Tobago since 1950," in N. Girvan and O. Jefferson (eds.), Readings in the Political Economy of the Caribbean (Kingston, 1971), and N. Girvan, Foreign Capital.

13. N. Abdullah, The Labour Force in the Commonwealth Caribbean (St. Augustine, 1977).

14. R. Henry, "A Note on Income Distribution and Poverty in Trinidad and Tobago," Research Papers, No. 8 (Port-of-Spain, 1974).

15. This issue is examined in some detail with the use of data for Trinidad and Tobago in J. Harewood and R. Henry, Inequality in a Post Colonial Society: Trinidad and Tobago, 1956-1981 (St. Augustine, forthcoming).

16. Government of Trinidad and Tobago, White Paper on Public Sector Participation (Port-of-Spain, 1972).

17. Results are found in T.M. Farrell, R. Henry, D. Phillips and A. Seabrun-Lewis, "Grenada: Employment and Household Survey, 1980," Department of Economics (St. Augustine, 1981).

18. The thrust to diversify the agricultural base in Grenada is examined in R. Henry and G. Sammy, "CARIAGRO: Grenada and St. Vincent as Prototypes in Agro Industrial Development," mimeo (St. Augustine, 1983).

13. Linking Tourism and Agriculture to Create Jobs and Reduce Migration in the Caribbean

Luther G. Miller

I. Introduction

Caribbean governments have been drawn increasingly toward coping with the consequences of internal and international migration. The movement of workers from rural to urban areas has created new social and educational demands on the governments. The subsequent movement of people from urban areas to other countries has reduced the pool of skilled and professional talent. To cope with urbanization and unemployment, governments have expanded the public sector and kept food prices low. The latter, in turn, has discouraged agricultural production, thus accelerating migration.

Though rich in land and poor in foreign exchange, the Caribbean imported $736 million of food from the United States in 1980. the English-speaking Caribbean alone spent over $600 million on food in 1980 or nearly $100 per capita.[1] Some of this food was consumed by tourists. A central question for future Caribbean economic development is whether the nations of the region can forge and implement a strategy to link the agricultural and tourist sectors to achieve the following objectives: (1) increase jobs in both sectors, (2) reduce labor migration to the urban areas and abroad, and (3) reduce the waste of foreign exchange on imported food. In this chapter, I will outline such a strategy, explaining why it has not yet been implemented and how it can and should be implemented. My thesis is that only concerted government policy can link agriculture and tourism in the Caribbean to benefit both sectors, accelerate the region's development, and reduce the pressures to emigrate.

II. The Economic Impact of Tourism

Domestic and international tourism is a

significant and often vital component of all the Caribbean economies. International tourism involves a potential transfer of wealth from developed to developing countries and is an important propellant for an industry, which in many countries shows the greatest growth potential of all economic sectors. The role of tourism in economic and social development has made its growth a strategic priority in the plans of most Caribbean governments. For numerous countries aspiring to rapid development, and even for those that have already attained it, encouraging tourism can be one of the most effective and least costly formulas for obtaining socioeconomic advancement, since it uses human resources intensively while utilizing a relatively small investment of financial capital.

International tourism is growing, particularly in Third World countries. The tourism industry has retained its resilience despite the oil crisis of the 1970s and a decade of inflation culminating in the economic recession of the early 1980s. In the last thirty-two years, the number of international tourists has declined only twice--in 1974 and in 1982. In developing countries, tourism has grown faster than the export sector. Despite a decline in overall trade, international tourism receipts grew by 4 percent in 1982. The developing countries' share of nearly $100 billion of tourist revenues was estimated at 25 percent to 30 percent.[2]

Caribbean countries account for 2.6 percent of total international arrivals. The trend in Caribbean tourism has been similar to that of the rest of the world: steady growth since 1970 with two hiccups caused by the poor general economic climate in 1975 and 1981. The number of visitors to the Caribbean grew from 4.23 million in 1970 to 7.34 million in 1983 (see Table 13.1).

An estimated $4.45 billion was spent by tourists in the Caribbean in 1983. The two principal beneficiaries of this expenditure were the Bahamas and Puerto Rico, each receiving around $700 million and together accounting for one third of total receipts (see Table 13.2).

Visitor spending represented from 37.5 percent of export value in Montserrat to 3.5 percent in Trinidad and Tobago in 1980. Only in the agriculture or mineral-rich countries is the amount spent by visitors relatively small compared to that from merchandise exports.[3] But even in these countries, tourism ranks among the top three sources of foreign exchange. Between 10 percent and 20 percent of the foreign exchange produced by tourism is converted into government revenues, depending on the degree of development of each country.

Table 13.1

Tourist Arrivals in the Caribbean
(thousands of people)

	1970	1980	1981	1982	1983	% Change 1983/82
OECS* Countries	177.1	324.5	296.3	292.3	327.9	+ 12.2
Anguilla	1.0[1]	5.7	6.2	6.7	7.8	+ 16.2
Antigua	63.4	86.6	84.7	87.0	101.1	+ 16.2
Dominica	13.5	14.4	15.9	19.0	19.6[2]	+ 3.2
Grenada	30.4	29.4	25.1	23.2	35.0[1]	-
Montserrat	9.5	15.5	15.6	14.6	15.0[1]	+ 2.7
St. Kitts/Nevis	13.5	32.8	35.5	34.5	34.2	- 0.9
St. Lucia	29.5	79.7	68.6	70.2	77.4	+ 10.2
St. Vincent & Gren.	16.4	50.4	44.7	37.1	37.7	+ 1.7
Other CARICOM**	591.6	1028.1	1007.9	1033.6	1156.5	+ 11.1
Barbados	156.4	369.9	352.6	303.8[1]	328.3[1]	+ 8.1
Belize	42.0	63.7	62.1	62.0[1]	62.0[1]	-
Jamaica	309.1	395.3	406.4	467.8	566.2	+ 21.0
Trinidad & Tobago	84.1	199.2	186.8	200.0[1]	200.0[1]	-
Netherlands Antilles	289.1	620.3	654.3	683.1	645.5	- 5.5
Aruba	75.0	188.9	221.3	220.2	195.2	- 11.4
Bonaire	7.4	25.2	28.7	30.3	27.8[1]	- 8.4
Curacao	106.6[1]	184.7	176.3	174.4	115.0[1]	- 34.0
St. Maarten	100.6[1]	221.5	228.0	258.2	307.5	+ 19.1
Bahamas	891.5	1181.3	1030.6	1101.1	1200.0[1]	+ 9.0
Bermuda	302.8	491.6	429.8	420.3	446.9	+ 6.3
France (D.O.M.)	80.6	314.9	389.8	365.6[2]	370.0	+ 1.2
Guadeloupe	47.2	156.5	132.8	189.4[2]	194.0[2]	+ 2.4
Martinique	33.4	158.5	157.0	176.2	176.0	-
U.S. Territories	1460.8	2007.4	1917.1	1903.7	1879.8	- 1.3
Puerto Rico	1088.4	1627.4	1573.4	1564.7	1529.8	- 2.2
U.S. Virgin Islands	372.4	380.0	343.7	340.0	350.0[1]	+ 2.9
Other Countries	447.0	1277.1	1306.7	1350.2	1312.7[1]	- 2.8
British Virgin Islands	33.5	97.0	109.6	113.7	118.9	+ 4.6
Cayman Islands	22.9	120.2	124.6	121.2	130.8	+ 7.9
Costa Rica	154.9	345.5	333.1	371.6	326.0[1]	- 12.3
Dominican Republic	63.0	301.1	339.9	341.2	340.0[1]	-
Haiti	33.7	138.0	139.2	139.0[1]	139.0[1]	-
Suriname	20.0[1]	48.4	48.0	40.0[1]	40.0[1]	-
Turks & Caicos Is.	2.0[1]	11.9	12.3	13.3	13.0[1]	-
Venezuela	117.0	215.0	300.0	210.2	305.0[1]	- 2.5
Total	4241.0	7234.0	6933.0	7150.0	7339.0	+ 2.6

[1] Denotes Caribbean Tourism Research and Development Centre (CTRC) Barbados estimates

[2] Denotes new series

*Organization of Eastern Caribbean States
**Caribbean Common Market

Source: Data from Caribbean Tourism Research and Development Centre, Barbados.

Table 13.2

Estimates of Visitor Expenditure
(U.S. million dollars)

	1979	1980	1981	1982	1983
Anguilla	1.7	2.6	2.4	2.5	
Antigua/Barbuda	36.3	42.0	43.7	43.8	
Aruba	108.7	127.5	156.4	148.3	
Bahamas	561.7	595.5	639.1	654.5	730.0
Barbados	207.8	253.7	264.1	251.1	251.1
Belize	7.4	7.0	7.5	7.5	
Bermuda	240.1	280.0	287.9	302.8	
Bonaire	3.4	3.8	5.1	6.6	
British Virgin Is.	38.6	42.3	53.8	65.5	81.5
Cayman Islands	36.2	44.6	52.7	54.9	
Costa Rica	72.9	81.0	93.7	131.1	
Curacao	119.0	149.1	158.3	155.4	
Dominica	2.3	2.1	3.0	4.4	
Dominican Republic	130.8	167.9	223.2	228.9	
Grenada	14.3	14.8	17.3	17.3	
Guadeloupe	72.3	110.9	93.5	107.5	
Haiti	62.8	46.3	55.5	55.5	
Jamaica	194.3	241.7	284.3	337.8	399.2
Martinique	71.5	74.6	75.2	81.6	
Montserrat	4.0	4.5	5.6	5.3	6.0
Puerto Rico	565.0	625.4	608.6	699.2	690.8
St. Kitts/Nevis	6.0	8.7	9.6	9.4	
St. Lucia	33.5	33.6	28.8	37.0	
St. Maarten	87.2	108.8	117.5	123.5	
St. Vincent	10.5	13.7	25.2	25.9	
Suriname	18.2	18.2	20.0	20.0	
Trinidad & Tobago	110.0	142.2	146.7	150.0	
Turks & Caicos Is.	3.4	4.2	4.8	4.1	
U.S. Virgin Islands	299.1	304.3	317.5	315.8	
Venezuela	178.0	246.0	185.4	194.8	
Total	3322.0	3797.0	3986.0	4247.0	4450.0

Source: National and Caribbean Tourism Research and Development
Centre estimates.

Tourism is a major direct and indirect employer of labor in the Caribbean. Lodging alone entails 82,000 jobs, and an additional 188,000 persons are employed in ancillary jobs, including taxi drivers, restaurant workers, and shop attendants. Also, tourism generates employment by utilizing local labor on a wide variety of jobs, not only in the local travel and service industry, but also in complementary sectors of production, such as construction, agriculture, and light industry. Since the services offered to visitors are not threatened by mechanization, the development of tourism may be a key strategy in the struggle against unemployment--a problem of growing concern in the Caribbean (See Table 13.3).

Table 13.3

Employment Generated by Tourism in the Caribbean Area

Country	Population	Employed Labor Force	Employment Generated By Tourism	% of Employed Who Work in Tourism
Antigua & Barbuda	76,138	23,222	5,490	23.6
Dominica	74,089	15,130	802	5.3
St. Kitts/Nevis	48,699	13,566	1,781	13.1
St. Lucia	120,000	31,800	5,805	18.2
Barbados	249,110	103,352	14,430	14.0
Jamaica	2,172,200	703,400	15,944	2.3
Trinidad & Tobago	1,152,000	447,300	6,530	1.5
Puerto Rico	3,415,000	807,000	42,172	5.2
U.S. Virgin Islands	105,000	35,940	11,705	32.6
Bahamas	231,000	84,288	41,058	48.7
Costa Rica	2,163,000	665,072	11,590	1.7
Venezuela	14,401,000	3,818,900	36,600	1.0

Source: Data from Caribbean Tourism Research and Development Centre.

III. Constraints on Linkages

A de facto linkage exists between tourism and virtually every other sector of the economy, particularly construction, light industry, furniture manufacturing, agriculture, and fishing. However, these linkages are weak. With a little government

effort, Caribbean economies could benefit substantially
from greater linkages between tourism and other
sectors. The results could be increased job formation,
market expansion, and efficiencies of scale.

Despite the potential advantages of increasing the
links between tourism and other sectors of the economy,
particularly agriculture, Caribbean development
specialists have so far taken only a narrow view of the
economic relationships involved. In comtemporary
analysis, the linkage between tourism and agriculture
is sometimes defined by the proportion of tourist food
dollars retained locally, without any reference to the
performance of the local food and marketing sectors.

Another definition uses the "equivalent tourist
population" concept, which determines additional demand
for food as a direct result of tourism. Under this
formula, the increased food demand generated by tourism
exceeds 15 percent in only four Caribbean countries:
Bermuda, the British Virgin Islands, the Cayman
Islands, and St. Maarten; in twenty-three of the thirty
Caribbean Basin countries, food demand is increased by
less than 5 percent.[4] However, the weakness of such an
approach is inherent in its definition: By defining
demand on a purely per capita basis, the formula
overstates the effective demand of the local population
and downplays the role of tourists. In reality, only
the high income local population can afford to buy the
high-quality food normally consumed by tourists.
Therefore, any discussion of linkages between
agriculture and tourism must take into account the
greater spending potential of the tourist market when
compared to the local market.

Most analyses overlook the real crux of the
problem of linking agriculture and tourism, which is
not so much the size of tourist food demand but the
food-supplying capability of the local economy.
Despite a great agricultural production potential, the
Caribbean region as a whole, and in particular the
hotel sector, has relied heavily on food imports to
satisfy the needs of the tourist industry. As long as
insufficient production distribution of agricultural
produce and of fisheries persist, the region will
continue to rely on imports.

The economies of the Dominican Republic, St.
Vincent and the Grenadines, St. Lucia, and Grenada
illustrate trends in food demand and agricultural
development for the entire Caribbean. In these
countries, agricultural development is constrained
because of three fundamental factors: (1) Demand for
local fresh produce is low because prices are
frequently high, both in relative and in absolute
terms; (2) the quality of local produce is variable and
often low, and local products often do not meet the

demands of sophisticated consumers; and (3) the availability of supplies is inconsistent.

Agricultural development is often constrained by the small size and limited demand of the local market. Supplies may fluctuate sharply, causing significant price variations when compared to the relatively steady prices of imported foods. This situation is aggravated by the atmosphere of mutual mistrust that prevails among farmers and wholesalers because of a history of both sides reneging on price agreements.

The care and handling of produce is frequently inadequate to deliver high-quality items from production to consumption. Farmers may leave crops in the sun too long, store them in unsuitable packaging material, or damage them on the way to market. The fruits and vegetables themselves may be of the wrong variety to meet market requirements. Local farmers are often biased against changing their traditional crop production or lack information on the types and qualities of food needed by the tourist industry. In addition to their general tendency to resist change, farmers are hurt by high production costs. Produce may be poorly raised because fertilizer and other necessary inputs are too expensive or the farmer is not knowledgeable enough to use them correctly. Private and public sector investment is insufficient.

In general, the agricultural sector in most Caribbean islands has experienced declines during the past few decades. Much of the land is mountainous with variable rainfall and uneven soil quality. For centuries, the development of export crops, such as sugarcane and bananas, has been given priority over the production of food crops for domestic consumption. Export crops, usually grown on modern plantations, often continue to occupy the most productive land whereas small-scale food production is largely relegated to lower-quality marginal land.

Many disillusioned farmers migrate to the cities to find alternative employment, thus contributing to the decline in agricultural production. This trend has increased unemployment rates and caused the growth of depressed areas, heightening demand for government spending on social programs. Often the younger and more educated farmers migrate to neighboring islands or to the United States and Canada, although in recent years, use of this North American "safety valve" has diminished.

IV. Integrating Agriculture and Tourism

The failure to meet tourist food demand results in large part from the problems inherent in the agricultural system, and the solution involves interrelationships between a wide span of institutions, for the roots of these problems can be identified in production and marketing. Many groups involved in the system provide locally produced goods and services for tourist consumption. In addition to farmers, these include hotel and restaurant personnel, wholesalers, retailers, market researchers, managers of training institutes, agricultural extension workers, promotion specialists, and financial leaders.

Although the tourism industry alone may not be enough to save the agricultural sector and neutralize emigration, it can play a vitally important role in stimulating agricultural demand and should be promoted along with schemes to expand local markets or increase food exports. The stimulation of agricultural demand through tourism will only be accomplished, however, if the integrated nature of the food production and marketing system is acknowledged and if development programs are directed at the system as a whole and not at individual or unconnected points in the system.

In addressing the problems of price, quality, and supply, each step of the production, distribution, and consumption process should be examined. From the consumers' viewpoints, tourists often prefer the type and taste of food typical of their home countries. Although the majority of tourists still come from North America, at least until the recent recession increasing numbers have been arriving from Europe, South America, and particularly the neighboring Caribbean islands. The willingness to experiment with local cuisine may be growing. Tourists seem to be getting younger, on average, and increasingly interested in experiencing local culture if prices are reasonable.

Tourists (as well as residents) expect a high standard of food preparation and service when they eat in restaurants, especially those found in or around the larger hotels. Restaurateurs might better meet their customers' requirements by upgrading the skills of kitchen staff in preparing and presenting local foods. Waiters should be trained to answer questions about local cuisine and even learn a few techniques to "sell" these foods. Including local specialities in hotel and restaurant advertising is an effective way of promoting foods that may be new to visitors. Any program to increase tourist (and resident) consumption of local foods requires a great deal of promotion, particularly in the early stages. In addition to menu preparation and presentation, important elements in such a campaign are mass-media advertising, exhibitions, and culinary shows.

As tourism has increased, average income and vacation expenditure per tourist have declined, signaling a relative shift from full-service hotels to self-contained apartments. The range of distribution outlets catering to this section of the tourist market must change and expand correspondingly. The retailers have tried to increase tourist consumption of local foods by offering conveniently packaged, easy to prepare products in attractive displays. For tourists who choose to prepare their own meals, time-saving convenience foods are important. Despite the downward pressure on prices, tourists still expect to buy high-quality food products since they are, for the most part, accustomed to obtaining good quality at reasonable prices in their home grocery stores. Ease of use, simple cooking instructions, and ingredient information must all be present if the tourist is to be encouraged to purchase local food.

Visitors will not wish to spend a great deal of time searching for local products. Prominent displays and advertising of local food are important to bring it to the tourists' attention and introduce the idea of experimenting with probably unfamiliar products. Tourists will depend for assistance on the people with whom they come into contact during the entire food-buying process. Sales may be improved if the retailer provides literature on how to cook various local foods and is well trained to provide helpful advice. Through providing these services to tourists, retailers will also be in a position to provide the same services for local residents, thus further expanding the market.

The tourist market for local foods is neither homogeneous nor static. It exhibits many of the characteristics of the tourist's own food consumption behavior at home. Market research is essential in the following areas: surveying the reaction of tourists to local foods and their presentation; testing new local products; monitoring food trends in tourists' countries of origin; and evaluating distribution outlets. To contribute to informed purchasing decisions, market researchers must collect and analyze data on agricultural trends as well as on the tourist market.

The farmer's role is to ensure an adequate supply of the commodities demanded. The farmer must be prepared to operate the farm as a year-round business. The quality of produce must be acceptable, and the price within the range that prospective buyers are willing to pay. These require effective dissemination of timely market research findings and good production planning. Too often agricultural marketing boards are poorly staffed and under-financed, resulting in lost opportunities for the farmer.

The role of the agricultural extension worker is to guide farm management, particularly in choosing the correct varieties of produce to be brought to market.

To do this, the extension worker must not only interpret market demand data but also supply the farmer with information about planting, expected yields, and so on.

Wholesalers also have a pivotal role in this system: ensuring quality, freshness, appropriate packaging, dissemination of market information, efficient storage facilities, adequate processing, and advertising. Food processing in the region is now limited not only by the lack of low-priced regular food supplies, but also by the high cost of imported processing equipment and materials and by insufficient technical expertise. Financial institutions are needed to provide credit to farmers and wholesalers and offer flexibility in their repayment schedules. A credit insurance scheme may have to be devised to reduce the risk of insolvency among farmers and wholesalers.

Institutional cooperation is vital to intensify the tourism-agricultural linkages in the Caribbean. In each country, a committee consisting of the Ministry of Tourism, Ministry of Agriculture and Fisheries, Ministry of Industry and Commerce, Hotel and Restaurant Association, and Food Wholesalers Association should be established under the coordination of the Ministry of Tourism. The main responsibility of this committee would be to analyze the problems that divert local food supplies away from the tourist sector and formulate a coordinated effort to ease these problems. The Ministry of Tourism must also take an active role in promoting menus with high local food content.

It is important to review legislation and implement the legal changes necessary to encourage greater production and linkages. The government should limit the quantity of imports of specific produce where local supply is adequate or could become adequate in the short term. A protectionist policy may be necessary, given the propensity of the hotel sector to use imported produce.

So far government actions have not been conducive to intensifying the linkages between agriculture and tourism because of unfavorable pricing policies that have adversely affected the supply capability of the agricultural sector and resulted in sluggish growth of agricultural output. In general, an overvalued exchange rate has made imported food products especially attractive.

Although the recommendations presented here will not automatically solve the problems previously described, once the process of linkage begins, momentum will build to sustain the program and bring about even more linkages. Even if all the food consumed by tourists is locally produced, sold, prepared, and served, a substantial leakage of foreign exchange may

occur if profits are taken outside the host country.
Only between one-third and one-half of all tourist
expenditure for food reaches the producer, wholesaler,
and retailer; the rest goes toward food preparation and
service, including overhead costs and profit. The
"leakage" of foreign exchange resulting from the
purchase of imported goods and services, management
fees, repatriation of profits and earnings by foreign
corporations and nonnational employees, and other
payments abroad is estimated at 58 percent.[5]
     The promotion of linkages between the food
industry and the tourist industry will help to stem
this "leakage" abroad of earnings and to increase
participation and profits among local businesses. The
benefits from improved linkages include not only
foreign exchange earnings but also the use of idle land
and labor. Increased employment opportunities within
the Caribbean countries themselves will reduce the
pressures to emigrate and potentially improve the skill
level of the local labor force.

Notes

1.   See testimony by Robert Pastor, "Agricultural Development and the Caribbean Basin," before a Joint Hearing of the House Committee on Agriculture and Foreign Affairs, July 20, 1982, p. 10.

2.   World Tourism Organization, General Secretariat, World Compendium of Tourism Statistics, 1983 (Madrid, Spain.

3.   Data prepared by Caribbean Tourism Research and Development Centre, Barbados.

4.   As coined by Roger Doswell, the "equivalent tourist population" is tourist arrivals multiplied by average length of stay divided by 365.   (Table published by Caribbean Tourism Research and Development Centre, "A Study of Linkages Between Tourism and Local Agriculture," Barbados, March 1984.)

5.   Ibid.

Part 5

Migration and Development: International and U.S. Options

14. Policy Initiatives of the Multilateral Development Banks and the United Nations Specialized Agencies

G. Arthur Brown

I. Introduction

The Caribbean countries, most of which are islands and the majority small--even microscopic--economies, have always experienced large waves of both in- and out-migration. Movement from one island to another, to areas in the region, or to the United States, Canada, and the United Kingdom has been a prospect to members of virtually every family in the Caribbean region at some time. Migration is one of the career possibilities for the adolescent in much the same way that a family might consider a teenager's going into agriculture, qualifying in a traditional profession, or seeking a particular job in the home town. This acceptance of migration as one of life's options has resulted from the history of these islands and from the economic and political circumstances present at various times. If this basic fact is not taken into account, the range and quantity of migration that has occurred will not be understood.

Unlike large areas of Central and South America, the Caribbean islands have no indigenous population: All the islands have been peopled by the descendants of settlers, slaves, or indentured workers. This absence of strong roots in the country explains to a great extent the attitude of the Caribbean peoples toward migration. Although the changed circumstances since the postwar period and political power have contributed to the welding together of a more coherent society, the historical facts cannot be ignored in any analysis or understanding of migration patterns and in the formulation of policies in this area. It is important also to recognize that although many similarities exist between the islands, their migration patterns show many important differences. A comparatively old, settled country like Barbados has over the years been an

exporter of population. Guyana and Trinidad until
recently were recipients of population.

No one set of policies can be developed even for
the collection of very small islands known as the
Leeward and Windward Islands. A further factor is that
island peoples living in a small geographical area
surrounded by the ocean throughout all history have
exhibited a greater tendency, and have no doubt greater
urges, to move out across the ocean than those living
in large land masses. The possible psychological
reasons for these movements involve both the push
arising from an apparently limited environment and
limited opportunities to the people and the pull
provided by the relative ease of sea transport and--in
the case of the Caribbean--the magnet of the large
surrounding land mass. When these factors are combined
with the fluctuating economic fortunes that are
traditional to the islands, they compose the perfect
recipe for large movements of out-migration. Large
migration flows took place from various Caribbean
islands until the Second World War, as a result of
adverse economic pressures at home combined with
economic opportunities abroad.

In the postwar period, there were significant
shifts in the direction and character of the
migration. Large-scale migration to the United Kingdom
took place from all the islands. From 1948 to 1962, an
estimated 250,000 to 300,000 persons from the English
Caribbean migrated to Britain. The passage of the
Commonwealth Immigration Act in 1962, however,
virtually halted this opportunity. The migrants to the
United Kingdom were essentially unskilled people;
however, they included a large number of persons who
were literate and capable of filling such jobs as bus
conductor, subway station attendant, messenger, and
factory worker. No noticeable movement of skilled and
professional people to the United Kingdom occurred
during this time.

Following the granting of independence to most
islands in the 1960s and the passage of the 1965
Immigration Act in the United States, a new wave of
migration to the United States developed, which grew
from a yearly average of 17,000 people during the 1953-
1965 period to an annual average of 68,000 in the 1967-
76 period. The migration to the United States and the
migration to the United Kingdom differ in an important
respect: Those who migrated to the United States
already had established family connections there.
Indeed, in a normal pattern, one or two family members
would be sponsored and accepted by relatives in the
United States when conditions in the migrants' home
country were not satisfactory. A very large proportion
of these migrants also were sponsored to undertake

higher professional and technical education in the
United States. Before the establishment of a
university in the islands, this was the most important
means for training skilled and professional people in
the Caribbean.

After 1976, a marked change occurred in the type
of migration from the Caribbean, particularly from
Jamaica and Guyana. For the first time, the motivation
for migration changed: The push became the dominant
motif, not only because of the lack of confidence in
the future quality of life but also because of
political issues such as freedom and rights. This
political motivation was not present in previous
Caribbean migration to Great Britain, and the economic,
social, and political impact of this migration on the
sending countries was of a totally different dimension
from the impact of previous migration.

The official announcement by the government of the
People's National Party (PNP) in Jamaica in 1974 of the
adoption by the Party of Democratic Socialism,
accompanied by pro-Cuban and Soviet thrusts and the
denigration of the private sector, resulted in the
migration of well-established professional and skilled
people, senior civil servants, executives in the
private sector, and middle-level supervisory and
foreman classes.

Although as time passed it became clear that the
rhetoric was more extreme than the action in such
fields as the private sector, the rhetoric was
unfortunately believed. When the rhetoric was coupled
with an increase in violence and crime, much of which
was politically motivated, the professional and skilled
classes were overtaken by fear: Fear not only of
losing property, job, or business and income but also
of being caught up in the violence, and, probably the
worst fear of all--that travel would be stopped. These
fears explain why migrants took elaborate steps to
conceal the intention to migrate, including purchasing
return tickets, continuing to give business
appointments to clients for dates after which they
would have left, and not advising close friends of
their departure. In many instances, houses were left
fully furnished; cars were driven to the airport and
left; children were not advised of their leaving but
picked up at school and taken straight to the
airport. These movements were not organized on a group
basis; they were all done on an individual basis. The
two main receiving countries, the United States and
Canada, appeared to have been willing to facilitate
this movement, particularly between 1976 and 1980. The
Guyana situation was not dissimilar except that the
politically motivated migration from there took place
over a longer period.

How does one relate these different migration waves to economic development? My general conclusion is that migration until the end of the Second World War, for the reasons already stated, was beneficial to the individuals and to the sending countries. The migration, largely of unskilled persons, relieved population pressure at a time when no conscious effort was being made to undertake any type of economic planning or economic development. The migration after 1976 was definitely harmful to the economy because of the large loss of people with professional and managerial skills.

A discussion of migration and development only becomes relevant in circumstances in which policy options can influence the size of the economy, the size of population, its quality, and its utilization. The postwar growth of the Caribbean economies until the early years of the 1970s indicates that a positive policy of economic development, combined with good management, can promote growth and a better quality of life.

II. Brief Review of the Caribbean Economies

Table 1.1 lists some basic economic facts about the English-speaking Caribbean. These show that small islands with relatively small populations have been able to achieve a significant standard of living for their people. Among all developing countries, these Caribbean countries are in the upper quartile of any category of grading for developing countries, whether based on financial indicators such as per capita gross national product (GNP) or social indicators such as life expectancy, literacy, and infant mortality. The World Bank Development Report gives the highest per capita GNP for a low-income country (Ghana) as $400 (in 1981 dollars), and the average as $270.[1] For middle-level countries, the highest (Paraguay) is $1,630, and the average is $850. Trinidad, according to the bank's figures, had a per capita GNP higher than that of Ireland, and Barbados was high among the upper-middle-income countries. In the social field, however, the Caribbean countries stand out compared with other developing countries. Life expectancy, for example, is between seventy and seventy-two years at birth in the Caribbean. The world average even for upper-middle-income countries is sixty-five years, and for lower-middle-income and low-income countries, it is fifty-seven. Adult literacy is in the ninetieth percentile compared with 76 percent for upper-middle-income countries and 52 percent for low income countries.[2]

That a country such as Barbados that has no mineral resources and is dependent on agriculture and tourism, was able to reach a per capita GNP of US$3,500 in 1981 speaks well for its economic management. One must also assume, in the absence of evidence to the contrary, that it was not harmed by the considerable out-migration that took place during the last fifty years. Certainly when compared with other developing countries that are similar in size and natural resources but that do not have the same proportion of their population migrating, there is no evidence that Barbados would have been better off without this migration as none of these countries, with the exception of Singapore and Hong Kong, enjoys a higher per capita income.

With regard to the other islands and the two mainland territories, the population/natural resources ratios have no discernable influence on per capita GNP. Criteria for what may be called the appropriate population are hard to come by. In terms of maximizing economic development and living standards, the one lesson that comes through when looking at developing countries worldwide is that the crude use of population size, population ratios, and unemployment levels cannot give answers as to whether the population size is ideal or whether migration will hinder economic development. Certainly no a priori study of Barbados's population/natural resource parameters would have shown that it would be so much better off than Guyana.

If one can draw any conclusions about the reasons for the region's progress, the following should be accorded high significance: (1) the number and proportion of professional and highly skilled, middle-level skilled, and experienced members of the labor force compared with the total labor force; (2) the efficiency of management of the economy; and (3) the level of confidence in the government and country by the skilled and professional group. The term "experienced" here describes the large number of workers who, although not initially possessing skills, over the years of working at the same task have acquired a proficiency enabling them to make a substantial contribution. Contrasted to this, are the unskilled and inexperienced groups, largely among those under twenty-five years and female members of the labor force who constitute the main component of the unemployed force. In Jamaica, for example, the unemployment rate in 1979 among males aged thirty-five and over was 8.9 percent, whereas among females aged fourteen to nineteen, it was 82.3 percent.[3]

The three elements described are interwoven. Lack of confidence at (3) clearly affects the persons at (1). Bad management at (2) influences the confidence at (3). It may be surprising that capital and natural resources are not mentioned as priorities in this scheme. In fact, in Guyana and Belize, which possess large natural resources such as good agricultural land, water, and, in the case of Guyana, minerals and potential hydropower, development of these factors does not automatically follow.

III. The Caribbean Community and Integration Attempts

The distribution of population among the Caribbean islands, Guyana, and Belize was very much an accident arising from the decision of plantation owners to import slaves or indentured laborers. The subsequent shifting around of population by migration within the Caribbean area was essentially a mid-nineteenth century and early twentieth century happening. Some of the movements, particularly from Barbados and some of the smaller islands to Guyana and other Caribbean destinations, were significant and did influence population distribution in Guyana and Trinidad as receivers. However, had the British government as the metropolitan power devised a migration policy for the area when it could have, the population distribution would have been more economically rational, and many of the anomalies now present would have been avoided.

Many Caribbean people believe that if before the emergence of strong local political leaders and the taste of power in their individual islands, the British had merged the islands into a federal structure, a migration strategy could have been formulated for the area as a whole. The ideal time for such a decision would have been in the mid-1930s--a time when there was widespread depression in the sugar industry--the main industry in the islands and territories, and when the dependence on Britain was great.

Had the British envisaged independence as the ultimate goal for their colonies, they would have been concerned at the fate of islands like St. Vincent and Dominica making their way in the world alone and would, therefore, have started the federal exercise at a time when they had complete legal and de facto authority over the area. Only in the 1950s did any serious attempts begin to be made to bring the area into a federal structure. By then, however, there was universal sufferage and elected parliaments, local leaders had emerged and had ministerial portfolios including that of chief minister, the elements of industrial development had commenced, and differences in economic opportunities and quality of life had emerged between the different islands and territories.

By the time the federal government was formed after protracted negotiations in 1957, it was nothing more than a hostage to the individual national governments. It had no real taxing power, and its main

economic thrust was to move toward the forging of a
free trade area and common external tariff. But
because of this, many special interests arose in each
territory; the exceptions allowed and the length of
time proposed for the transition to free trade and
customs union made a mockery of any real attempt to
weld the economies together.

Against this background, in all negotiations for a
federal structure the one important area in which a
federation would have been significant--freedom of
movement of peoples within the federal region--was not
addressed. As a result, attempts to establish free
trade within the region, which could have meant the
demise of the relatively weaker industries in one set
of islands to the advantage of the stronger industries
in other territories within the federation--totally
failed. This result was inevitable if those workers
out of work in the islands with weaker industries had
no hope of seeking employment in the islands with
stronger industries. It is a truism that freedom of
movement of capital and physical factors of production
within an agreed area must be accompanied by freedom of
movement of people if the arrangement is to be viable
and fair and equitable to members of the agreement.

The imbalances in economic strength among the
different countries meant that there would have been an
automatic flow of people from the Leeward and Windward
Islands to Barbados and Trinidad composed of largely
unskilled and middle-level workers and a possible flow
of skilled and professional people to Jamaica. At that
time, none of the potential host countries would have
welcomed such inflows. The dissolution of the
federation was due partly to the feeling among the
ordinary people that nothing was in it for them; they
could lose jobs but not seek jobs elsewhere. In the
case of Jamaica, nothing was known of the rest of the
area by the ordinary worker. When this situation is
combined with the ineptness of the leaders, the petty
jealousies, and the strenuous attempts to maintain a
power base at home, the added fear of further taxation
merely to pay for another layer of government made the
collapse of the federation inevitable only three years
after its formation.

The subsequent attempts at closer arrangements
following the demise of the federation are equally
interesting because of the failure to learn the lessons
of the past and the need to be primarily concerned with
the peoples' welfare and interest. The Treaty of
Chaguaramas, which gave rise to the Caribbean Common
Market (CARICOM), was an ambitious attempt by the
members of the defunct federation to try again to move
closer together. This time they decided to attempt
only to establish a Caribbean Community, although many

ambitious declarations were made about harmonizing
foreign policies, external trade policies, and so on,
and, of course, about setting up a free-trade area and
a common external tariff. But the question of movement
of people was still avoided with the inevitable result
that CARICOM, although starting auspiciously in the
1970s, has since been merely bumping along seeking
formulas for its survival at various emergency
meetings.

In 1979, concerned by the malaise that had
descended on CARICOM, the governments appointed a group
to chart a course for the Caribbean Community in the
1980s. This high-powered group, after discussing
extensively the "people role" in the community, could
not agree on an outright recommendation for free
movement of people even though many members recognized
that this was absolutely crucial for the economic
integration policies to work.

It is instructive to read two sections of the
report, one dealing with the "Coordination of External
Trade Policies" and the other with "Establishment,
Services, Movement of Capital, and Labor and CARICOM
Enterprise Regime."[4] In regard to the coordination of
external trade policies, the group's report is very
positive, although in the absence of a political
federation, the requirement to harmonize external trade
policies and contacts with third countries would be
totally impractical. The socialist government of
Jamaica in the 1970s could not possibly have harmonized
its policies with the capitalist Barbadian government
regarding economic relations with Cuba and the Soviet
Union. On the other hand, in the area of local control
and decision-making, namely, movement of capital and
labor within the region, the weak and tentative
recommendations are in striking contrast. Reference is
made in one paragraph to the need to "encourage" the
movement of capital and labor and in another paragraph,
it is observed that although there should be "gradually
increasing liberalization of the factor movement," the
group "could not advocate complete freedom of movement
of people."

To complete the picture, it should be noted that
not only was complete freedom of movement of people
ruled out but also no intermediate migration strategy
was developed. The only understanding ever reached in
this area is that if work permits are being issued (and
they are required in all islands) and the choice is
between an application from a CARICOM citizen and one
from a non-CARICOM citizen, where both are equally
suitable for the job, preference should be given to the
CARICOM citizen. The reason generally given for the
failure to reach agreement was the wide disparity
between economies. Trinidad, for example, which had

the highest per capita income, feared that it would be
swamped with migrants from the smaller islands if there
were freedom of movement. As in all these cases, there
was also the fear of large migration upsetting the
position of a political party in the constituencies
where the migrants settled.

For the near future, attitudes may harden in the
CARICOM region against further liberalization of
movements of people. The reason is not only the very
depressed state of the economies of Jamaica and the
smaller islands but also that Trinidad and Tobago has
lapsed into a declining economy and has therefore
become more protectionist in its policies. Apart from
movement of professionals occasioned by the shortage of
skills, we can write off any return to liberalization
of migration in the CARICOM region for at least the
next ten years.

The Caribbean experience is a good example of the
difficulties involved in planning and agreeing on a
coherent migration strategy between states. If
reaching an understanding is so difficult between
countries that have close ties with one another, how
much more difficult must it be between countries
without these relations either to reach agreement or to
take bilateral actions that take into account the
problems and needs of potential sending countries.

IV.   The United Nations and Migration Policies

Various UN agencies have been concerned with
manpower planning, demographic issues, internal and
external migration, and the relationship of these
issues to economic development. No one agency has a
prime responsibility to oversee the integration of all
aspects of the population resources and environment
issues, and although each agency has stressed the need
for viewing these matters in a coherent whole, each has
its official priority areas of concern.

The International Labour Office (ILO) is not only
the oldest UN specialized agency but also the agency
first involved in advising governments to approach
development planning through an analysis of manpower
supply and demand, taking into account the imbalances
that inevitably arise between the relative need for
skilled and unskilled workers. Many countries in the
early 1950s set up manpower planning units that for the
first time enabled governments to deal with people as
their most important resources. These manpower plans
were in turn linked with financial plans. They pointed
up the amount of capital needed to ensure employment at
various proportionate levels of the labor force, and
they made estimates of the skilled/unskilled breakdown
and highlighted the need for training to ensure a

better accord between skilled and unskilled. Internal and external migration assumptions were also factored in, and migration policies were needed to realize the assumptions.

These were brave beginnings. Regrettably, in many plans the capital assumptions were never realized and the manpower plans remained paper plans. Manpower units, instead of being the driving force of economic plans, are now largely statistical units where they have survived. These units failed for the reasons that economic planning units failed: They were regarded as instruments for the medium term, and staff was needed to deal with the day-to-day pressing issues. Their best people were being constantly raided. Whenever budgetary cuts were to be made, these units suffered disproportionately. But two other factors came into play here. There has never been a true commitment on the part of governments to using planning departments-- economic, manpower, agricultural, or any other. Ministers were concerned with today's issues. This was compounded by the fact that many planning operations became overly theoretical, obsessed with input/output matrices, and they lost touch with the real world around them.

The ILO has been concerned with migration issues from the prewar period, and its convention no. 97 concerning Migrations for Employment, revised in 1949, is often used as a guideline by both sending and receiving countries for the treatment of migrants.[5] A more comprehensive convention--the UN convention on the rights of all migrant workers and their families--has been under discussion since 1979, but so far agreement has not been reached. This convention would be a charter of rights for the migrant worker, dealing with minimum wages, Social Security benefits, rights of dependents to join, remittance of earnings, access to health, housing and education benefits, and so on. In other words, it would provide the migrant worker with some protection against exploitation.

It was recognized that illegal migrants would be most exposed to exploitation, and ILO convention no. 143, concerning migration in abusive conditions and the promotion of equality of opportunity and treatment of migrant workers, deals with some basic human rights issues that should be respected.[6] For example, due process of law should always be used in any deportation proceedings, and the illegality of a migrant's status should be determined by judicial process, and not by arbitrary police action.

The concern with the population explosion in the last twenty-five years following improvements in health drew inter-governmental bodies into dealing with the population question. The forecast that world

population would reach 6.1 billion persons in the year
2000, following an increase of 700 million in the ten
years from 1970 to 1980 (3.7 billion to 4.4 billion)
created concern. But even more worrying is the fact
that although the annual growth rate in developed
countries has settled at 0.7 percent, in the developing
countries the average annual rate of growth is 2.1
percent, with that for many countries, particularly
African ones, being far in excess of this figure. The
UN Fund for Population Activities was specially set up
in the early 1970s to deal primarily with the family-
planning side of the population issue, collaborating
with the World Health Organization on the health side
and with the Department of International Economic and
Social Affairs of the UN Secretariat on economic and
social issues. The UN Economic and Social Council
(ECOSOC) is the intergovernmental body that oversees
these issues. The ECOSOC authorized the first World
Population Conference, which took place in Bucharest in
1974. This conference prepared the World Population
Plan of Action, and the following principles enunciated
in the World Plan are of interest:

(a)   The principal aim of social, economic and
      cultural development of which population goals
      and policies are an integral part is to
      improve levels of living and the quality of
      life of the people.

(d)   Population policies are constituent elements
      of socioeconomic development policies never
      substitutes for them.

(j)   In the democratic formulation of national
      population goals and policies, consideration
      must be given, together with other economic
      and social factors to the supplies and
      characteristics of natural resources and to
      the quality of the environment.

      The second world population conference took place
in Mexico City in July 1984. At this conference a
convergence of view became apparent that greater
attention must now be paid to the integration of
population, resources, and environmental factors in
development plans. The close relationship between
population factors and the following broad sector was
emphasized--food and nutrition, resources and the
environment, education and health.
      Noting the fact that since the Bucharest
conference, interest in migration and population
distribution had increased, one of the papers
commissioned for the Mexico City conference is on

population distribution, migration and development.[8] The basic premise of the group was "that migration and population distribution should be interpreted as reflecting socioeconomic inequity and inefficiency both internally and internationally--and not merely as a cause of social and economic problems." The group saw a direct connection between rural development and urban migration and international migration. It urged that the overemphasis on the adverse effects of internal migration and urbanization that characterized the earlier discussions and the 1974 world plan of action be changed and that what was needed was a combination of rural and urban strategies so that a comprehensive plan would be developed that dealt with population distribution policies. Although the paper recognized the connection between internal migration, economic development policies, and international migration, the recommendations do not deal with the adoption of a structured policy by the sending countries for international migration. The majority of the recommendations deal with the actions and attitudes to be undertaken and displayed by the receiving countries.

Reference to the "basic premise" previously quoted probably provides an explanation for the shift in attitude and the strategy proposed, namely that population distribution reflects socio-economic inequity internally and internationally. Since the internal distribution issue was seen largely in terms of the problem of urbanization, the inequity is seen to exist in the international area and inequity can only be corrected or removed by the party that has the advantage of being the better-off party. Hence, the responsibilities of the developed or richer countries are emphasized since they would be the receiving countries to correct these "inequities" and to have more liberal immigration policies. In essence, therefore, apart from concern about the brain drain, developing countries were seen as needing only to facilitate the movement outwards of their people, whom they hoped would be mostly unskilled workers.

A number of other UN organizations deal with the issues of population, manpower planning, and internal and international migration. The four major multilateral financing organizations providing assistance to Caribbean countries are the World Bank and its affiliate, the International Development Association (IDA), the Inter-American Development Bank, the Caribbean Development Bank, and the UN Development Programme. In addition, there are a number of bilateral donors, principally the United States, Canada, United Kingdom, and other European countries. Because of the small size of some islands and their number, donors and multilateral finance institutions

determined that it would be more efficient and less
time consuming if some umbrella mechanisms were
available to look at overall aid needs and
availability. The Caribbean Group for Cooperation and
Economic Development was formed, consisting of all
interested donors, on one hand, the English-speaking
Caribbean governments plus Haiti, the Dominican
Republic, and Suriname, on the other. Annual meetings
are held at which economic reviews are made of each
country and of the external aid likely to be available
on the basis of pledges or statements of interest by
the donors.

Since 1978, more than $6 billion has been pledged
or committed to the countries in this group for both
capital and technical assistance. Jamaica has been the
largest recipient, absorbing some 40 percent of total
available resources. Assistance covers a wide range of
economic activities ranging from agriculture and
fisheries to education and transportation. The UN
agencies provided technical assistance in 1983
amounting to $38.5 million, and the World Bank provided
technical assistance (as distinct from capital loans)
of $17.6 million in that year.

Population projects received only a small
proportion of the total assistance, but assistance to
the critical areas of rural development, food and
nutrition, education and health, and employment-
creating projects influences population distribution
and internal and international migration.

The World Bank has been the active member of the
World Bank group in Latin America and the Caribbean
because only Haiti qualifies to borrow from the soft
loan affiliate of the bank--the International
Development Association (IDA). This means that
initially, all loans to Latin America and Caribbean
regions are at market-related rates--approximately 11
percent in 1983. In 1983, the World Bank/IDA made
twelve loans to the Caribbean countries totaling $205
million, of which loans amounting to $120 million went
to Jamaica. Table 14.1 presents information on the
sector breakdown of loans to Latin America and
Caribbean region. During the last ten years,
agricultural and rural development has been at the top
of the list of World Bank loans to the region, followed
by transportation and power. This ranking is also true
for the worldwide allocation of loans for the bank and
IDA over the last three years, and in the case of the
IDA, agriculture and rural development have absorbed
nearly 40 percent of loans in 1983. The distribution
for the Caribbean is approximately the same. The bank
has observed that, in many countries, countrywide
economic growth requires improvement in the quality of
life in rural areas where the majority of people still

Table 14.1

World Bank/IDA Lending to Borrowers
In Latin America and the Caribbean
(US$ million)

Sector	Annual Average 1974-1978	1979[a]	1980[a]	1981[a]	1982[a]	1983[a]
Agricultural and rural development	$ 406.5	$ 405.0	$ 408.0	$ 923.2	$ 694.5	$1029.6
Development finance companies	123.8	245.0	269.0	184.0	415.8	427.4
Education	48.7	52.5	32.0	82.0	112.8	59.8
Energy - oil, gas and coal	-	-	78.5	27.0	102.0	81.2
Power	258.3	346.0	708.0	698.0	394.4	89.4
Industry	144.8	185.5	87.0	255.0	205.3	304.5
Nonproject	12.1	156.5	80.0	27.0	76.2	60.2
Population, health and nutrition	11.2	-	-	-	13.0	33.5
Small-scale enterprises	30.5	7.0	202.0	-	26.0	446.1
Technical assistance	4.9	-	-	1.5	8.8	10.2
Telecommunications	35.2	-	44.0	-	40.0	-
Tourism	22.6	52.5	-	-	-	-
Transportation	302.4	468.5	371.0	355.0	651.7	447.3
Urban transportation	44.1	176.5	88.0	254.0	206.8	46.2
Water supply and sewerage	72.8	169.8	316.0	346.5	40.6	424.2
Total	$1518.0	$2264.8	$2684.0	$3153.2	$2987.9	$3459.6
Of which IBRD*	$1476.8	$2232.8	$2595.0	$3119.0	$2962.9	$3396.6
IDA	41.2	32.0	89.0	34.2	25.0	63.0

[a]Fiscal year

*International Bank for Reconstruction and Development (World Bank)

Source: World Bank, World Development Report 1983 (Oxford University Press, 1983)

live. Failure to come to grips with rural development
makes providing jobs and incomes for the unskilled
migrants from the rural to the urban areas impossible,
resulting in increases in slums, crime, social unrest,
and migration. But rural development policies require
a political commitment from the government; in many
cases, however, this commitment does not extend beyond
mere expressions of good intentions.
     The bank has shown that special techniques are
needed for successful rural development projects
involving community understanding and participation,
and that traditional development techniques will not
work. One interesting change in World Bank philosophy
and policy has been the recognition of the need for
devising and adopting appropriate technologies to the
needs of the rural areas; such technologies include
community involvement in water and sanitation, the use
of simple hand pumps, low-cost housing, and small-scale
irrigation. These solutions are a far cry from the
earlier belief that the large dam and power station and
the mechanization of agriculture are the cure-all. The
bank has now accepted the importance of loans in the
soft areas of education, health, and population
planning, where economic benefits are not readily
quantifiable in monetary terms. In a study comparing
the capital requirements for capital-intensive versus
appropriate-technology methods, the bank found that in
nine product lines the capital/labor ratio was $2,955
for appropriate technologies compared to $15,142 for
the same product using conventional methods.[9] Thus, a
given sum of money can go so much further when applied
with appropriate technology.
     The bank has undertaken two major research studies
in migration: (1) migration patterns in Western Africa
and (2) labor migration and manpower in the Middle East
and North Africa.[10] The bank stated that the first
study will enable it to understand the determinants and
consequences of migration in West Africa and that such
understanding is directly relevant to the World Bank
rural development and education projects in the area.
The first phase of the second study involved the
preparation of projection of manpower supply and demand
for major labor-importing and -exporting countries.
     The World Bank and IDA have made loans directly to
support population programs. IDA has lent some $110
million worldwide in support of such programs between
1975 and 1982.[11] Loans have covered family-planning
programs, maternal and child health care, education and
information programs, nursing schools, and so on.
Lending in this area is relatively new for the bank and
IDA. Between 1982 and 1983, IDA lending for population
health and nutrition doubled from 0.9 percent of all

loans to 1.7 percent, and for the World Bank, from 0.3 percent to 0.8 percent.[12]

The Inter-American Development Bank (IADB) is a substantial source of funding for the Caribbean countries. Jamaica, for example, has secured loans from the IADB amounting to $406 million for the period 1969-1983, and the breakdown of sectors is interesting.[13]

	IADB Loans (In Thousands of Dollars)
Industry	$ 154,000
Education, science and technology	55,000
Agriculture and fisheries	55,000
Energy	43,000
Expert financing	40,000
Environmental and public health	23,000
Urban development	16,000
Transport and communications	13,000
Tourism	5,000
Preinvestment	2,000
Total	$ 406,000

Unlike the loan distribution for the World Bank/IDA, agriculture is not the leading sector; however, the IADB has very strongly supported education, health, and environmental projects. This bank also has supported Latin America integration projects; it has loaned $2 billion for integration projects in the period 1960 to 1983 and made grants of $193 million for the same purpose.[14] However, these integration projects were not linked to any formal migration policies and programs between the countries concerned.

The third institution specifically geared to making loans to the Caribbean countries is the Caribbean Development Bank. The bank has grown considerably in its operations over the last five years: As of 31 December 1983, its accumulated lending amounted to $435 million.[15] The largest sector lending was to the areas of transportation and communication, which absorbed 27 percent, followed by manufacturing with 26 percent. Education absorbed only 3 percent, and health, 1 percent. One explanation for this profile could be that the island governments felt that their agricultural and social sector loans were being adequately provided by the World Bank and IDA.

Interestingly, the smaller islands have put priority on
loans for transportation and communication.
   The Caribbean countries have been substantial
beneficiaries of the UN system, the World Bank, and the
multilateral financing institutions, in addition to
receiving generous support from bilateral donors.
Taking into account their small size and population,
these islands have been on a per capita basis in the
top quartile of aid recipients, and for some donors,
the islands are among the highest recipients of aid on
a per capita basis. This aid, when combined with other
resource inflows, has been used for the whole gamut of
economic and social activities, and it is questionable
whether some islands have the absoptive capacity to use
efficiently significantly increased aid.
   The objectives of these assistance programs have
been to improve the human resources base by financing
education and training programs, to improve the
infrastructure of roads, transportation,
communications, water supply, and power to expand
agricultural and industrial production and thereby
increase employment, to improve public health, and to
improve the public services. All these objectives no
doubt converge to improve the quality of life and
provide increased incomes, and as such, they should act
as a damper on migration. However, none of these
programs was designed with its impact on in- or out-
migration in mind or using migration strategies as a
policy input. As indicated in manpower planning,
assumptions about migration were made as an exogenous
input. No policies had as an objective to influence
migration and migration patterns, although the results
of the above programs would have had an indirect
influence either on restraining migration or
encouraging a reverse flow of persons who had
previously migrated or of new migrants.
   The more recent interest of the World Bank and
other funding agencies in integrated rural-development
programs and in low-cost appropriate-technology
programs, although not directly geared to influencing
in- or out-migration, clearly has had a powerful
influence on migration decisions. Puerto Rico is often
cited as the classic case of a country with an
aggressive economic development program based on
capital-intensive high-technology applications, which
although greatly increasing GDP destroyed substantially
more jobs in the low-cost-technology cottage and
similar industries than were created in the new
industries. This fueled a large-scale out-migration of
those thrown out of work.
   Notwithstanding this example, the same mistakes
have continued to be made in many development
programs. For example, no real attempt has been made

to avoid using output per manhour as a measure of
efficiency and productivity. Such a measure is
obviously influenced by the ratio of capital to
labor. Alternative measures such as cost per unit of
output are not influenced by the capital/labor
factor. These countries of high unemployment have no
mandatory requirements that, for every project,
alternative combinations of actors of production should
be routinely examined and a decision made on the basis
of the combination of factors utilizing the largest
labor component compatible with competitive unit cost.

UN and external-aid experts have not built these
policies into their advice, and this area requires
change. No attempt is made to assist the government in
building an integrated program in which the
interrelationship of all sectors is worked out. Each
sector is looked at separately, and special-interest
groups both among the external donors including UN
agencies and within the government seek the advancement
of a particular sector without regard to whether the
sum total makes sense. In this situation, the ideal of
linking population and manpower programs, including
migration, into an integrated program has little chance
of realization, particularly if the government ministry
concerned is relatively weak and the external special
interest group in this field has little money to offer.

No rational solution will be available until all
external-aid agencies recognize that the present
uncoordinated, chaotic system is actually
counterproductive and they are prepared to collaborate
with the government is working within a coherent
plan. Such collaboration not only requires
coordination of donor inputs into designated programs
but, even more important, coordination of externally
financed programs with the domestic budget. Countless
examples can be found of externally financed schools,
hospitals, water supply schemes, and research
organizations that collapse once external aid is
withdrawn, because no attempt was made to ascertain
whether the domestic budget could bear the cost of the
teachers, the nurses, or the maintenance of the
hospitals. Therefore, a long road must be traveled
before the benefits of external assistance can be
ensured to be commensurate with the inputs, and only
within this context will it become possible to ensure
that population and migration policies can become
active ingredients in the overall economic strategy.

One objective of the Caribbean Group is to help
ensure that the Caribbean countries determine their
economic and social priorities in such a way that they
are realistic and feasible in terms of economic growth,
employment, foreign exchange, and so forth, but also
that bilateral and multilateral donors would respect

these priorities, avoid overlapping and competition for projects, and help secure the achievement of one set of objectives.

A new urgency has been introduced over the last three years--the need for governments to review and totally restructure their economies. This urgency has arisen from the debt crisis and the fact that ultimately countries in trouble find they have no alternative but to turn to the International Monetary Fund (IMF). Invariably, the IMF prescribes that the country must adjust its economy by reducing the monetary claims on resources needed to meet foreign-exchange debt requirements. Thus, imports must be made more expensive and exports encouraged by devaluing the currency, the budget deficit has to be reduced, domestic credit curtailed, and short-term foreign borrowing restricted. All these policies are aimed at restricting and curtailing demand and, therefore, standards of living. These austerity programs no doubt have had and will have adverse effects on people's views about remaining in these countries and undoubtedly act as stimulants to migration.

The IMF now occupies a preeminent position by virtue of its great influence on helping design overall economic development strategies, including population plans, which affect the future standard of living of hundreds of millions of people. The World Bank, the companion international organization to the IMF, realized some time ago that the policies of restraint prescribed by the fund inevitably led to negative growth. To counteract this, a companion program was needed, aimed at stimulating economic development at the same time. Hence, structural adjustment loans were introduced. Before these loans are granted, they have to fit into some overall economic strategy that is compatible with the IMF program.

At no time has the opportunity existed for the two major international organizations, supplemented by the actions of the UN agencies and bilateral donors, to come to grips with the need for a coherent approach to the development of countries now in economic straits. The leverage is there, the countries are desperate, and funds are available, if agreement can be reached on a course of action. The role international institutions can now play far outweighs any opportunities and influence they may have had in the past; they can ensure that the population dimension is taken into account in the overall planning now possible.

320

Notes

1. World Bank, <u>World Development Report 1983</u>
(Oxford University Press, 1983). The classification of
countries as low income, lower middle income, etc. to
be found in this report.

2. <u>Ibid.</u>

3. Government of Jamaica, <u>Economic and Social</u>
<u>Survey of Jamaica</u> (Kingston, 1979), p. 16.15.

4. Caricom Secretariat, <u>The Caribbean Community</u>
in the 80's: <u>Report By a Group of Caribbean Experts</u>,
11 January 1981, pp. 67-68.

5. International Labour Office, <u>Convention and</u>
<u>Recommendations</u> (Geneva, n.d.).

6. <u>Ibid.</u>

7. United Nations, <u>Report of the United Nations</u>
<u>Population Conference, 1974 - Bucharest 19-30 August</u>
<u>1974</u> (New York, 1974).

8. United Nations, <u>Recommendations of the Expert</u>
<u>Group on Population, Resources Environment and</u>
<u>Development</u>, Preparatory Committee for the
International Conference on Population 1984, 23-27
January, E/Conf./76/PC/8(New York, 1984).

9. World Bank, <u>The World Bank and the World's</u>
<u>Poorest</u> (Washington, 1980), p. 22.

10. World Bank, <u>World Bank Research Programme</u>,
Reference Nos. 671-26 and 671-63, (Washington, various
dates).

11. World Bank, <u>IDA in Retrospect</u> (Washington,
1982), p. 53.

12. World Bank, <u>Development Report 1983</u>, <u>Supra</u>.
<u>fn</u>. #1.

13. Inter-American Development Bank, <u>Annual</u>
<u>Report 1983</u> (Washington, 1983), p. 78.

14. <u>Ibid.</u>, p. 16.

15. Caribbean Development Bank, <u>Annual Report</u>
<u>1983</u> (Bridgetown, 1983).

15. Using Migration to Enhance Economic Development in the Caribbean: Three Sets of Proposals

Robert A. Pastor
Rosemarie Rogers

I. Introduction

The predominant view in the Caribbean is that emigration is a personal right and that it serves the economic and social interests of the home countries. Therefore, Caribbean leaders generally reject any policies that might interfere with Caribbean emigration and indeed are reluctant to even view migration as a policy issue for fear it might be interpreted as interfering with a personal right. However, as this book documents, emigration is not as fully beneficial to home countries as initially believed. Indeed, in some cases, the costs of emigration for sending nations may exceed the benefits.

In balancing personal rights with social costs, governments have the responsibility to protect the former, while trying to identify ways to reduce the costs of emigration to national economic development and to increase the benefits.

In the Caribbean, only the government of Cuba uses emigration to further its national economic and political goals. It has used emigration to weaken internal political opposition; irritate or harm unfriendly governments; expel criminals, delinquents, and other undesirable persons; earn money for the state; and extend Cuba's influence abroad.[1] Except for Cuba, the Caribbean generally has a laissez-faire approach to emigration and return migration. However, several nations and international organizations are beginning to perceive the link between migration and economic development, and as this relation is better understood, new policies are likely to be proposed that will endeavor to utilize migration to enhance development.

In this chapter, we shall first identify the development problems that relate to migration. Then, we shall explore and analyze programs developed by

countries in other regions of the world to try to
utilize migration to enhance economic development. The
term "migration-for-development programs" will refer to
all the various services and programs devised by
sending and/or receiving countries to use return
migration and/or migrants' savings to enhance the
economic development of the sending country. Such
programs include reintegration services, return
incentive schemes, and employment-creation projects in
the sending countries. The latter projects have been
undertaken by individual migrants or by groups of
migrants and aided by the sending and/or receiving
countries. Our purpose is to evaluate which programs
succeeded and which failed and why, so that we can
consider ways to adapt some to the Caribbean. Finally,
we shall offer three sets of proposals specifically
tailored to the Caribbean.

II. Migration-Related Development Problems

The three major migration-related development
problems faced by most Caribbean governments are (a)
unemployment, (b) scarcity of managerial and
professional talent, and (c) inadequate investment in
both private and public sectors. For the Caribbean
countries, emigration generally reduces unemployment,
but it also reduces skilled manpower. To the extent
that aid and investment are constrained or even
precluded because of the absence of good managers and
skilled workers, emigration also reduces investment and
adversely affects the region's economic development.
At the same time, although remittances may be large and
important as a source of foreign exchange, they remain
an unused opportunity for investment and, in some
cases, may even be harmful to development--namely, when
they increase inflation and imports.[2]
World Bank reports on the Caribbean often note
that the region has a relatively high proportion of
skilled people per capita for the developing world.
Management expertise is lacking primarily because too
many persons with requisite skills are leaving or have
already emigrated.[3] Although a few of the World Bank's
studies have recognized the link between emigration and
administrative roadblocks to development, not one
suggested the need to fashion a policy to deal with
them. For example, a recent World Bank report on
Jamaica noted that though the doubling of emigration in
the 1970s had the beneficial effect of slowing the rate
of population growth--to about 1 percent in 1980--it
also adversely affected development, since
"professionals and skilled workers comprehend a large
portion of the outflow in recent years."[4] Six months
later, another World Bank report described the "main

problems that demand the new Government's [Prime Minister Edward Seaga's government] attention;" high on the list of problems were the "decline in service quality" and "an acute scarcity of skilled, managerial and technical personnel, particularly in the public sector, mainly as a result of massive emigration in recent years." Nevertheless, when a few pages later the report recommended priority areas for government policy, none of the thirteen specific recommendations had even a remote association with manpower or migration policies.[5]

Similar reports have been written for other Caribbean countries. Concerning Haiti, one continually finds assertions that the major constraints on development are "the shortage of skilled labor" and "inadequate administration of the public apparatus." One report noted that "these constraints are so overwhelming that foreign assistance, though expected to be limited, does not seem to represent a major bottleneck in the medium-term development prospects of Haiti."[6] The same seems to be true for Dominica: "The limited capability domestically to prepare and execute projects is emerging as a constraint on the rate of absorption of available external resources."[7]

In March 1980, the Caribbean Common Market appointed a group of Caribbean experts to prepare a strategy for Caribbean economic development and integration in the 1980s. William Demas, president of the Caribbean Development Bank, chaired the group, and a rather comprehensive report with specific recommendations was completed in January 1981. Of the six development challenges identified by the group as being the most important for the 1980s, two were "upgrading the level of economic management" and "alleviating the unemployment situation." The group concluded that "the economic difficulties experienced by the region have been compounded by pronounced weaknesses in national economic management." It recommended a number of steps: The highest priority would be to recruit and pool the use of foreign experts and the last one was to encourage the return of highly skilled nationals. Although one may disagree with the ordering of the priorities, at least it showed recognition of the fact that migration can be linked to development problems. The group also recognized that in the 1980s the Caribbean will be sharing Cuba's problems of absorbing the baby boom of the last two decades into the labor force. The group recommended a number of steps, particularly encouraging labor-intensive technologies.[8]

In May 1983, Jamaican Prime Minister Edward Seaga stated that more than 18,000 Jamaican professional and skilled workers emigrated between 1977-1980--the equivalent of more than half the number of persons who graduated from higher training institutes or industrial training schools in Jamaica during that period. Jamaica's economic development was impeded as a result. He added that "some have returned since 1981, not because of any specific plan on my part, but because of the improvement in the climate" of Jamaica. Nonetheless, he acknowledged the need for such a plan. On July 31, 1983, in a letter to overseas Jamaicans, Seaga invited them to participate in "word, deed and attitude to the processes of reconstruction" by either investing in a home in Jamaica or opening a foreign exchange account in Jamaica. In his 1984 budget presentation, Seaga formulated this idea as an investment program by which overseas Jamaicans can invest in houses in Jamaica through the Urban Development Corporation.

Prime Minister Seaga also pursued the issue of the brain drain in a speech to the United Nations Development Programme (UNDP) in Geneva on June 12, 1984, in which he proposed the creation of an international fund for manpower resources. With UNDP support, he hosted an international conference in Kingston on February 5-7, 1985, to review his proposal for a Human Resources Facility to provide technical assistance to the developing countries that had lost so much of their skilled manpower. According to Seaga, "an astonishing 75% of the 500,000 professional and technical workers admitted to the U.S. as immigrants from 1969 to 1979 come from the developing world."[9]

In short, beginning to emerge in the region is a recognition of the linkage between migration and development and of the need to develop national policies that will make that linkage as positive as possible for the individual and for society.

III. Other Migration-For-Development Programs: Analysis and Relevance

In this section, we shall explore several migration programs from other regions. Although we recognize the uniqueness of the schemes and the diverse societal contexts for which they were formulated, we also believe that significant lessons and insights can be garnered from these other experiences and that some schemes might be adaptable to the Caribbean. The incentive schemes are expensive and include a variety of services such as information, training, technical advice, and direct financial subsidies. The more successful schemes are affordable partly because they involve cooperation between host and sending countries. The number of spontaneous returns of migrants far exceeds that which might be attributed to planned inducements.

A. Reintegration Services and Return Incentive Schemes

Several sending countries have instituted reintegration services to ease the reentry of returning migrants.[10] Such aid is also the essence of return incentive schemes, which attempt to attract migrants to return who might otherwise not do so and which are usually formulated for specific groups of migrants,[11] for example, for migrants selected by skill (in Algeria) or educational level and sometimes specialty (in Colombia, Korea, India, and Great Britain, and in the "return of talent" programs of the Intergovernmental Committee for Migration). Although considerable variation is evident, reintegration services and return incentive schemes have similar elements, which are mutually reinforcing. One important element is employment, which may involve recruitment for specific employment opportunities, maintenance grants for one or two years to scientists who are expected to find permanent employment during this time, or systematic information about employment opportunities.

In evaluating a Colombian return incentives program, respondents cited the absence of direct help with finding employment as one of the main limitations of the scheme.[12] On the other hand, a series of Algerian recruitment efforts among skilled migrants residing in France to fill specific job openings in Algeria turned out to be remarkably unsuccessful.[13] Thus the availability of work itself, although perhaps a necessary condition for successful return incentive schemes, is not a sufficient one, since many migrants did not leave their home countries because of unemployment, but rather for better opportunities. Responses to hypothetical questions in several European host country surveys, however, show that many migrants were ready to return home even if wages and working conditions were not as high as those in the new country. The Algerian scheme showed, too, that the combination of incentives was crucial.

Various schemes provide training to migrants for specific jobs in the home countries. In the European context, such training programs have been developed by several host countries, as a form of aid to the sending countries but also as a means of reducing their foreign populations. The leader in these efforts has been France, which has concluded bilateral agreements with a number of emigration countries, either for the sole purpose of organizing migrants' vocational "training for return" (for example, the Franco-Senegalese Agreement signed on December 1, 1980) or to organize "repatriation assistance" on a broader scale, of which

vocational training is one element (for example, the
Franco-Algerian Agreement, as specified in the
government circular of March 3, 1982).[14]
    Another important dimension of a number of return
incentive programs is assistance in obtaining housing,
through either preferential treatment of returnees in
the assignment of public housing or subsidies for
purchases or rent. In Israel, this feature engendered
resentment among the local nonmigrant population.
Other features of reintegration and return incentive
schemes are the payment of transportation costs for the
migrants and their families; the lifting of
restrictions on certain imports, or permission to
import certain items duty-free or at reduced rates;
permission to maintain foreign currency accounts in the
home countries (extended also to migrants who are still
abroad); and, in some programs, assistance with
educational expenses for the migrants' children.
    Evaluations of return incentive programs show that
they are moderately successful. In its last year of
operation, the Israeli scheme was used by 199
migrants. In its single year of operation (1972), the
Colombian scheme, which was aimed only at university
graduates, was used by 248 returnees. When these
beneficiaries were asked about the specific role played
by the schemes in their return, 9 percent of the
Israeli and 10 percent of the Colombian respondents
asserted that the schemes had indeed been the decisive
factor; for others, they had been one factor among
several. For still others, they had acted as
"triggers"; that is, these migrants had wanted to
return but had not yet made specific plans, and whether
they would have returned eventually without the
incentives is uncertain. Members of a last group had
decided to return independently of the incentives or
were already in the home country when they learned
about them but availed themselves nevertheless of the
benefits offered. (From the data on the French return
bonus scheme one can also infer that a considerable
portion of those claiming the bonuses would have
returned in any case.)
    Two difficulties with the realization of such
schemes have been noted. First, the local population
may feel that the migrants are a privileged group
already and that they are now being rewarded for what
may be viewed as selfish or unpatriotic behavior. This
issue is acknowledged but not really addressed in the
discussions of most return incentive schemes. In the
discussion of reintegration measures, van Gendt
defended the programs by stressing that the various
services for returning migrants are offered on a one-
time or short-term basis only. Second, the costs of
such schemes are clearly high and have to be measured

against the importance of the need to reattract
particular manpower living abroad, as opposed to, or in
addition to, seeking to employ individuals still in the
country who might leave (or with measures intended for
reintegration only against the costs of having a less-
well-reintegrated return population). Availability of
funds from outside sources perhaps justifies the costs
of such programs more easily and may also serve to
minimize resentment from the nonmigrant populations.

B. Employment Creation by Individual Migrants

In a variety of migration contexts, reference is
made to the target migrant--the person who goes abroad
temporarily to work and save enough money for a
specific purpose and then returns. His purpose might
be to construct a home, to purchase agricultural land,
to acquire a dowry or a bride price, or to establish a
coffee shop or a taxi service at home. With few
exceptions, these activities have been spontaneous,
planned only by the migrants and their families,
without policymakers paying attention to them. They
have been discussed in the literature in anecdotal
fashion or at best in limited case studies but have
hardly been systematically described or evaluated for
large samples. For example, the most frequent comments
made by observers of European labor migration concern
the fact that too many of the migrants' "targets" have
been consumption items (housing is included here) and
that activities involving employment generation have
been concentrated almost exclusively in the tertiary
sector, where they were poorly planned, often
duplicative, and therefore prone to failure. Yet in
Southern European villages when asked who are the most
successful local return migrants, the villagers nearly
always refer to individuals who engage in some
entrepreneurial activity. Various reintegration
services are useful to such returnees. One example are
permits to import farming machinery or to import the
trucks or cars needed to set up a transport business.

A highly integrated scheme to aid migrants with
job creation projects in their home countries was
developed in the Netherlands in the mid-1970s to
benefit six labor-sending countries in southern Europe
and North Africa.[15] The latest published evaluation of
the project was in 1980.[16] The migrants were offered
help in the preparation of modest feasibility analyses
and in the more detailed planning of their proposed
projects, and then financial assistance in the form of
subsidized loans and outright grants. The planning--
including the procurement of documents, permits, and so
on--was largely the applicants' responsibility; this
requirement served to eliminate the less capable or

less motivated. Projects were selected for support according to their promise of employment creation (direct and indirect), their potential demonstration effects in technology and/or management, and their fairness and legality in the proposed treatment of their employees.

Three hundred and eight of 873 projects proposed over four years (1976-1980) had been rejected by the time of the evaluation. Seventy-nine projects had reached the implementation stage, and the remaining 487 projects were at varying stages of preparation and decision-making. Forty-two of the projects being implemented were in the primary sector, 26 in the secondary, and 11 in the tertiary sector. The average financial assistance per project (loans and grants) was 85,000 guilders (approximately $37,000); with the migrants' funds added, the average project investment was 150,000 guilders ($65,000).

Other than the financial assistance costs, the programs' administrative costs were relatively small, involving a director, an administrator, and two consultants. By 1978, "counterparts" were being identified in the countries of origin, that is, individuals or organizations who could be called on to serve as local consultants in the project planning and implementation process. In addition, a variety of training sessions were organized in the Netherlands and in the home countries for migrants whose projects were in an advanced state of preparation.[17]

C. Employment Creation Projects by Groups of Migrants

The best documented cases in which migrants contributed savings toward the creation of new industries or new branches of existing industries were in Turkey and Yugoslavia, and more recently, Greece. The Turkish and Yugoslav efforts differ in several important respects, but in both countries the idea was first developed spontaneously by a group of migrants. Later, officials in a home or host country expressed interest and offered support for the projects.[18]

The first Turkish Workers' Company was founded in 1965 by a group of migrants--professionals and blue collar workers--in Cologne. The concept aroused considerable interest, and by 1978 forty-five companies were in operation, boasting an average of 125 newly created jobs, with an average of 1,813 shareholders (the majority of them migrants) per company; another forty companies were at various stages of realization, and another seventy-three companies were being planned.[19] The first companies attracted migrant investors from various parts of Turkey, but later

investors tended to be concentrated in the local or
surrounding regions in which the new companies were
being established.

In the 1970s, the average cost of a share was
12,500 Turkish lira (approximately $900)--only a
fraction of a typical migrant's savings during his
sojourn abroad.[20] The migrants' motivations for
participating in these schemes were not only--perhaps
not even primarily--economic. By the late 1970s, few
if any of the companies had paid dividends, and since
the number of shareholders far exceeded the number of
jobs created, few migrants could expect to find work in
the companies, and some would not have been
interested. The migrants were motivated partly by
patriotism and partly to contribute toward the
development of their home regions--"so that the younger
generation would not have to leave." The proportion of
migrants participating in these schemes is
impressive. By the late 1970s, depending on how the
calculations are made, somewhere between 10 and 20
percent of all post-World War II Turkish migrants to
Europe participated in these investments.[21]

Various Turkish laws initially made such ventures
difficult. Turkish commercial law applied mainly to
small family companies, and the requirement that one-
fourth of a company's founding capital be transferred
to Turkey in local currency before the company could be
registered created serious problems because of
inflation. The German Ministry of Economic
Cooperation, however, became very interested in these
projects and has supported them through the provision
of subsidized credits as well as managerial training.
Since 1976 the companies have been supported by a
special fund, financed in equal parts by the Turkish
and German governments. By the early 1980s, 128
companies are reported to be in production (having
created 17,162 new jobs, or an average of 134 jobs per
company), another 77 are at the investment stage, and
21 are being planned. However, the failure rate has
been high: "These 226 companies represent only a
little over half of some 400 enterprises created since
1963-64."[22]

Yugoslav experiments with collective action for
employment generation began in the early 1970s.
Migrants from a Croatian village committed themselves
in a referendum to contribute 500 German marks
(approximately $150) toward the creation of a small
textile factory in their community. This effort was so
successful that a number of migrants from the same area
later decided to extend more substantial loans to the
factory for the creation of two subsidiary plants in
neighboring villages, so that their family members
would have access to employment opportunities. This

effort became the model for many others. Some twenty
projects were reported in the 1970s. In a study in
1981 of Yugoslav migrants in France and Germany, the
respondents were found to be familiar with about twenty
other projects, which had not been mentioned in the
earlier reports.[23]

The Yugoslav projects differ from the Turkish ones
in several respects. With a single exception, migrants
have not created new enterprises but rather have
extended loans to expand existing enterprises. In the
projects for which data are available, the value of the
loans was on the average ten times larger than the
shares bought by Turkish migrants (the range was from
3,000 to 20,000 German marks). Fewer "depositors"
participated in the Yugoslav projects. The majority of
the migrants anticipated that they or a family member
would obtain employment in the newly created branch
enterprise. Many of the contracts between the
enterprises and the migrant-depositors indeed promised
them priority consideration in hiring, and the
enterprises promised to repay the loans after a certain
number of years.

Despite the spontaneous origin, the initiative for
the later projects has come either from individual
enterprises or from the local communities. The
Yugoslav federal authorities have supported the
projects more through general exhortations than through
specific policies. All projects needed funds in
addition to the migrants' loans: These were supplied
by the enterprises or the banks, or as subsidized
credits from various state or regional funds for the
development of underdeveloped regions in Yugoslavia.
The projects are generally located in Yugoslav regions
with high out-migration. Enterprises find such
initiatives attractive for a combination of economic
and social reasons--the availability of credits,
including credits from various societal organizations
that would otherwise not be available, and fulfilling
policymakers' expectations of facilitating the return
of migrants. The most productive enterprises in the
country's most developed regions, however, have shown
little interest in such initiatives.

The projects have attracted migrants who have
strong ties to the communities in which the enterprises
are located: Deposits, whether by a husband or a wife,
were usually made in the community from which the
husband came; in a few cases they were made in or near
the wife's home. The migrants most attracted by the
projects--apart from a few who seemed to be primarily
motivated by social conscience--were interested in the
employment opportunities and generally saw no other
alternatives for return. They were not always the
candidates most desired by the enterprises (for reasons

of age, health, or lack of skills) and when some were refused employment, considerable resentment resulted.[24]

In summary, the Turkish and Yugoslav cases suggest that several points should be considered in planning collective employment generation projects. First, such projects are likely to attract investors from other parts of the home country only if the projects are located in urban growth centers, not in less-developed and rural regions. Second, the migrants who are potentially the most interested in such projects are not those who are the most likely to organize them. In Turkey, the organizational impetus tended to come from professionals or highly skilled migrants, even if most of the shareholders were found among the less skilled; later, some speculators joined as well. In Yugoslavia, the migrants looked for leadership to managers of local enterprises, bank officials, or the leaders of their communities.

Third, it is necessary to be very explicit about the conditions under which migrants agree to participate in such efforts. Perhaps, the most crucial question is access to the newly created jobs, and it is important not to create false expectations. Finally, in some Yugoslav communities, the migrant-depositors or their relatives working in the enterprises experienced some resentment from other members of the local population. Talk circulated about "buying jobs," criticism that "those who have thousands of marks or francs to deposit are wealthy enough already--they don't need jobs," and so forth. Such reactions serve as reminders of the need to be sensitive to the possible reactions of the local nonmigrant population whenever projects involving returning migrants are formulated.

IV. Using Migration for Development: Three Proposals for the Caribbean

The experiences in other migration contexts offer some valuable insights and lessons for the Caribbean. They also demonstrate that alternatives exist to the coercive approach of Cuba or the laissez-faire approach of the rest of the Caribbean. The successful programs in other areas were expensive, and many involved cooperation between sending and receiving countries. To attract returning migrants, incentive programs should offer specific employment, which need not approximate the migrants' current wages and other benefits but should be highly attractive by local standards, and, when necessary, they should provide housing. The programs' effectiveness increases to the extent that they also provide transportation, expenses for educating the returning migrants' children, exemption from duties for the migrants' possessions and for their investment, and permission to maintain foreign currency accounts. Of the employment-creation schemes, the most successful involved some spontaneous interest on the part of migrants, some support from sending countries, and some aid from receiving countries.

A proposal to use migration for development should try to enhance the development of the sending country and increase the well-being of the individual emigrant and his family. As a rule, programs should offer incentives rather than penalties to encourage participation. In addition, in recognizing the United States as part of the larger Caribbean community--the result of recent immigration[25]--proposals should attempt to increase the social welfare of the entire community and to increase and improve the ties between the people and the countries in the region.

Proposals should be responsive to the three migration-related development problems previously noted. Obviously with unemployment such a serious problem in the Caribbean, large numbers of unskilled workers should not be encouraged to return home unless they plan to contribute to employment-creation projects.

To address the problem of the lack of skilled manpower and management, the best strategy for most Caribbean countries would be to use scarce resources for two purposes: to make the local educational systems more relevant to the local job markets and to ensure job placement for young Caribbean graduates who study at home or abroad. Although Caribbean governments should try to reattract some of their skilled long-term emigrants, it would be far more sensible--given the large, young population entering the job markets--for governments to use most of their resources to improve the relevance of their educational systems and their manpower programs and to provide specific employment opportunities for Caribbean youth who have just completed their university education abroad. As previously noted, most return-incentive programs engender resentment among local populations. Although a certain degree of resentment may be unavoidable, a better policy by and large would be to develop new roots--and jobs--for the young professionals who have just completed their schooling abroad than to uproot those professionals with already established families and careers abroad.

Proposals should recognize and build upon the special characteristics of Caribbean immigration to the United States. The Caribbean community in the United States is large, skilled, remarkably successful, and extraordinarily well organized. For example, immigrants from St. Vincent maintain eighteen different associations in the New York metropolitan area. A total of ninety-five different Jamaican community associations have been set up in fifteen states and the District of Columbia, with more than one-third of the groups in New York.[26] Communicating with these groups would be easy if programs were developed that encouraged return migration.

In developing proposals, the fact should be recalled that the Caribbean (along with Israel) already receives the highest level of foreign aid per capita in the world. The Caribbean Group alone mobilized over $8 billion of aid to the entire region--excluding the largest country, Cuba--from 1978 to 1985. The United States, Canada, the United Kingdom, France, the Netherlands, and Venezuela--all have large bilateral aid programs with countries in the region. International development organizations, as well as regional funds such as those of the European Economic Community and the Organization of Petroleum Exporting Countries (OPEC), also have sizable aid programs to the region.

The proposals offered in the following sections attempt to (1) utilize remittances to create jobs in the area; (2) formulate incentives for skilled and entrepreneurial persons to return; (3) discourage--but not preclude--future emigration by professionals, managers, and skilled manpower; (4) encourage some migrants to return and use their savings for job creation; (5) utilize international development assistance programs more rapidly and effectively; (6) improve and expand export opportunities for the region; (7) improve economic and social ties between the United States and the nations and peoples of the region; and (8) encourage regional economic integration, particularly of the smaller eastern Caribbean states.

The three sets proposals for "international cooperation for migration-for-development" are: (1) Caribbean national and regional remittance banks to utilize remittances more effectively for economic development; (2) return incentive programs aimed at closing the medium-term--five to ten years--management gap by developing a network and a pool of U.S.-based Caribbean professionals; and (3) a program to encourage young local graduates to remain home and those who study abroad to return by visa enforcement and a system of "forgivable loans."

A. Caribbean Remittance Banks

Remittances remain a sizable untapped economic opportunity for the Caribbean (and for many countries in the developing world.) Although data are not solid, one World Bank study, using data from the International Monetary Fund, estimated that selected developing countries had received $24 billion in remittances in 1978, representing about 13 percent of those countries' exports. Estimates for Jamaica--one of those countries--fluctuated from $17 million in 1968 to $56 million in 1972 to $41 million in 1977, and as a percent of Jamaica's exports, from 7 percent in 1967 to nearly 20 percent in 1973 to 10 percent in 1978. For selected countries in the Caribbean Basin, total remittances were estimated to have increased from $30 million in 1968 to $600 million in 1978. The same study found that the overall level of remittances was not affected by foreign exchange or other incentive schemes; however, such schemes did affect the way remittances were spent (i.e., consumption or savings).[27]

We propose the establishment of Caribbean national and regional remittance banks as mechanisms that could utilize emigrant remittances for economic development. The larger Caribbean governments could establish national remittance banks under the active supervision of the World Bank, the Caribbean Development Bank, and other international financial institutions. The smaller states of the eastern Caribbean might want to consider a regional bank associated with the Organization of Eastern Caribbean States and the Eastern Caribbean Currency Authority as well as the other institutions previously listed; such a regional bank could still allocate funds on a national basis.

These banks would ensure that emigrants' remittances would not be lost and indeed would be invested in ways that would offer them a good rate of return, a financial stake in enterprises, and at a certain point, job opportunities for them or their families in such enterprises. The World Bank (or Inter-American Development Bank) would actively supervise the banks (perhaps through the International Finance Corporation), much as they do their loans, to assure emigrants that their investment would not be jeopardized by a change in government or political instability. The banks would transfer agreed-upon proportions of the emigrants' remittances to their families, directly and as dividends from the investments.

These remittances could in turn be used as the governments' counterpart funding for international development projects. (The Caribbean Development Facility (CDF) was first established by the Caribbean Group in 1979 to help provide counterpart funding required by all international financial institutions (IFIs) for almost all projects; until that time, many

projects either had been delayed or had not been
approved merely because the Caribbean governments did
not have the matching funds. Even with the CDF,
certain projects are held up because of inadequate
counterpart funding.) In effect, Caribbean governments
could use remittances to increase foreign aid and use
foreign aid as an incentive to migrants to increase
their remittances because the aid would, in effect,
constitute matching grants for the remittances.[28]

A remittance bank could operate as follows.
Working with the World Bank and other institutions, it
would identify promising projects in the private
sector. The IFIs would then agree to fund one-half of
the investment, and the remittances would provide the
other one-half. Apart from having to pay a nominal
administrative fee to the bank, the emigrants would
thus increase their investments, perhaps even double
them, depending on the proportion of the IFI loan that
was concessional. (If they withdrew their investments
before five years elapsed, they would receive only the
money deposited, without interest.) Then, as the
projects came on stream, the emigrants could either
receive annual dividends at competitive or nearly
competitive rates, which they could pass on to their
families, or reinvest. Since no project is riskfree,
employment or a return on the investment could not be
guaranteed. However, the active supervision of the
World Bank would significantly reduce such risks below
those of other private-sector investments, and job
opportunities could be offered on a priority basis to
emigrants who invested a certain amount of money, to be
determined at the beginning.

The incentives for emigrants to use such banks
would be that (1) their remittances would not be lost,
as now sometimes occurs; (2) the banks would guarantee
that the emigrants' families would receive whatever
portion of their remittances they chose to send them;
(3) the emigrants' investments would be augmented by
IFI loans or grants and ensured by IFI supervision; (4)
the emigrants would be contributing to their country's
development; and (5) they would receive priority in
obtaining employment in these projects in the future.
The benefits to the home countries would be that (1)
they would receive some foreign exchange that
previously had gone straight for consumption to
individual households, often leading to increased
imports or even demand-led inflation; (2) they would
expedite a larger number of loans from international
development banks; (3) they would be expanding their
own private sectors in ways that give more people a
stake in their society; (4) they would have a channel
for encouraging the return of some skilled or
entrepreneurial emigrants; and (5) in the case of the

eastern Caribbean, the countries would have an additional mechanism for encouraging regional cooperation. It would be a kind of alien-employee ownership plan.

How much demand might exist for such a remittance bank? Such investments are unlikely from people who have left their country for political reasons or who have lost confidence in their home country. For those who already send substantial remittances, a good proportion of those funds is used to maintain the standard of living of the emigrant family while the principal wage-earner is away. Since the survey data on the use of remittances are spotty, and no questions have been asked about how remittances might be spent if other opportunities arose, it is impossible to ascertain what proportion would be available for remittance banks. However, two points can be made. First, as others in this book have demonstrated, the proportion of the remittances as a percent of the emigrants' income is often quite high for all types of migration-- temporary workers, skilled and professional workers and illegal migrants. This extraordinarily high savings ratio--sometimes exceeding 50 percent among agricultural workers according to Terry McCoy's chapter in this book--suggests that Caribbean workers can save when they are in the United States; it is not unrealistic to expect their families to save in the Caribbean for a good reason.

Second, at least part of the reason why so much of the remittances is used for consumption or to renovate houses is simply because there is a dearth of investment opportunities. Few, if any, intermediaries are available to assist emigrants or workers to channel their savings into productive enterprises and to accumulate sufficient capital to make an investment viable. Emigrants' conceivably might not use the bank, but just because they are currently spending remittances to maintain a certain income level is not a sufficient explanation for not using the bank. Perhaps the best way to find out whether such a bank would be used and useful would be to do a market survey among Caribbean emigrants in a particular community--say in New York or Miami--and to begin with a single pilot project on one island and only expand if it works.

Another transitional approach to phasing in the remittance banks would be to provide incentives for those private banks in the United States that rely on emigrants' deposits to invest in the Caribbean. Perhaps A.I.D. might be prepared to oversee and guarantee some of these investments.

Would the IFIs want to undertake a supervisory role when the cost is relatively high for the limited size of the scheme? The banks undoubtedly prefer to use their resources and devote their attention to the larger countries; the issue for the United States and other donors is whether these small economies in the Caribbean merit a relatively larger role for the banks. Without that interest, it is unrealistic to expect the banks to play the kind of role envisaged in this proposal.[29]

B. Closing the Management Gap: Return Incentive Programs for the Skilled.

Even if the Caribbean governments trained the next generation of managers and succeeded in keeping most of them in the region, they still would have a serious medium-term (five to ten year) management gap. This gap is identified in many reports by the World Bank, the Group of Caribbean Experts, and the UN Economic Commission for Latin America. If all Caribbean professionals and managers who emigrated or are currently working in international institutions returned to their countries, this gap would probably be closed. However, such a mass return is unlikely under any conceivable circumstances.

Many Caribbean emigrants already return to the region on their own without special inducements. Therefore, one would expect that effectively designed return incentive programs should increase the numbers of returning emigrants. Such programs, however, are likely to be expensive, and to the extent that returning migrants would be given desirable jobs whereas those who never left remained unemployed, they are likely to breed resentment.

Caribbean governments would have difficulty fully funding such programs, but they could make some commitments to them by providing support personnel to ease the reintegration of returning migrants, by providing local scholarships for children of returning migrants, or by locating housing. Fortunately, several groups have both the resources and incentives to develop and fund such programs and recruit groups of migrants.

International Institutions. Many talented Caribbean officials staff the international financial institutions (World Bank, Inter-American Development Bank, Caribbean Development Bank, International Monetary Fund), UN Development Program, other UN specialized agencies, and many other international organizations. Some worked for the political party in their country now out of power, and they may not be welcomed by the incumbent administrations; others have worked abroad for so long that they are unlikely to consider returning. But a number of officials who

still feel attached to their home country would like to
contribute to its development provided they could be
assured of obtaining a post commensurate with their
experience.

The IFIs would be good places to start organizing
return incentive programs and recruiting for them.
Although there is agreement that many of the IFIs staff
should come from the developing world, an important
question that has not been addressed is whether this
staff needs to be or should be permanent. Although
international civil servants should be treated
equitably, those especially needed by their developing
countries could perhaps be offered employment contracts
for limited time periods, say, two to six years (albeit
with the possibility of renewals or of moving elsewhere
in the organization). Those who accepted their home
countries' offers would be returning not only with
skills and experience in managing international
projects but also with general skills in how to deal
with IFIs--a major responsibility for many officials
from the developing world.

The World Bank, using the Caribbean Group, could
take the lead in developing an inventory of Caribbean
staff working in international organizations (IOs).
This "return migration group," which would be charged
with overseeing the program, should consult with the
Caribbean governments and then make appropriate job
offers to individuals whose assignments in the
international organizations were about to be
completed. Participation in the program would be
voluntary. Some who accepted the job offers would
serve in their home government; others might supervise
the projects that they had been overseeing from
Washington, with the view of managing the facilities
when completed.

For special cases, the IFIs should consider
encouraging the return of senior international civil
servants by subsidizing or "topping off" their salaries
above what the local governments could provide,
although perhaps not as high as they might earn in
their positions at the IFIs.

Donor Governments and Return Migration

Projects. The largest numbers of skilled Caribbean
emigrants have gone to those countries--the United
States, the United Kingdom, Canada, France, the
Netherlands--that also happen to be the major sources
of development assistance to the Caribbean. Each of
these governments, but particularly those of the United
States and Canada, have recently expanded their
bilateral aid programs, and most of these programs are
managed primarily by either private voluntary
organizations or consulting firms. The demand for

personnel to work on such projects has increased
sharply in the last few years and is likely to continue
to grow in the next five years. Yet few Caribbean-born
personnel are hired because most consulting firms
cannot afford the time or financial costs involved in
such recruitment.

However, it should be neither difficult nor
expensive to develop a professional network for
recruiting Caribbean personnel--a pool of U.S.-based
Caribbean professionals. The key newspapers,
organizations, and churches used by each immigrant
group are easily identifiable: Through advertisements
and interviews, aid agencies could develop a data bank
of names of potential return migrants. Information on
this pool of Caribbean professionals could then be made
available to consulting firms or private voluntary
organizations with an added injunction that a certain
percentage of their personnel--increasing each year--
should, if possible, be recruited from this pool.

In addition, the U.S. Agency for International
Development (A.I.D.) and other bilateral aid agencies
could invite people from this pool as well as others
(reached through advertising) to submit proposals for
employment creation projects in their home countries.
Such a program could be modeled on the Dutch program
described earlier, and it might be able to work in
conjunction with the remittance banks. Emigrants'
projects would be funded by the bilateral aid agencies,
and they would return to create and manage their own
projects or enterprises. Given Canada's commitment to
double aid to the region and similar commitments by the
European Economic Community and the United States, and
given the strong interest in stimulating the private
sector and in addressing the brain-drain problem, such
return migrant projects appear to be quite feasible and
attractive.

Private Investors and Traders: Using
Transplanted Talent. Caribbean governments have
increasingly come to rely on foreign investments as
stimuli for economic development and as sources of
employment, technology, and foreign exchange. The
Caribbean Basin Initiative will undoubtedly provide an
additional stimulus to further investment. In
addition, as transportation costs become more important
and as the U.S. quotas on textiles from the Far East
become more constraining, textile firms are likely to
move their manufacturing facilities to the Caribbean
area. For all these reasons, increased foreign
investment is expected in the region, particularly if
the U.S. economic recovery is sustained.

Some Caribbean governments--for example, Haiti's--
explicitly require foreign investors to associate with

local partners, but most foreign investors and traders are already aware of the benefits of working with local managerial personnel even when the host governments do not require it. The perfect manager would be a native of the particular Caribbean country who had lived in the United States for an extended period. One would expect therefore that foreign investors and traders would be eager to tap into a data bank of potential Caribbean return migrants; perhaps they would be willing to pay a sufficiently high fee that would fund the establishment and maintenance of such a data bank. The return of Caribbean managers after an extended stay in the United States might also lead to increasing trading opportunities, as these people may have had substantial experience with U.S. markets.

The Intergovernmental Committee on Migration. The International Committee on Migration (ICM, formerly ICEM) has operated a "return of talent" program to Latin America from Europe since 1974 and from the United States since 1981. Under this program ICM recruits Latin American nationals who reside in the United States as well as Europeans and others for specialized and professional positions in Latin American countries. The services offered include job placement, travel assistance, and salary incentives. Currently fifteen Latin American countries participate in the program. Since 1964 the organization has moved more than 28,000 professionals, technicians, and highly skilled workers to Latin America in all its programs.[30] In 1983, after receiving requests from African governments and multilateral funding, ICM expanded the program to Africa. Representatives of Caribbean governments could approach ICM with a proposal for a similar program.

C. Investing in the Next Generation

The United Nations Conference for Trade and Development (UNCTAD) estimated that between 1961 and 1972 the developing countries invested the equivalent of $42 billion in the health and education of professional and skilled workers who subsequently emigrated to the United States, Canada, and the United Kingdom.[31] To address this problem, several analysts proposed that developing countries impose a "compensation" or "education tax" on professionals, managers, and other skilled personnel who are trained at public expense and subsequently emigrate. The tax could be computed according to various formulas, and the revenues could be spent in many different ways. Three variations on such a tax have been proposed: (1) The sending governments could assess the emigrants

directly, or they could negotiate tax-sharing
arrangements with the receiving countries; (2) a
moderate supplementary tax could be levied on the
incomes of skilled emigrants under a global tax system;
and (3) International Monetary Fund (IMF) compensatory
facilities could be used to help those governments that
have large fluctuations in migrants' remittances.[32]
Another option would be for the United States as a
receiving nation to deduct a portion of the Social
Security tax paid by the emigrant and transfer that to
the emigrants' home country.

Although these options merit consideration, we
suggest a different approach. To ensure that Caribbean
students educated in the United States return home when
they complete their studies, the United States should
vigorously enforce its visa laws, insisting that
Caribbean students not overstay. For those Caribbean
students receiving government scholarships (both
Caribbean and U.S.) for study abroad, Caribbean
governments ought to make sure that the field of study
is relevant to their nation's needs and that the
students will be placed in jobs that will use their new
skills when they return.

For those students receiving university-level
education in the Caribbean, governments might consider
providing "forgivable student loans" to all those who
use their new skills in their country. Those who
choose to emigrate within a certain appropriate
interval would not have their loans forgiven; they
would have to repay them.[33] Although this technically
would not be an "education tax," it might be considered
as such. The United States currently penalizes
countries for using such a tax. The Jackson-Vanik
amendment of the Trade Act of 1974 prohibits trade
under most-favored-nation status with governments that
either prohibit emigration or inhibit it through an
"education tax." As a first step toward assisting
Caribbean nations to reduce the brain drain, the United
States should clarify its interpretation of an
"education tax" and if necessary, consider repealing
that provision.

V. Summary

Although emigration from the Caribbean has long
been viewed as beneficial to the region's economic
development, it is increasingly clear that it also
represents an impediment and a lost opportunity. After
analyzing migration-for-development programs for other
regions and identifying those factors that were most
effective while also relevant to the Caribbean, we
propose a set of programs that would reduce the cost of
emigration to Caribbean development and multiply the

benefits. The proposals include Caribbean remittance banks, incentive programs to recruit U.S.-based Caribbean professionals from private and public life, and a set of measures to encourage the next generation of Caribbean professionals to use their skills in their home countries.

An alternative is presented that is between the statist approach to emigration of the Cuban government and the wholly individualistic approach of the rest of the Caribbean governments. It uses the available ways to reconcile the personal right to emigrate with the collective concern for economic development. It involves steps by Caribbean governments, by donor governments like that of the United States interested in the region, and by the international development institutions. To the extent that economic development is a primary concern of those interested in the Caribbean, increased attention should be given to migration as a central factor in the development equation.

Notes

We appreciate the comments of Sergio Diaz-Briquets, Richard Feinberg, Nicholas Carter, William Demas, and Gretchen Brainerd on earlier drafts.

1. Michael S. Teitelbaum, Latin Migration North: The Problem for U.S. Foreign Policy (New York: Council on Foreign Relations, 1985), pp. 35-38.

2. International Labor Organization, Time for Transition (Geneva: ILO, 1975), p. 65.

3. For example, World Bank, Caribbean Group: Current Situation and Prospects, Report No. 3937-CRG, May 24, 1982, pp. 8-9. This report cited the conclusion of a World Bank study group on the economic problems of the micro-states at a meeting in Antigua in April 1981.

4. World Bank, Jamaica: Development Issues and Economic Prospects, January 29, 1982, p.3.

5. World Bank, Jamaica: Structural Adjustment, Export Development, and Private Investment, June 3, 1982, pp. 17-19.

6. World Bank, Economic Memorandum on Haiti, May 25, 1982, pp. ii-v.

7. World Bank, Economic Memorandum on Dominica, May 25, 1982, p. iii.

8. The Caribbean Community in the 1980s: Report by a Group of Caribbean Experts, appointed by the Caribbean Common Market Council of Ministers (Georgetown, Guyana: Caribbean Community Secretariat, 11 January 1981), pp. 30-38.

9. Interview and discussion with Prime Minister Edward Seaga, Woodrow Wilson Center for Scholars, Washington, D.C., May 13, 1983 by Robert Pastor. The two programs were outlined in "Prime Minister's Message To All Jamaicans Overseas," Panama Star and Herald, July 31, 1983, p. B-6. For the follow-up on his letter to overseas Jamaicans, correspondence from Lorna Murray, Planning Institute of Jamaica, 29 June 1984. Address by Rt. Hon. Edward Seaga to the Governing Council of the UNDP, Geneva, 12 June 1984. Edward P.G. Seaga, "Developing Nations Need 'Manpower Bank,'" Miami Herald, January 28, 1985, p. 61.

The late Prime Minister Tom Adams of Barbados also proposed the issue of immigration policy as one area of possible fruitful collaboration among the eastern Caribbean states. ("Caribbean Nations Creating Regional Force," Foreign Broadcasting Information Service, November 18, 1983, p. S1.)

10. Rien van Gendt, Return Migration and Reintegration Services (Paris: OECD, 1977).

11. The two exceptions, of which we are aware, are sui generis: from 1968 to 1970 Israel conducted a program to encourage the return of any citizen who had left between 1952 and 1964 (Nina Toren, "The Effect of Economic Incentives on Return Migration," International Migration, Vol. 9, No. 3, 1975, pp. 134-144), and in the late seventies France unilaterally instituted a "return bonus scheme" intended to induce her foreign migrants to leave (Andre Lebon, "L'aide au retour des travailleurs etrangers," Economie et Statistique, No. 113, 1979, pp. 37-46). The French scheme was first aimed at unemployed migrants only, but this restriction was dropped after it had been in operation for a few months.

12. German Mesa R. et al., Evaluacion del Programa de Retorno de Profesionales y Tecnicos. (Bogota: Ministerio de Trabajo y Seguridad Social, Fondo Colombiano de Investigaciones Cientificas, 1978).

13. Stephen Adler, "The Organization of Return Migration: A Preliminary Analysis of the Recent Experience of France and Algeria," Document MI/76/3, Paris: OECD, 1976.

14. Organization of Economic Cooperation and Development (OECD), Continuous Reporting System on Migration, SOPEMI Report 1982 (Paris: OECD, 1983), pp. 90-91.

15. The project was initially part of a larger program of Reintegration of Emigrant Manpower and the Promotion of Local Opportunities for Development (REMPLOD), set up in 1974 to assist these countries. However, after two years of research and experimentation the program moved from its initial, narrower goal of supporting return projects to the general goal of creating employment opportunities in the sending countries--for migrants and nonmigrants alike. Nevertheless, it was decided to reserve a small part of the budget specifically for aid to employment creation projects by returning migrants.

16. Foundation Netherlands Centre Foreigners, "The Experimental Scheme of Returnee Development Projects for Foreign Workers: Policy and Its Implementation by the NCB-IMOS Office," Report covering the period August 1976 - October 1980 (Utrecht, December 1980). See also Dik U. Stroband, "Background Information on the Dutch Policy with Reference to the Remigration Projects of Migrant Workers" (Utrecht: Netherlands Centre Foreigners, 1977), and interviews undertaken in 1979 by Rosemarie Rogers with Mr. Stroband as well as two researchers from the REMPLOD team. (See Rosemarie Rogers, "Incentives to Return: Patterns of Policies and Migrants' Responses," in Mary M. Kritz, Charles B. Keely, and Silvano M. Tomasi, eds., Global Trends in Migration: Theory and Research on International Population Movements (Staten Island, New York: Center for Migration Studies, 1981), pp. 338-364.)

17. For detailed descriptions and evaluations of some of these projects, emanating mainly from the sending countries, see, for example, "Cooperativas para el retorno," Carta de España (monthly publication of the Istituto Espanol de Emigracion, Madrid), No. 282, May 1983, p. 46; "Cooperativas para el retorno,"Carta de Espana, No. 292, April 1984, pp. 14-20; and Patricia Goldey, "Migration, Co-operation, and Development: An Examination of a Pilot Project in Portugal," in Daniel Kubat, ed., The Politics of Return: International Return Migration in Europe (Rome: Center for Migration Studies, 1984), pp. 45-53.

18. Ross Fakiolas "Problems and Opportunities of the Greek Migrants Returning from Western Europe," Athens: Centre of Planning and Economic Research, mimeographed paper, 1980. Murat E. Gunce, "Turkey: Turkish Workers' Companies," Arbeiten aus der Abteilung Entwicklungslanderforschung, No. 71. Bonn: Friedrich-Ebert-Stiftung, 1978.

19. Turkei Report, 1978, Nos. 1 and 2.

20. Rinus Penninx and Herman van Renselaar, A Fortune in Small Change: A Study of Migrant Workers' Attempts to Invest Savings Productively Through Joint Stock Corporations and Village Development Cooperatives in Turkey (The Hague: NUFFIC/IMWOO/REMPLOD, 1978), p. 445.

21. Ibid., p. 234; M. Werth and N. Yalcintas, "Migration and Re-Integration: Transferability of the Turkish Model of Return Migration and Self-Help Organizations to other Labour-Exporting Countries."

346

World Employment Programme, International Migration for
Employment Research Working Paper No. 29, Geneva: ILO,
1978, p. 80.

22. OECD, SOPEMI Report 1982, p. 131. See also
"Enterprises and Employment in Emigration Regions: The
Investment of Private Savings and the Role of Financial
Institutions - The Turkish Experience," contribution
from Turkey to the Meeting of Government Experts on
"Private Savings for Enterprise Development in
Emigration Regions: The Role of Financial
Institutions," Izmir, 2-5 April 1984.

23.   Mladen Vedris, Od deviznih usteda do radnih
mjesta u domovini, Migration Report No. 38, Zagreb:
Centre for Migration Studies, 1978; Ulaganje usteda
vanjskih migranata u drustveni sektor privrede,
Migration Report No. 33, Zagreb: Centre for Migration
Studies, 1977; "The Utilization of Migrant Workers'
Hard-Currency Savings in Productive Economic
Activities," Yugoslav Report for the OECD Joint Project
"Service for Returning Migrant Workers," Zagreb: OECD,
1975; Marko Beros, "Policies, Measures and Instruments
for the Attraction and Utilization of Savings," Ibid.;
Mirjana Morokvasic, "Yugoslav Workers in France and
Germany: Strategies for Settlement and Strategies for
Return," in "Return Migration to Yugoslavia: Policies,
the Innovative Return Migrant, and Prospects for
Economic Development," final report submitted by
Mirjana Morokvasic and Rosemarie Rogers to the
Rockefeller-Ford Program on Population and Development
Policy, 1982.

24.   Rosemarie Rogers, "Employment Creation
through Migrants' Loans to Enterprises in Yugoslavia,"
in "Return Migration to Yugoslavia: Policies, the
Innovative Return Migrant, and Prospects for Economic
Development," final report submitted by Mirjana
Morokvasic and Rosemarie Rogers to the Rockefeller-Ford
Research Program on Population and Development Policy,
1982.

25.   For the development of the thesis of the U.S.
as a Caribbean nation, see Robert Pastor, "Our Real
National Interests in Central America," The Atlantic
Monthly, July 1982, pp. 27-39.

26.   For the lists of Vincentian and Jamaican
associations, we are grateful to Joyce Toney of St.
Vincent and New York City; correspondence May 18, 1984.

27.   Gurushri Swamy, International Migrant
Workers' Remittances: Issues and Prospects, World Bank

Staff Working Paper No. 481, Washington, D.C., August 1981, pp. 1, 7, 53, 9, 8, 36-40.

28. The use of remittances as counterpart funding would be much more complicated than is implied in this brief description and would require the cooperation of the international development banks to be acceptable. In effect, governments would have to take title to the foreign exchange and substitute that for local currency expenditures. (Nicholas Carter assisted us in understanding the obstacles to implementing this aspect of the proposal.)

29. Our gratitude to Arthur Brown and Nicholas Carter for pressing us to address these two questions. They deserve the credit for helping us refine the proposal, but we accept the responsibility for any remaining errors or limitations.

30. ICM is undertaking an evaluation of the effectiveness of its Return of Talent program in Latin America and expects to complete it by the fall of 1985. A recent ICM report suggested that one measure of the effectiveness of the program, which returned 4,500 professionals to Latin America in the decade ending December 31, 1984 is the continued request by the governments for more assistance. (Gretchen Brainerd, Washington Representative, Intergovernmental Committee for Migration, "The Return of Talent Programs for Latin America and Africa: Evidence of Effectiveness," Washington, D.C., 28 December 1984.)

31. For an intensive analysis of the subject and a number of proposals, including several of those proposed in this paper, see United Nations Conference on Trade and Development, The Reverse Transfer of Technology: A Survey of Its Main Features, Causes, and Policy Implications (N.Y.: United Nations, 1979, TD/B/C.6/47).

32. J. Bhagwati and M. Parington (eds.), Taxing the Brain Drain, I: A Proposal, and J. Bhagwati (ed.), The Brain Drain and Taxation, II: Theory and Empirical Analysis (N.Y.: North-Holland Publishing Company, 1976); W. R. Bohning, "Migration, The Idea of Compensation, and the International Economic Order," World Employment Program, International Migration for Employment Working Paper #2-26/WP45, Geneva: International Labour Organization, December 1979.

33. Both Michael Teitelbaum and Jagdish Bhagwati, whose thinking on the "emigration tax" has evolved since his earlier work, were particularly helpful in suggesting alternative approaches to the brain-drain problem.

16. U.S. Immigration Policy and Caribbean Economic Development

Harris N. Miller

I. Introduction

The United States is pulled both by its global responsibilities and by its special concern for its third border in the Caribbean.[1] For immigration policy, the key question is whether the United States should maintain a single, global standard or develop a special policy for the Caribbean because of past practices and the region's strategic importance to the United States.

U.S. policy has not been consistent. On the one hand, U.S. officials talk about special relationships with our Caribbean neighbors, and, in fact, one important provision of the Immigration and Nationality Act (INA) -- the basic law governing U.S. immigration and refugee programs -- gives preferential treatment to natives of a Caribbean nation. The Cuban Adjustment Act of 1966, an outgrowth of strong anti-Castro sentiment, permits Cuban nationals who reach U.S. shores to adjust to legal status, a privilege not afforded nationals of other countries.

On the other hand, U.S. immigration policies are meant to be universal and nondiscriminatory, especially after changes in the legal immigration quota system in the 1960s and 1970s and the passage of the Refugee Act of 1980. All nations have the same ceiling on legal immigration to the United States, contrary to policy during earlier periods when the United States discriminated against selected countries in Europe and Asia. Prior to the 1980 Act, people fleeing persecution from Communist and certain Middle Eastern countries were given preference, but today refugees are supposed to be judged by a universally applicable standard.

This seeming contradiction in U.S. policy toward the Caribbean between special relationship and

348

universality is not unique to immigration. Many observers have noted a gap between the promises of a special relationship between the United States and Latin America and the reality of that relationship. Abraham Lowenthal has argued that this gap arises because little consideration is given to the particular impact of policies on Latin America when these policies are global in nature;[2] Robert Pastor acknowledged the gap but disagreed with Lowenthal's analysis that Latin American considerations have been given short shrift in immigration.[3]

In this chapter I discuss some alternative approaches to a special immigration relationship between the United States and Caribbean nations. I first assess the impact of present immigration policies on emigration from the region. Next, I discuss the major immigration reform legislation before Congress, drafted by Senator Alan Simpson (R.-Wyo.) and Congressman Romano Mazzoli (D.-Ky.)--commonly known as the Simpson-Mazzoli bill--and analyze its likely impact on the Caribbean. Then several alternative policies are presented, with a discussion of possible effects of each.

II. Current Immigration Policy Toward the Caribbean

In discussing current U.S. immigration policy toward the Caribbean, it is important to understand the difference between legal immigration--lawful movement of people to the United States either for a fixed period or permanently--and illegal immigration-- movement of people to the United States either without legal authority or legally for a fixed period that they overstay without authorization. Though the data in this area are uncertain, illegal immigration from the Caribbean to the United States appears to be much larger than legal immigration.[4]

Legal Immigration

Three of the various types of legal immigration are examined here. First, permanent immigrants are people who come to the United States because they fit into the preference system developed in 1965 and modified twice since. The preference system determines the priority for people wishing to emigrate to the United States, and sets numerical limits. Second, nonimmigrants are people who come here temporarily: Many are short-term visitors and business people; others come for longer periods to work or study. Finally, the asylees (those seeking asylum) are people who are or who claim to be fleeing persecution in their homelands and want to live in the United States.

Permanent immigrants are the easiest group to understand because, in theory at least, the level and types of people who enter the country are defined and controllable. The watershed year for U.S. legal immigration policy is 1965 when Congress repealed the "national-origins" quota system, which had discriminated against southern and eastern Europeans and Asians and replaced it with a more neutral system based on family reunification and, to a lesser extent, skills. A ceiling of 170,000 was placed on immigrants from the Eastern Hemisphere (Europe, Asia, and Africa), with an annual limit of 20,000 per country. Immediate relatives were exempt from the ceiling.

The Western Hemisphere was given special treatment, with no ceiling from 1965 to 1968 and then an overall ceiling of 120,000 with no preference system and no individual country limitations. The three-year delay in the ceiling was meant to allow the Select Commission on Western Hemisphere Immigration to study the pros and cons of a Western Hemisphere ceiling, particularly because of fears that it would adversely affect U.S. relationships with Mexico and the Caribbean. However, the commission made the rather timid recommendation of a further delay in implementing the ceiling until 1969--a recommendation Congress ignored.[5]

In 1976, the INA was amended to place the Western Hemisphere under the preference system, with a 20,000 per country limitation, and in 1978, the Western and Eastern Hemisphere ceilings were combined to a worldwide ceiling of 290,000, subsequently reduced to 270,000. By 1978, the special treatment of legal immigrants from the Caribbean and other Latin American nations had ended to a large extent.

However, several other aspects of the complicated legal immigration system made the system less restrictive for the Caribbean nations than might first appear. The INA contains a 600 per country limit on colonies, those numbers being deducted from the mother country's ceiling. In 1965, many of the Caribbean islands were still colonies. However, when they achieved independence, their ceilings were raised to 20,000, a major difference. Another factor is that the 20,000 per country and the 600 per colony ceilings do not apply to those classified as immediate relatives--spouses, minor children and parents of U.S. citizens--which often turn out to be a large percentage of those wishing to emigrate. Finally, the populations of most Caribbean nations are small, so the number of emigrants is often a large proportion of their people.

What have all these legal immigration policies meant in practical terms for the Caribbean nations? First, the 1965 reforms generally created a radical shift in the source countries for immigration to the United States. During the first sixty-five years of the twentieth century, 75 percent of legal immigrants came from European nations; now, over 80 percent come from Latin America and Asia. The Caribbean sent 123,000 legal immigrants to the United States in the 1950s, over 470,000 in the 1960s, and almost 750,000 in the 1970s. Even during the 1970s, dramatic increases took place from Jamaica, which sent the largest number of legal immigrants in 1981, jumping from 13,427 in 1972 to over 23,500 in 1981.[6] In 1983, the Dominican Republic and Jamaica ranked sixth and seventh in the world in number of immigrant visas issued by the Department of State, just behind Mexico, the Philippines, Korea, India, and mainland-born Chinese.

However, the demand for those who wish to emigrate legally to the United States outruns the numbers allocated to many countries, leading to backlogs. As of January 1984, Jamaica had almost 60,000 people with visas approved who could not enter the United States because of the limitations of the preference system and the 20,000 per country ceiling. Many of these people will have to wait several years to enter the United States legally. The lines are even longer in the Philippines where some people will have to wait more than twelve years. Worldwide, more than 1.5 million people are registered to enter the United States legally, many more than the system can accept. And the number grew over 12 percent from 1983 to 1984, with no sign that the growth is abating.[7] In sum, slightly more than 70,000 people emigrate legally from the Caribbean to the United States each year, with the bulk from Jamaica and the Dominican Republic.

In 1981, over 600,000 Caribbean citizens entered the United States as nonimmigrants--on a temporary basis. However, over 85 percent of these were short-term visitors for business or pleasure. This group had little impact on permanent immigration, except for those who overstayed their entry visas and remained illegally in the United States.

Two subgroups of the nonimmigrants deserve special attention--foreign students and temporary foreign workers. The latter, known as H-2s after the apposite provision in the INA, enter the United States to work in areas in which U.S. workers are not available.

Though over 300,000 foreign students are in the United States at any one time, the Caribbean nations have contributed a relatively small number--between 10,000 and 12,000 per year. The largest number enter from the Bahamas, with the Dominican Republic, Haiti, Jamaica, and Trinidad and Tobago sending over 1,000 each. The Caribbean also sends a small number--less than 1,000--exchange visitors who come with government assistance for special advanced training. Table 16.1

Table 16.1

Caribbean Foreign Student Population
In the United States, 1983-84[a]

Country	Foreign Students
Anguilla	3
Bahamas	1,480
Barbados	320
Br. Virgin Islands	42
Cayman Islands	23
Cuba	1,790
Dominica	29
Dominican Republic	740
Guadeloupe	4
Haiti	1,300
Jamaica	2,330
Martinique	11
Montserrat	2
Netherlands Antilles	580
St. Christopher-Nevis	24
St. Lucia	46
St. Vincent and Grenadines	40
Trinidad and Tobago	1,800
Turks and Caicos Islands	12
Unspecified	211
Total	10,867

[a]These data come from a yearly report on foreign students in the United States published by the Institute of International Education, entitled Open Doors: 1983/84 (New York).

provides data on the Caribbean foreign student population in the United States.

Because the Immigration and Naturalization Service (INS) has only begun to develop an effective means of monitoring whether nonimmigrants actually leave the United States at the end of their entry period, it is difficult to know how many of these students complete their studies and return home. Some who have tried to look at this issue believe as many as one-third of all foreign students remain in the United States either without finishing their education or after doing so. Some of these remain legally by marrying U.S. citizens or adjusting under the skilled preference immigration categories; others simply remain illegally.

During the past four years, concern about abuses of the foreign student program led the INS to tighten regulations to monitor the immigration status of foreign students to reduce illegal overstays. Also, the Simpson-Mazzoli bill contains provisions to discourage abuses of the program.

The H-2 workers come to the United States from the Commonwealth Caribbean to work in the sugarcane fields of Florida and to pick tobacco and apples in New York and other East Coast states. The United States has been admitting approximately 20,000 H-2 workers each year for agriculture, 13,000 of whom come from the Caribbean.[8]

There are many critics of the H-2 program, particularly regarding the wages and working conditions of the imported labor. However, for the agricultural employers who use them, the workers themselves, and the home countries that welcome the earned remittances and the willingness of the United States to absorb some of its labor, the H-2 program is viewed as beneficial. H-2 workers enter the United States under contracts negotiated between the growers and the home countries. With very few exceptions, the H-2 workers return home after their period of work in the United States. Because their earnings are high compared to wages in their home countries, the H-2 workers do exceptionally well, which creates keen competition for the available H-2 slots.

Under international law and U.S. law, refugees and asylees are people who have been persecuted or have a well-founded fear of persecution based on race, religion, nationality, membership in a particular social group, or political opinion. Until the Refugee Act of 1980, only people escaping from Communist countries and certain Middle East nations were refugees under U.S. law, but the 1980 act applied the status to people fleeing any nation if they can establish they have been persecuted or face a well-founded fear of persecution. Refugees are people outside their home countries, but not in the United States, such as the Vietnamese who flee Vietnam in boats and arrive in Thailand, Hong Kong, and other Southeast Asian nations. These countries do not want to resettle these people permanently, expecting instead that the United States, Canada, Australia, France, and other developed countries will take them. By contrast, asylees are people who have fled directly to the United States from their home countries.

For the Caribbean, Cuba and Haiti are the countries for which the terms "refugees" and "asylees" are most relevant. Since Castro took over in 1959, nearly 1 million Cubans have come to the United States, a large percentage of them claiming to flee political persecution. In 1966, Congress enacted a special law, the Cuban Adjustment Act, which gave these Cubans an unusual right to have their status legalized even if there are questions about whether they are truly fleeing persecution.

The most recent influx of Cubans came in 1980, when 125,000 people, including 2,000 to 3,000 undesirables--criminals or people with severe mental illness--fled to the United States. The exodus from Cuba's Mariel harbor has had a major impact on immigration policy in the United States. The undesirable elements created severe law enforcement problems that led to several thousand of them being imprisoned or jailed. Immigration relations between the United States and Cuba, which have ebbed and flowed over the years, became very hostile.

Two recent decisions have helped to resolve some of the lingering difficulties arising from the Mariel exodus, though two other longer term issues have been created. First, the INS, after leaving the Marielitos in a questionable legal status for four years while Congress debated the first two versions of the Simpson-Mazzoli bill, has begun adjusting them to legal status using the 1966 Cuban Adjustment Act. By the end of 1985, most of them, except the undesirables, should have legal status.

Second, after four years of episodic negotiations, the United States and Cuba reached an agreement on December 14, 1984 under which most of the undesirables will be returned to Cuba, and the United States will once again accept Cubans under the normal permanent immigration program. The longer term issue involving the undesirables is that many do not want to go back and, with the help of lawyers, will tie up the legal system perhaps for years to prevent their return.

The longer term issue for U.S. immigration is that as many as 300,000 Cubans may be eligible to emigrate to the United States because of family relationships. Because of the preference system and the 20,000 per country ceiling, these people cannot all come at once. Indeed, there is some question whether any can come. In May 1985, in retaliation for the establishment of Radio Marti, Cuba suspended the migration agreement.

Haitians have been coming illegally in fairly large numbers and legally in relatively small numbers to the United States for years, but in 1980 before and after the Cuban boatlift, the number of Haitians arriving on U.S. shores increased substantially. And because they arrived at the same time as the Cubans, in many people's minds the 25,000 or more who arrived in 1980 became linked with the Marielitos.

A great debate has arisen over whether these Haitians are economic migrants fleeing the poverty of their homeland or asylees fleeing persecution. Because the INS chose to detain many of the Haitians in the early 1980s, whereas most of the Cubans were allowed to remain free, many claimed the Haitians were being discriminated against because they were black. The civil rights and civil liberties communities and many members of Congress got into a running battle with the INS until the Haitians were released. The legal case arising from their detention is still in the federal courts.

Unlike the Cubans who for the most part can only come to the United States when Castro allows or encourages them, the Haitians continued to come after the 1980 period, leading the Justice Department, in conjunction with the U.S. Coast Guard, to begin to intercept them at sea and return them to Haiti before they could arrive in the United States. That program continues today and has substantially reduced, though not eliminated, the flow of Haitians.

Two issues remain unresolved. First, the Haitians who arrived during 1980 and subsequently remain in a legal limbo are not eligible--as are the Cuban arrivals under the 1966 act--for special treatment. Provisions of the Simpson-Mazzoli bill would have legalized their statuses along with those of the Cubans, but they were not enacted. Such Haitians can apply individually for asylum, but few are likely to meet the INS criteria. Their best hope is special legislation.

Second, Haitians continue to try to come to the United States, at least some of whom may have legitimate asylum claims. Often in unseaworthy vessels, they head for the United States directly or via the Bahamas, some to drown at sea, others to be overtaken by the Coast Guard, and a few to reach U.S. shores successfully and evade detection. Although the Coast Guard patrols and various diplomatic entreaties to the Haitian government have reduced the flow, they have not stopped it. Many Haitians pay to come to the United States, and the smugglers who take advantage of them will continue to abet the desire to flee for a better life. The U.S. government is going to have to treat the asylum claims of those who do reach U.S. shores seriously.

Illegal Immigration

For all the analysis of legal immigration, most observers believe the number of illegal immigrants from Caribbean nations simply overwhelms legal immigrants.

Many experts in the State Department and INS believe
that as many as 130,000 illegal Caribbean immigrants
come to the United States each year in addition to the
approximately 70,000 legal immigrants. Although this
estimate, as with any estimate of illegal immigration,
may be high, it certainly is conceivable. And there is
every indication that the number continues to grow.

Many of these illegal immigrants initially enter
legally as visitors for business or pleasure and then
remain after their period of entry has expired. They
melt into ethnic Caribbean communities in the United
States, usually with little fear that they will be
apprehended by the understaffed INS. Because the
department is aware of so many visa abusers from
Caribbean nations, they scan visa applicants from these
countries very carefully. Still, even the most
skeptical consular official cannot turn down every
applicant, especially when the applicant has relatives
to visit in the United States. The official may
believe the applicant will never return to his or her
homeland, but the visas are still issued--over 600,000
in 1981.

Many illegal immigrants enter with expertly forged
documents, the production of which is a big business.
They arrive often at an overcrowded Miami International
Airport, where there is tremendous pressure on the
airport inspection officials from INS and U.S. Customs
to process international arrivals quickly. To inspect
each entrant adequately would grind the arrival process
to a halt, so the inspectors are left to stop only the
most obvious forgeries. Once the entrants are past the
inspectors, they too can quickly melt into their
communities, with little likelihood of being
apprehended.

The estimates of how many illegal immigrants live
in the United States vary tremendously, and the
estimates of how many come from any particular country
or region vary even more. The U.S. Census Bureau has
talked in terms of 3 million to 6 million illegal
immigrants in the United States, whereas other sources
have projected an illegal population closer to 12
million. What percentage of the illegals are from
Caribbean nations is even harder to determine. Most
believe--without any real data to justify their
conclusions--that well over 1 million illegal
immigrants from the Caribbean nations live in the
United States, and that number grows by 100,000 or more
each year. The largest sending countries are those
that also send large numbers of legal immigrants.[9]

In sum, each year as many as 200,000 Caribbean
citizens come to the United States to live, perhaps
one-third under the legal immigration system. Under
current law, the number of legal immigrants is likely

to continue to grow, especially if the migration
agreement with Cuba is ever implemented. And, unless
major changes are implemented in U.S. policy to stem
the illegal flow as contemplated in the Simpson-Mazzoli
bill, discussed in the next section, the illegal
immigrant population will probably expand also.

III. The Simpson-Mazzoli Bill

U.S. ambivalence on immigration is perhaps best
demonstrated in its policies on illegal immigration.
On the one hand, the United States is a sovereign
nation, with more than occasional lapses into jingoism,
that wants to control its borders. "America firsters,"
labor union members worried about their jobs, and
population control advocates have been among those who
have called for strict control of U.S. borders against
illegal entry.

On the other hand, those who take Emma Lazarus's
words on the base of the Statue of Liberty literally --
"give me you tired, your poor" -- various ethnic
groups, civil libertarians, and employers who are happy
with the cheap and docile labor provided by illegal
immigrants have worked together to prevent any serious
attempts to limit immigration. The INS has been
seriously underfunded and understaffed, with little
augmentation between World War II and the early
1980s. (INS apprehensions are now running at over 1
million per year, but no one knows how many are
repeaters, and large numbers undoubtedly evade the
immigration authorities.) A 1952 provision of the INS,
known as the Texas Proviso because it was promoted by
the agricultural interests from that state, made it
clear that although it is illegal for an illegal
immigrant to work in this country, it is not illegal
for an employer to hire an illegal immigrant. Thus,
there are few disincentives for an employer not to hire
an illegal immigrant.

For the last fifteen years, the federal
government, in fits and starts, has tried harder to
control illegal immigration. In the mid-1960s after
the United States ended the large temporary-worker
program from Mexico, known as the Bracero Program, the
number of illegal immigrants grew markedly. Most INS
officials believe that the people being apprehended
were simply the Braceros, now entering illegally. But
whatever the cause, illegal immigration became an
issue. Those who saw immigration as a law-and-order
issue joined organized labor, which saw the illegal
flow as a threat to jobs.

In 1972, with the support of President Richard
Nixon, the House of Representatives considered a bill
authored by Congressman Peter W. Rodino, Jr. (D.-N.J.),

making it illegal for an employer to hire an illegal
alien. Despite objections from the agricultural
employers, who wanted to continue to use their cheap-
labor sources, and some Hispanic groups, who claimed
the bill would lead to discrimination against
Hispanics, the Employer Sanctions Bill overwhelmingly
passed the House. However, the Senate Judiciary
Committee never took action because then Chairman James
Eastland (D.-Miss.) was responsive to agricultural
interests. Rodino got the bill through the House again
in 1974, but Eastland once more refused to consider
it. And in 1975, with a provision added that would
have legalized many illegals already in the United
States, Rodino pushed it through the House Judiciary
Committee, but it died without further action.

President Jimmy Carter brought forward another
version of an employer sanctions/legalization package
in 1977, but once again Congress was not ready to face
the issue. Instead, Congress established a Select
Commission on Immigration and Refugee Policy, which was
first headed by former Florida Governor Reuben Askew,
and then Notre Dame University President Theodore M.
Hesburgh. It was composed of Carter administration
officials, Congressional leaders, and public citizens
charged with studying the issues and making
recommendations.

In a voluminous report issued in March 1981, the
commission called for the same basic immigration policy
package--employer sanctions and a legalization
program. They also recommended numerous changes in the
legal immigration provisions of the INA, the procedures
for asylum, and the temporary-worker program.

President Ronald Reagan, in response to the
Hesburgh Commission report, established his own task
force, headed by Attorney General William French Smith,
to make recommendations. In July 1981, Smith put
forward a plan including sanctions and legalization.
Though there were differences between the commission
proposals and Smith's, the broad outlines were the
same.

Change in party control of the Senate and the
retirement of two House members in 1981 brought two
relative newcomers to prominence in Congress in the
immigration field. Freshman Senator Alan K. Simpson
(R.-Wyo.) had some background in the area, having
served on the Hesburgh Commission. Congressman Romano
Mazzoli (D.-Ky.), though beginning his sixth term, had
never even served on the House Judiciary Subcommittee
on Immigration, Refugees, and International Law when he
took over as chairman, at the behest of his long-time
friend Father Hesburgh, in spring 1981.

Thus began a four-year saga, the conclusion of
which is still uncertain.[10] Simpson and Mazzoli have

been imitating Sisyphus during sessions of the last two Congresses--struggling valiantly to push a major reform bill up the side of the treacherous immigration mountain and into law. In both 1982 and 1984 they came very close but were foiled as they ran out of time.

Although the future of the Simpson-Mazzoli bill is in doubt, it is important to understand its contents and how it might affect Caribbean migration and economic development. For whether it passes or not in the 99th Congress, many of its longer term objectives are likely to become reality through changes in the law or changes in the administration of existing immigration laws.

The major emphasis of the bill, to paraphrase the Select Commission, is to keep open the front door of legal immigration by closing the back door of illegal immigration. Most U.S. citizens and their elected representatives do not distinguish between the methods of entry of newcomers to U.S. shores. The Select Commission, Simpson, Mazzoli, and many supporters of their bill fear that as long as the illegal population is large and continues to grow, there may be a move to curtail the more easily identifiable and more easily controlled legal immigration. Even though there is almost universal agreement that legal immigration is a net benefit to U.S. society, it could be restrained in the name of controlling overall immigration.

The Simpson-Mazzoli bill, following from the Select Commission, the recommendations of the four U.S. Presidents from Nixon through Reagan, and the work of Congressman Rodino, contains two basic elements to limit illegal immigration -- employer sanctions and increased enforcement by the INS.

The argument in favor of sanctions is straightforward. Illegal immigrants come here to take jobs, and since there is no legal punishment for the employers who hire the illegals, the employers encourage their arrival. Therefore, the best way to end the job lure that brings the illegal immigrants is to impose a graduated series of penalties--including criminal penalties for systematic, flagrant violators-- against employers who knowingly hire illegal aliens.

Linked to this argument is one for an increase in the funding and personnel of the INS. Even without the bill, at the urging of Simpson and Mazzoli and their colleagues on the Appropriations Committees, Congress has begun a steady funding and personnel increase for INS. The Border Patrol has been strengthened with more people and more sophisticated technology. Investigation and apprehension of illegal immigrants are also being increased. INS is moving toward more sophisticated tracking systems to detect those who enter legally but then overstay their visas.

A third important element of the Simpson-Mazzoli
bill is the legalization program, more commonly
referred to as amnesty, that will allow many of those
who entered illegally to apply for legal status and, if
they meet certain criteria, eventually become U.S.
citizens.

Legalization is the most controversial portion of
the bill, with few U.S. citizens willing to condone
illegal behavior. The supporters of the program argue,
however, that though these people are technically here
illegally, many were welcomed here by past U.S.
unwillingness to deal with illegal immigration.
Proponents also note that the deportation of large
numbers of illegal immigrants is impractical and
undesirable.

To make sure that the most deserving are
legalized, the program makes eligible only those who
arrived in the United States prior to a fixed date
(which has shifted during the Congressional debate) and
who have maintained a solid work and community record
since their arrival. Criminals, welfare abusers, and
others with questionable backgrounds will not be
eligible. The Simpson-Mazzoli bill also contained a
special provision in the last Congress to legalize the
status of Cubans and Haitians who arrived before
January 1, 1982, to eliminate that sticky political
problem.

The Simpson-Mazzoli bill proposes numerous
revisions in the H-2 temporary-worker program for
agriculture, meant to respond to the complaints of the
Western agricultural community, that they need foreign
workers to harvest their crops. The Western
agricultural community, now so dependent on illegal
aliens (most growers admit that 50 to 75 percent of
peak harvest workers are illegals), wants a program
responsive to its needs, unlike the current H-2
program. Even though the Simpson-Mazzoli bill does not
offer what many growers want, it would facilitate entry
for more foreign workers if U.S. workers are unwilling
to fill the jobs.

The bill also changes the asylum process to give
the decision-makers independence from INS and the State
Department. When the Simpson-Mazzoli bill was first
introduced in 1981, many, especially supporters of the
Haitians seeking asylum, argued that the INS was judge,
jury, and executioner for the asylum seekers. Since
then, INS has used its regulatory authority to give
more independence to those adjudging asylum claims, and
at least some of the furor surrounding the asylum
process has abated. However, a great deal of
controversy has arisen over the State Department's
recommendations on asylum claims from El Salvadorans,
demonstrating that this issue is far from settled.

A fifth important element of the Simpson-Mazzoli bill would tighten the foreign student program to make it more difficult for such students to remain in the United States legally after completing their studies. As the bill moved through the legislative process, various exceptions were carved out for foreign students with expertise in the sciences because of demands by universities and high-technology industries for their services. What remains, though, is a program meant to encourage students to return to their home countries after they complete their studies.

A final element of the original Simpson-Mazzoli legislation, which was deleted in the House and in the conference between the two houses in September 1984, was a package of changes in the legal immigration provisions of the INA. These changes were to reflect more realistically the demand for legal immigrant visas than the present system established in 1965. However, Chairman Rodino of the House Judiciary Committee successfully argued that the focus of the bill was on illegal, not legal, immigration and that the reforms of the preference system should await implementation of legalization and future study.

One element of the legal immigration reform section, however, did remain--a provision to raise the per country ceiling for Mexico from 20,000 per year to 40,000 per year. (The ceiling was also raised for Canada, but the Canadians do not use their full quota.) Supporters of this proposal argued that it reflects the enormous demand for visas from Mexico and the United States' special relationship with that country. Others, however, see it as a return to the odious national-origins system, and, because it discriminates in favor of Mexico, intrinsically discriminatory against all other countries.

Consequences for the Caribbean

If enacted, the central provisions of the Simpson-Mazzoli bill will have an impact on the Caribbean. The estimated 100,000 or more people from the Caribbean who enter the United States illegally each year would be substantially reduced under the provisions of the bill. No one believes that sanctions and increased enforcement will totally stop the flow of illegal immigration, but they will reduce the numbers. Also, many Caribbean citizens already here illegally may not be able to find jobs because of sanctions and may decide to return to their home countries.

The effect on those Caribbean nations that have become accustomed to using the United States as a safety valve for surplus labor could be important-- though the long-term effects may be positive as well as negative. Caribbean nations' leaders might spend some time thinking about this eventuality, though they probably will only deal with it after passage of the bill.

The legalization program will allow many Caribbean citizens living underground in the United States to achieve legal status, eventually becoming U.S. citizens. At that point, they can petition to bring other relatives to the United States, thus increasing the demand for visas from the Caribbean nations and the backlog of those waiting to come. Some also believe that once legalized, many of these people will be able to earn more reasonable wages.

The changes in the H-2 program, coupled with the imposition of sanctions against employers who now hire illegals, may lead to a substantial expansion of the H-2 program. Although most of the Congressional debate has focused on Western agricultural employers and their alien labor from Mexico, the Caribbean nations present a large labor pool that many employers may find desirable. Those Caribbean workers who now enter under the H-2 program have established a very positive image with their employers as hard-working and honest, a reputation that may benefit other workers. It is unlikely that the number of imported H-2 workers would come anywhere near the number of Caribbean workers who now enter illegally, and such H-2 workers could only stay temporarily. Yet, an expanded H-2 program could provide a new type of safety valve for Caribbean countries.[11]

Relatively few Caribbean foreign students enter the United States each year, and it is difficult to gauge the impact of the changes in the foreign student program on the Caribbean. In small countries in the Caribbean, the loss of even a few well-trained and highly motivated individuals could affect long-term economic development, so encouraging students to return should be beneficial.

The changes in the asylum procedures will likely affect only one country's nationals in the short term -- those of Haiti -- and it appears unlikely the decision on a few individuals will have much immediate impact on economic development in that country. Nevertheless, an asylum process that reached judgments that reinforce the negative image that many people in the United States have of Haiti, based on its poor record on human rights, will not help Haiti's attempts to attract U.S. investment and tourists.

Finally, the one change in legal immigration--the increase in visa numbers for Mexico--proposed in the conference version of the Simpson-Mazzoli bill, will have only a marginal impact on the Caribbean nations. However, the Caribbean nations and the rest of the

world may expect longer term changes in the legal
immigration system. Chairman Rodino's arguments
against changes in the current legal immigration
program have merely postponed, not resolved, the issue.

IV. What We Are Doing and What We Could Be Doing

No one can say with any certainty what impact
current or future U.S. immigration policy has or may
have on Caribbean economic development. Nevertheless,
it is useful to examine those policies discussed in
terms of economic development issues and to consider
what changes should be made and their effects on the
Caribbean.

It is important to understand the current debate
on immigration in its historical context. Immigrants
to the United States have proved throughout history to
be hearty, often escaping from the direst circumstances
to emerge with amazing successes. Every ethnic group
has its stories of the poor immigrants who have risen
to the heights of government, industry, sports, or the
arts. Some groups have taken longer than others, and
not all immigrant families succeed. But the overall
economic and social strength of the U.S. has depended
greatly on the achievements of immigrant groups. There
is no reason to think that the most recent U.S.
immigrant arrivals will be any different. The Asian
immigrants of the last twenty years are achieving
notable successes already. The Cuban arrivals in
Florida have done very well also.

Many believe these successes have a Darwinian
explanation. The best and the brightest become
immigrants. Even those without special skills or
education have the spirit and motivation that brings
them, their children, or their grandchildren to the
forefront in the new world. If this thesis is
accurate, then any program that encourages or allows
legal immigration from developing countries to the
United States deprives those countries of the people
who may contribute most to their nation's economic
development. The conventional wisdom that the
Caribbean nations need to export surplus labor may, in
fact, be a double-edged sword, with the safety valve of
emigration as one edge and the loss of the ambitious as
the other.

Often this debate is framed in terms of developing
countries losing skilled people, people with advanced
training acquired either in their home countries or,
frequently, abroad. Certainly, this is a topic of some
import. Yet when we are talking about a country with
less than 1.5 million people, such as Jamaica, which
has an outmigration to the United States each year of
40,000 people or more, to speak only of the several

hundred among these with college and advanced degrees is to see the trees and miss the forest.

What does all this mean in terms of U.S. immigration policy? First, regarding permanent immigration, U.S. policy, which emphasizes the rights of families to reunite, has dramatically increased legal Caribbean immigration to the United States since the mid-1960s. These numbers are likely to increase even more as extended families use their emigration opportunities. Legalization would create demands for bringing in other relatives.

The primary objective of U.S. immigration policy-- reuniting families--is unlikely to change, though some attempts were made during the debate on the Simpson- Mazzoli bill and more may be made in the future to rearrange the preference categories and limit the overall ceiling. It is unlikely that any special increases for the Caribbean island nations will be approved. Mexico has achieved a special relationship with the United States, especially in the immigration area, which is why the Simpson-Mazzoli bill proposes extra immigration numbers. But the preference for an even-handed policy toward all other nations is widely held on Capitol Hill and in the executive branch. Some in the State Department even privately oppose the proposed increase in legal immigrants for Mexico because it removes the appearance of universality in legal immigration.

The chances for change are reduced further by the lack of consensus about the response to the question of whether increased legal immigration would be positive or negative for the Caribbean. If one could demonstrate conclusively that it would benefit the United States or the sending countries, an argument for an increase could be made. But such is not possible.

Given the frequently heard argument about the importance of skilled people to economic development, consideration might be given to trying to limit the skilled preference categories under which Caribbean immigrants come to the United States, especially the third preference which allows the admission of people with particular skills. Limiting the right of these people to emigrate to the United States might encourage them to stay in their home nations where they could contribute to economic growth.

Several factors argue against such a policy, however. First, the number of third-preference admissions has been and continues to be very small from the Caribbean nations -- less than 350, including family members, in 1981. Although in the context of the relatively low levels of economic development in the Caribbean losing any people with skills can be harmful, it is hard to accept that such a dramatic policy change would be adopted for such small numbers or, if adopted, would have much impact.

Second, people with skills that merit the third preference classification can find another developed-country destination. So a U.S. limitation would not be effective unless other developed countries agreed to employ the same limitation. Third, Congress seems reluctant to limit the admission of people with skills, especially high-technology skills. The provisions of the Simpson-Mazzoli bill pertaining to foreign students would limit the ability of foreign students to remain in the United States by adjusting their immigration status from foreign student to third preference. However, as indicated, major exceptions were made for students with high technology skills.

Finally, if such a policy were proposed, singling out Caribbean immigrants would be seen as discriminatory. Limitations on third preference would have to be considered in the context of all nations, or, at least, all developing nations. And, for the reasons indicated, adoption of such a policy is unlikely and would probably not achieve the desired objective.

What of nonimmigrant admissions? Because the number of Caribbean foreign students admitted is relatively small, little immediate impact of changes in policy is likely. Recent changes in the INS regulations for monitoring foreign students have made it more difficult for students to remain in the United States illegally. This may encourage more students to return home after completing their studies rather than taking menial jobs in the underground economy in the United States. The changes proposed in the Simpson-Mazzoli bill would force a larger percentage of students to return home. The other major group of nonimmigrant admissions--H-2 workers--could become especially significant both for the U.S. labor market and for the sending Caribbean nations if the Simpson-Mazzoli bill achieves its major objective--limiting illegal immigration.

An effective limitation on illegal immigration would deprive many U.S. employers of their major source of labor. Illegal immigrants are spread throughout the work force, holding jobs in agriculture, hotel, restaurant, cleaning, and other service industries, manufacturing, especially the garment factories, and construction. The majority of these illegal immigrants are concentrated in the southeastern and southwestern United States and most major urban areas.

At the same time, the inability of the Caribbean sending countries to export tens of thousands of illegal emigrants to the United States will, at least in the short term, provide labor surpluses, often in nations that already have major surpluses. Although some of these workers will be able to travel to other islands and other nations -- Canada, for instance, also has a large illegal migrant population, much of it from the Caribbean -- the Caribbean governments may welcome a program for sending a percentage of these people abroad to work.

One way to deal with this issue is simply not to pass the Simpson-Mazzoli bill, and to allow the relatively free flow of human resources to continue. Undoubtedly, many Caribbean island leaders would join with many U.S. employers in endorsing such a move. However, even if the Simpson-Mazzoli bill does not pass, the U.S. government appears to be determined to limit illegal immigration, as evidenced by the dramatic growth of INS resources during the past three years. This policy makes it unlikely that the issue will simply disappear. Also, taking no action on illegal immigration may in the long run be more harmful to the Caribbean nations because it may lead to much stricter limitations on legal immigration.

U.S. employers will have at least five ways to react to the loss of illegal labor, if the Simpson-Mazzoli bill is effective. They can close their businesses, which may happen in industries that have existed only because they have access to inexpensive, exploitable labor. They can move their bases of operations to other countries with lower labor costs. This may happen in some cases, and may even benefit the Caribbean nations if they become the home for some of these employers. They can mechanize operations currently done manually. Many labor economists argue that illegal labor has actually hindered economic progress in some industries because inexpensive labor has removed the incentive for those industries to mechanize. However, not all jobs can be done with machines.

Fourth, the employers can hire U.S. workers. This course is the one hoped for by organized labor and many other backers of employer sanctions who believe illegal immigrants take jobs from U.S. workers. To the extent illegal immigrants are employed in relatively well-paying jobs, especially in manufacturing and construction, many U.S. workers may be available and willing to take those jobs. This is especially true if, as some economists contend, the presence of illegal immigrants depresses the wages and working conditions of employees.

U.S. workers may not come forward for some jobs at the lower end of the pay scale or for which the work is very unpleasant. Many growers argue that this is true for their labor force, though they claim to pay reasonable wages with adequate working conditions. To

fill these jobs, an expanded H-2 program makes sense.
Before any H-2 workers are admitted at present and in
any modified program, market tests must first be
performed to determine the availability of U.S.
workers. If the U.S. workers do not come forward to
take the jobs, a flexible H-2 program needs to be
constructed that will allow the temporary admission of
workers.

The H-2 program as currently constituted cannot
require employers to hire from a particular nation, and
nothing in the debate on the Simpson-Mazzoli bill so
far indicates that the legislation will contain such a
provision. Most of those who have worked on the H-2
provisions of the Simpson-Mazzoli bill have focused on
the employee needs of West Coast agriculture, with the
projection that most of the temporary workers will be
from Mexico.

However, agriculture in the southern and
southeastern United States also reputedly has its share
of undocumented workers, at least some of whom will
need to be replaced by temporary foreign workers.
Agricultural employers will have to develop sources of
labor for these workers. The appropriate U.S.
government officials, in conjunction with the employer
groups, should work with the Caribbean island nations
to develop those labor pools for the H-2 program.

A larger question remains about the undocumented
aliens who are not working in agriculture. The H-2
program is designed for temporary workers who take
temporary jobs, not for temporary workers who take
permanent jobs. Most nonagricultural H-2 workers are
in seasonal jobs, such as those employed by resorts.
The Simpson-Mazzoli legislation does nothing to change
the H-2 program for workers outside agriculture.
Whether an effective Simpson-Mazzoli program would
create permanent jobs in nonagricultural employment
that only foreign workers could fill remains to be
seen, but if so, further modifications in the H-2
program would be needed.

These modifications would require rethinking
programs for temporary-workers, making them closer to
the European gastarbeiter or guestworkers, many of whom
take jobs in industry, not in temporary employment
fields such as agriculture. These guestworkers
frequently became permanent residents of their host
countries, creating difficulties that have surfaced
during the last few years of high unemployment in
western Europe.

If such programs were developed for the U.S. labor
market, Caribbean workers would be a possible source of
labor. Though the existing H-2 program is not without
problems, it has worked reasonably well in terms of
providing employers with labor and having the workers

return to their home countries when their contracts for employment have ended.

V. Conclusion

Large numbers of Caribbean people emigrate to the U.S. each year, many legally, probably a larger number, illegally. The most likely and serious change in U.S. immigration policy that would affect the Caribbean nations would be the passage of the Simpson-Mazzoli bill to limit the flow of illegal immigrants. Although any changes in U.S. policy are likely to effect Caribbean economic development, shutting off this safety valve might force the Caribbean nations to deal more realistically with their population and surplus-labor problems. In the short term, it could cause some economic distress, which could be, potentially, politically destabilizing. Such a possible result makes the success of programs like the Caribbean Basin Initiative even more imperative.

Some of the potential illegal immigrants could come to the United States under temporary worker programs, especially the H-2 agricultural program with modifications proposed in the Simpson-Mazzoli bill. And if the U.S. labor market without large pools of illegal labor also demands temporary nonagricultural foreign labor, the Caribbean islands could also be a source for these workers.

Notes

I wish to thank some very helpful individuals on
Capitol Hill, the Department of State, the Immigration
and Naturalization Service, the Congressional Research
Service, and Dr. Robert Pastor for assistance in
preparing this paper.

1. In this paper, I use the term "Caribbean" to
refer to the Caribbean island nations and
dependencies. Mexico is excluded because its unusual
immigration relationship with the U.S. merits separate
treatment. Similarly, the Central American countries
that could be considered part of the Caribbean Basin
require separate analysis.

2. Abraham Lowenthal, "Ronald Reagan and Latin
America: Coping with Hegemony in Decline," in Eagle
Defiant, Kenneth A. Oye, Robert J. Lieber, and Donald
Rothchild (eds.), (Boston: Little Brown, 1983), pp.
320-21.

3. Robert Pastor, "U.S. Immigration Policy and
Latin America: In Search of the 'Special
Relationship,'" in Latin America Research Review, V.
19, No. 3, pp. 35-56.

4. Understanding the collection and presentation
of immigration data is an art unto itself, especially
when one considers that the actual number of illegal
immigrants is, by definition, unknowable. The
Immigration and Naturalization Service and the
Department of State, the two government agencies most
responsible for who enters and leaves the U.S. legally,
collect and present their data in different formats.
The INS reports almost always contain numerous caveats
about missing data. The publication of the data is
always badly out of date -- and of questionable
accuracy.
My estimates on illegal immigration are based on
my own work in immigration the past four years,
estimates by the Census Bureau for the Select
Commission on Immigration and Refugees Policy and a
later downward revision, interviews with researchers in
the area, and discussions with officials of the INS and
State Department.

5. Report of the Select Commission on Western
Hemisphere Immigration (Washington, D.C.: Government
Printing Office, 1968).

6. The Dominican Republic has been the largest

source of legal immigrants to the U.S., but Jamaica jumped passed it in 1981, and may continue to be the number one sending country for some time.

7. See 1983 Report of the Visa Office, Bureau of Consular Affairs, Department of State (unpublished).

8. For a detailed analysis of the H-2 program, see Chapter 8 of this book.

9. Once again, the data for illegal immigration are very uncertain. These estimates come from various officials, none of whom wish to be quoted by name.

10. For a review of the progress of Simpson-Mazzoli through the 98th Congress, see Harris N. Miller, "'The Right Thing to Do': A History of Simpson-Mazzoli," in the Journal of Contemporary Studies, Vol. 7, No. 4 (Fall, 1984), pp. 58-78, and in The New Immigration and American Democracy, Nathan Glazer (ed.) (forthcoming).

11. The INS may try to change the H-2 program administratively. See The New York Times, January 27, 1985, p. 1.

17. Economic Development, U.S. Economic Policy, and Migration: Establishing the Connections in the Caribbean

Peter Hakim
Sidney Weintraub

Can the United States manage its economic policy toward the Caribbean in ways that would diminish incentives for Caribbean migration to the United States?[1] Two sets of issues need to be addressed:

o   First, can a strategy for economic and social development be devised that would reduce migration pressures in the Caribbean? Would it be advantageous for Caribbean countries to adopt such a strategy? Do they have the capacity, resources, and determination to carry it out? Would other important political, social, and economic objectives have to be compromised?

o   Second, what changes in U.S. economic policy would be required to support a migration-reducing development strategy? Is the United States prepared to make those changes? What commitment of new resources would have to be made to Caribbean development?

We are not proposing that the economic policies of the Caribbean nations or of the United States be guided by the objective of reducing migration. Policies that promote social and economic development are desirable in their own right, whatever their impact on migration. Our intention is to explore how migration issues can be taken into account in development plans. We ask what policy measures might be effective in reducing pressures for migration and what the costs and benefits of these measures would be for both the United States and the Caribbean.

I. Relating Migration to Economic Development

Much about migration and economic development remains poorly understood. Debates continue over the ends and means of economic development, over what policies will lead to what outcomes, and over how to implement different policies. The issues are central to any development program: inward- versus outward-oriented economies; centralized versus decentralized economic management; influence of prices versus structural inpediments to growth; social versus "productive" investments; the respective roles of the private and public sector; and austerity versus expansionary fiscal policies.

Even though many causes of international migration have been identified, we cannot yet explain the size of migration flows between countries, let alone predict how marginal economic changes will affect the magnitude or short-term direction of the flows. Will migration decrease if wage differentials between two neighboring countries are halved or if unemployment is reduced by half in the sending country? Will a marginal increase in national income lead to a marginal increase or decrease in emigration? What impact does a change in national income have on the composition of migration flows?

The relation between migration and economic development is complex and indirect. We can suggest at least three conflicting hypotheses regarding the effect of economic development on Caribbean migration to the United States.

The null hypothesis. Disparities in economic opportunity are powerful factors that encourage migration. Current economic disparities between the United States and virtually every country in the Caribbean are so immense that even extraordinary development gains in the Caribbean countries could hardly reduce migration pressures. Income per capita in the United States is more than ten times the average for the Caribbean.

There are fifteen independent Caribbean nations (excluding Cuba) with a total population of about 17 million; only four of them, with a combined population of 2 million, had per capita gross national products (GNPs) greater than $2,000 in 1982; six, with a combined population of 6.4 million, had per capita GNPs of less than $1,000; and five, with a total population of 8.2 million, reported GNPs from $1,000 to $2,000. Per capita GNP for the United States in 1982 was over $13,000.[2]

Although income per capita is at best a rough indicator of economic opportunity, other indicators also show wide disparities between the United States and the Caribbean. Wage and consumption differentials are enormous. Open unemployment in the Caribbean as a whole is in excess of 20 percent, and underemployment is estimated to be even greater; nearly 50 percent of the Caribbean work force is without regular employment.

These disparities notwithstanding, we know that "economic push factors" (i.e., the perceived lack of economic opportunities) are not the only determinants of migration flows from the Caribbean to the United States. Established habits and patterns of migration coupled with extensive social networks between Caribbean nationals and their compatriot communities in the United States may be working to sustain migration levels regardless of changes in the push factors. The relative status of individuals in their own communities may be a more significant determinant than cross-country income differentials. Political events can override the influence of changing economic and social conditions.[3]

The perverse hypothesis. A second plausible hypothesis is that economic development in the Caribbean will increase pressures for migration to the United States, at least in the short term. Development will cause dislocations for many Caribbean people, and the more rapid and encompassing that development is, the greater the dislocations will be. Economic development will also enhance the capacity of Caribbean people to emigrate (by providing them with new skills, more education, and higher incomes) and generate even higher aspirations for income and consumption. These added pressures for migration could overwhelm the effects of any new opportunities that development makes available.

The common assumed hypothesis. A third hypothesis is that sustained development would indeed create opportunities--for productive employment, higher wages, satisfaction of basic needs, improved services, better future for children, and expanded consumption--that will allow people to lead productive and satisfying lives in their own societies and thereby reduce incentives for migration.

Available data are not adequate to test these three hypotheses. Instead, policy must make some leaps in the dark. Regardless of its consequences on migration, economic development will be pursued by the countries of the Caribbean. Consequently, the policy issue--if one is concerned about migration--is what strategy for economic development would be most effective over the longer term in reducing incentives for migration. Phrased differently, what development strategy would be most effective in allowing people to satisfy their social and economic aspirations within their own countries?

The search for a development strategy that might influence migration patterns over the long term can proceed either empirically or theoretically. Both approaches present substantial problems. Empirically, one could examine the historical experience of one or more countries and attempt to relate migration flows over time to evolving development patterns, stages and outcomes. To our knowledge this kind of analysis has not been attempted on any country. It would probably be extraordinarily difficult to reach any strong conclusions given the limited data on both economic development and migration, the variety of factors other than development affecting migration, and the time lags between changes in social conditions and their effects on individual decisions.

Sergio Diaz-Briquets employs another empirical approach: he attempts to relate migration flows from a sample of countries to development patterns and results in those countries. (See Chapter 2.) Diaz-Briquets argues that lower rates of emigration from Panama and Costa Rica, as contrasted to Cuba and the Dominican Republic, are a consequence of differing patterns of development. He concludes that

> economies that are more broadly diversified, that can generate adequate rates of economic growth, and that give sufficient attention to social objectives appear to be more likely to produce adequate numbers of productive jobs and more capable of satisfying latent needs of the populations. Under these conditions, and as long as a situation conducive to substantial economic growth persists, these economies can successfully reduce push factors usually associated with emigration.[4]

What is proposed is that "migration-reducing" development involves the achievement of satisfactory rates of economic growth, low levels of unemployment, diversified economic activity, improvements in social welfare, and equitable distribution of the benefits of growth. The analysis is essentially qualitative rather than quantitative, and thus weights are not assigned to the several migration-reducing variables identified.

Although his conclusions are reasonable, their wider applicability still needs to be tested. Diaz-Briquets himself suggests that other factors may be more important for the smaller countries of the Caribbean. Moreover, the study focuses primarily on development outcomes and does not give attention to the economic policies that produced those outcomes. The value of his study would be increased if it were based on a wider selection of countries using more sophisticated quantitative analysis and a more precisely defined set of policy variables.

Lacking a secure empirical basis, we are forced to rely principally on thoughtful theoretical speculation in the search for a migration-reducing development strategy. Alejandro Portes's article, "International Labor Migration and National Development," is the most fully elaborated attempt to engage in such speculation. He proposes an inward-oriented development strategy that includes expanding the production of basic manufactured goods; relying less on imported models and patents; developing domestic technology; and regulating externally induced consumer pressures.[5] The core of his argument is that "export-led development is likely to promote emigration" because it (1) exposes developing countries to the "fashions, consumption standards, and expectations of advanced countries"; (2) "contains a built-in bias against increases in the returns to labor"; and (3) subjects countries to a dependency on insecure external markets.[6] He presents little evidence to support these assertions, and most economists would disagree with his analysis.

A fundamental problem arises in drawing a distinction between inward- and outward-oriented development for small Caribbean islands. The World Bank, a leading proponent of export-led development, has argued for a combination of export expansion and import substitution.[7] Portes himself recognized that the controversy "may ultimately prove a false one."[8] The dichotomy is not a helpful guide to policy for most Caribbean countries. Internal markets in the Caribbean are extremely small (the largest Caribbean country has a smaller population than Hong Kong), and foreign trade and investment already account for a major portion of economic activity.

The search for a migration-reducing development strategy should start by identifying which determinants of migration could realistically be influenced by economic change.[9] In the Caribbean, the determinants most susceptible to economic intervention appear to be the high rates of unemployment and underemployment. Development affects the growth of population and labor force participation only indirectly and slowly. Even over long periods, economic development can do little to reduce wage and consumption differentials between the United States and Caribbean countries. Economic development will not diminish the aspirations of Caribbean peoples, who are continually exposed to North American consumption standards and life-styles and are well-informed about economic opportunities in the United States.

Would employment growth reduce migration pressures? Studies have shown that most migrants come from the ranks of the employed, but little is known about their job productivity or security. Moreover, many migrants are self-employed, an ambiguous status that suggests they may not have been able to obtain regular jobs. Employment creation will not bring quick results--and may even have a perverse effect in the short term--but it may be the only economic intervention that could reduce migration over the long term. Certainly, migration is unlikely to diminish in the absence of substantial growth in employment.

There are other reasons for emphasizing employment promotion in economic development plans. First, it might help resolve what is probably the most persistent and disquieting problem facing Caribbean societies: the limited opportunities and abysmally low incomes of a large share of their populations. Emphasis on employment should lead to a more equitable distribution of development benefits and help alleviate poverty generally. Thus, even if employment growth does not ultimately reduce migration, it serves more vital objectives. Having arrived at this unobjectionable recommendation to expand employment, we now must ask the harder question of how it can be done.

Few developing countries have been able to absorb labor satisfactorily and avoid high rates of unemployment and underemployment. Underemployment and low productivity are pervasive in rural areas throughout Third World countries. In urban areas, where rural-urban migration has bloated populations, a dual labor force has emerged. A minority of workers is incorporated into a "modern" sector; these workers receive reasonable salaries and have access to social benefits, whereas the remainder has depressed wage rates, sporadic employment, low productivity, and few social benefits. Raymond Carr, writing about Puerto Rico, described the situation as "a raft of well-paid workers floating on a sea of unemployed."[10]

This pattern is common throughout the Caribbean. In 1981, open unemployment exceeded 20 percent in five of the six independent nations of the Organization of Eastern Caribbean States (OECS).[11] The situation was worse in the larger nations of the Caribbean. Jamaica had an open unemployment rate of more than 27 percent in 1981, and underemployment was estimated to be of equal magnitude.[12] Haiti's open unemployment in 1981 was nearly 12 percent, but an additional 40 percent of the economically active population was reported to be underemployed.[13] Unemployment in the Dominican Republic was about 20 percent, with an equal or higher rate of underemployment.[14] None of the smaller Caribbean nations for which statistics are available had unemployment rates of less than 10 percent in 1981.[15]

II. Employment-Promoting Development

Specialists tend to agree on what policies are required to reduce unemployment in developing countries.[16] Economic growth is essential. More specific policy directions include greater attention to agriculture, particularly to developing small-farmer production; industrial development policies that encourage labor absorption and reduce subsidies to capital; promotion of exports and decreased import protection; and stronger programs for human resource development and family planning. Within the Caribbean, tourism is an area that also deserves attention.

Agricultural Development

Agriculture is an important source of employment in most countries of the Caribbean. In Haiti, 74 percent of the labor force is in agriculture; in the Dominican Republic, 49 percent; and in Jamaica, 35 percent.[17] Rural employment in the smaller countries is less but still significant; in 1970, agricultural workers accounted for about 30 percent of the labor force in the six independent OECS states.[18] The share of national income accounted for by the agricultural sector in the Caribbean is substantially lower than the share of workers it employs. This difference reflects the low productivity of rural labor and limited investments in agriculture throughout the Caribbean. What rural investment has taken place has largely been directed to primary export crops like sugar in the Dominican Republic, coffee in Haiti, and bananas in the Windward Islands.

Raising rural productivity and incomes in the Caribbean would require efforts to diversify agricultural production, with particular emphasis on small-farm production of food crops and nontraditional exports. Agricultural diversification in the Caribbean, if it were possible at all, would be painful and expensive, but it may be the only way to avoid continuing economic and social decline in rural areas. The sugar and banana industries, the largest agricultural enterprises in the region, are in precarious straits and have only limited prospects for recovery.

A long-term agricultural development strategy directed toward small-farm production would involve investing in rural infrastructure (roads, schools, irrigation systems); building greater capacities for agricultural research and extension (perhaps on a regional basis); assuring the availability of agricultural credit and supplies; and eliminating price

controls that discourage food production. In several
Caribbean countries, the strategy may also require some
redistribution of land.

Increased agricultural productivity will not by
itself increase employment; the reverse may be more
likely. But, in other settings, the previously
outlined policy measures have led to expanded
production of basic foods and export crops; the added
production, in turn, resulted in the growth of rural
industries for food processing and the manufacture of
farm inputs and simple consumer goods.[19] Where it has
succeeded, the development of small-farm agriculture
has fostered an employment-oriented demand structure;
i.e., it has raised demand for labor-intensive
products.[20] Moreover, expanding local food production
would help check the growing food import bill of
virtually all Caribbean countries. This kind of
agricultural development is probably a necessary
component of any strategy for employment growth in the
Caribbean.

Industrial Development

Table 17.1 shows the share of industry in the
gross domestic product of different countries of the
Caribbean. Labor absorption and industrial growth
rates have varied significantly from country to country
during the past decade.

Industrial development in the Caribbean, as
elsewhere in Latin America, has been relatively capital
intensive, and its contribution to employment has
consequently been more limited than it might have
been. Labor absorption could be expanded in industry,
and particularly in manufacturing, by reducing or
eliminating subsidies to capital, including low or
negative rates of interest, low or nil tariffs for
importing capital goods, and special tax benefits. The
removal of these subsidies, however, may result not in
more labor-intensive investment but in less overall
investment. If subsidies are required, they should be
directed toward reducing the costs of labor rather than
capital (e.g., by governments covering social security
payments and other social benefits). Similarly,
policies that make labor more expensive, such as
restricting the dismissal of unneeded workers, may have
to be relaxed.

Expanding exports would also contribute to
employment growth. The small domestic markets in the
Caribbean cannot sustain continuing industrial
expansion, and prospects are limited for enlarging
markets through a common market arrangement. Without
increased exports, the growth of import-substituting
industries, which depend on imports of intermediate
products will be constrained by foreign-exchange

Table 17.1

Industry and Manufacturing:
Shares of Gross Domestic Product,
Percent of the Work Force, and Average Growth Rate, for
Selected Caribbean Countries, 1982.

	Industry[a] (% of GDP)	Manufacturing (% of GDP)	Industrial Employment (% of work force)	Av. Annual Growth Rate of Industry 1970-1982
Dominican Republic	28	16	18	6.9
Haiti	24	13	7	7.3
Jamaica	32	16	18	-3.5
Trinidad and Tobago	52	13	39	4.0
OECS countries	25**	9**	-	-

[a]Industry includes manufacturing, mining, construction, electricity, water, and gas.

*United Nations, ECLA, Economic Survey of Latin America (Santiago, 1983). These figures are for 1981.

**Caribbean Development Bank, Annual Report 1983 (Bridgetown, 1983).

Sources: World Bank, World Development Report 1984 (Oxford University Press, 1984), except as noted.

shortages. As a rule, moreover, export industries are more labor intensive than import-substituting industries.

Promoting export growth will require lowering overvalued exchange rates and reducing (although not necessarily eliminating) barriers against imports which in the Caribbean include quotas as well as tariffs. By reducing protection gradually, the potential damage to import-substituting industries could be anticipated and contained.

Caribbean countries may be in a position,

particularly since the passage of the Caribbean Basin
Initiative (CBI), to attract increasing foreign
investment for assembly or enclave industries. These
industries, which import mostly raw materials and
intermediate products and process them for export,
would be potential sources of new employment. Because
they are only weakly integrated into the wider economy,
however, assembly industries often move on when lower
wages and/or other competitive advantages emerge
elsewhere. Thus, they may not permanently solve, and
could even compound, unemployment problems.

Promoting the development of small and medium-size
businesses (employing from a few to 100 workers) would
also contribute to labor absorption. Most research
suggests that smaller enterprises tend to use less
capital per worker and are able to hire labor that is
less skilled. In Mexico, for example, fixed assets per
job in small manufacturing firms in 1975 averaged about
25 percent of those of their larger counterparts.[21]
Smaller firms also may have great multiplier effects,
since they tend to rely primarily on local raw
materials and to supply goods and services for larger
enterprises and domestic consumption.

The simple removal of existing biases against
small industries would contribute substantially to
their development. These firms should have the same
access to government and private credit, foreign
exchange, and raw materials as larger enterprises.
Special programs for small-business development have
had a mixed record. They have often provided support
that is irrelevant or unsustainable. Sometimes they
have encouraged capital intensity or dependence on
advanced technology. But when such programs are well
conceived and competently managed, they can provide
needed technical assistance and training to small
entrepreneurs and their workers and help smaller
businesses gain access to credit, raw materials, and
markets.[22]

Tourism

Tourism is a significant source of income and
foreign exchange for nearly every Caribbean country.
Increasing the number of tourists and their length of
stay in the Caribbean would expand employment
opportunities--although efforts by any single country
to stimulate tourism may simply draw visitors from
elsewhere in the Caribbean. Substantial variations
occur from country to country in the ratio of jobs
created per tourist dollar, which suggests some
possibility for increased labor absorption in the
tourist industry. The differences, however, may simply
reflect wage differentials among the countries. (The

data themselves also may not be reliable.) The largest
gain would be achieved by reducing the leakage abroad
of foreign exchange from the tourist industry. Luther
Miller estimated that leakage is about 58 percent of
earnings--the result primarily of importing goods and
services for tourists and repatriation of profits and
management fees.[23] He made several imaginative
proposals to reduce the leakage and generate additional
employment by establishing stronger links with other
sectors of the economy, particularly agriculture.
Although small in most places, the increased demand for
local food products could be significant in a few
countries.

Education and Training

Economic development requires qualified managers,
technical specialists, and skilled workers. Investment
in human resources to increase labor skills and
mobility would be central to any strategy for
employment growth in the Caribbean. Such investments,
however, will also facilitate emigration. Nancy Foner
estimated that 51 percent of Jamaicans trained in
professional and management skills from 1977 to 1981
migrated to the United States.[24] The loss of managers
and other skilled persons may be an unavoidable cost in
the short run.[25]

Population Programs

Programs to control population will take fifteen
years or more to slow labor force growth and thereby
contribute to reduced unemployment and
underemployment. This slow effect, however, is not a
reason for neglecting population programs since
virtually all measures to promote employment and limit
emigration are likely to become effective only over
long time spans. Aside from the Dominican Republic,
population growth rates are generally lower in
Caribbean countries than in other developing countries
(in part, the result of emigration), but they are
considerably above those in the industrialized
countries.[26] Failing to check population growth will
almost certainly present long-term obstacles to
economic development in the Caribbean and contribute
both directly and indirectly to unemployment
problems.[27]
This basic package of measures to promote
employment growth would, of course, have to be refined
and tailored to the needs of each Caribbean country.
The major difficulty, however, is not designing a
development strategy: It is making it work in

practice--securing the necessary private and public resources; developing the technical capacity required to translate policy prescriptions into workable programs; mobilizing government bureaucracies, enterprises, and financial institutions; and overcoming political resistance.

For the next several years the nations of the Caribbean are likely to confront adverse economic conditions and difficult problems of adjustment. They have to lower expenditures to conform with available resources, contend with sizable external debt payments, align their economies to a changed international situation, and contain domestic political pressures. Efforts to manage these problems will shape their economic agendas for years to come.

Migration of skilled and unskilled persons is likely to continue unabated for many years regardless of the success of Caribbean nations in tackling their immediate economic problems and in introducing measures to expand employment. Despite the loss of many skilled and enterprising people, however, migration should contribute to economic development in the short-run and perhaps lead to reductions in pressures for further migration.

The World Bank reported that net benefits of migration can be large and suggested that "it may even be beneficial for countries to facilitate emigration. . . ."[28] Emigration reduces the number of unemployed and may increase the productivity of those remaining at home. Because most migrants are of child-bearing age, emigration results in diminished birthrates and declines in population growth. Finally, remittances can make a substantial contribution to foreign exchange earnings. Table 17.2 provides an estimate of amounts remitted to the three largest countries of the Caribbean. For Haiti and the Dominican Republic, remittances equal about 25 percent of export income and for Jamaica, 10 percent. For Haiti and the Dominican Republic, annual remittances exceed U.S. bilateral assistance. Dawn Marshall estimated that remittances represent a smaller share of foreign exchange earnings in the countries of the eastern Caribbean; of the four countries on which she reported (Barbados, St. Vincent, St. Lucia, and Grenada), only in Grenada did they exceed 10 percent of export income.[29]

III. The Contribution of U.S. Economic Policy

Economic development in the Caribbean will depend not only on the policy choices made by the Caribbean nations themselves but also on external factors beyond their control. The most significant external factors are the health of the U.S. economy and U.S. economic policy toward the region. U.S. trade, investment, and

Table 17.2

Remittances of Emigrant Workers for
Selected Caribbean Countries, 1982

	Total (US$ millions)	% of Merchandise Exports
Dominican Republic	$190	25
Haiti	95	25
Jamaica	75	10

Source: World Bank ,World Development Report 1984 (Oxford
University Press, 1984), p. 244.

aid are all important to the Caribbean. For a few
smaller countries, tax policies and the promotion of
tourism may have some, although probably lesser,
significance.

As shown in Table 17.3 trade revenue is a sizable
share of GDP for virtually all Caribbean countries;
most of that trade is with the United States. More
than 60 percent of all Caribbean exports go to the
United States compared with less than 35 percent for
Latin America as a whole. The U.S. share in Caribbean
trade rose from 1970 to 1980, while it declined for
Latin America.[30] The major determinant of Caribbean
export levels is probably the condition of the U.S.
economy. A drop in U.S. demand between 1980 and 1982
led to a sharp decline in exports; the decline was more
than 20 percent for Jamaica and the Dominican Republic,
whereas for Haiti it was about 35 percent.[31] U.S.
economic recovery should revive Caribbean trade--
although prices of major Caribbean commodity exports
remain low and Caribbean countries apparently are not
expanding production sufficiently to take full
advantage where U.S. demand is growing.[32]

Even though it is early to assess its impact, the
Caribbean Basin Initiative (CBI) provides a useful
framework for examining U.S. trade and investment
policy toward the Caribbean. The centerpiece of the
CBI is the twelve-year exemption from U.S. tariffs
granted to certain imports from Caribbean and Central

Table 17.3

Exports and Imports as a Percent of Gross Domestic Product
And Share of Exports Directed to the United States
For Caribbean Countries, 1981

	Exports as % of GDP(1981)	Imports as % of GDP(1981)	% of Exports to the U.S. (Av. 1979-1981)
Dominican Republic	17*	22*	68
Haiti	14	26	69
Jamaica	48	58	42
Trinidad/Tobago	45	35	69
Guyana	61	82	23
Barbados	61	74	26
Bahamas	82**	83**	84
Belize	89	107	n.a.
Dominica	37	82	n.a.
Grenada	38	65	n.a.
St. Kitts	73**	112**	n.a.
St. Lucia	59	111	n.a.
St. Vincent	68	89	n.a.
Suriname	53	63	37

*World Bank, World Development Report 1984 (Oxford University Press, 1984).
**Caribbean Development Bank, Annual Report 1983 (Bridgetown, 1983).

Sources: World Bank, World Tables, Third Edition, vol. I (Johns Hopkins University Press, 1983), for exports and imports as percentage of GDP, except as noted. Inter-American Development Bank, Annual Report 1983 (Washington, 1983), for percent of exports to the U.S.

American countries. These exemptions, however, are unlikely to produce much immediate economic gain for the Caribbean because they affect only about five percent of the region's exports. Before the CBI, 87 percent of Caribbean and Central American imports entered the U.S. duty-free, and some goods will continue to face tariffs or, as in the case of sugar, quotas. Significantly, tariffs remain on such particularly labor intensive items as textiles, shoes, and other leather goods. U.S. labor unions resisted the inclusion of these items in the CBI legislation. Indeed, the U.S. tariff structure is generally weighted against imports with a high labor content.

Feinberg and Newfarmer estimated that the short-run growth in Caribbean and Central America exports will total no more than $100 million, or about one percent of 1980 exports.[33] Other estimates are even lower. The longer-run potential is considerably greater because the new trade incentives should stimulate foreign and domestic investment in the region to produce goods eligible for duty-free treatment.[34]

The principal gains that might accrue from one-way free trade thus depend on the added investment that the new trade preferences can induce. This will take time to materialize. Although a proposed tax credit to promote U.S. investment was eliminated by Congress, the United States has actively encouraged investor interest in the Caribbean. Many U.S. businessmen have been exploring prospects there but so far little new investment has occurred.

To the extent that the CBI contributes to economic growth in the Caribbean, it will help create employment opportunities. But it may attract investment in both labor- and capital-intensive industries. One lesson from the Puerto Rican experience is that capital-intensive investment will predominate when subsidies are extended to capital, as they are in many Caribbean countries. Aside from removing tariffs on textiles and leather goods and perhaps expanding sugar quotas, little can be done to direct U.S. trade and investment policies toward more labor-absorbing growth.

Aid is a more flexible instrument of economic policy. Unlike trade or investment, it can in principle be shaped to advance specific development objectives--such as employment creation. It could also be used to increase the capacity of Caribbean countries to take advantage of U.S. trade and investment policies.

There has been a continuing U.S. aid effort in the Caribbean, which was increased sharply beginning in 1982 with the CBI appropriation of $140 million (Table 17.4).

Tables 17.5 and 17.6 show that foreign assistance generally and U.S. bilateral aid specifically account for a significant part of available development resources for the three most populous Caribbean countries. The same is true for many other Caribbean nations. Doubling the current level of bilateral aid, for example, would add $300 million to the Caribbean economies, a sum that exceeds the likely gains in trade from the CBI. This suggests that bilateral U.S. assistance could contribute importantly to employment growth in the Caribbean, if it were so designed. Specifically, AID resources could support the economic development strategy discussed, providing assistance for:

Table 17.4

U.S. Economic Assistance to the Caribbean, 1979 to 1985
(US$ millions)

	1979	1980	1981	1982	1983	1984	1985[a]
Dominican Republic	$ 48	$ 56	$ 39	$ 80	$ 56	$ 93	$113
Haiti	25	26	35	34	44	45	54
Jamaica	18	15	74	137	110	115	140
Other Caribbean	38	53	31	54	71	81	80
Total	$129	$151	$179	$304	$281	$334	$387

[a]Amount requested

Sources: Agency for International Development, U.S. Overseas
Loans and Grants and Assistance from International Organizations
(Washington, 1982); FY 1984 Congressional Presentation (Washington,
1983); and FY 1985 Congressional Presentation (Washington, 1984).

o   Small-farmer agriculture, including credit,
     rural infrastructure, agricultural
     diversification, soil and water conservation,
     and regional research and extension
     capacities. (Although PL 480 shipments can be
     used productively and help reduce food
     imports, they must be accompanied by measures
     to avoid depressing local food prices.)

o   Reforms that reduce or eliminate subsidies to
     capital.

o   Programs for developing small businesses.
     (For example, AID recently provided $41
     million in the Dominican Republic for loans to
     small manufacturers and farmers.)

o   Vocational, technical, and management
     education to produce skills needed in local
     industry and agriculture.

o   Programs for family planning, women, and
     public health.

Table 17.5

Foreign Assistance to Selected Caribbean Countries:
Annual Average for 1982 and 1983
(US$ millions)

	AID	World Bank	IDB	Carib. Dev. Bk.
Dominican Republic	68	21	126	-
Haiti	39	37	21	-
Jamaica	124	127	64	13

Sources: Agency for International Development, FY 1984
Congressional Presentation (Washington, 1983); World Bank, World
Development Report 1982 (Oxford University Press, 1982) and World
Development Report 1983 (Oxford University Press, 1983); Inter-
American Development Bank, Annual Report 1983 (Washington, 1983);
Caribbean Development Bank, Annual Report 1983 (Bridgetown, 1983).

Table 17.6

U.S. Economic Assistance to Selected Caribbean Countries:
Annual Average for 1982 and 1983
(US$ million)

	% of Gross Domestic Investment	% of Exports
Dominican Republic	5	9
Haiti	22	11
Jamaica	19	17

Source: World Bank, World Development Report 1984 (Oxford
University Press, 1984).

Much of the AID program is already directed to these and other employment-promoting activities, and we would want to conduct a more detailed analysis before proposing specific modifications. Making employment creation AID's first priority, however, would require greater attention to the total development programs of Caribbean countries and their capacity to create jobs and absorb labor productively. In turn, this would mean strengthening AID's capacity for analyzing the employment consequences of alternative policies and programs. In addition, AID would want to develop Caribbean capacities for research, analysis, and data-gathering on employment. AID's success in fostering employment growth in the Caribbean will require not only identifying appropriate projects but also encouraging policy reforms and helping attract local development financing into job-creating activities.

Giving priority to employment in U.S. aid programs need not affect the activities of multilateral agencies--although the United States could encourage them also to assign more attention to job creation. Smaller assistance agencies, like private voluntary groups (PVO) and the Inter-American Foundation, can also contribute to employment growth in the Caribbean. They are well-suited to work with small farmer groups and informal urban businesses that are often bypassed by larger bilateral and multilateral funders. Their programs to mobilize the modest savings and entrepreneurial skills of small producers and proprietors can be particularly significant in small Caribbean countries.[35]

The overall contribution of U.S. economic policy to Caribbean development will depend on its consistency as much as on its content. Sharp changes in sugar quotas caused by pressures from domestic producers or fluctuations in aid levels reflecting perceived security concerns can cause serious economic disruptions for the small Caribbean countries. No matter how well they are conceived, U.S. policies will only be effective in promoting growth and employment in the Caribbean if they are consistently applied over time.

IV. Conclusions

1. The relationship between economic development and migration in the Caribbean is complex. In the short term, at least, it is uncertain whether economic development will reduce or increase migration measures-- or simply not affect them.

2. Caribbean societies will continue efforts to develop their economies. The challenge is to find a development strategy that can create sufficient

opportunities to satisfy the aspirations of Caribbean people within their own societies. This is a difficult task that will take time.

3. Among migration push factors, high rates of unemployment and underemployment in the Caribbean may be most susceptible to economic intervention. Employment-oriented development should result in greater equity and help reduce poverty generally.

4. Policy measures for employment growth include promoting small-farm production and rural diversification; removing subsidies to capital that discourage labor-absorbing industrial development; reducing barriers to the efficient use of labor; fostering small-business development; expanding exports; improving labor force skills; and reducing population growth.

5. It is easier to devise an employment-promoting development program than to make it work in practice. Reducing unemployment and underemployment in the Caribbean would be difficult under the best of circumstances; current adverse economic conditions make it even more so. It is not clear that Caribbean nations have the institutional capacity, resources, and political determination to implement a program for employment growth. And even if they were successful, migration pressures are likely to remain strong for years to come.

6. U.S. economic policy is critically important to the economies of the Caribbean. Most Caribbean trade is with the United States; the United States dominates foreign investment; and the U.S. is the largest source of bilateral aid to the Caribbean.

7. The Caribbean Basin Initiative (CBI) provides a useful framework for studying the effects of U.S. trade and investment policy on the economies of the region. The benefits of the CBI's trade provisions are likely initially to be small; over time, however, they might induce significant new investment in the region. Expanding U.S. sugar quotas would produce the sharpest immediate boost to economic development and employment growth in several Caribbean nations; this, however, would tend to perpetuate Caribbean dependency on a declining industry, and discourage agricultural diversification and small-farm production.

8. Although U.S. trade and investment policies can promote growth, they cannot be readily shaped to foster labor-absorbing growth. The incentives for labor-intensive investments must come largely from the policy choices of the Caribbean countries themselves. The CBI's potential contribution to employment creation (as well as to economic growth), however, could be enhanced by extending its duty-free provisions to currently excluded products like textiles and leather

goods, which have a high labor content.

9. Bilateral aid is a flexible instrument for supporting employment growth. U.S. assistance to the Caribbean is substantial, and many of its programs are consistent with an employment-promoting strategy. AID could probably contribute more by assigning higher priority to employment generation and by encouraging appropriate policy reforms. This would require that AID and the Caribbean countries improve their capacities for analysis of the employment consequences of different policies and programs. There is also considerable scope for other development assistance agencies, large and small, bilateral and multilateral, to contribute to employment creation.

10. Even if the Caribbean countries devised and successfully carried through an employment-promoting development strategy, and U.S. economic policies fully supported this strategy, migration flows are unlikely to diminish greatly in the short run and prospects for the longer run are uncertain. But migration pressures in Caribbean societies will certainly not decline and may even accelerate without a sustained and successful effort to expand employment opportunities.

Notes

1. In posing the issue this way, we are leaving
aside the important question of whether or not the
United States should seek to limit immigration. U.S.
policy appears increasingly directed toward some
limitation, although it is still open to debate whether
reducing immigration is in the best interest of either
the U.S. or the Caribbean.

2. World Bank, World Development Report 1984
(Oxford University Press, 1984), p. 219.

3. Our analysis will focus primarily on economic
variables, but political events and decisions are
central to all of the issues we discuss. Politics will
shape and constrain U.S. and Caribbean policy choices
and importantly affect the decisions of potential
migrants.

4. Sergio Diaz-Briquets, "Impact of Alternative
Development Strategies on Migration: A Comparative
Analysis," Chapter 2 in this book.

5. Alejandro Portes, "International Labor
Migration and National Development," in Mary Kritz
(Editor), U.S. Immigration and Refugee Policy: Global
and Domestic Issues (Lexington Books, 1982), p. 87.

6. Ibid., p. 84.

7. World Bank, Development Report 1984, p. 32,
Supra. fn. #2.

8. Portes, "Labor Migration and National
Development," p. 87, Supra. fn. #5.

9. We are not arguing that development policy
should be directed toward reducing emigration. It must
give first attention to economic and social objectives,
e.g., expanding opportunities, increasing income, and
achieving greater equity.

10. Raymond Carr, Puerto Rico: A Colonial
Experiment (Vintage Books, 1984), p. 210.

11. Caribbean Development Bank, Annual Report
1983 (Bridgetown, 1983), p. 22.

12. Ibid., p. 22.

13.   United Nations, Economic Commission for Latin America, Economic Survey of Latin America 1981 (Santiago, 1983), pp. 471-472.

14.   F. Desmond McCarthy, "Macroeconomic Policy Alternatives in the Dominican Republic: Analytical Framework," World Bank Staff Working Papers, Number 649 (World Bank, 1984), p. 30.

15.   Caribbean Development Bank, Annual Report 1983, p. 22 Supra. fn. #11.

16.   Lyn Squire provides an extensive bibliography on issues of employment in developing countries, Employment Policy in Developing Countries: A Survey of Issues and Evidence, World Bank Research Publication (Oxford University Press, 1981).

17.   World Bank, Development Report 1984, p. 258 Supra. fn. #2.

18.   Sidney Chernick, The Commonwealth Caribbean: The Integration Experience, World Bank Country Economic Report (Johns Hopkins University Press, 1978), p. 19.

19.   See John W. Mellor and Bruce F. Johnston, The World Food Equation: Interrelations Among Development, Employment, and Food Consumption," Journal of Economic Literature, Vol. 22 (1984), pp. 531-574 for a good review of the research done on the relation of agricultural development to economic growth and employment. They also present a sizable bibliography.

20.   Ibid., p. 568.

21.   World Bank, Trade and Employment Policies for Industrial Development (World Bank, 1982), p. 40. This short book provides a useful summary of the policy issues involved in labor-intensive industrial growth and small business development.

22.   Michael G. White, "Small Business in the Caribbean: A Study of Programs Supporting Small Business Development and Entrepreneurship," report prepared for the Inter-American Foundation (Rosslyn, 1984). This report reviews programs in various Caribbean countries established to promote small business.

23.   Luther G. Miller, "Tourism and Agricultural Linkages in the Caribbean," Chapter 13 in this book.

24. Cited in Robert A. Pastor, "Introduction: The Policy Challenge," Chapter 1 in this book.

25. Because our analysis is largely concerned with broad policy issues, we have not attempted to distinguish among different types of migration. Social and economic change, however, will affect the composition as well as the magnitude of migration flows. The brain drain, or the emigration of skilled persons, for example, presents different issues from the emigration of unskilled labor. It is possible to reduce one while encouraging the other.

26. World Bank, Development Report 1984, p. 254 Supra. fn. #2, and Caribbean Development Bank, Annual Report 1983, p. 22 Supra. fn. #11.

27. World Bank, Development Report 1984, pp. 51-207 Supra. fn. #2, presents a comprehensive discussion of the relation of population to economic development and examines available measures for checking population growth.

28. Ibid., pp. 101-102.

29. Dawn Marshall, "Migration and Development in the Eastern Caribbean," Chapter 4 in this book.

30. Inter-American Development Bank Annual Report 1983 (Washington, 1983), p. 113.

31. World Bank, World Development Report 1982 (Oxford University Press, 1982), p. 124 and World Bank, Development Report 1984, p. 234, Supra. fn. #2.

32. Richard E. Feinberg, "The Caribbean Basin Initiative: First Steps Towards Implementation," presented at the conference "The Caribbean Basin Initiative and the Puerto Rican Economy," sponsored by the Caribbean Institute and Study Center for Latin America (Inter-American University, April 1984), p. 19.

33. Richard E. Feinberg and Richard Newfarmer, "The Caribbean Basin Initiative: Bold Plan or Empty Promise?" in Richard Newfarmer, (Editor), From Gunboats to Diplomacy: New U.S. Policies for Latin America (Johns Hopkins University Press, 1984), p. 217.

34. Feinberg, "Caribbean Basin Initiative: First Steps," p. 9 Supra. fn. #32.

35. We do not delude ourselves. The proposals suggested for creating employment will not

revolutionize the Caribbean labor situation. In the
short run, emigration to the U.S. almost certainly will
be necessary to alleviate problems of unemployment and
underemployment. Perhaps the most effective
contribution that the U.S. could make to Caribbean
economic development would be to combine an employment-
generating policy with freedom for Caribbean people
from the smaller islands to enter the United States.
Many of these persons already enter the United States,
often illegally. If they could do so legally, it is
conceivable that the number of additional entrants
would be limited. We have not pursued this in our
chapter because our task was to examine how U.S. policy
could diminish incentives for Caribbean migration, not
how it could encourage migration on more favorable
terms. Moreover, under current circumstances, it is
unlikely that the U.S. would be willing to consider
seriously this suggestion. And there is another
problem: Opening the U.S. to migration from the small
islands of the Eastern Caribbean would lead to
pressures for a similar opening to Haitians,
Dominicans, Jamaicans, and Trinidadians, who are more
numerous.

Part 6

Toward a Synthesis
in Theory and Policy

18. Caribbean Basin Interdependence: The Future Movement of People and Goods

Clark R. Reynolds

I. Increasing Interdependence of the Region

The Caribbean Basin is a geopolitical concept that nevertheless reflects a growing pattern of regional interaction. This chapter sets the problems of migration and development in the Caribbean in a larger context that includes Central America, Panama, Mexico, Venezuela, Colombia, the United States, and Canada.

Throughout the region, labor flows have always reflected the gulf between individual aspirations and economic opportunity. At first, migration was involuntary, under slavery, the encomienda system, debt peonage, and other dehumanizing institutions that were imposed in much of the Caribbean, Mexico, and Central America not to mention the United States. Since emancipation, voluntary migration has become the norm, and labor movement has far surpassed that of the earlier periods. Rising population pressures on the land and a growing gap between economic opportunities at home and abroad have caused an increasing percentage of workers to seek employment elsewhere, often at great hardship and risk. In some of the Commonwealth Caribbean countries an estimated one-third of the work force has at one time been part of this migratory process.[1]

From the most extreme examples of exploitation--in which labor was reduced to a commodity and forced to relocate at the will of the employer--to today's "undocumented migration" that overcomes legal and institutional barriers, migration has placed a high cost on those attempting to improve their lot and on their families. Far from being a smoothly operating means of economic adjustment, labor migration is often a very imperfect means of avoiding the consequences of an uneven distribution of land and other resources or unequal opportunities for education, employment, and

quality of life. These discrepancies are often
associated with imperfections in the flow of capital,
technology, and trade.

Despite important linguistic, cultural, ethnic,
and political differences, the societies of the
Caribbean Basin have become interwoven through a long
history of migration among themselves and with the
nations of Asia, Africa, Europe, and North America.
Ironically perhaps, this distorted and often cruel
pattern of labor movement has contributed to the
region's unusually cosmopolitan character and lent an
important global dimension to the issue of Caribbean
migration. Given the relative size, resource
dependence, level of development, and vulnerability to
the world market of these countries, they face similar
economic social, and political challenges, even though
each is unique. In this regard, as the global economy
becomes increasingly interdependent, the region
exemplifies a much wider ranging interaction of trade
and factor movements. By the same token, the analyses
and policy recommendations of this book have a
potential impact that goes well beyond the Caribbean.

II. Toward an Eclectic Theory of International Migration

Conventional neoclassical theories of trade and
factor market adjustment have suggested that, apart
from natural and artificial barriers to exchange, a law
of one price should apply for goods, services, and
factors of production between markets. Indeed under
extreme assumptions, in a purely competitive, static
world, trade alone was expected to move factor prices
toward equality. Much attention was given in the
development literature to the free operation of markets
for goods and services, neglecting discussions of labor
mobility within and between countries. Where low wages
persisted, it was implicitly assumed that barriers to
trade, investment, and technology transfer might well
account for the gap in incomes of unskilled labor.
Divergent wages for skilled labor were attributed to
differing educational levels (investment in "human
capital") or to offsetting noneconomic characteristics
in the respective job markets. In cases where capital
was scarce and labor abundant, investment was supposed
to flow from capital-abundant areas to low-wage
regions, causing productivity, employment, and wage
levels to converge. Although the literature on factor
price equalization admitted the possibility that
convergence might bring down wages in the labor-scarce
regions, [2] this possibility was all but neglected in
the development literature.

This litany might seem absurdly simplistic, if it

were not the basis for the theoretical links between
value, investment, productivity, and wages in much of
the theory underlying contemporary development
policy. One can go through the main textbooks of the
period and find little analysis of interacting factor
movements between rich and poor regions. It is as
though migration were in fact a second-best approach to
factor market adjustment, reflecting barriers to trade
and investment that, if removed, would make labor flows
between countries unnecessary except for social or
political reasons. The excellent literature on earlier
migratory flows between Europe and the United States
and other regions of late settlement, which focused on
the international transmission of the trade cycle, [3]
did not significantly influence development economics
as applied to contemporary development problems.
Internal migration did find a place in the development
literature but not in terms of the relationship to
international factor movements.

More recently wage differentials within and
between countries have been explained by more taxonomic
models built upon theories of labor market
segmentation. In such approaches, labor markets are
arbitrarily partitioned for social, political, or other
institutional reasons to benefit some at the expense of
others. Power relations enter the employment process,
permitting wage levels to diverge from a competitive
norm even with considerable factor mobility. Low-wage
labor may move in pursuit of better paying jobs, but
access to the market is blocked by migration policy or
unions or questions of race, sex, or social
background. (An interesting application of this
approach to Caribbean migration is presented in Chapter
12 by Ralph Henry and Kim Johnson.)

Segmentation theories are offered as more
realistic alternatives to neoclassical analysis, since
they take account of power relations and institutional
characteristics of labor markets in practice. Despite
their rather descriptive and ex post facto character,
they help to explain the wide disparities in wages,
hours, and working conditions that do exist between
persons of similar capabilities in rich or poor
countries and that apply to those of differing age,
sex, race, or social background in the same country.
However, they fail to deal with the economic dimensions
of bargaining space within which wages must fall if
they are not to exceed the average value product of
labor (value added divided by the number of labor units
employed per period.)

Moreover, workers may exercise monopoly power over
management because of natural or artificial barriers to
entry that they or their organizations may also
impose. This power, along with the monopsony power

that employers may impose on labor in elastic supply,
helps account for the variations in wage levels, but
all such variation must occur within the space
determined by labor's average value product.

(In neoclassical economic analysis, under
conditions of pure competition, labor receives its
marginal value product, as do all other factors of
production, so that the total value added is
absorbed. However, with market imperfections some
factors may absorb more and others less than their
marginal value product, depending upon their relative
bargaining power. When part of the value added is
represented by economic rent, this component is subject
to bargaining among the various factors -- labor,
management, entrepreneurs, owners of land, plants and
equipment, and technology, and of course the state
through taxes, licenses, and other fees.)

In this chapter I contend that in the Caribbean
all such approaches have some degree of relevance to
the migration process, and all have policy
implications. For example, each of the economies
depended for its initial development on rents earned
from the export of raw materials and primary
products. The use of labor was traditionally designed
to extract the maximum amount of rent by minimizing the
cost of factor inputs. Since the price of the raw
materials and primary products depended on incomes in
external markets, rather than on domestic purchasing
power of labor, the minimization of wages had no effect
on the shape of the demand curve or on the amount of
resource rents that could be extracted. On the other
hand, those rents fluctuated with the price of the
commodity in the international market (unit value
fluctuated, so that average and marginal value product
fluctuated, and of course rents fluctuated that much
more since they were a return to a resource in
relatively inelastic supply).

What this meant is that the demand for cane
cutters fluctuated with the world market for sugar
rather than with domestic conditions, so that local
wage levels tended to be influenced by the
international economy whether wages were determined by
neoclassical conditions (wage = marginal value product,
with marginal value or price fluctuating with
international market conditions regardless of the
stability of marginal physical product) or by a less-
competitive bargaining process (since the scope for
bargaining was limited by the average value product of
labor and that too fluctuated with the international
price of sugar).

The more control employers had over labor, the
lower wages could be depressed toward subsistence
level. Over time, as shown in Chapter 11 by Courtney

Blackman, the Caribbean markets tightened and slackened as world market conditions waxed and waned, regardless of the intrinsic productivity of Caribbean labor. Intraregional migration tended to reinforce the trade cycle: Tight conditions exacerbated in the upswing as labor moved in search of higher wages (following rising unit values), and slack conditions worsened by return migrants in the downswing. Since the price of such commodities tended to move with the international trade cycle, little offsetting tendency existed among the island economies, all of which exported to European and North American markets.

During times of prosperity in Europe and North America (times of rising raw material and primary product export prices), immigrants from the Caribbean were in demand in the metropolitan countries. This added to the destabilizing cyclical character of migration. It also, however, permitted increased control over the supply of labor especially in those activities (such as mining and high unit value export crops) that had a high rent share of value added. In such sectors workers, if properly organized, could bargain for a greater share of the rents, even if the resulting wages significantly exceeded the offer price of labor elsewhere in the local or neighboring economies. The Ricardian rents on commodity exports permitted such rent-partitioning to occur, since inframarginal producers could still earn significant rents, even with the higher wages. The problem is that this tended to lead to a two-tier labor market within the country: Certain rent intensive exports permitted high wages despite the low productivity and income of workers elsewhere in the domestic economy. In a number of countries the governments tended to favor labor in the bargaining process, especially when employers were foreign individuals or corporations and especially when the rents accruing to the firm were not reinvested in the country.

Although this type of behavior applies throughout Latin America, it has particularly important implications for the Caribbean Basin export economies as they attempt to develop effective employment strategies. A two-tier labor market tends to lead to distorted migratory patterns. For example, there tends to be a queuing of labor willing to wait for the high-wage positions (which by their very nature are limited, so as to be able to extract a share of the commodity rents). The Todaro theory applies to such partitioned markets whether the high wages are in rent intensive raw material exports or in other activities. (Todaro's model was designed to explain why wages can be maintained at higher levels in some sectors than in others, since the job seekers from the low wage sectors

are willing to queue up for the jobs until the high
wage, times the probability of getting the better job,
equals the low wage at the point of origin.)[4]
     Depending upon the extent to which market power
can be monopolized by employers or employees, there is
a socioeconomic struggle for scarcity rents that may
affect both the level and the functional distribution
of value added in a given firm, industry, and even
national economy. Where those conditions differ
between markets or economies, wage differentials may
well persist, although the migration and queuing
process operate to break down those differentials, just
as trade and investment flows apply similar pressures
in markets for goods and services from which the demand
for labor is derived.
     Not surprisingly, the iron law of factor price
equalization is honored in the breach. Unskilled labor
in the Dominican Republic earns more than its
counterpart in more densely populated Haiti, even
though considerable migration takes place between the
two countries. Similarly, wage levels for unskilled
labor diverge sharply between Central American
countries, so that the earlier migration from El
Salvador to Honduras (persons seeking jobs and arable
land) provided one proximate cause of the Soccer War.
It can be argued that competition for land and jobs
contributed to the breakdown of relations between the
two countries, disrupting further progress of the
Central American common market.[5] Costa Rica, with its
relatively high wages, attracted considerable migration
from the rest of the region even before the conflicts
in Nicaragua and El Salvador, and now, that its economy
is in crisis, immigrant labor is perceived to be
depressing employment conditions for nationals of the
country.
     We have seen in a number of the chapters in this
book historical examples of migration among the
countries of the Caribbean Basin in response to
differential wage and employment opportunities. The
case has been made (e.g., by G. Arthur Brown in Chapter
14) that even today intraregional migration is subject
to considerable market imperfection (without invoking a
regional version of the segmentation theory). It is
argued that better coordination of regional labor
movement, combined with more appropriate employment-
enhancing development policies, might well improve the
tightness of the Caribbean labor market--increasing the
efficiency of resource allocation, improving the
balance of regional development, and widening the
distribution of its benefits. It could be said that
the persistent application of policies ill suited to
the region's labor abundance, including limits to
intraregional labor mobility, actually contributes to

job search outside of the region including in the United States.

III. Migration as a Reflection of Imperfections in the International Labor Market

Much has been written about a new international division of labor, including the appropriate characterization of it as a "new form of the old international division of labor" (see Chapter 12 by Henry and Johnson). Whatever the term used, we are experiencing increasing cross currents of migration, trade, and investment among countries to a degree unprecedented since the beginning of this century. This process is leading to a much greater degree of labor market interdependence. The internationalization of labor and capital markets, trade, and technology transfers is tending to disrupt long-standing institutional arrangements such as those described for the creation and partitioning of economic rents. Indeed I shall argue that much of the migration between rich and poor countries is a direct reflection of the dual labor market that those institutions have tended to establish and protect.

What is missing in much of the literature on the new international division of labor are the potentially positive employment effects in the developing countries from an awakening spirit of enterprise--which Schumpeter in his wildest dreams did not envision--that is rewriting the history of corporate capitalism. New firms, venture capitalists, and offshoots of traditional transnational enterprise are competing for what might be termed entrepreneurial profits or "innovation rents," bringing a fresh dynamic to the international economy.

As investors work to maximize the return over costs by moving the locus of labor-intensive production to low-wage regions, they tend to continue to sell the bulk of their output in the high-income home market. This global pursuit of entrepreneurial rents, which takes firms into the developing world, is a very different process from that of import-substituting industrialization that characterized much of Latin America in the 1950s and 1960s and that was fostered by the regional associations in Central America and the Caribbean.

In the import substituting industrialization phase, firms did not have to be efficient, since competition was restricted by tariffs, licenses, and other barriers, and since it was not necessary to sell in the international market to make a reasonable return on capital. Even the restricted local market (upper income households for many of these firms) was adequate

since the high costs of production could be offset by
high prices. The effective subsidies for such firms
came from a rechanneling of resource rents, away from
capital and labor in the rural sector and toward
capital and labor in the urban industrial sector. The
old system of rent partitioning that had evolved in
segments of the rural labor market (e.g., for organized
labor producing high-unit-value mineral and
agricultural exports) was now taken over by urban
unions, which competed with firms for a share of the
new monopoly profits. The result was a new two-tier
urban wage structure, in which union labor was able to
earn wages considerably above those in the informal
sector, just as organized plantation workers were able
to earn wages above those in peasant agriculture.

Such import substituting industries did earn
profits in excess of a normal return on capital, but
those profits might be called "protection rents" rather
than the innovation rents from the new pattern of
international enterprise, since they reflected legal
barriers to entry rather than a return to product or
process innovation or entrepreneurial skill.
Protection rents have a far less dynamizing function
than innovation rents as they earned precisely because
firms are protected against competition that would
otherwise force costs and prices downward to the
benefit of the consumer. They are the capitalist
corollary of market segmentation.

It is almost as though the neoclassical theory
were suddenly being vindicated, at least on the down
side, as capital moves in search of low-cost labor. It
is not necessarily "capital" seeking labor, however, as
firms tend to use the maximum financial leverage from
local sources to permit the highest possible return on
equity.[6] To the extent that this process occurs in the
Caribbean, it could dampen pressures to migrate outside
of the region. But such cheap labor-seeking investment
tends to break down the old rent partitioning
agreements, not only in the developed countries but in
privileged segments of the Third World labor market. A
new tier is introduced into the international labor
market--that of the industries that attract the latest
phase of international capital, that are forced by the
nature of the market process to be efficient, and that
retain their rents in the home country. If local labor
attempts to partition the rents in its favor, either
through organization or political pressure, the firms
are likely to pull up their shallow roots and relocate
elsewhere. Even in California high-tech firms (such as
Atari) are known to suddenly relocate assembly
operations from the Silicon Valley to Asia, tending to
make a reality of the iron law of factor price
equalization but in the downward direction.

Given such behavior, which is often imposed on these highly competitive industries, where even high technology has a half-life that is numbered in months rather than years, one may wonder whether the labor market implications are not comparable to those of the old plantation economies where workers were forced to compete with each other at subsistence wages, never seeing the rents that they produced. Only this time the plantation workers assemble electronic instruments or sew baseballs rather than cut cane.

IV. Threats to the Two-Tier International Labor Market

The problem of privileged labor in the formal sector of developing countries is similar to that of union workers in the United States and other industrial countries that after a long struggle with management has found itself in a position of rent-sharing. The economic space that made this possible in the United States was the fact that part of the high productivity of labor (value added per worker) represented rents to product or process innovations that were protected against competition by patents, licenses, and oligopoly power. It was possible to provide a normal return on capital and still have rents left over to be shared between labor and management. (The high corporate salaries and golden parachutes of U.S. executives constitute an important element of rent-sharing in that economy.) Unions were able to bargain for a share of rents in exchange for minimizing strikes, slowdowns, and other disruptions of industry and for playing a benign role in politics.

The two-tier labor market that we described in developing countries applies to a far greater degree between them and the industrial nations. The evolution of a dual international labor market from the end of the last century to the early years of the twentieth century has been described in brilliant detail by W. Arthur Lewis.[7] He sees its origins in the different agricultures of the temperate and tropical regions. Tropical agriculture is shown to have experienced less productivity growth (accessibility to investment and technological change) than temperate agriculture. This growth, when combined with the much more densely populated and more rapidly reproducing tropical regions, has tended to sustain the dual wage structure even in the primary sector of the Caribbean versus the United States. The implications of this analysis for contemporary international conditions, including those of the Caribbean region, are developed in his Princeton lectures.

What is missing from the Lewis analysis of international labor market dualism is the process of protection and rent generation in the "temperate" countries; the latter countries kept the labor markets tight and prevented productivity from falling to the "tropical" level by erecting barriers to entry that were successively employed against low-cost migrant labor and until the 1960s against those whose ethnic origin were associated with the "tropical" regions. It might well be argued that the artificial tightness of the U.S. labor market (which has nevertheless accommodated a successive wave of job seekers at the low end of the market, as described by Piore)[8] is now being broken down by a new wave of migration from the "tropical" countries. Not surprisingly a backlash is beginning in organized labor and spreading to all sectors of society; some perceive their incomes to be threatened whereas others fear the loss of their social and political supremacy.

V. Production Sharing and Market Sharing

Given the changing structure of the international economic system and its implications for the labor market, a new strategy is needed to minimize the impact on workers in sheltered markets of the global diffusion of productive employment. In previous periods of relative labor supply growth for the industrial countries, wage spreading did occur (a divergence in real-wage levels between skilled and unskilled labor with particular benefits for property owners and the managerial class), as analyzed for the United States at the turn of the century by Morely and Williamson.[9] Such divergence, as wages at the low end were depressed by factors such as the unprecedented migration from Eastern Europe at the time, was asssociated with radical working-class movements and populist pressures in the major political parties. The outcome was a compromise in the form of greater scope for collective bargaining, the imposition of quotas for legal migration, and a crackdown on labor radicalism, beginning in the 1920s but extending into the period of the Great Depression. The United States achieved an internal socio-economic compromise that led to the rent-sharing insitutions that have been in operation until now. Only in the last few years have those institutions and policies been seriously challenged. In the world of the 1980s and 1990s, the old compromises will not hold up. Firms in the United States, in conjunction with political parties, can no longer reach an entente with organized labor that will permit a viable pattern of rent-sharing for the foreseeable future. That is, in part, because the new internationalization of production transcends national boundaries and is required, by competitive market

forces, to seek the lowest cost inputs wherever they
may be so as to preserve a succession of precarious
rents from an ever-evolving series of product and
process innovations. In the past this was possible
within the boundaries of the United States because an
important share of innovation rents could be confined
to domestic firms and because those rents were
sufficient to support a high and rising level of real
wages, regardless of conditions offshore. Under such a
system migration could be allowed, within reason,
provided that it was not large enough to upset the de
facto rent-sharing agreement between domestic labor and
management. The Full Employment Act of 1946 was a high
point in this process. At the same time, some degree
of immigration of low-cost labor remained necessary to
provide workers for the menial services and for the
less attractive occupations on which the general
welfare depended. Hence the Mexican Bracero program
begun during World War II operated into the 1960s, and
the H-2 program for temporary workers (applied
primarily to the Caribbean, but now under discussion in
an extended form for Mexican labor as well) remains in
operation.

What is needed for the next generation is a set of
institutions that will permit workers from a widening
range of countries to participate in the rent
generating process, without destroying the
entrepreneurial dynamic of international development or
diverting it away from this hemisphere. Certainly the
strides being made in Asia cannot be ignored, and many
firms are looking to the Pacific Rim for future labor
market interdependence, owing to the weak unions and
relatively accommodating economic policies of those
countries. Perhaps not surprisingly, real wages in the
leading nations of the Pacific Rim are rising much more
rapidly than those in the industrial core and certainly
more than those in the Caribbean Basin. Indeed extreme
admirers of the Asian experience point to better income
distribution in some of the "Gang of Five" countries
than even Sweden enjoys. The same author projects the
gross national product (GNP) of the Pacific Rim
countries (including Japan, but not China or most of
those in Southeast Asia) to approach that of the
European Community or the United States by the year
2000.[10]

Given the degree of interdependence in the
Caribbean Basin and the U.S. perception of its security
interests that adds to the asymmetry of that
interdependence, the time for consideration of a mutual
development strategy capable of dealing with the forces
underlying regional migration and labor welfare is long
overdue. The Pacific Basin Initiative (PBI)
represented an attempt to encourage regional trade and

investment links with the United States. But the PBI
was not designed to come to grips directly with the
need for a reconciliation of employment and labor
income policies in both the United States and the
countries of the region. Indeed many of the incentives
of the PBI favor investment that may or may not be
labor-absorbing on a permanent basis, just as the
earlier program for Puerto Rico (Operation Bootstrap)
was established in the 1950s in part to ease the
migration pressure from that island to the United
States. While very successful in diverting investment
from the United States to the lower wage economy,
Bootstrap proved to have a limited long-term impact on
employment and regional industrial integration.

A new approach to production sharing and market
sharing is needed that goes well beyond offshore
assembly operations to accommodate a full integration
of domestic and international industry to service both
local and foreign markets. This challenge, of course,
is directed to the highly protected, small-scale, high-
cost local import-substituting industries and the labor
unions that depend upon them. It also represents a
threat to domestic autonomy from firms that, even when
they begin small as trading companies or venture
capital operations, are destined to become large and
powerful if they are successful, with global
flexibility from which to negotiate with the individual
states of the Caribbean. For that reason the approach
to production and market-sharing might well take on a
regionwide character; new or existing institutions from
the Caribbean Basin would provide an oversight function
that would safeguard regional interests and permit some
degree of rent-sharing. This need not be done directly
through a dual-wage structure that benefits a favored
group of workers; it could also be done through new
forms of profit-sharing that will nevertheless
safeguard incentives for research and development and
new investment in the region. Properly engineered,
such a program would also lead to both import
substitution and export promotion but in the context of
increased efficiency of production with a more rational
use of factors abundant in each of the economies
involved (with important implications for labor in the
Caribbean.)

An approach to production and market sharing for
new investment in the region would require favorable
attention not only from the United States, but from the
European Community, Japan, and other industrial
countries. There is no disputing the link between
development policy, trade, investment, and regional
migration for the United States in the Caribbean, just
as that with Mexico and Canada. In addition, as Mexico
develops through a similar set of production and

market-sharing relationships with the United States and the other industrial countries, its interaction with the rest of the Caribbean Basin is likely to grow as well. As with Mexico, any significant change in U.S. immigration policy is certain to have a profound impact on the welfare of the Caribbean Basin countries which, if handled without concern for the consequences, could more than offset the positive elements of the Caribbean Basin Initiative. Given the realities of increasing regional interdependence, it would be advisable for all parties concerned to work toward the coordination of employment, migration, and development policies, even if such coordination means a major new initiative in U.S.-Caribbean relations.

Notes

1. Ransford W. Palmer, Caribbean Dependence on the United States Economy (New York, 1979).

2. W.F. Stolper and P.A. Samuelson, "Protection and Real Wages," Review of Economic Studies, Vol IX (1941), pp. 58-74.

3. Brinley Thomas, Migration and Economic Growth. A Study of Great Britain and the Atlantic Economy (Cambridge, 1973).

4. Michael P. Todaro, Migration and Economic Development (Nairobi, 1976).

5. William H. Durham, Scarcity and Survival in Central America: Ecological Origins of the Soccer War (Stanford, 1979).

6. Stephen H. Hymer, The International Operations of National Firms, A Study of Direct Foreign Investment (Cambridge, MA, 1976).

7. W. Arthur Lewis, The Evolution of the International Economic Order (Princeton, 1973).

8. Michael J. Piore, Birds of Passage (Cambridge, 1979).

9. Samuel A. Morley and Jeffrey G. Williamson, "Demand, Distribution, and Employment: The Case of Brazil," Economic Development and Cultural Change Vol. 23 (1974), p. 33.

10. Staffan Burenstam Linder, "Political Economy of the Pacific Century," manuscript, Hoover Institution, Stanford University, 1974.

19. Relating Migration and Development Policies: Summary and Conclusions

Robert A. Pastor

I. Connecting Migration and Development

Imagine an analysis of the Third World in the 1970s that never mentioned petroleum. Or consider a study of Europe in the decade after the Second World War that overlooked the emergence of a European Community. A study of U.S.-Caribbean relations that ignored the transforming impact of migration on development in the entire region should be similarly implausible. But until this book, one would have been hard pressed to locate a study relating migration and development in a forest of other works that focus on the resurgence of the Cold War in the Caribbean.

The urgent security crises that engulf the region cannot be ignored, but unless one also pays attention to underlying problems and emerging developmental patterns, one might very well face a continual succession of crises. In the longer course of history, human migration and economic development will shape the region more than any transient breakdown of political order in a particular country, even the exceptional case of the Cuban revolution. William McNeill has tried to locate the importance of migration in history. He described the large-scale movements of people, such as those currently taking place in the Caribbean Basin. The massive flows of migration, McNeill wrote, are "analogous to currents in the earth's magma that direct the motion of tectonic plates. As the collision of tectonic plates provoke geological spectaculars--mountain ranges, earthquakes, volcanoes--so also in human affairs, it seems likely that political spectaculars like the rise and fall of civilizations rested on these basic currents of human migration."[1]

Even though security problems in the Caribbean region still rivet the attention of the United States,

by the year 2000, a new generation of Americans might
criticize their parents for failing to comprehend the
relationship between security, migration, and
development and for failing to see the emergence of a
new Caribbean area community in which the United States
is a member. Indeed, by the year 2000 people might
very well point to the new human bonds that connect the
region as being relatively more important than the
disparity in wealth and power that today separates the
United States from the rest of the Caribbean area.

This book is an attempt to reach beyond the
headlines and explore the connection between two
powerful phenomena shaping the Caribbean Basin:
migration and development. We have traveled a good
distance from our discussion in the first chapter on
the two errant assumptions that continue to guide
policy on these issues. Although some assume that
poverty continues to push Caribbean emigrants, we have
deepened our understanding of the kinds of development
that accelerate migration. Although others assume that
emigration is a crucial escape valve for releasing
social pressures from fragile nations, we have
identified the costs and the opportunities of
migration.

In this chapter, I will try to summarize the
journey by reviewing the findings, discussing the
evolution of Caribbean and U.S. perspectives on the
policy implications, and summarizing the policy
recommendations that emerged from the various
analyses. In Chapter 3, Anthony Maingot describes the
Caribbean area as a single socio-cultural area where
people move in search of values and beliefs that
transcend national borders. "The costs of ignoring"
this transnational culture, according to Maingot, "are
too great; the potential benefits for harnessing it for
development [are] too enticing." In this spirit and
with this objective, I shall try to capture the essence
of this book.

II. The Impact of Development on Migration

Development signifies change, and one of the
changes, which is an inevitable concomitant of
development, is migration. As economies expand and
diversify, as improvements in health reduce mortality
and increase the population, and as communications,
transportation, and education offer people access to
the modern world, people move within their countries
and abroad. In addition to the economic impetus to
move, powerful social, cultural, political, and
psychological forces have facilitated and increased
migration in the Caribbean region.

Although some migration is inevitable and

beneficial to society, rapid rates of internal and international migration are costly: Families are divided, and local and national governments are forced to divert scarce resources to meet the more expensive social and educational needs of an expanding urban population. Rapid migration can also hasten the decline of agriculture and expand the demand for food imports, even though foreign exchange might be scarce. High emigration rates of professional and skilled workers can reduce the capacity of the government and the private sector to promote development precisely when a nation's expectations and needs are rising.

The issue for those concerned with Caribbean economic development is not whether to preclude migration but whether projects and strategies can be identified that could contribute to development by slowing the pace of migration. Our concern is at the margins: to preclude excessive rates of emigration that can be costly to sending as well as receiving societies. A related issue is whether nations can productively employ their populations if emigration is curtailed by the United States and/or other receiving countries.

It is implausible that every variable pushing and pulling people to migrate could be affected so that the income and opportunity gap would be closed between the United States and the Caribbean countries, reducing migration to a trickle. Some people from the small Caribbean countries will always seek the diversity of opportunities only attainable in large industrialized countries like the United States. Moreover, the social networks of an enlarged Caribbean socio-cultural area imply that some level of migration will always occur.

However, development projects and strategies, that accelerate migration, however unintentional, can be identified as can those that could reduce the rate of migration. Although recognizing the historical and socio-cultural motives for migration, Diaz-Briquets suggests in his analysis that development strategies skewed to a single objective, whether economic growth or equity, are more likely to increase levels of migration than those that balance these objectives. More specifically, "urban-biased" policies, which maintain low food prices and provide no technical assistance, credit, or fertilizer to farmers, in effect, discourage farming and encourage food imports. These strategies are likely to quicken migration. As urban areas grow more congested, and capital-intensive investments create fewer jobs, many will consider the option of looking for work abroad.

Because rapid rates of internal and international migration are costly to society, governments should

take migration into account in formulating development
strategies and seek strategies that could reduce the
migration rate. Such development strategies would
emphasize (a) assisting the agricultural sector to feed
both local people and tourists; (b) expanding
employment; (c) relating manpower policy more directly
to a nation's development needs and its demographic
profile; and (d) balancing income distribution with
diversified economic growth.

III. Varying Effects of Migration on Development

    Trying to measure the costs and benefits of
migration to Caribbean development is fraught with a
host of difficulties. First, the data are often either
unavailable or unreliable. Second, some of the major
items in the equation are not easily quantifiable, and
even those that can be quantified, such as the cost of
educating future emigrants, are subject to markedly
different interpretations (if average costs are used,
for example, rather than marginal costs). Nonetheless,
some approximations are possible.
    A useful point of departure is to first
conceptualize and identify the costs and benefits. The
costs of emigration could include the country's
investment in the emigrant's education, health, and
welfare; performance and efficiency loss in the public
and private sectors as a result of the loss of skilled
workers and managers; indirect effects on government
decisions concerning population and employment (the
more people that leave the less the government may
think it has a problem), and the overall impact on the
dependency ratio. The potential benefits of emigration
to the sending country are derived from remittances,
acquisition of skills, reduced unemployment, reduced
rates of population growth, and increased opportunities
for trade and investment.
    The costs and benefits depend on the rate and
cause of migration, and they vary within a nation (at
the level of households, communities, and nations),
between nations, and between different types of
migration. The costs and benefits also vary according
to the types of migration--permanent or temporary,
legal or illegal, return, refugee, or immigrant--and to
the social, political, and economic structure in the
country of origin. They also depend on the emigrant--
whether he is a professional, skilled, or unskilled
worker.
    The assessment in this book of the different types
of migration leads to the following conclusions.
Temporary emigration, particularly when part of a
structured program such as H-2, and permanent
immigration (to the Caribbean) appear to benefit the

Caribbean countries most. The impacts of <u>permanent
emigration</u> of skilled or professional workers and
<u>return migration</u> are harder to assess because they
depend on whether the emigrant can be replaced easily
in his work place and whether they affect the
productivity of a large number of associated workers.
Sometimes the departure of a talented administrator can
leave an administrative void; this concern is
particularly serious in smaller countries where
difficulties in implementing development projects can
often be traced to the absence of managerial personnel.

The impact of <u>return migration</u> depends on the
reasons for the return and whether the person can
readily apply his skills. It also depends on whether
the individual has acquired any skills abroad and
whether he is predisposed and able to apply them when
he returns. With these considerations in mind,
Elizabeth Thomas-Hope concludes that in the short-term,
return flows have a "positive effect" on the individual
and the family; living standards and housing are
improved by the return and particularly if capital and
goods are remitted. However, she argues that this
effect must be assessed in the light of longer-term
ties of dependency on life styles, expectations, and
consumption patterns, which are reinforced by the
circular flow of migrants. Return migration could
become "a major potential resource for Caribbean
societies," she writes, if governments formulated and
implemented policies aimed at utilizing the migrants'
skills.

Even though the survey data on <u>illegal migration</u>
are unavoidably problematic, Papademetriou discerns
several distinct and interesting patterns from his and
other surveys. First, Caribbean illegal migrants are
well-educated by the standards of their country of
origin; they stay in the United States for extended
periods; and their earning levels are often comparable
and sometimes higher than those of legal permanent
residents who have been in the United States for
comparable periods. Although few illegal migrants
originally intend to stay very long, most do. Of
greatest interest is that little distinction is
apparent in the profile between Caribbean area citizens
in the U.S. as permanent legal residents and those here
illegally. The key difference is not between legal and
illegal but between Caribbean and Mexican migrants; the
former are better educated, earn higher incomes, and
send home much higher levels of remittances.

Although <u>migration</u> generally benefits the
receiving nation, it does not necessarily cost the
sending nation. As Patricia Anderson noted, a gap
often exists between a nation's social need for skilled
personnel and its effective demand. A skilled

individual may be constrained from utilizing his full
potential in his home nation for social, political, or
financial reasons or simply because opportunity is
lacking compared with that which he might find in the
United States.

The family is a major beneficiary of emigration
because it is the main recipient of remittances, which
are often quite substantial. Remittances are generally
spent to maintain or improve the family's standard of
living (consumer goods) or to improve housing. Except
for the H-2 program, which requires workers to send
some wages home, Caribbean governments do not touch the
foreign exchange nor, with one recent exception
(Jamaica; see Chapter 15), have governments developed
mechanisms that could encourage the use of remittances
for investment purposes. However, remaining families
also bear significant, though less tangible, costs as a
result of emigration: The high rate of dependency (the
ratio of those unable to work because they are too
young, too old, physically unable, or compelled to look
after others over those in the labor force) is severely
exacerbated by emigration. In other words, remittances
may be a deceptive "benefit" of migration when the
family's principal wage-earner is supporting his
dependent family from abroad rather than supporting
them and contributing to the community at home.
Moreover, as Marshall rather cogently demonstrates, the
benefit of remittances are often marginal as compared
to the loss of managerial skills.

The development potential and success of the
sending country and the rate and cause of emigration
will also affect the extent to which emigration
contributes or hurts that country. Arthur Brown argues
that emigration from the Caribbean--and particularly
Jamaica--before the mid-1970s was primarily motivated
by economic reasons and was more beneficial to the
region than the more recent emigration, which was
related to political dissatisfaction. In the cases of
Jamaica, Guyana, and Haiti, rapid and large-scale
emigration primarily for political reasons by
professionals adversely affected the development of
these countries. In the eastern Caribbean, where the
departure of even a few managers affects the home
countries, emigration can be a serious developmental
liability. However, a steady flow of all types of
migrants over a long period, as in the case of Barbados
during the last two decades, has not visibly harmed
that country's development prospects.

In general, with all the caveats and variables
noted, the costs of emigration are sustained by the
sending nations whereas the benefits--such as they are--
accrue to the emigrants, their families, and the
receiving nations. However, emigration of unskilled,

surplus, or unemployed labor during a depression can
be regarded as beneficial to the sending nation
whether it is temporary or permanent. Several
authors, including Papademetriou, Thomas-Hope, and
McCoy, believe that the benefits of migration to the
sending nations could be multiplied by informed
government policies.

The purpose of using the cost-benefit analysis
is not so much to compute a net benefit or cost for
emigration but rather to understand the differential
effects of migration--on communities and nations, and
with respect to different types of migration-- to
devise ways to enhance the benefits of migration to
Caribbean development while reducing the costs.
Ransford Palmer suggests that an analysis that
disaggregated the costs and benefits at the level of
the sector, the firm, and the household would be more
useful in formulating policy. This may be true, but
such a microeconomic analysis would require the
generation of vast quantities of new data, none of
which is currently available.

Some authors find the cost-benefit analysis
limited or even misleading. Patricia Anderson
suggests that an alternative yardstick for measuring
the impact of emigration would be to assess whether
it contributes to the maintenance or the erosion of
the sociopolitical system in the home country. This
approach is useful in encouraging scholars to
distinguish political costs and benefits from
economic ones, but it might very well prove even more
difficult to define and measure than a more
conventional cost-benefit analysis.

IV. From Ambivalence to Consensus: A Basis for
Policy

Two firmer conclusions emerge from this book:
that both migration and development are increasingly
important in the region, and that the relationship
between the two is complex but comprehensible and
subject to some degree of policy manipulation.
Discussion about the policy significance of these
conclusions, however, diverges because of national
differences, but mostly because of different
disciplinary and professional perspectives. At an
abstract, structural level, Patricia Anderson and
Ralph Henry argue that neither development nor
emigration can be greatly affected unless and until
the structural dependency--which locks the Caribbean
economies into a stultifying embrace with the United
States--has changed. An alternative structural
perspective, articulated by Courtney Blackman, Clark
Reynolds, and Alejandro Portes, views migration not

as a problem but as a process of adjustment within a
broader transnational labor market. Using this view,
they see migration as an issue that transcends
national boundaries, defying individual governments
to address it effectively.

Most chapters, however, focus on the level at
which national governments make policy, and the
assumption is implicit that governments can indeed
affect both development and migration. The authors
agree that strategies to promote economic development
are beneficial and can be effective but are
ambivalent about what to do about migration. This
ambivalence is deeply rooted and explains why neither
the United States nor the Caribbean had heretofore
moved to develop a policy relating migration and
development. The United States views itself as a
nation of immigrants and yet is troubled by the
recent large influx of immigrants, particularly
illegal migrants and refugees. Although the United
States recognizes that the brain drain reduces the
development capacity of lesser developed countries
(LDCs), the United States still needs and benefits
from young immigrants trained in the sciences,
engineering, and computer skills. Besides, as
Bhagwati suggests, many "more brains [are] draining
away in LDC societies" because of social or political
constraints or lack of opportunity than are lost by
migration.

Caribbean attitudes match the ambivalence of
U.S. ones. Although Caribbean people consider
immigration a way of life and a right, they also
recognize that significant developmental costs are
incurred by some types of migration. On the one
hand, the Caribbean wants to reduce the brain drain;
on the other, the Caribbean elite wants to preserve
the option of migration. While the Caribbean wants
the United States to keep a wide open door to its
emigrants, Caribbean Common Market (CARICOM)
governments close the door to immigrants even from
other CARICOM countries.

As a result both the United States and the
Caribbean have been of many minds on the subject of
migration policy, and the prevalence of de facto
rather than deliberate emigration and immigration
policies is a reflection of these mixed attitudes.
For these and other reasons, policies on migration
and its relationship to development have lagged
considerably behind the phenomenon, as William Demas,
president of the Caribbean Development Bank, put it
so well. However, as a result of the dialogue
stimulated by the research project, both U.S. and
Caribbean attitudes have become clearer and the gap
separating them has narrowed. U.S. authors have

become more sensitive to the impact of U.S. immigration policy on Caribbean economic development. Caribbean scholars and policymakers, including Courtney Blackman, Arthur Brown, Dawn Marshall, and Patricia Anderson acknowledge that Caribbean development planning has been remiss in failing to take migration into account, and they recommend changing this. Marshall suggests that Caribbean governments should look more closely at ways that migration could be used to benefit them, and Blackman, in his chapter, suggests a number of ways this could be done.

In reaching these conclusions, the participants in the research project first addressed two questions: What is lost by failing to relate migration to development? What could be gained by policies that relate migration to development? It is easier to point to development failures, which have a migration component, than to suggest that an awareness of the relationship of migration to development could have prevented that failure. For example, Arthur Brown, Patricia Anderson, and Ralph Henry describe how Jamaican Prime Minister Michael Manley sought a development model that would enhance self-reliance and reduce dependency, but the rhetoric he used to mobilize support for his program actually accelerated the rate of professional emigration with serious adverse economic consequences. Emigration was clearly one of the causes and one of the consequences of the development failure. Whether a more complete understanding of the ramifications of migration and the costs to development might have modified the strategy is speculative, but conceivable.

Another example is afforded by the development plans formulated by the microstates of the eastern Caribbean. As Dawn Marshall writes, failure to take into account the propensity for emigration sometimes makes the difference between the success or failure of a particular development project. A third example is the Caribbean Basin Initiative (CBI), which has paid more attention to trying to create jobs than to who might fill them or what impact "enclave" manufacturing might have on migration and the rest of the economy. The result might very well be an increase in migration, though the CBI promised the opposite. These development failures have multiple causes, but among them is the conceptual failure to understand the relationship between migration and development.

Those are examples of development failures. What could be gained by taking migration into account? I will review some of the proposals offered in this book.

V. Policy Recommendations

Caribbean Emigration and Immigration Policies

Historically, Barbados and several other Caribbean islands promoted emigration of their citizens, but today most countries have no policies whatsoever on emigration and highly restrictive policies on immigration. Several authors recommend changes in both. Although aware that emigration can often be costly to Caribbean development, Courtney Blackman argues that policies aimed at containing capital and restricting labor within national boundaries have the opposite effect since they are perceived as threatening basic freedoms and the middle class. Instead, Blackman recommends that the migration-and-development policy, which is most likely to succeed in the long term, is one that is most liberal and least restrictive. A similar point about the structural vulnerability of the open Caribbean socio-cultural area is made in different ways by Maingot, Anderson, Henry, and Brown--four Caribbean representatives of very diverse perspectives. Henry's analysis is in many respects the most compelling: He finds that the Caribbean countries that tried most vigorously to cut the cord of dependency found that it had tightened to the point of almost strangling the economies. The more cautious, laissez-faire governments in the region have become less dependent in the long run.

Blackman pursues the logic of this argument the furthest. He recommends that "governments should liberalize their national policies with respect to the movement of people, especially skilled workers within the region." He recommends a Caribbean-wide agreement to remove all restrictions on the movement of people, and, "to facilitate this, exchange control restrictions on the transfer of funds within the region and on non-resident borrowing" should also be removed. In other words, although recognizing the costs of the brain drain and capital flight, he recommends that the best way to shut those valves is to open them all the way. He also recommends that governments promote seasonal labor migration and deduct part of their earnings to ensure the financial security of dependents left behind.

To deal with the scarcity of managerial skills, Blackman urges governments in the region to encourage the return of Caribbean migrants with such skills, by advertising abroad and providing various concessions on bringing household goods or cars home. Also, he urges governments to reduce the level of taxes. Better use could be made of Caribbean communities abroad as possible markets for specialized goods and as sources of investment. But his principal recommendation derives from the open systems theory, which he believes more accurately depicts the dilemma of the Caribbean than the dependency theory. The key to development in the region, according to Blackman, is to maintain a stable political and economic climate: "Caribbean governments should bear in mind that the outcome of economic and political disorder is often the flight of both skilled workers and capital--two essential elements of development and modernization."

Trevor Hope's analysis of the historical impact of immigration on Caribbean development leads him naturally to the conclusion that Caribbean governments should encourage immigration, but if that is improbable, at least, they should not preclude or unduly restrict immigration. Arthur Brown, however, reminds us that Caribbean Common Market (CARICOM) leaders have not even agreed to permit the free movement of workers in CARICOM, let alone outside the region. Changing these laws would not be easy, but there is some indication that several Caribbean governments are considering relaxing immigration restrictions to entice Hong Kong businessmen to invest and immigrate to the Caribbean.[2]

U.S. Immigration Policies

Although migration has many causes, U.S. immigration policy remains a powerful determinant of the level and type of Caribbean immigration. One only has to look at the dramatic increase in the numbers of immigrants after the 1965 liberalization of the immigration act.[3] For the last decade, the average annual level of legal Caribbean immigration has been about 73,000 people. Harris Miller estimates that nearly twice that number overstay their nonimmigrant visas each year, joining an expanding population of illegal aliens. How could the United States sensitize its immigration policy to Caribbean development, and what should it do?

Regarding permanent legal immigration, Harris Miller considers a number of options to tilt U.S. immigration policy to favor the Caribbean, but he rejects them in favor of a universal, global policy. This view was also strongly supported at the Wye Conference by Arnold Leibowitz, who noted that U.S. immigration policy had taken a long time to arrive at the point where it did not discriminate against any ethnic, national, or racial group and that it would be a mistake to return to earlier, discriminating standards, even for an "affirmative purpose." Of

course, the Simpson-Mazzoli bill includes a special
quota preference for Mexico and Canada, but Leibowitz
opposes that provision and argues that even if the bill
passed, it should not be extended.[4] Miller rejects the
idea of changing the occupational preference system so
as to reduce the brain drain from the Caribbean or
other developing countries. He feels that such
immigrants contribute enormously to the United States
and should have the right to emigrate here. Besides,
the occupational preference category amounts to a
relatively small percentage of total immigrants as
compared to relative preference.

With regard to illegal migration, Miller makes a
strong case for passing the Simpson-Mazzoli bill, which
would reduce illegal migration by prohibiting employers
from hiring those who are in the United States
illegally. Miller believes that passage of the bill
would lead to the curtailment of illegal migration, but
the effect of that would be mitigated by the amnesty
(legalization) provisions of the bill, which would give
Caribbean immigrants expanded opportunities under
family reunification programs. Papademetriou agrees
that passage of the Simpson-Mazzoli bill would have a
neutral effect on Caribbean migration to the United
States; illegal aliens would be replaced by legal
permanent residents and family members. Since he found
little difference between the average legal and illegal
Caribbean emigrant, one could therefore conclude the
bill would make little difference for economic
development in the Caribbean.

As the temporary-worker program (H-2) is very
beneficial to the Caribbean nations, McCoy and Marshall
both suggest that the program should be expanded and
reoriented to the smaller nations in the eastern
Caribbean. The reasons for reorienting the program are
that remittances have a very considerable, positive
impact on the small economies of the eastern Caribbean,
and also these nations have fewer alternatives than,
say, Jamaica. McCoy makes a series of additional
recommendations to improve the temporary-worker program
and make it more sensitive to the developmental needs
of the Caribbean. These include (1) removing the
distinction between foreign and domestic agricultural
workers, which would mean temporary workers would pay
income and Social Security taxes, but these would then
be remitted to the migrant via a remittance bank; (2)
developing a new inter-governmental organization for
allocating positions more equitably and to workers from
the smaller eastern Caribbean islands; (3) providing
agricultural training programs in land-grant
universities for the migrants before they return home;
(4) more effective use by Caribbean governments of the

23% mandatory savings plan for development purposes; and (5) giving statutory recognition to the developmental consequences of the program. The New York Times reported in January 1985 that the Immigration and Naturalization Service is considering dramatically expanding the program by administrative action.[5]

A recurrent problem in formulating migration policies is the inadequacy or unavailability of data. Therefore, we recommend that both U.S. and Caribbean governments upgrade their capabilities for data gathering on immigration and consider establishing policy analysis units to review the data and their implications.

Caribbean Development Strategies

Consistent with the Blackman thesis on the need for a stable, gradual approach to politics and development, Diaz-Briquets recommends a development strategy that balances economic growth with equity as most likely to reduce the pressures of migration in the region. He also stresses the importance of a political development model that is open and accomodating and therefore more likely to avoid abrupt changes.

All the authors recognize the limited options available to such small, open economies. Regional integration through a common market is essential given the limited markets, but even if the common market were to truely remove all trade barriers, the region would still be too small for an import-substitution strategy to be effective. Blackman, Brown, Hakim, and Weintraub all agree that the best prospects for expanding employment are through trade, aid, and foreign investment and promoting linkages within the economies. As Blackman says, "sophistication, not closure, is the corrective for dependence." The Caribbean Basin Initiative offers some hope, but the key issue is how to use the CBI to enhance rather than supplant local initiative. This probably will require redesigning local training programs and may also require that foreign investors collaborate more with local enterprise and research institutions.

As the decline of agriculture drains scarce foreign exchange and stimulates migration, increased emphasis on the agricultural sector is essential. Modernization of agriculture could increase and diversify production to serve domestic markets and also tourists. Luther Miller provides a number of specific proposals to establish and strengthen linkages between local agriculture and tourism to save foreign exchange, expand employment opportunities in the rural and urban areas, and thereby slow migration. As for traditional

crops like sugar, which face difficulties in
international markets, the United States ought to
consider expanding its domestic commodity programs to
insulate Caribbean economies from the chilly winds of
wide fluctuations in international prices and to permit
greater export opportunities for Caribbean crops.

Ernest Preeg proposes a specific development
program for Haiti that takes into account the reduced
opportunities for emigration as a result of the
successful interdiction efforts undertaken by the U.S.
Coast Guard and border patrols from the Dominican
Republic. He suggests that the international aid
community jointly sponsor a development program aimed
at increasing productivity in the agricultural sector
and redirecting the rural/urban migration toward the
provincial cities. He also recommends that the United
States accept more legal immigrants from Haiti but
recognizes that is unlikely until more Haitian
permanent residents are living in the United States,
which could occur if the Simpson-Mazzoli bill passed.

Ralph Henry recommends that the only manpower
strategy that would permit Caribbean countries to fully
utilize their labor would be a "human-resource
strategy," similar to the model pursued by several
Asian countries. Specifically, he suggests that such a
strategy have the following five components: (1)
cooperative research projects with industrialized
countries on advanced technology, such as biogenetics;
(2) altered terms of trade that would permit small
Caribbean countries to invest in "knowledge-intensive"
exports; (3) scholarship programs in science and
technology that require students to return to their
homeland; (4) flexible manpower and educational
planning programs; and (5) encouragement of return
migration by skilled managers.

Hakim and Weintraub are skeptical that a change in
development strategy or U.S. policy could have much of
an effect on the flow of Caribbean migrants to the
U.S. Nonetheless, they propose a development strategy
that takes migration into account; it places greatest
emphasis on employment creation. They accept that
employment creation will not yield quick results and,
indeed, could have a perverse effect in the short term,
but in their opinion "it may be the only economic
intervention that could reduce migration over the long
term." They also recommend a five-pronged strategy
that includes emphasis on the following: (1)
agriculture, primarily for the purpose of creating
productive jobs; (2) industrial development, which
removes disincentives to invest in labor; (3) export
promotion; (4) family planning and manpower programs;
and (5) tourism promotion. Aid, they believe, can be

more effective than trade to promote development,
reduce migration pressures, and expand employment.

International Arrangements for Migration and Development

Almost everyone recognizes that the problems and
opportunities related to migration and development
require the cooperation of some or all countries of the
area. Anderson recommends a bilateral agreement
between the United States and Jamaica; others suggest a
regional arrangement; and still others suggest
international initiatives. Anderson proposes that the
United States and Jamaica recognize that migration is
just one part of a larger system and to maintain the
stability of that system, both governments should agree
to (1) maintain present levels of immigration; (2)
increase the numbers of lower-skilled contract labor
from Jamaica; and (3) permit short-term contract labor
for highly skilled individuals.
Bilateral aid agencies and international
development banks should also consider evaluating
existing aid programs to ascertain their impact on
migration. Arthur Brown proposes the need for
integrated planning by international donors as well as
national governments: Such planning would view
population and labor migration as integral components
of economic development. He notes that development
efforts only pay lip service to comprehensive planning,
thus failing to integrate the objectives of different
economic and social sectors. To achieve sectoral
integration, more attention should be given to long-
range objectives. Brown also suggests that the use of
more labor-intensive appropriate technologies should be
increased and that priority be given to rural
development and population programs. In his view, the
international development community can have
substantial influence in bringing about these changes
in focus. As Diaz-Briquets suggests, however, the
primary responsibility rests on Caribbean governments
to pursue balanced and equitable development
strategies.
Rosemarie Rogers and I developed several proposals
for using migration to enhance economic development.
First, we propose national and regional remittance
banks to provide an incentive for migrants (and their
families) to invest their remittances in their home
countries. Such banks would be supervised by the
international development banks, and could use
remittances, which as Richard Feinberg suggests, could
be considered as returns on human capital or as
leverage to multiply private-investment opportunities.
Second, we propose establishing several manpower

pools to encourage Caribbean experts, who currently reside abroad, to apply their talents in their home countries. These manpower pools could be organized and funded separately by the international development banks, bilateral aid agencies, private investors and merchants, and the Intergovernmental Committee on Migration. The international development banks repeatedly indicate that a significant constraint on expending loans to the region is the lack of managers. If such loans could include funding for Caribbean emigrants, then two problems--the need for investment and skilled manpower--could be addressed simultaneously. Jamaican Prime Minister Edward Seaga proposed the establishment of an international fund for manpower resources to be supported by the United Nations Development Programme, and to help nations like Jamaica to compensate for the "brain drain." Trevor Hope suggests that a less expensive and more effective way to address the problem of the brain drain would be for the Caribbean to permit immigration of skilled and professional workers. Blackman concurs with this recommendation.

Third, Rogers and I propose that Caribbean governments would make better use of their scarce resources if they helped young graduates to set down roots in their countries than if they tried to uproot those who settled abroad a long time ago. Harris Miller estimates that one-third of all foreign students in the United States remain when they complete their studies. We recommend that the United States cooperate with Caribbean (and other Third World) governments to encourage the return of these students by strict visa enforcement and by ensuring that foreign students only pursue graduate programs relevant to their countries' needs. Dawn Marshall estimates that between 1953 and 1972, 81 percent of all new Grenadian doctors left Grenada for foreign countries. We propose that those who study at universities in the Caribbean at public expense receive forgivable loans for their education, provided they remain and work in their country for an appropriate period. Those who emigrate would have to repay their loans.

VI. A Strategy and a Compact

The authors of this book have proposed a number of specific recommendations that governments and international organizations could adopt to manage the issues of migration and development more effectively. However, these recommendations can only have an enduring impact on the region's development if they are placed in the context of a broader strategy and program. That requires, first, an understanding of the

region's special development dilemma, and second, a
specially tailored strategy to respond to it.

Whether the development dilemma is described as
"dependency," "underdevelopment," or by another term,
all the authors agree that the nations of the region
share similar problems: They are small in size and
population; they have limited resources; they rely on
trade, aid, and foreign investment for a large
proportion of their gross domestic product; and they
are close to the United States, a highly unequal
competitor. Together these characteristics mean that
major forces shaping their nations' destinies originate
abroad, whether they are the fluctuating price of sugar
in the international market, interest rates charged by
U.S. banks, hurricanes, marines or guerrillas.

William Demas defined economic viability and
development for small Caribbean states as requiring "a
process of sustained increases in production and
productivity."[6] For nations as open and vulnerable to
external shocks as those of the Caribbean, sustained
development can only occur if they reduce their
fragility, if they construct buffers that protect them
from harsh winds that blow across the islands without
warning and leave a devastated landscape.

Both internal and international policies are
available to exploit the comparative advantage of the
region while reducing its vulnerability. A crucial
instrument for achieving both objectives is
diversification. The more numerous and different a
country's exports are, the less vulnerable it is to the
shifting price of one. The more markets a country has,
the more opportunities it has to expand production.
Second, in addition to expanding and altering the
number of products they export; nations can try to
insulate the market of one of their products. That is
the objective of international commodity agreements,
such as those for coffee, sugar, or tin: to moderate
the fluctuations in price through an international
organization that buys and sells a specific commodity
to keep the price within an agreed band.

Third, nations can expand their markets through
regional integration or special trade preference
schemes (e.g., the Lome agreement or the Caribbean
Basin Initiative). Fourth, nations can upgrade their
human resources through improvements in education or
training, or by a special human-resource strategy, as
proposed by Henry and Johnson. Finally, governments
can stimulate local production to substitute for
current imports; this strategy would be especially
appropriate for food. All these steps, plus others
recommended previously, would reduce the degree to
which nations in the region would be the objects of
international manipulation.

The United States shares with the Caribbean an interest in economic development for the simple reason that it shares with the region the consequences of instability and underdevelopment. Moreover, as the Caribbean reduces its dependency, it becomes a better trading partner. Therefore, neither U.S. nor Caribbean interests are served by a bilateral framework for cooperation that reinforces the one-sided, dependent relationship and discourages regional cooperation. In advising against bilateral aid in the mid-1960's, Senator J. William Fulbright stated the issue most clearly: "The crucial difference between bilateral and international aid is the basic incompatibility of bilateralism with individual and national dignity. Charity corrodes both the rich and poor, breeding an exaggerated sense of authority on the part of the donor and a destructive loss of self-esteem on the part of the recipient."[7] Although the Caribbean Basin Initiative contributes to the region's development by expanding its markets, the CBI's framework is essentially bilateral, requiring separate agreements between the United States and each Basin nation.

As an alternative, we propose a Caribbean Basin Compact, a cooperative program involving all the nations of the region and other nations and international organizations interested in contributing to the region's development. The basis for this compact is the recognition of the (asymmetrical) interdependence of the nations in the region and the interconnectedness of the various problems they face, particularly those of migration and development.

The Caribbean Group for Cooperation in Economic Development, established in 1978 at the initiative of President Jimmy Carter and under the auspices of the World Bank, would be the perfect vehicle for drafting the terms of such a compact. The group is composed of more than thirty nations and fifteen international organizations and meets annually to review development plans and reports for each Caribbean nation, to encourage an increase in the resources to be loaned for development, and to review regional projects. Between mid-1978 and early 1985, the group provided $8 billion in foreign aid to the region.[8]

The governments associated with the Caribbean group could use an annual meeting to request that the staff of the World Bank undertake a regional development plan for the entire Caribbean Basin, including the United States. Utilizing the concept of the mutual development strategy proposed by Reynolds in Chapter 18, the staff could draft a manpower policy for the region that takes into account the comparative advantage of different nations in the region, and

includes a coordinated approach to migration and
production-sharing.

The United States might offer additional
investment resources if the region were to use the
resources for employment-expansion, population
programs, and invigorated agricultural policies.
Within the context of such a regionwide plan, the
international development banks could try to identify
the geographical and functional areas with the greatest
potential for future employment. A regional plan on
migration could include immigration policies for some
of the smaller Caribbean nations. Encouraging
immigrants might be a better investment than
contracting with expatriates. In the context of such a
plan, the United States might join with other
governments to assist them to recover--perhaps through
dual national taxation--some of the education costs
invested in emigrants.

Future annual meetings could serve as
opportunities for the United States to explain its
economic policy, for other Finance Ministers to
sensitize the United States to the potential impact of
its proposed policies on the region, and for all to
contemplate modifications of policies to mitigate
adverse effects and expand cooperative approaches.

In short, the compact would be both a development
plan and a process of continuing consultation. It
would not deny the sovereignty of the small nations of
the region; on the contrary, it would offer them new
opportunities to develop, while at the same time,
permitting them to reduce their vulnerability. For the
United States, it would offer a constructive plan to
promote development and stability on its "third border"
while at the same time demonstrating to the world its
desire to forge uniquely balanced and respectful
relationships with the many small nations that share
the Caribbean.

Caribbean emigration to the United States is not a
solution to the development problem of the Caribbean.
In most cases, it is part of the problem. But
migration is also a bond that transcends borders and
ties the nations of the Caribbean Basin together into a
new community. That new community should learn from
the creativity and dynamism of the Caribbean Basin
immigrant. All the nations touched by the immigrant's
journey should together consider ways to harness that
human energy for the future development of the entire
region.

Notes

This chapter is not only an attempt to summarize the
findings, analyses, and recommendations of the other
authors in this book; it also tries to summarize
numerous comments made at two separate conferences to
consider these papers. As such, I will occasionally
refer to the authors and a number of commentators in
this chapter.

1. William McNeill, "Migration in Historical
Perspective," Population and Development Review, Vol.
10, No. 1, March 1984, p. 7.

2. Frances MacLean, "Caribbean Basin Projects
Draws Interest -- Finally," Washington Post, January
27, 1985, p. F2.

3. Robert Pastor, "The Impact of U.S. Immigration
Policy and Caribbean Emigration: Does It Matter?" in
Barry Levine (ed.), Caribbean Exodus (N.Y.: Praeger,
1985).

4. Arnold Leibowitz, "Caribbean Development As
the Goal of U.S. Immigration Policy: The Tail Seeking
to Wag the Whale," paper prepared for a Conference on
"Migration and Development in the Caribbean," Aspen
Institute's Wye Plantation, Maryland, September 14-16,
1984.

5. Robert Pear, "U.S. Plans to Ease Alien Labor
Rules," New York Times, January 27, 1985, p. 1.

6. In an important essay, Demas writes that "the
question of economic viability of a country [in the
eastern Caribbean] is a non-issue, if by viability we
simply mean the ability of a formally sovereign State
and its people to survive. This is surely possible.
The real issue is whether the level of living to which
the people of the State can reasonably aspire can be
achieved on a sustainable basis, without 'excessive'
external financial and economic and therefore probably
political dependence and loss of effective (as distinct
from formal) sovereignty." He argues that the issue is
really "one of degree" -- whether excessive dependence
can be reduced, whether sustained growth can be
achieved -- and he concludes optimistically. (William
Demas, "The Viability of the OECS States," statement to
the Board of Governors of the Caribbean Development
Bank, Antigua, May 13 and 14, 1981, p. 4).

7. J. William Fulbright, <u>The Arrogance of Power</u> (N.Y.: Random House, 1966), p. 225.

8. Telecon with Nicholas Carter, World Bank, March 5, 1985.

About the Editor and Contributors

Robert A. Pastor, editor of this book, directed the research project on "Migration and Development in the Caribbean," at the School of Public Affairs, University of Maryland in College Park, where he taught and did research from May 1982 to September 1985. He is currently professor of political science at Emory University and Director of the Latin American and Caribbean Program at the Carter Center at Emory. In 1985-86, he is on leave of absence as a Fulbright Professor at El Colegio de Mexico. Dr. Pastor was the Director for Latin American and Caribbean Affairs on the National Security Council from 1977 to 1981. Prior to that, Dr. Pastor was the executive director of the Linowitz Commission on U.S.-Latin American relations, a private group of distinguished citizens that issued two reports on U.S. policy toward Latin America. He has taught at Harvard University where he received his Ph.D. in political science and an M.P.A. from the John F. Kennedy School of Government. He is the author of Congress and the Politics of U.S. Foreign Economic Policy.

Patricia Anderson is a demographer at the Institute of Social and Economic Research, University of the West Indies in Mona, Jamaica. Her principal research interests include labor market analysis and labor migration. From 1969 to 1980, Dr. Anderson worked at the National Planning Agency in Jamaica. She received her Ph.D. from the University of Chicago and a B.A. from the University of the West Indies.

Courtney Blackman, a native of Barbados, became
the first governor of the Central Bank of Barbados in
1972. He was formerly associate professor of
management at Houston University and has taught in
secondary schools in Jamaica, Ghana, and Barbados.
From 1968 to 1971, Dr. Blackman was associate economist
and later assistant secretary of the Irving Trust
Company in New York. Dr. Blackman received his Ph.D.
from the Columbia University School of Business in 1969
and his B.A. in modern history from the University of
the West Indies, Jamaica. His published works include
The Balance of Payment Crisis in the Caribbean: Which
Way Out?

G. Arthur Brown, a graduate of the London School
of Economics, assumed his present post as associate
administrator of the UN Development Programme in
1978. Previously, he was governor of the Bank of
Jamaica for ten years following a career in the civil
service of Jamaica where he was financial secretary to
the government and head of the civil service. Mr.
Brown has been a part-time lecturer in public finance
at the University of the West Indies.

Sergio Diaz-Briquets, associate director of the
research project, is a private consultant in
Washington, D.C. He was formerly associated with the
Population Reference Bureau in Washington, D.C., and
the International Development Research Centre in
Ottawa, Canada. A specialist in population and
development issues, he holds a Ph.D. in demography from
the University of Pennsylvania. The author of several
books and scholarly articles, including The Health
Revolution in Cuba, he is now engaged in research on
the link between economic development and emigration.

Peter Hakim, consultant to the Inter-American
Dialogue, was previously vice president for research
and evaluation at the Inter-American Foundation (1980-
1985), program officer for International Resource and
Environment Programs (1975-1980), and program advisor
in science and technology for Chile and Argentina at
the Ford Foundation (1971-1974). Mr. Hakim has
published and lectured on the subject of nutrition and
development programs. He holds an M.P.A. in public and
international affairs from the Woodrow Wilson School at
Princeton University.

Ralph Henry is senior lecturer in economics at the
University of the West Indies, in St. Augustine,
Trinidad and Tobago. Dr. Henry has held posts as
senior planning officer with the Trinidadian Ministry
of Labour and with the National Planning Board. His

main interests lie in manpower economics, agro-
industries and worker-participation schemes in
Caribbean-type countries. He received his Ph.D. in
economics from the University of Alberta in 1972 and
his B.Sc. in economics from the University of the West
Indies in 1967.

Trevor Hope is a journalist and historian engaged
in research on Caribbean migration. He has published
on European affairs and historical subjects and is
currently working on material relating to historical
perspectives on Caribbean migration. Dr. Hope took his
first degree at St. Andrew's University (Scotland) and
postgraduate degrees at Columbia University, New York,
and the Institute of History of the Romanian Academy of
Social and Political Sciences.

Terry L. McCoy is currently acting director of the
Center for Latin American Studies at the University of
Florida in Gainesville. He also holds appointments in
the Departments of Political Science and Sociology. He
has conducted research on Caribbean migration and U.S.
immigration policy.

Anthony P. Maingot is professor of sociology and
director of the graduate program in international
studies at Florida International University. His
recent essay, "Ideology, Politics, and Citizenship in
the American Debate on Immigration Policy: Beyond
Consensus," in Mary Kritz's U.S. Immigration and
Refugee Policy received much favorable attention. His
principal research interests focus on the political
sociology of the Caribbean. Dr. Maingot received his
Ph.D. from the University of Florida in Gainesville in
1967.

Dawn I. Marshall is a research fellow at the
Institute of Social and Economic Research (ISER),
University of the West Indies at Cave Hill, Barbados.
She was counterpart chief technical adviser to the Man
and the Biosphere Project, "Studies on Population,
Development and the Environment in the Eastern
Caribbean." Currently she coordinates the Caribbean
section of the Eastern Caribbean Migration Project.

Harris Miller is president of Harris Miller and
Associates, a government-relations firm in Arlington,
Virginia. He was formerly legislative assistant to the
House Judiciary Subcommittee on Immigration and Refugee
Policy and most recently a consultant to its chairman,
Hon. Romano Mazzoli. Mr. Miller was a Democratic
candidate for Congress in the Tenth Congressional
District of Virginia in 1984. He received an M.Phil.

in political science from Yale University and a B.A.
from the University of Pittsburgh. He has written
extensively on immigration and refugee policy,
including most recently an article on the history of
the Simpson-Mazzoli bill, which will be published in a
book on immigration edited by Nathan Glazer.

Luther Gordon Miller is a specialist in tourism
development at the Caribbean Tourism Research and
Development Centre in Bridgetown, Barbados. He is also
a fellow of the Economic Development Institute of the
World Bank. His professional interests include the
economic and social impact of tourism in the Caribbean
and the optimum developmental model for the region and
its island economies. Mr. Miller received his M.B.A.
from Concordia University in Montreal, Canada.

Demetrios G. Papademetriou is executive director
of Population Associates International. From 1980 to
1983, he served as the executive editor of the
International Migration Review. He has taught at the
University of Maryland, Duke University, and the New
School for Social Research, where he is a member of the
graduate faculty in international political economy.
Dr. Papademetriou, a political scientist, has chaired
and participated on a large number of national and
international panels on migration. His research has
been supported by a number of foundations and the
results published in over ten journals. His latest
book is The Unavoidable Issue: U.S. Immigration Policy
in the 1980s (with Mark J. Miller).

Ernest H. Preeg is a career foreign service
officer who served as U.S. ambassador to Haiti from
1981 to 1983, deputy assistant secretary for
international finance and development from 1976 to
1977, and director of the Office of European Community
and OECD Affairs from 1974 to 1976. He has published
books and articles on U.S. foreign and economic policy
and regional affairs. Dr. Preeg wrote his chapter when
he was a visiting fellow at the Overseas Development
Council in 1984, and he has been a fellow at the
National Planning Association, the Brookings
Institution, and the Council on Foreign Relations. He
received his Ph.D. in 1964 and M.A. in 1962 in
economics from the New School for Social Research.

Clark Reynolds is professor of economics at the
Food Research Institute at Stanford University and
principal investigator for the Binational Project on
U.S.-Mexico Relations. He is also director of the
Monticello West Foundation. Dr. Reynolds has been
senior fellow at the Brookings Institution and member

of the faculty of Yale University, the Stockholm School
of Economics, the National University of Mexico, and El
Colegio de Mexico. He has been a frequent consultant
to the U.S. and other Western Hemisphere governments,
to international organizations, and to banks in the
region. Dr. Reynolds received his Ph.D. and M.A. in
economics from the University of California at Berkeley
and A.B. magna cum laude from Claremont College.

Rosemarie Rogers is professor of international
politics at The Fletcher School of Law and Diplomacy at
Tufts University. Her research interests have been
primarily in the areas of ethnic studies, the
development of computer-based methodologies for the
social sciences, and international migration. She has
most recently edited a book entitled Guests Come to
Stay: The Effects of European Labor Migration on
Sending and Receiving Countries (Westview Press, 1985),
and she is now completing a book on the content,
sources, and effects of European migration policies
from the post-World War II period to the present. She
holds a Ph.D. degree in political science from the
Massachusetts Institute of Technology.

Elizabeth Thomas-Hope is lecturer in geography at
the University of Liverpool and associate research
fellow of the Centre for Caribbean Studies at the
University of Warwick, United Kingdom. From 1982 to
1984 she was Overseas Development Institute (ODI)
visiting fellow at the Institute of Social and Economic
Research, University of the West Indies, Mona,
Jamaica. She holds a D.Phil. degree from the
University of Oxford and masters degrees from the
University of Aberdeen (Scotland) and Pennsylvania
State University. Dr. Thomas-Hope was chairman of the
Society for Caribbean Studies in the United Kingdom
(1981 to 1983) and has published on Caribbean affairs,
migration issues and Third World development. Among
recent publications, she has edited Perspectives on
Caribbean Regional Identity (Liverpool : Centre for
Latin American Studies, University of Liverpool,
monograph series no. 11, 1984) and co-authored A
Geography of the Third World (London: Metheun, 1983).

Sidney Weintraub is Dean Rusk Professor at the
Lyndon B. Johnson School of Public Affairs at the
University of Texas at Austin. Prior to joining the
faculty, he held positions as deputy assistant
secretary of state for economic affairs and assistant
administrator for the U.S. Agency for International
Development. He has been a senior fellow with the
Brookings Institution with which he is still
associated.

List of Participants: The Conference on Migration and Development in the Caribbean, Held at the Wye Center, Maryland, September 14–16, 1984

Dr. Patricia Anderson
Institute of Social
and Economic Research
Kingston, Jamaica

Mr. Paul Balaran
Ford Foundation
New York, New York

Mr. Charles Becker
University of Maryland
College Park, Maryland

Mr. Peter Bell
Carnegie Endowment for
International Peace
Washington, D.C.

Dr. Jagdish N. Bhagwati
Columbia University
New York, New York

Hon. Courtney N. Blackman
Governor
Central Bank of Barbados
Bridgetown, Barbados

Mr. Gladstone Bonnick
Inter-Agency Resident Mission/
International Development Banks
St. Johns, Antigua

Ms. Gretchen Brainerd
Inter-Governmental Committee
for Migration
Washington, D.C.

Hon. G. Arthur Brown
United Nations Development
Programme
New York, New York

Dr. Peter Brown
University of Maryland
College Park, Maryland

Mr. Raymond Burghardt
National Security Council
Washington, D.C.

Mr. Malcolm Butler
Agency for International
Development
Washington, D.C.

Dr. Nicholas Carter
The World Bank
Washington, D.C.

Dr. Elsa Chaney
Georgetown University
Hemispheric Migration Project
Washington, D.C.

Dr. Hollis Chenery
Harvard University
Cambridge, Massachusetts

Hon. D. R. Clarke
The World Bank
Washington, D.C.

Hon. William Demas, President
Caribbean Development Bank
St. Michael, Barbados

Dr. Sergio Diaz-Briquets
Consultant
Washington, D.C.

Dr. George Eads
University of Maryland
College Park, Maryland

Ms. Patricia Ellis
MacNeil-Lehrer
Arlington, Virginia

Dr. Richard Feinberg
Overseas Development Council
Washington, D.C.

Dr. Manuel Garcia y Griego
El Colegio de Mexico
Mexico City, Mexico

Dr. Jeffrey Garten
Lehman Brothers
New York, New York

Mr. Peter Hakim
Inter-American Foundation
Washington, D.C.

Dr. Ralph Henry
University of the West Indies,
St. Augustine, Trinidad

Dr. Trevor Hope
Historian
Liverpool, England

Dr. William E. Kirwan
University of Maryland
College Park, Maryland

Hon. A. David Knox
The World Bank
Washington, D.C.

Mr. Arnold Leibowitz
Attorney
Washington, D.C.

Dr. Vaughan Lewis
Organization of Eastern
Caribbean States
Castries, St. Lucia

Dr. Anthony Maingot
Florida International
University
Miami, Florida

Dr. Dawn I. Marshall
Institute for Social and
Economic Research
Bridgetown, Barbados

Representative Romano Mazzoli
U.S. House of Representatives
Washington, D.C.

Hon. Val McComie
Organization of American States
Washington, D.C.

Dr. Terry McCoy
University of Florida
Gainesville, Florida

Hon. M. Peter McPherson
Agency for International
Development
Washington, D.C.

Mrs. Doris Meissner
Immigration and Naturalization
Service
Washington, D.C.

Mr. Luther Miller
Caribbean Tourism Research and
Development Centre
Christ Church, Barbados

Hon. Alan Nelson, Commissioner
Immigration and Naturalization
Service
Washington, D.C.

Dr. Ransford Palmer
Howard University
Washington, D.C.

Dr. Demetrios Papademetriou
Population Associates
Fairfax, Virginia

Dr. Robert Pastor
University of Maryland
College Park, Maryland

Dr. Patricia Pessar
Georgetown University
Washington, D.C.

Dr. Alejandro Portes
Johns Hopkins University
Baltimore, Maryland

Honorable Ernest Preeg
Overseas Development Council
and Department of State
Washington, D.C.

Ms. Lillian Pubillones-Nolan
House Foreign Affairs Committee
Washington, D.C.

Mr. Jeffrey Puryear
Ford Foundation
New York

Dr. Clark Reynolds
Stanford University
Stanford, California

Dr. Riordan Roett
Johns Hopkins University-SAIS
Baltimore, Maryland

Dr. Rosemarie Rogers
Fletcher School of Law and
Diplomacy
Medford, Massachusetts

Dr. Alan B. Simmons
International Development
Research Centre
Ottawa, Canada

Hon. Charles Skeete
Inter-American Development Bank
Washington, D.C.

Dr. Oded Stark
Harvard University
Cambridge, Massachusetts

Deborah Szekely, President
Inter-American Foundation
Rosslyn, Virginia

Dr. Michael Teitelbaum
Alfred P. Sloan Foundation
New York, New York

Mr. Jerry Tinker
Senate Judiciary Committee
Washington, D.C.

Dr. Elizabeth Thomas-Hope
University of Liverpool
Liverpool, England

Dr. Lydio Tomasi
Center for Migration Studies
New York, New York

Dr. Sidney Weintraub
University of Texas
Austin, Texas

List of Participants: The Conference on Migration and Development in the Caribbean, Held at the Wilson Center, Washington, D.C., January 23, 1985

Barry Ames
Office of Rep. Les Aspin
Washington, D.C.

Felicity Barringer
The Washington Post
Washington, D.C.

Everett Bauman
The Wilson Center
Washington, D.C.

Charles Becker
University of Maryland
College Park, Maryland

Everett E. Bierman
House Committee on Foreign
Affairs
Washington, D.C.

L. Francis Bouchey
Inter-American Security Council
Washington, D.C.

Harold Bradley
Center for Immigration Policy
Georgetown University
Washington, D.C.

Jodi Brayton
Senate Judiciary Committee
Washington, D.C.

Sergio-Diaz-Briquets
Migration & Development Project
University of Maryland
College Park, Maryland

G. Arthur Brown
United Nations Development
Programme
New York, New York

William Buzenberg
National Public Radio
Washington, D.C.

Dawn Calabia
Office of Rep. Stephen Solarz
Washington, D.C.

Paul Carlsen
Office of Rep. Mike Lowry
Washington, D.C.

Jorge Salazar-Carillo
Florida International
University
Miami, Florida

Nicholas Carter
The World Bank
Washington, D.C.

Mario Castillo
House Agriculture Committee
Washington, D.C.

Timothy Christenson
Office of Sen. Rudy Boschwitz
Washington, D.C.

D. R. Clarke
The World Bank
Washington, D.C.

Richard Clark
Office of Rep. Les Aspin
Washington, D.C.

Roger Conner
Federation of American
Immigration Reform
Washington, D.C.

Lyn Conway
Office of Rep. Romano Mazzoli
Washington, D.C.

Richard Day
Office of Sen. Alan Simpson
Washington, D.C.

Nicholas Dimarzo
Catholic Community Services
Washington, D.C.

Joseph Eldridge
Washington Office on
Latin America
Washington, D.C.

Arthur P. Endres
Subcommitte on Immigration
Office of Rep. Peter Rodino
Washington, D.C.

Patricia Weiss Fagen
Refugee Policy Group
Washington, D.C.

Jeffrey Farrow
House Committee on Interior and
Insural Affairs
Washington, D.C.

Jose Feliciano
U.S. Department of Agriculture
Washington, D.C.

John Felton
Congressional Quarterly
Washington, D.C.

Hon. Maurice A. Ferre
Mayor, City of Miami
Miami, Florida

Michael Finley
House Foreign Affairs Committee
Office of Rep. Dante Fascell
Washington, D.C.

Maureen Fletcher
Office of Rep. Jim Wright
Washington, D.C.

Richard Fletcher
Inter-American Development Bank
Washington, D.C.

Robert Fox
Inter-American Development Bank
Washington, D.C.

Alexa Freeman
Office of Rep. Charles Schumer
Washington, D.C.

Hugh Fremantle
The Wilson Center
Washington, D.C.

Jane Garcia
Office of Rep. Robert Garcia
Washington, D.C.

Helen Gonzalez
Mexican American Legal Defense
and Education Fund
Washington, D.C.

Louis W. Goodman
The Wilson Center
Washington, D.C.

Ben Haddad
Office of Rep. Bill Lowery
Washington, D.C,

Peter Hakim
Inter-American Dialogue
Washington, D.C.

Carl Hampe
Subcommittee on Immigration
and Refugee Policy
Senate Judiciary Committee
Washington, D.C.

Margaret Daly Hayes
Council of the Americas
Washington, D.C.

Susan Herrera
Congressional Hispanic Caucus
Washington, D.C.

Sheldon Himmelfarb
Office of Sen. Charles McC.
   Mathias, Jr.
Washington, D.C.

Steve Horblitt
Office of Del. Walter E. Fauntroy
Washington, D.C.

Marian Houstoun
Department of Labor
Washington, D.C.

Earl Huyck
National Institute of Health
Bethesda, Maryland

Patricia Ingram
Office of Sen. Russell B. Long
Washington, D.C.

Charles Keely
Population Council
New York, New York

Joshua Koltun
Office of Rep. Barney Frank
Washington, D.C.

Dorothy Krahn
Immigration & Naturalization
Service
Washington, D.C.

Mary Kritz
The Rockefeller Foundation
New York, New York

Paul Latortue
Center for Business Research
University of Puerto Rico
San Juan, Puerto Rico

Nancy Lieber
Democratic National Committee
Washington, D.C.

Christina Lund
International Affairs
Office of Management & Budget
Washington, D.C.

Christopher Madison
National Journal
Washington, D.C.

Hon. Romano Mazzoli
United States House of
Representatives
Washington, D.C.

Constantine Menges
National Security Council
Washington, D.C.

Doris Meissner
Immigration and Naturalization
Service
Washington, D.C.

Lorenzo Meyer
The Wilson Center
Washington, D.C.

Harris Miller
Harris Miller & Associates
Arlington, Virginia

Maureen Taft-Morales
Freelance Journalist
Washington, D.C.

Richard M. Morse
The Wilson Center
Washington, D.C.

John Nahan
Immigration & Naturalization
Service
Washington, D.C.

Alan Nelson
Immigration & Naturalization
Service
Washington, D.C.

Richard Newfarmer
The World Bank
Washington, D.C.

David North
Center for Labor & Migration
Studies
New Transcentury Foundation
Washington, D.C.

Richard A. Nuccio
Roosevelt Center for American
Policy Studies
Washington, D.C.

Alan L. Otten
The Wall Street Journal
Washington, D.C.

Robert Pastor
School of Public Affairs
University of Maryland
College Park, Maryland

Demetrios Papademetriou
Population Associates
Fairfax, Virginia

Robert Pear
The New York Times
Washington, D.C.

Catherine Pearson
Caribbean/Central American Action
Washington, D.C.

Patricia Pessar
Center for Immigration Policy
Georgetown University
Washington, D.C.

Amanda Pitt
Office of Rep. Mervyn M. Dymally
Washington, D.C.

Ben Proctor
Office of Rep. Jim Wright
Washington, D.C.

Jeff Pryce
Office of Rep. Edward J. Markey
Washington, D.C.

Lillian Pubillones
House Foreign Affairs Committee
Washington, D.C.

Dan Purtell
National Council of La Raza
Washington, D.C.

Michael Ratigan
Office of Sen. William
Armstrong
Washington, D.C.

George Reid
The World Bank
Washington, D.C.

Timothy Reiser
Office of Sen. Patrick J. Leahy
Washington, D.C.

Hon. Bill Richardson
U.S. House of Representatives
Washington, D.C.

Luz Rojas
Inter-Governmental Committee
for Migration
Washington, D.C.

Jon Rosenbaum
Office of U.S. Trade
Representative
Washington, D.C.

Mara Rudman
Office of Rep. Gerry E. Studds
Washington, D.C.

Nina Serafino
Foreign Affairs Division
Library of Congress
Washington, D.C.

Hon. Charles E. Schumer
U.S. House of Representatives
Washington, D.C.

Hon. Alan K. Simpson
United States Senate
Washington, D.C.

Barry Sklar
Office of Sen. Claiborne Pell
Washington, D.C.

Nina Solarz
Citizen's Committee for
Immigration Reform
Washington, D.C.

Saul Sosnowski
University of Maryland
College Park, Maryland

Sharon Stephan
Congressional Research Service
Washington, D.C.

Larry Storrs
Congressional Research Service
Washington, D.C.

Futi Sunia
Office of Rep. Mervyn Dymally
Washington, D.C.

Bill Taylor
Office of Sen. Bill Bradley
Washington, D.C.

Stephanie Tiferman
Office of Rep. James H. Scheuer
Washington, D.C.

Jerry Tinker
Office of Sen. Edward Kennedy
Washington, D.C.

Joyce Vialet
Congressional Research Service
Washington, D.C.

W. Robert Warne
U.S. Department of State
Washington, D.C.

Index